AA

Atlas of the World

Printed for PR Books Ltd, 2008

1st Edition July 2007 for the Automobile Association

Publisher's notes:
Published by Automobile Association Developments Limited
whose registered office is Fanum House, Basing View,
Basingstoke RG21 4EA, UK. Registered number 1878835.

Copyright © Hema Maps Pty Ltd
Brisbane, Australia
www.hemamaps.com
Based on original data © Research Machines PLC

ISBN: 978 0 7495 6118 5

A CIP catalogue record of this atlas is availabale
from The British Library.

Disclaimer
The contents of this atlas are believed to be correct at the
time of latest revision. However, the publishers cannot be
held responsible for any loss or damage occasioned to any
persion acting or refraining from action as a result of any use
or reliance on material in this atlas, nor for any errors,
omissions or changes in such material. This does not affect
your statutory rights.

Cover design:
© Automobile Association Developments Limited.

Printer
Printed in U.A.E. by Oriental Press, Dubai.

Front cover photographs:
AA World Travel Library:
tl C Sawyer; tc A Kouprianoff; tr K Paterson; cl N Sumner;
c C Sawyer; cr B Davies; bl D Corrance; bc G Marks; br P Kenward.

Photographs:
p11 L Cook/Science Photo Library
p13 R Royer/Science Photo Library
p15 R Edmaier/Science Photo Library
p17 K Svenson/Science Photo Library

Atlas of the World

Contents

Europe

Asia

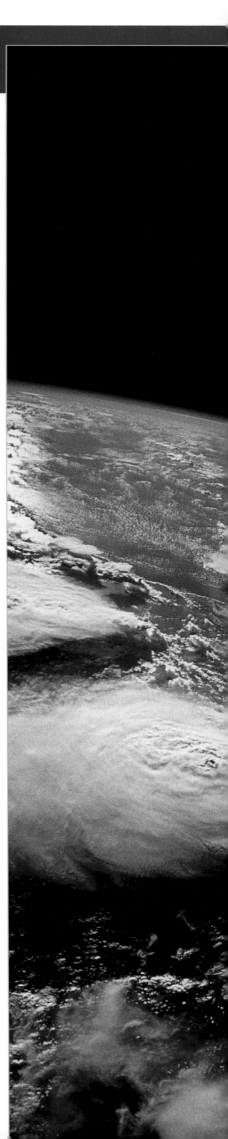

Key Map

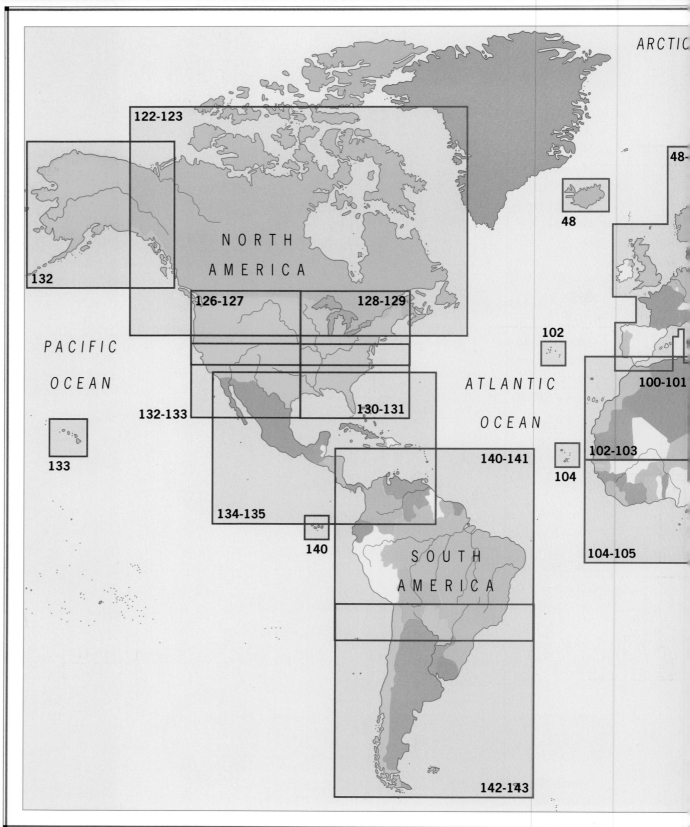

ARCTIC

122-123

48-

48

NORTH

AMERICA

132

PACIFIC

OCEAN

102

ATLANTIC

100-101

126-127

128-129

OCEAN

132-133

130-131

102-103

133

104

140-141

SOUTH

104-105

134-135

AMERICA

140

142-143

KEY TO CONTINENTAL RECORD SYMBOLS

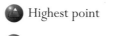 Highest point

 Lowest average annual rainfall

 Longest river

 Lowest point

 Highest average annual rainfall

Largest lake

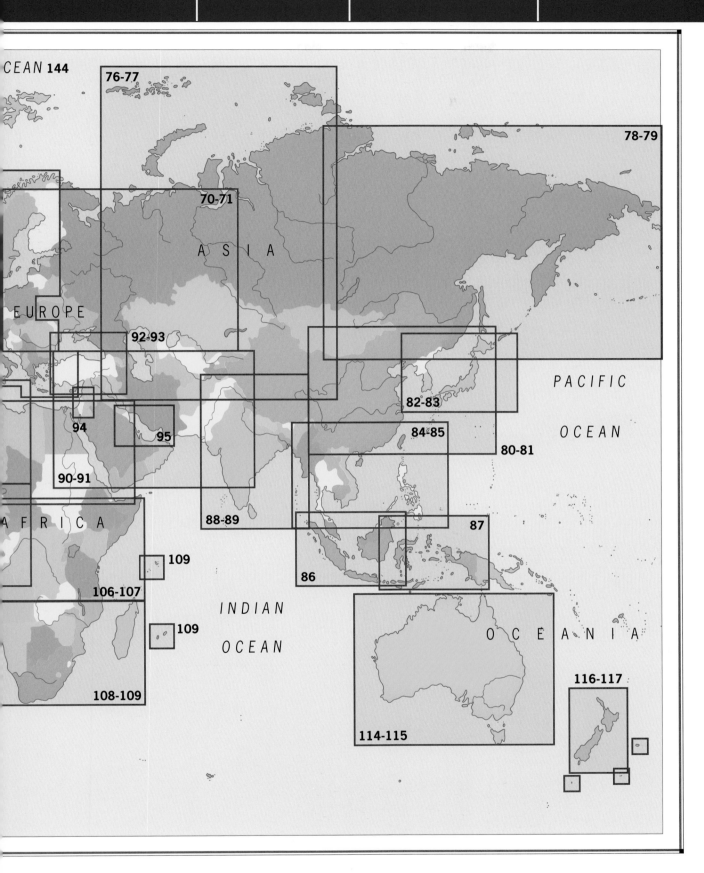

The first eight symbols show the most extreme value of the feature described, as well as its location.
If that description is in **bold**, it is not only the continental record, but also the World record.

Coldest place

Hottest place

Estimated population

Population density

Land area

Number of countries
(including dependencies)

World

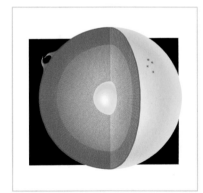

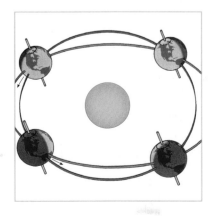

Our Star and our Neighbours

The Earth is one member of a Solar System of nine planets orbiting our local star – the Sun. All these bodies formed from a single cloud of gas and dust around 4.5 billion years ago as it was compressed, possibly by shockwaves from a giant supernova explosion. The centre of the cloud collapsed most rapidly, becoming denser and attracting more material until eventually it reached a point so hot and dense that nuclear reactions began inside it. These reactions continue today and are the source of the sunlight that heats our planet and sustains life. The Sun is critical to the regulation of our climate and environment – fine alterations in Earth's orbit are thought to cause periodic ice ages, so we are fortunate that the Sun is not likely to change drastically for another 5 billion years.

On a shorter scale, the Sun's output does have slight fluctuations. A cycle of sunspot formation (comparatively cool regions of the Sun's surface caused by magnetic activity), reaches a maximum every 11 years. From 1645–1705 almost no sunspots were seen, a dip in solar activity which coincided with a 'mini-Ice Age' of unusually low temperatures on Earth.

Once the Sun had formed, a disk of material would have been left outside the newly-formed star, which condensed to form the planets. Particles in the gas and dust cloud collided and stuck together, becoming increasingly larger bodies. Eventually these 'proto-planets' were pulled into a spherical shape by their increasing gravity.

The Solar System we see today reflects the composition of that gas and dust cloud, and divides into two regions. The inner portion contains the four terrestrial (Earth-like) planets – from Mercury orbiting close to the Sun, through Venus and Earth, to Mars. Beyond the orbit of Mars lies the asteroid belt, a ring of rocky debris, outside which are the gas giants, enormous planets created where the cloud bulged with huge quantities of gas.

The inner rocky worlds

The terrestrial planets are all very different. Mercury is a small, baking world, quite similar to our own Moon, and covered in craters. Venus is shrouded in a thick atmosphere of carbon dioxide and toxic molecules, with a surface pressure 95 times that of Earth's atmosphere, and temperatures of 470°C.

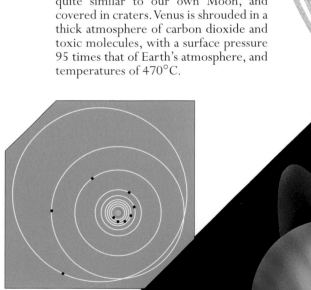

▶ **THE SUN**

The Sun is a massive ball of hydrogen gas **[B]**, *1.39 million km across. Energy is generated at its heart, where temperatures exceed 15 million°C, by nuclear fusion – the joining together through a chain reaction of two hydrogen atoms to form one helium. In the process, a large amount of excess energy is released, carried to the surface of the Sun in giant convection cells, and then radiated across the Solar System from the top of the 'photosphere' – the visible disk of the Sun, with a temperature of 5500°C.*

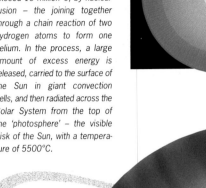

B

◀ **THE SOLAR SYSTEM**

The solar system consists of 9 planets **[A]**: *Pluto* [1], *the smallest, is the furthest away from the Sun, though once in every 248.6 years its orbit crosses inside Neptune's path. Neptune* [2], *the outermost of the gas giants, has a diameter of 49,400km, and orbits every 164.8 years.*

Uranus [3] *is similar in size to Neptune and orbits every 84 years. All the gas giants have ring systems, but Uranus's are second only to Saturn's. The planet is tilted at over 98° to the plane of the Solar System, so it seems to roll around its orbit.*

1

2

3

4

A

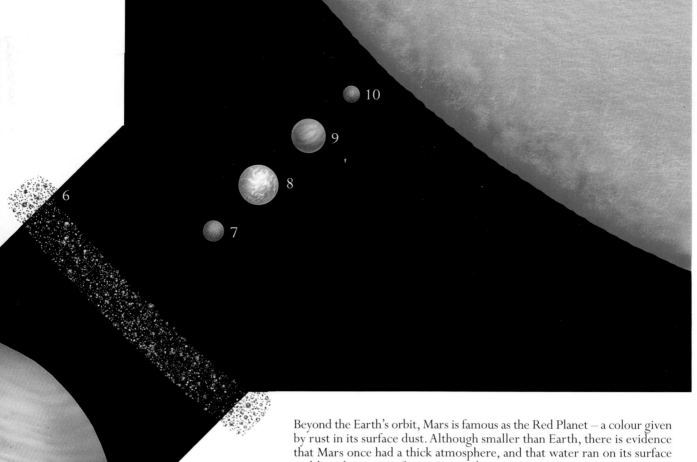

Beyond the Earth's orbit, Mars is famous as the Red Planet – a colour given by rust in its surface dust. Although smaller than Earth, there is evidence that Mars once had a thick atmosphere, and that water ran on its surface – although now it is frozen into polar ice-caps.

The gas giants

The outer Solar System contains worlds quite different from those nearer the Sun – the gas giants. Largest of these is Jupiter, more massive than all the other planets in the Solar System put together, with churning weather systems that include the Great Red Spot, a storm large enough to engulf Earth. Beyond Jupiter lies Saturn, with its spectacular ring system of icy particles, and then the smaller giants Uranus and Neptune. Space probes have shown that Jupiter, Uranus and Neptune also have thin ring systems, although these are nothing to match Saturn's spectacle.

All four of these worlds have large families of moons orbiting round them. Jupiter has a vast family of moons, including Io, the most volcanic body in the Solar System, whose eruptions launch yellow plumes of sulphur into space, scarring its surface with streaks. The most interesting member of Uranus's satellite system is Miranda – a small, deeply-cratered world which displays so many variations in terrain that it must have suffered some great cataclysm in the past. Neptune's giant satellite Triton has active geysers shooting water, ammonia and methane 8km above its surface.

Saturn [4] is noted for its spectacular ring system – the planet has a diameter of 105,000km, while the rings stretch out to 300,000km. It orbits the Sun every 29.5 years, and has a huge family of satellites.

Jupiter [5] orbits the Sun every 11.9 years. With a diameter of 137,400km it is the largest planet in the Solar System. It has complex weather systems, including the Great Red Spot, a storm with a diameter larger than the Earth's.

Between Jupiter and Mars is the asteroid belt [6], rocky debris left over from the Solar System's formation. Inside it lie the terrestrial planets. Mars [7], the red planet, circles the Sun in 1.9 years, and has a diameter of 6790km. Its surface is scoured by massive dust storms, and it shows evidence of running water on the surface in its past. Next in towards the Sun is our own

blue planet, the Earth [8], with a diameter of 12,700km. Within the orbit of the Earth lies its near twin Venus [9], circling the Sun in 225 days, and with a diameter of 12,100km. The atmosphere of Venus, however, is a poisonous mixture of carbon dioxide and other gases, with clouds of sulphuric acid. Mercury [10] is the second smallest planet with a diameter of only 4,880km, and a solar orbit that lasts 88 days. Its proximity to the Sun (58 million km) makes it a scorched world with no atmosphere, and a cratered surface similar to that of the Moon. It orbits the Sun once every 88 days.

◀ *The Sun is just one of over 200 billion stars in the vast spiral of the Milky Way galaxy, like every other star that we see with the naked eye in the night sky. It lies roughly two-thirds of the way towards the edge of the galactic disc, orbiting the centre at a speed of 250 kilometres per second, taking 200 million years to complete each revolution. This view is what the galaxy would look like to an observer outside. But because of our position in the plane, we see the dense star clouds as a pale band across the sky.*

The Earth and the Moon

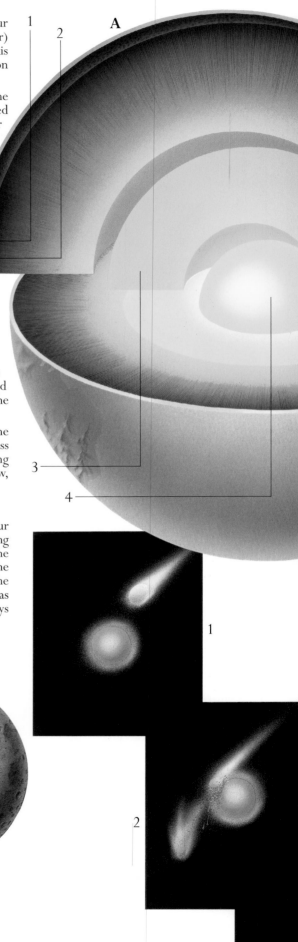

The Earth's satellite, the Moon, is so large by comparison with our own world (at 3746km, it is over one-quarter the Earth's diameter) that astronomers consider the two together as a 'double planet'. This massive size and proximity means that the Moon has a great influence on the Earth itself, for example through the tides.

The origins of the Moon are open to debate – some believe that the Moon is a chunk of debris flung off when the still-molten Earth collided with another body the size of Mars, in the early days of the Solar System. Since then, the two bodies have had very different histories. The Moon's small size meant that it cooled more quickly and its low gravity made it unable to hold onto an atmosphere – the factor which has been crucial in shaping our own planet's terrain. In fact, the Moon has altered so little that it provides valuable information about the history of the early Solar System. The lack of an atmosphere also means that, unlike Earth, the Moon is not shielded from the extremes of heat from the Sun. Temperatures at noon climb to 150°C, while at night they can plummet to -200°C. These acute differences can even cause moon-quakes as the surface stretches and contracts.

A familiar face

The Moon's surface divides into two distinct types of terrain, which can be easily distinguished with the naked eye from Earth. The bright highlands are highly cratered areas created more than 4 billion years ago during an era of bombardment by rock particles from space. The numbers of these particles dwindled until only a few massive chunks were left, which created enormous impact basins as they crashed into the Moon's surface. The gnarled highlands contrast sharply with the smoother, darker Maria (from the Latin for seas).

After the cratering had died away, the Moon seems to have undergone a brief period of intense volcanic activity. Red-hot fissures opened up across its surface, out of which huge volumes of lava poured, flooding low-lying areas. These lava lakes solidified to form the Maria, marked by only a few, very small craters.

Lunar attraction

The changing direction of the Sun and Moon from Earth cause our monthly cycle of tides. Twice a month, at full and new moon, the high Spring Tides occur, with Moon and Sun lined up, or directly opposed, so the tidal effect is at its strongest. Such tidal effects have influenced the Earth-Moon system as a whole. Over millions of years, the friction of the oceans' movement has slowed the lunar 'day', so it now lasts exactly as long as the time the Moon takes to orbit Earth, with the result that it always keeps the same face turned towards us.

▶ **STRUCTURE OF THE MOON**
The Earth's satellite, the Moon [B], has a structure that reflects its different size, and possibly origin. Because it is a much smaller body – around one-twentieth the volume of the Earth – it has a higher surface area to volume ratio. It cooled down more rapidly early in the history of the Solar System, and is now inactive. The lunar crust [1] is actually thicker than Earth's – an average of 70km, though it is thinner on the Earth-facing side, possibly due to the tidal effects of the Earth's gravity. This could be a possible explanation of why the smooth 'seas' are found far more on this side, formed from eruptions of lava through the thin crust. Beneath this lie layers of solidified, cold rock, which decrease in rigidity. At the centre there may be a cold core [2], although its existence is still debated.

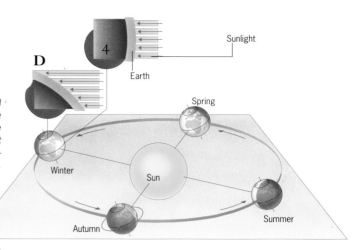

◄ THE STRUCTURE OF THE EARTH

The Earth has the shape of a squashed ball or a spheroid **[A]**. It has a diameter at the poles of 12,703km, but is wider at the Equator, thrown outward by the rapid daily spin which causes a 'bulge'. The crust [1], on which lie the continents and oceans, is a thin layer of rock varying in depth between 10 and 20km. Below this lies a mantle [2], divided into two regions. The upper mantle extends down to 3000km, and divides into the mainly solid lithosphere and the mostly molten aesthenosphere. Beyond this, the molten rock of the upper and lower mantle extends down towards the molten outer [3] and solid inner [4] cores of iron and nickel, around 7000km across, at the centre of the Earth. It is the rotation of this core that is believed to generate the Earth's magnetic field, in an effect similar to that of a dynamo.

► THE EARTH'S SEASONS

The Poles of the Earth are tilted at 23.5° **[D]**. As it orbits the Sun, different parts of the globe receive a varying amount of sunlight through the year-long cycle of the seasons [3]. For six months of the year, the Northern Hemisphere is tilted towards the Sun, which therefore appears higher in the sky, giving warmer temperatures and longer days [1]. Six months later, when the Northern Hemisphere is tilted in the other direction, the days are shorter and the Sun stays closer to the horizon [2]. The situation is reversed in the Southern Hemisphere. The Tropics of Cancer and Capricorn are lines around the globe at the lines of latitude +/- 23.5°. They mark the northernmost and southernmost points where the Sun appears directly overhead.

Fossil records show that there were once 400 days in each Earth year, so the same effect must also be slowing its rotation as well. Hence in the distant future, the spin of the Earth could be so slow that its day and year are equal, so that one scorched side of the planet will permanently face the Sun.

Complete coverage

Very occasionally, as the Moon orbits around the Earth and it in turn moves around the Sun, all three bodies – Sun, Earth and Moon – line up exactly and an eclipse is seen. If the Earth blocks out the Sun shining onto the full Moon, a rather unspectacular lunar eclipse happens. Far more spectacular are solar eclipses, when the new Moon passes right across the face of the Sun. By chance the Moon and Sun have discs in the sky that are almost the same size. This means that total solar eclipses can only be seen for short periods of time from tiny regions of the Earth. The effect is breathtaking as the Moon covers the bright central disk of the Sun, and reveals the wispy white corona of gas streaming out from the Sun's surface.

◄ HOW THE MOON BEGAN

The Moon orbits too far from the Earth to be a captured asteroid. Instead, it is thought to have been formed when a body the size of Mars collided with the still-molten Earth during the formation of the Solar System, some 5 billion years ago [1]. The collision resulted in a stream of debris being thrown off into orbit round the Earth [2], and this eventually condensed to form the Moon [3]. The iron-rich cores of the two original bodies combined and remained within the Earth, becoming its very dense central region, whilst the Moon formed from the two lighter outer sections. This may explain why the Earth is thought to have a more complicated structure than the Moon, and also the lack of iron in Moon rock.

E

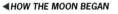

◄ HOW THE MOON AFFECTS THE EARTH'S TIDES

The proximity of the Moon to the Earth, coupled with its size, causes strong gravitational forces between the two worlds, which is shown in the tides [E].

As the Moon exerts a gravitational pull on the Earth, it draws the seas towards it, and creates a bulge in the seawater on one side of the planet. At the same time, the Earth itself is attracted towards the Moon, pulling it away from the sea on the opposite side of the globe and creating a smaller tidal bulge on the opposite side. Because the Moon is relatively slow-moving, the tidal bulges in the sea remain in almost the same place, while the Earth rotates under them [1,2,3,4]. As each bulge passes a point on the Earth roughly once each day, seashores experience two high and two low tides each day (although the shape of an inlet can alter their spacing). As the Moon circles the Earth once a month, the tides occur at different times each day.

▼ During the brief minutes of the eclipse, the corona of the Sun can be seen.

Normally this is an invisible halo, made up of two distinct regions of gas which overlap, the K-corona and the F-corona. The latter reaches out many millions of kilometres from the Suns surface while the K-corona extends for a mere 75,000km.

A World in motion

We think of the ground as being steady and immovable: in fact the surface of the Earth is in a constant state of movement, propelled by the intense heat of the interior. Although our planet is 12,700km wide, the crust on which the continents and oceans lie is only a few tens of kilometres thick at its deepest. This thin crust is broken into slabs or plates, which float on top of an inner molten layer, the mantle. Where these plates collide with each other or slowly draw apart are areas of violent activity, subject to earthquakes and studded with volcanoes. This drama is not restricted to dry land: satellite photography has shown that the two-thirds of Earth's surface under the ocean is just as fascinating, with features such as chains of volcanic mountains that stretch for 60,000km around the globe.

The idea that the continents are slowly moving was first put forward to explain how the coastlines of different continents appear to fit together like pieces of a jigsaw puzzle. For example, the eastern coast of South America nestles snugly into the western coast of Africa. Such continental drifts can be traced back to a point around 250 million years ago, when all the land masses on Earth were joined into a supercontinent called Pangaea (from the Greek for all earth), surrounded by a single vast sea, the Tethys Ocean. This supercontinent slowly disintegrated into the major land masses we know today.

Geologists call their model for the movements of the Earth's crust plate tectonics. This describes the surface, both continents and ocean floor, as being split into plates whose movements are driven by the churning of the molten rock in the inner mantle. The largest plates are as wide as the Pacific Ocean, while others are much smaller. Their thickness varies from around 10km beneath the oceans, to 30km under major land masses, and up to 60km where a plate has to support the weight of a mountain range. In general, ocean floor plates are made of dense basaltic rocks, while the continents are formed from less dense granite.

Earthquakes

Most of the areas where plates are separating are hidden beneath the ocean. At the fault between the plates molten rock wells up through a fissure and solidifies, creating new ocean floor. Only in a few places can this process be seen on dry land, notably in the volcanoes of Iceland, which sits on a fault called the Mid-Atlantic Ridge.

Plates can meet in a number of ways. At earthquake zones they grind past each other in opposite directions, being compressed so that they store huge amounts of energy. This is released in calamitous movements of the ground – earthquakes. The most famous earthquake zone of all, the San Andreas Fault in California, is a region where the North American and Pacific Plates are moving past each other. Earthquake prediction hinges on the theory that major quakes are preceded by 'quiet' periods during which the plates lock together, and store up the energy. Not all the plate boundaries are earthquake or volcano zones – the Himalayas are the result of a head-on collision between the relatively fast-moving Indo-Australian Plate, and the Eurasian Plate. These two continental plates buckled upwards, forming the mountain range, and halting the Indo-Australian plate's movement. Conversely, not all volcanoes are at plate boundaries. The volcanic Hawaiian Islands, for instance, lie in the middle of the Pacific Plate.

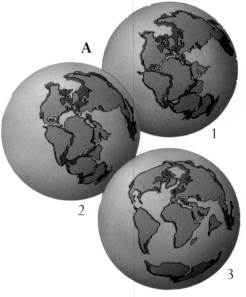

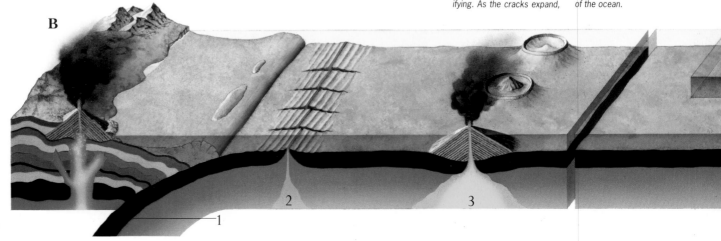

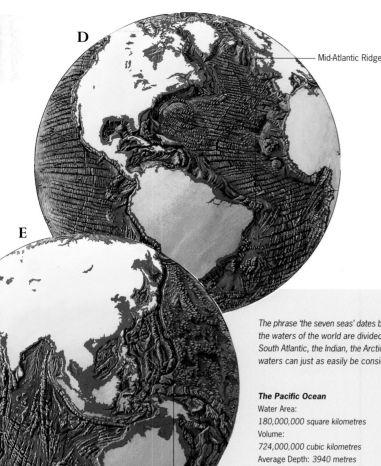

Mid-Atlantic Ridge

D

E

Marianas Trench

◀ THE ATLANTIC AND THE PACIFIC

The floors of the two largest oceans reveal important differences in their structures.

The Atlantic Ocean **[D]** is divided by the Mid-Atlantic Ridge that runs for its entire length, from Greenland down to the Antarctic Plate. This is a region where the Earth's crust is stretching, new floor being pumped out so that the Atlantic is gradually widening. As the rock is pulled apart, large slabs sink, creating the series of rifts that run parallel to the ridge along its length. Only in a few places does the ridge emerge above the sea, most spectacularly in Iceland, the shape of which is constantly being redefined by volcanic activity.

In contrast, the floor of the Pacific Ocean **[E]** shows signs of many different seismic activities. It is surrounded by the so-called 'ring of fire' – volcanic zones where the oceanic plates dive below continental ones and create volcanoes. At other places, oceanic plates converge, creating trenches where one plate dives below the other, such as the Marianas Trench, the deepest place on Earth.

THE SEVEN SEAS

The phrase 'the seven seas' dates back to the seas known to Muslim voyagers before the fifteenth century. Nowadays, the waters of the world are divided into seven oceans – the North Pacific, the South Pacific, the North Atlantic, the South Atlantic, the Indian, the Arctic and the Antarctic. But divisions such as these are in reality arbitrary, as all these waters can just as easily be considered as parts of one continuous global ocean.

The Pacific Ocean
Water Area:
180,000,000 square kilometres
Volume:
724,000,000 cubic kilometres
Average Depth: 3940 metres

The Atlantic Ocean
Water Area:
106,000,000 square kilometres
Volume:
355,000,000 cubic kilometres
Average Depth: 3310 metres

The Indian Ocean
Water Area:
75,000,000 square kilometres
Volume:
292,000,000 cubic kilometres
Average Depth: 3840 metres

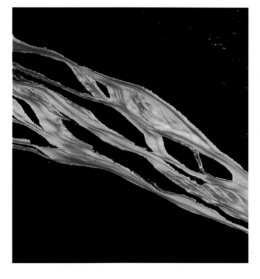

◀ *Lava which erupts from the earth's surface can take on a number of forms Aa, or block lava, is runny, and quickly forms a hard pastry-like crust when it cools. Pahoehoe lava has a sheen to it like satin and often consolidates in rope-like forms. When this kind of lava comes into contact with the sea it takes on the form of a jumbled heap of pillows, hence its name pillow lava.*

▼ SEA CHANGE

A coastal region **[C]** is shaped by the forces of longshore drift. Sand is pushed along the shore by ocean currents to build up spits [1], bars [2] and sometimes enclosing bays to form lagoons.

A river carries vast amounts of sediment out to sea, which is deposited to form a delta [3]. Under the sea, the accumulation of sediment forms the continental shelf [4], a region that slopes gently out from the coastline for about 75km, to depths of 100-200m. In places it is cut through by submarine gorges, formed either by rivers when the sea level was lower or by the undercutting effect of river currents flowing out to sea. The shelf gives way to the steep continental slope, which dives to depths of several kilometres. From the base of the slope, the continental rise extends up to 1000km from the coast into the ocean.

C

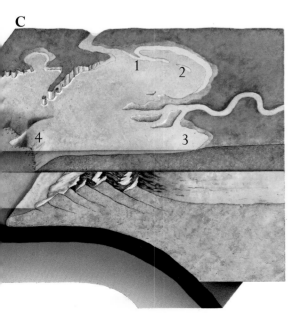

This chain of volcanic mountains is caused by a semi-permanent 'hot spot' where molten magma rises from the depths of the mantle through the crust, and spews out of a volcano. Although the hot spot in the mantle is stationary, the Pacific Plate, and with it the volcano, is continually moving. Hawaii itself is only the most recent in a chain of 107 volcanic vents formed by the plume. As the plate moves on, each volcano becomes extinct, and a new one forms further along the chain. Many thousands of these 'hot spot' volcanoes are known – mostly beneath the ocean surface – so there must be hundreds of hot plumes in the mantle to have created them all.

While plates are being destroyed in the subduction zones where they collide, new plate material is being produced all the time deep beneath the ocean surface. The sea floor is just as geologically fascinating as the continental land surface, and is still awaiting full exploration.

Occasionally, the volcanic activity of the mid-oceanic ridges reaches the surface, and forms islands. At other places, hot gases venting from the depths of the Earth create pools of warmth on the ocean floor, where life can flourish.

Shaping the World

Over billions of years, the harsh landscape created by geological activity such as plate tectonics and volcanism has been softened and sculpted by the eroding forces of ice, water and air. Glaciers have ground out valleys, and rivers have carved huge gorges, including America's Grand Canyon. At the same time the steady pounding of the seas and oceans eats away and remodels coastlines.

Studies of the changing climate in the past show that the Earth has gone through periodic 'ice ages' when the ice-caps pushed into temperate regions closer to the Equator. These periods were critical in shaping the landscape that we see today – during the last Ice Age, which ended 10,000 years ago, an ice sheet covered most of Northern Europe, Asia and North America. The ice ages can be dated by drilling out an ice core from a polar cap. Each year a layer of new ice is laid down, which in colder years – during ice ages – is thicker. These records surprisingly reveal that over the last 4 million years, successive ice ages have gripped Earth for longer than the warmer periods in between.

Variations in the Earth's climate are thought to be the result of cyclical changes in its orbit, which becomes more, then less, elongated. According to these models the Earth's average temperature should currently be on the increase – which means that the measured increases in temperature cited as evidence of global warming and the greenhouse effect may have a natural cause.

Getting in shape

During the ice ages, massive glaciers formed across the globe. As these vast, slow-moving rivers of ice rolled forward, the sheer weight of ice ground down rocks in their paths, leaving a softened, altered landscape once they had retreated. These forces are still at work today: on Greenland and in Antarctica there are many glaciers which eventually find their way to the sea, where they break up into icebergs.

Although glaciers are the most dramatic form of erosion, there are others: over longer periods, rivers and seas can cut through rock and carve out valleys. Even rain has a profound cumulative effect on rock. Raindrops dissolve gases from the atmosphere and become dilute acid, chemically attacking igneous rocks formed from volcanic lava. In time, the particles broken off build up to great depths and are converted by pressure and heat into sedimentary rocks such as limestone. When these are subjected to the intense heat of the Earth's crust they become metamorphic rocks, such as marble and slate.

▼ **A WOBBLING WORLD**
The climate of the Earth is not constant but gradually varies over time in cycles of thousands of years **[B]**. The shape of the Earth's orbit around the Sun can vary between an almost perfect circle [1] and a pronounced ellipse [2] over a cycle of around 100,000 years. When the orbit is more elliptical, the climate of the Earth is more extreme. At the same time, another cycle changes the angle of tilt of the planet between a minimum 21.8° and a maximum 24.4° **[C]**. At the maximum inclination, every 22,000 years, the climate is most extreme, and the seasons are especially marked, with the Poles pointing further away from the Sun during winter. When the effects of these cycles are combined, they lead to ice ages of varying severity, the last of which ended around 10,000 years ago.

▶ **EARTH SCRAPER**
Glaciers **[A]** are dramatic rivers of ice slowly creeping down valleys and carving mountain ranges into a series of sharp peaks. They usually originate where ice or hard-packed snow builds up in a cirque [1], a basin near a mountain top. After a sufficient mass has built up, it will start to move under its own gravity, wearing down rocks by pressure, scraping and frost action, to form glacial spoil called 'moraines'. The boulders of moraine underneath the glacier act as abrasives, scouring the landscape. Lateral moraines [2] are rocks cut away and pulled along at the sides of the glacier. Where two ice-rivers meet, the lateral moraines can join to form a medial moraine [3] – a stripe of rubble down the centre of the glacier. As the glacier grinds along over rocks and boulders, the stresses induced can open up deep and jagged splits called crevasses [4]. A glacier terminates at a snout [5] which may empty into the sea, or a great lake. On dry land the shape of the snout depends on the climatic conditions, and especially the rate at which the snout melts compared with the rate at which the glacier advances. If the the two rates are exactly balanced, the snout remains in the same place, but

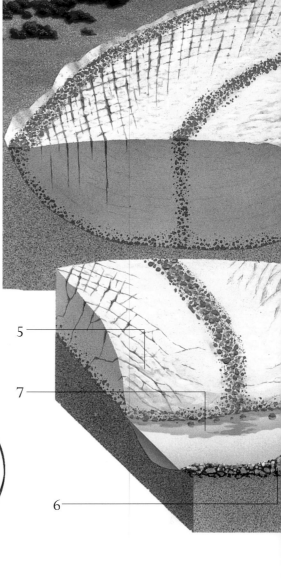

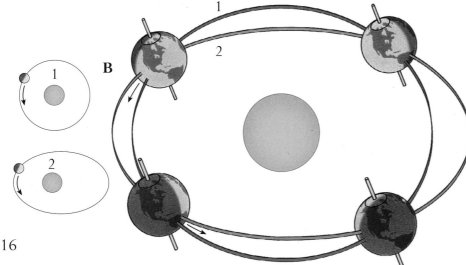

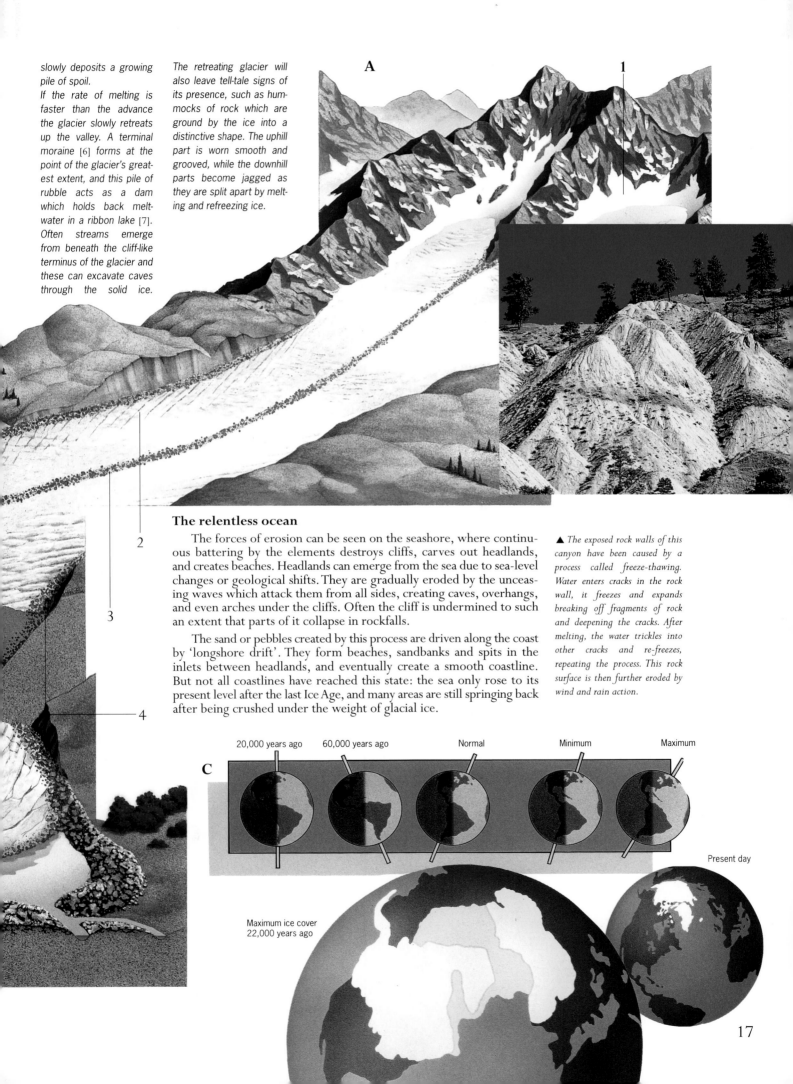

slowly deposits a growing pile of spoil.

If the rate of melting is faster than the advance the glacier slowly retreats up the valley. A terminal moraine [6] forms at the point of the glacier's greatest extent, and this pile of rubble acts as a dam which holds back meltwater in a ribbon lake [7]. Often streams emerge from beneath the cliff-like terminus of the glacier and these can excavate caves through the solid ice.

The retreating glacier will also leave tell-tale signs of its presence, such as hummocks of rock which are ground by the ice into a distinctive shape. The uphill part is worn smooth and grooved, while the downhill parts become jagged as they are split apart by melting and refreezing ice.

The relentless ocean

The forces of erosion can be seen on the seashore, where continuous battering by the elements destroys cliffs, carves out headlands, and creates beaches. Headlands can emerge from the sea due to sea-level changes or geological shifts. They are gradually eroded by the unceasing waves which attack them from all sides, creating caves, overhangs, and even arches under the cliffs. Often the cliff is undermined to such an extent that parts of it collapse in rockfalls.

The sand or pebbles created by this process are driven along the coast by 'longshore drift'. They form beaches, sandbanks and spits in the inlets between headlands, and eventually create a smooth coastline. But not all coastlines have reached this state: the sea only rose to its present level after the last Ice Age, and many areas are still springing back after being crushed under the weight of glacial ice.

▲ The exposed rock walls of this canyon have been caused by a process called freeze-thawing. Water enters cracks in the rock wall, it freezes and expands breaking off fragments of rock and deepening the cracks. After melting, the water trickles into other cracks and re-freezes, repeating the process. This rock surface is then further eroded by wind and rain action.

20,000 years ago   60,000 years ago   Normal   Minimum   Maximum

Present day

Maximum ice cover 22,000 years ago

17

Contrasting conditions

We talk so much about the weather because of its infinite changeability. As the Sun's radiation heats up the Equatorial zones of the planet much more than the Polar regions, it creates wide temperature contrasts. The hottest places on Earth can be a blistering 50°C in the shade, while in the depths of an Antarctic winter, levels as low as -70°C have been recorded. This variable heat produces hot air at the Equator, which rises, while cooler air further north and south sinks under it, producing wind patterns that stretch across the globe. These in turn create swirling eddies of air that can absorb water vapour over the sea, forming clouds, and deposit it as rain over land. Such air currents couple with the variable heat of the Sun to produce the wide variety of climates found on Earth, ranging from hot, rainless deserts to cool, wet, temperate coastal regions.

The atmosphere of the Earth just after it formed was an unbreatheable mixture of hydrogen and helium. In time this was replaced by an equally unbreatheable mixture belched out from volcanoes, which in turn has been modified by lifeforms to the air we breathe today. This is made up of 78 per cent nitrogen, 21 per cent oxygen, and a small proportion of carbon dioxide, which plants then recycle into oxygen. The remainder of the atmosphere is water vapour and small traces of other gases. The balance is a delicate one, perfectly suited to life as it has evolved, and the entire planet – both living things and minerals – is needed to maintain it.

The outer limits of the atmosphere stretch 2400 km above the surface, but the lower 15km, the troposphere, is the densest, holding nearly all the atmosphere's water vapour – which condenses under different conditions to create clouds. Beyond this region, up to 40 km high, lies the stratosphere, which contains a thin ozone layer that blocks out harmful ultra-violet radiation.

Climate types

Land near the Equator has weather patterns typified by those of southern Asia. For six months of the year cold dry winds blow from the land out to sea, giving arid conditions and little rain. In the summer the wind reverses direction and starts to blow warm air off the ocean. This air is heavy with water vapour and triggers torrential rainstorms over land.

Weather in the temperate latitudes of northern Europe is dominated by the jet stream, a band of high winds at altitudes of about 12km. It forms where warm air from the tropics meets cold Polar air, creating a jet of air travelling at speeds around 200kmh in summer, 400kmh in winter. The jet stream's direction develops in a similar way to a slowly flowing river, meandering and forming eddies. These are seen as high-pressure anticyclones, wind systems that create clear, dry weather, or low pressure depressions with associated clouds and weather fronts.

The circulation patterns of the oceans are just as important in regulating climate. In general, the oceans circulate in large eddies, clockwise in the Northern Hemisphere, anticlockwise in the Southern.

— Hadley cell

A

▲ CREATING WINDS

The amount of heat absorbed at the Equator is much greater than at the Poles. The temperature difference creates giant circulation cells which transfer heat from the Equator to the Poles [A]. The Hadley cell is driven by hot air rising from the Equator which cools and returns to the surface at 30° latitude. Some of this returning air is drawn back towards the Equator, creating the trade winds. The Ferrel cell guides warm air towards the Poles, creating winds which the Earth's rotation skews to become the Westerlies. Where these winds meet cold air blowing directly from the Pole, frontal depressions form giving unsettled weather. At the cell boundaries jet streams form – channels of high winds which encircle the planet. This circulation from the Equator to the Poles is complicated by the Earth's rotation, creating the Coriolis force which bends winds to the right in the Northern Hemisphere, and to the left in the Southern Hemisphere.

▶ Deserts can be created in many ways, and they may be hot or cold. The Antarctic, being one of the driest places in the world, is classed as a cold desert. The Sahara and the Arabian Deserts are classic examples of hot deserts. The photograph shows a sand dune in the Simpson Desert in Australia.
Winds blowing over the land constantly shift dunes in ever changing patterns.

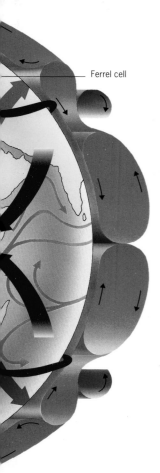

Ferrel cell

▶ A tornado can form during a very severe thunderstorm [C]. Hot air evaporating off land or sea rises rapidly through the atmosphere, condensing to form clouds. As surface air rushes inward the low pressure at the centre of the storm, the spin of the Earth makes the whole complex spin, producing a typhoon or hurricane (right). Tornadoes occur when the fast-rising thermals, which create a storm, begin to spin even more quickly, perhaps in response to the local geography. As the thermal winds up on itself, it draws a funnel of cloud down from the bottom of the storm towards the ground, where the winds often exceed 200kmh. The extreme low pressure sucks up material from the ground, flinging it out at the top of the tornado, sometimes to land several kilometres away. Waterspouts are similar vortices that form over water.

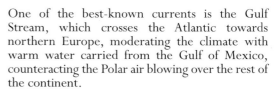

C

▶ **VARIETY OF CLIMATE**
The patterns of rainfall and temperature around the world divide the Earth into different regions of vegetation [B]. Seven cities around the world illustrate the wide variety of weather these produce.

New York has an east coast continental climate, with cold winters, hot summers and steady rainfall all year round. London's climate is marine west coast, similarly wet to New York's but with less variation between summer and winter temperatures. Omsk has typical steppe climate, with low rainfall and very cold winters followed by hot summers. Singapore's tropical climate gives almost constant hot and very wet weather. Manaus in Brazil's region of tropical savanna has constant high temperatures, with very dry summer months. A desert climate like that of Alice Springs has very high average temperatures (with a slight dip during the southern winter months), but almost no rain throughout the year.
The Nigerian capital, Lagos, has a constantly hot tropical rainforest climate, characterised by its extremely wet summer months.

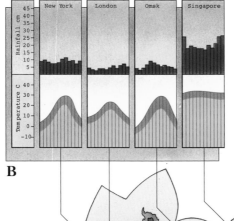

B

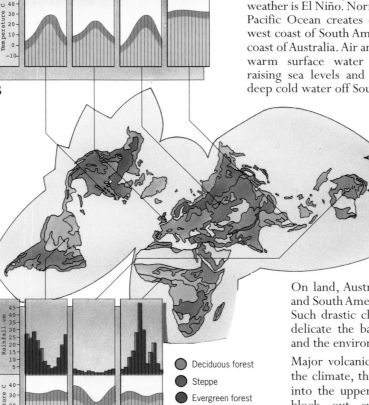

- ● Deciduous forest
- ● Steppe
- ● Evergreen forest
- ● Tropical rainforest
- ○ Tropical savanna
- ○ Desert
- ○ Tundra

One of the best-known currents is the Gulf Stream, which crosses the Atlantic towards northern Europe, moderating the climate with warm water carried from the Gulf of Mexico, counteracting the Polar air blowing over the rest of the continent.

Another example of the oceanic effect on the weather is El Niño. Normally, the circulation of the Pacific Ocean creates cold, dry weather on the west coast of South America, and rain on the east coast of Australia. Air and water currents circulate warm surface water westwards to Australia, raising sea levels and creating an upwelling of deep cold water off South America.

But as the warm water spreads eastwards it destabilises the trade winds, which reverse their direction. The ocean circulation reverses as well, with warm water off South America preventing the cold upwelling which brings up nutrients vital to fish stocks. On land, Australia experiences drought, and South America suffers torrential rain. Such drastic climatic changes show how delicate the balance is between climate and the environment.

Major volcanic eruptions can also affect the climate, throwing dust particles high into the upper atmosphere, where they block out sunlight. Sudden climate changes are believed to have caused mass extinction of life on Earth in the past, and as yet there is little humanity can do to counter, or even predict, these changes.

Peopling the Globe

The origins of humankind are very hard to determine. The fossil record of our ancestors is very patchy, and thus the story involves large amounts of guesswork. Archaeologists believe that between 7 and 10 million years ago, a human ancestor, called Ramapithecus, developed from the same stock as chimpanzees and gorillas. The route from these creatures to modern man can be traced in terms of changing skeletons. Bipedal motion required a sturdy pelvis, while the increasing intelligence of these progenitors can be followed through increasing brain capacities. Ramapithecus was succeeded by Australopithecus, whose later form is named Homo habilis, the handy man, because fossil evidence shows that it used simple tools.

Homo erectus appeared in Africa 1.7 million years ago and spread to the rest of the world roughly 1 million years ago. They were almost as tall as modern humans, with skull capacities twice as large as Homo habilis. This species lived longer in Asia than in Africa – it includes Peking Man, who lived 250,000 years ago. It was gradually succeeded by our species, Homo sapiens, which appeared in Africa more than 500,000 years ago. The expansion was a slow drift as bands of hunter-gatherers followed prey animals. There can have been no population pressure: 10,000 years ago the world population was between 5 and 10 million, about the population of New York City today. As people settled in various places, climate and food sources led them to evolve differently. For example, those in very hot Equatorial countries kept a dark skin to protect them from ultraviolet sunlight; those in colder climates developed lighter skins to maximise the effect of a weaker sun – vitamin D, essential to bone growth, is gained from sunlight.

At first only Africa, Asia and the warmer parts of Europe were colonised: America and Australia remained empty for thousands of years. Movement between continental land masses was made possible by climate changes. During the last Ice Age, much of the world's water was locked into the ice caps. Sea levels dropped dramatically, what is now the Bering Strait became a land passage, and vast stretches of ocean became navigable by small boats.

Hunters to farmers

For two million years, human ancestors lived as hunter-gatherers, following a nomadic pattern of life, with a diet of animals and seasonal fruits.

▼ **THE ICE AGE**
In the Ice Age, parts of Europe were covered in glacial sheets and the North Sea was a great plain [**A**]. The climate and terrain were very like Alaska today, and herds of reindeer roamed the area. These were a main food source for groups of hunter-gatherers, traces of whom have been found in Europe, mostly in the warmer areas (southern Spain, south-west France and along main rivers). These people followed the deer herds on their grazing migrations, augmenting their diet with small game as well as vegetables, berries and grains. As the climate became warmer various groups settled near coasts to become fisher-gatherers.

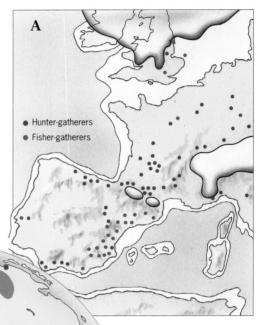

A

● Hunter-gatherers
● Fisher-gatherers

◀ **HOMO SAPIENS**
From central and southern Africa Homo sapiens spread out to populate the whole world [**B**]. The first migration spread from Africa eastwards across to Asia. Routes branched off to northern Africa and southern Europe. A second wave occurred 15,000 years ago, when glaciation provided a land bridge across the Bering Strait, allowing movement from northern Asia to the Americas.

B

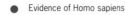

● Evidence of Homo sapiens

▲ Prehistoric Americans

C

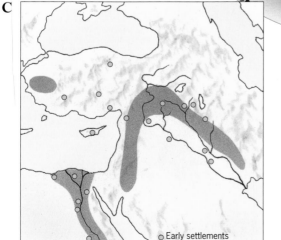

○ Early settlements

◀ **THE FIRST FARMERS**
The first farming settlements, which developed into the first cities, were probably founded around 10,000 years ago in the 'Fertile Crescent' [**C**], a band of land stretching from the Mediterranean to the rivers Tigris and Euphrates, in modern Jordan, Lebanon, Syria, Turkey and Iraq. Civilisation also flowered along the banks of the river Nile, similarly suited to agriculture. From simple farmsteads grew villages, towns, cities and eventually whole civilisations.

▲ *This skull of* Australopithicus africanus *is over 2 million years old. Africanus was the first hominid to leave the forest for the open plain.*

This changed between 20,000 and 10,000 years ago with the development of agriculture. About 15,000 years ago, as temperatures rose, primitive farming practices began to appear wherever the climate allowed it. The most important of these were Mesopotamia, the crescent between the rivers Tigris and Euphrates in modern Iraq, south-eastern Turkey and eastern Syria, the Nile valley, Central America and north-east China. Once wandering groups settled down the population soared, increasing from 5 to 300 million in 8000 years.

Small farming settlements developed into villages, then towns, then cities. Social and political organisations developed to control large groups of people. Gradually, the great civilisations grew, in the fertile fields of these first settlements. Along the Nile Valley, the Egyptians started to build a sophisticated culture around 3000BC, at the same time as the Sumerians were developing a system of city states in Mesopotamia. Similar civilisations appeared in China and Central America. Influences from these civilisations rippled outwards, laying down the pattern for the shape of the modern world.

▶ OUT OF AFRICA

It is now considered that the ancestors of humankind first appeared in Africa [D]. As well as indications of early Homo sapiens, the evidence for Africa's claims to be the cradle of humanity comes from fossils of Australopithecus and Homo erectus found in South Africa, Olduvai Gorge in Kenya, and Ethiopia. These are older than any others so far discovered in the world and so it seems likely that the human beings who evolved in Africa gradually spread out to other parts of the world. This is corroborated by fossils of a later date found in India, Java and China which indicate the direction of migration out of Africa. Early Homo sapiens fossils have also been found in China, southern Europe, North and South America and the Middle East. In Europe, the fossils found so far are confined to early forms of Homo sapiens and Neanderthal man, whose traces have been found in Germany, Hungary, France, Belgium, Greece, Czechoslovakia, Russia and the Middle East.

D

△ Homo erectus
▲ Homo habilis
● Australopithecus
■ Early paleolithic

E

● Caucasian
○ Mongol
● Negroid
◑ Indian/Caucasian
● Aboriginal
◐ Caucasian/Mongol
◑ Negroid/Caucasian

▲ FIRST MIGRATIONS

Human beings it seems could not stay long in one place [E].
At first, migrations were slow and took place over thousands of years. From their African prototype, people adapted physically, in response to extremes of climate, gradually evolving into the various races that populate the world today. These races developed in certain areas, as shown on the map above, however, the forces of the modern world from the age of discovery onwards created later movements that have spread people around the world. These modern migrations, some voluntary, others enforced as in the slave trade, are also shown.

The population explosion

There are more than 6 billion people in the world today. This figure is rising at a rate of 140 million each year, an increase of more than the population of Japan. But until comparatively recently, the rate of increase of the world population was low. Two thousand years ago, there were an estimated 300 million people on Earth; by 1650 this had increased to a mere 500 million. Then in only 200 years this number had doubled, and in the 150 years since then it has increased five-fold. In spite of recurrent famine and war, the world population seems set on an inexorable upward curve, doubling every 39 years.

This population explosion is a result of social developments since the Industrial Revolution. Proportionally there are the same number of births each year – or perhaps fewer. But the advances of improved sanitation and nutrition made possible by the industrial and scientific advances of the 18th and 19th centuries meant that fewer babies died at birth and that people lived longer.

At first these changes were confined to the countries of the developed world, in Europe and America, but as they have spread around the world, the population has ballooned. Now in most European countries the population remains stable, mainly because of the availability of reliable contraception. Indeed, in some countries the birth rate has fallen below the number needed to maintain stability; this will result in a top-heavy 'age pyramid', with too many grandparents and not enough grandchildren to support them. Some countries, such as France and Sweden, have tried to encourage people to have more babies through maternity payments and tax discounts for large families.

In the developing world the situation is different. There are many cultural and religious objections to the use of contraception. In a traditional agricultural community, too, a large family was desirable. As well as ensuring that the parents would have surviving children to look after them, many children provided a workforce to farm the land. But fewer people now live on the land, as farming becomes mechanised; and a large family in an urban industrialised setting just creates more mouths to feed. China, the most populated country in the world, has solved the problem, rationing families to one child each.

The rush to the cities

All over the world, more people live in cities than in the country, because it is no longer possible to make a living working on the land.

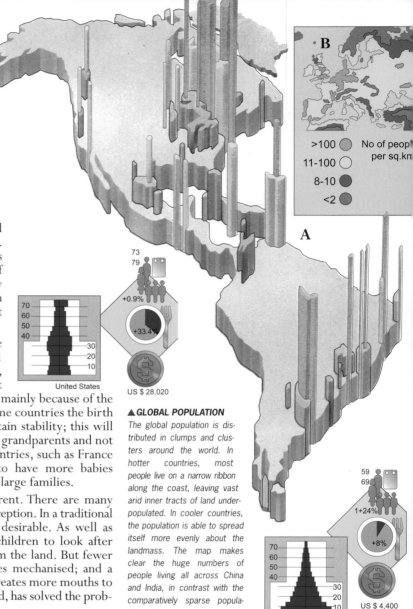

A **B**

>100 No of people per sq.km
11-100
8-10
<2

73
79
+0.9%
+33.4%
US $ 28,020
United States
70 60 50 40 30 20 10

59
69
1+24%
+8%
US $ 4,400
Brazil
70 60 50 40 30 20 10

▲ **GLOBAL POPULATION**
The global population is distributed in clumps and clusters around the world. In hotter countries, most people live on a narrow ribbon along the coast, leaving vast arid inner tracts of land underpopulated. In cooler countries, the population is able to spread itself more evenly about the landmass. The map makes clear the huge numbers of people living all across China and India, in contrast with the comparatively sparse population of much of the United States. The graphics around illustration **[A]** show for each continent the rate of population growth, the average longevity of men and women, the gross national product per capita (a measure of wealth), and the calorific intake per head as a

percentage of an adult's average daily requirement. These illustrate the gap in health and wealth between the developed world and the developing nations.

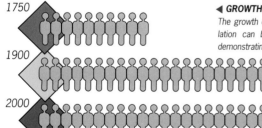

1750
1900
2000

◀ **GROWTH 1750–2000**
The growth of the human population can be shown **[D]** by demonstrating the number

of people that would occupy each 2km² of land of the Earth's surface at various eras: 1750, 1900 and 2000.

D

▶ **POPULATION GROWTH**
The Earth's population has swollen from a mere 250 million 1000 years ago (roughly the present-day population of the United States) to 6 billion today.

For most of the intervening period growth was very slow, and there were even slight declines caused by plagues

such as the Black Death. However, from about the time of the Industrial Revolution the rate of growth increased, accelerating further with each improvement in hygiene and healthcare.

A graph of world population growth over the past 300 years **[C]** can be split to show how the relative increases in each

continent have been staggered. Throughout recorded history, the population of Asia has been greater than that of all the other continents combined. However, during the 19th century the population of Europe grew at twice the rate of Asia's, thanks mainly to the improvements in living conditions brought about by sci-

entific advances and the Industrial Revolution. This rate of growth has slowed in Europe this century, whereas that of Asia has accelerated spectacularly – its population seems likely to have tripled in the fifty years from 1950. Over the last two centuries the populations of North and South America have

been increasing just as fast. In the 19th century this was due to immigration, whereas this century's gains can be attributed to better health and hygiene, improvements which have gradually spread to the developing world.

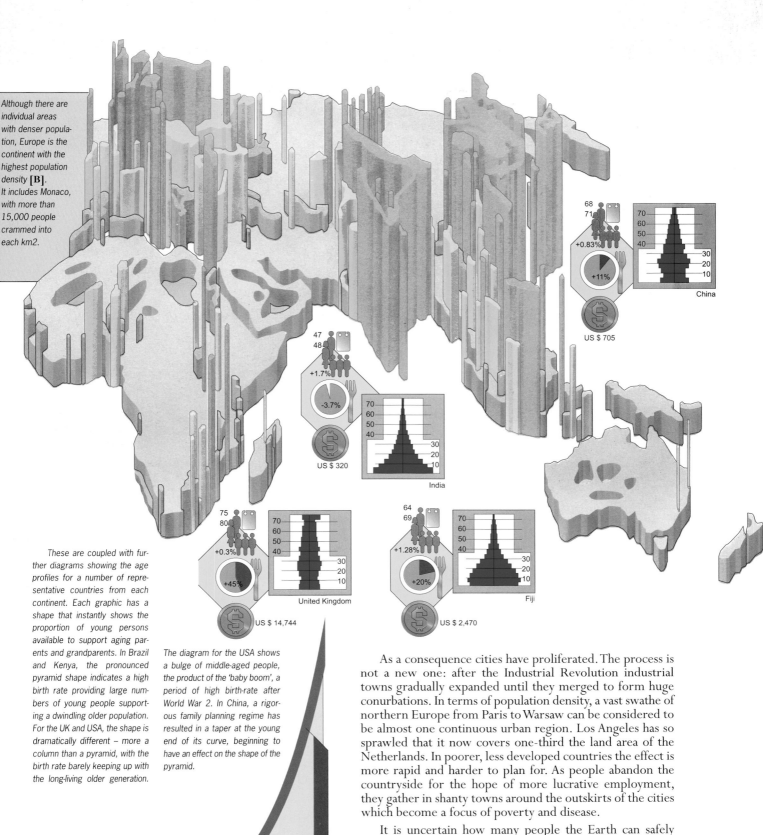

Although there are individual areas with denser population, Europe is the continent with the highest population density [B]. It includes Monaco, with more than 15,000 people crammed into each km2.

68
71
+0.83%
+11%
US $ 705
China

47
48
+1.7%
-3.7%
US $ 320
India

75
80
+0.3%
+45%
US $ 14,744
United Kingdom

64
69
+1.28%
+20%
US $ 2,470
Fiji

These are coupled with further diagrams showing the age profiles for a number of representative countries from each continent. Each graphic has a shape that instantly shows the proportion of young persons available to support aging parents and grandparents. In Brazil and Kenya, the pronounced pyramid shape indicates a high birth rate providing large numbers of young people supporting a dwindling older population. For the UK and USA, the shape is dramatically different – more a column than a pyramid, with the birth rate barely keeping up with the long-living older generation.

The diagram for the USA shows a bulge of middle-aged people, the product of the 'baby boom', a period of high birth-rate after World War 2. In China, a rigorous family planning regime has resulted in a taper at the young end of its curve, beginning to have an effect on the shape of the pyramid.

C

Years: 1750   1800   1850   1900   1950   2000

World population   790 million   980   1260   1650   2500   6200

As a consequence cities have proliferated. The process is not a new one: after the Industrial Revolution industrial towns gradually expanded until they merged to form huge conurbations. In terms of population density, a vast swathe of northern Europe from Paris to Warsaw can be considered to be almost one continuous urban region. Los Angeles has so sprawled that it now covers one-third the land area of the Netherlands. In poorer, less developed countries the effect is more rapid and harder to plan for. As people abandon the countryside for the hope of more lucrative employment, they gather in shanty towns around the outskirts of the cities which become a focus of poverty and disease.

It is uncertain how many people the Earth can safely hold and feed. Just as scientific discoveries have improved life expectancy and diminished infant mortality, so have crop yields grown. Population growth in the developing world has been accompanied by rising affluence and greater availability of education. History shows that richer and better educated countries tend to have low population growth.

Distribution of the resources would ensure a fairer share for everyone. At the moment, the Northern Hemisphere has four-fifths of the World's wealth to share on only one-quarter of the population, whereas the Southern Hemisphere, with the majority of the population to sustain, has to make do with one-fifth of the World's resources.

COUNTRY FACTS & FLAGS

AFGHANISTAN

Capital:	Kabul
Area:	647,500 km²
Population:	31,056,997
Currency:	Afghani (AFA)
Main Religions:	Sunni Muslim 80%, Shi'a Muslim 19%, other 1%
Main Languages:	Pashtu 35%, Afghan Persian (Dari) 50%, Turkic languages 11%, 30 minor languages 4%
Int Dial Code:	93
Map Page:	91

ALBANIA

Capital:	Tirana
Area:	28,748 km²
Population:	3,581,655
Currency:	Lek (ALL)
Main Religions:	Muslim 70%, Albanian Orthodox 20%, Roman Catholic 10%
Main Languages:	Albanian (Tosk is the official dialect), Greek
Int Dial Code:	355
Map Page:	68

ALGERIA

Capital:	Algiers
Area:	2,381,740 km²
Population:	32,930,091
Currency:	Algerian dinar (DZD)
Main Religions:	Sunni Muslim 99%, Christian and Jewish 1%
Languages:	Arabic (official), French, Berber dialects
Int Dial Code:	213
Map Page:	103

ANDORRA

Capital:	Andorra la Vella
Area:	468 km²
Population:	71,201
Currency:	Euro (EUR)
Main Religions:	Roman Catholic
Main Languages:	Catalan (official), French, Castilian
Int Dial Code:	376
Map Page:	61

ANGOLA

Capital:	Luanda
Area:	1,246,700 km²
Population:	12,127,071
Currency:	Kwanza (AOA)
Main Religions:	Indigenous beliefs 47%, Roman Catholic 38%, Protestant 15%
Main Languages:	Portuguese (official), Bantu and other African languages
Int Dial Code:	244
Map Page:	98

ANTIGUA AND BARBUDA

Capital:	Saint John's
Area:	442.6 km²
	(Antigua 281 km²; Barbuda 161 km²)
Population:	67,000
Currency:	East Caribbean dollar (XCD)
Main Religions:	Anglican (predominant), Protestant, Roman Catholic
Main Languages:	English (official), local dialects
Int Dial Code:	1 + 268
Map Page:	135

ARGENTINA

Capital:	Buenos Aires
Area:	2,766,890 km²
Population:	39,921,833
Currency:	Argentine Peso (ARS)
Main Religions:	Roman Catholic 92%, Protestant 2%, Jewish 2%, other 4%
Main Languages:	Spanish (official), English, Italian, German, French
Int Dial Code:	54
Map Page:	142

ARMENIA

Capital:	Yerevan
Area:	29,800 km²
Population:	2,976,372
Currency:	Dram (AMD)
Main Religions:	Armenian Orthodox 94%
Main Languages:	Armenian 96%, Russian 2%, other 2%
Int Dial Code:	374
Map Page:	93

AUSTRALIA

Capital:	Canberra
Area:	7,686,850 km²
Population:	20,264,082
Currency:	Australian dollar (AUD)
Main Religions:	Anglican 26.1%, Roman Catholic 26%, other Christian 24.3%, non-Christian 11%
Main Languages:	English, native languages
Int Dial Code:	61
Map Page:	114

AUSTRIA

Capital:	Vienna
Area:	83,870 km²
Population:	8,192,880
Currency:	Euro (EUR)
Main Religions:	Roman Catholic 74%, Protestant 5%, Muslim and other 21%
Main Languages:	German
Int Dial Code:	43
Map Page:	63

AZERBAIJAN

Capital:	Baku
Area:	86,600 km²
Population:	7,961,619
Currency:	Azerbaijani manat (AZM)
Main Religions:	Muslim 93.4%, Russian Orthodox 2.5%, Armenian Orthodox 2.3%, other 1.8%
Main Languages:	Azerbaijani (Azeri) 89%, Russian 3%, Armenian 2%
Int Dial Code:	994
Map Page:	93

BAHAMAS, THE

Capital:	Nassau
Area:	13,940 km²
Population:	303,770
Currency:	Bahamian dollar (BSD)
Main Religions:	Baptist 35%, Anglican 15%, Roman Catholic 13%, Pentecostal 8%, Methodist 4%, Church of God 5%
Main Languages:	English, Creole
Int Dial Code:	1 + 242
Map Page:	135

BAHRAIN

Capital:	Manama
Area:	665 km²
Population:	698,585
Currency:	Bahraini dinar (BHD)
Main Religions:	Muslim 81% (Shi'a & Sunni), Christian 9%
Main Languages:	Arabic, English, Farsi, Urdu
Int Dial Code:	973
Map Page:	95

BANGLADESH

Capital:	Dhaka
Area:	144,000 km²
Population:	147,365,352
Currency:	Taka (BDT)
Main Religions:	Muslim 83%, Hindu 16%, other 1%
Main Languages:	Bangla (official, also known as Bengali), English
Int Dial Code:	880
Map Page:	88

BARBADOS

Capital:	Bridgetown
Area:	431 km²
Population:	279,912
Currency:	Barbadian dollar (BBD)
Main Religions:	Protestant 67% (Anglican 40%, Pentecostal 8%, Methodist 7%, other 12%), Roman Catholic 4%
Main Languages:	English
Int Dial Code:	1 + 246
Map Page:	135

BELARUS

Capital:	Minsk
Area:	207,600 km²
Population:	10,293,011
Currency:	Belarusian ruble (BYB/BYR)
Main Religions:	Eastern Orthodox 80%, other (including Roman Catholic, Protestant, Jewish, and Muslim) 20%
Main Languages:	Belarusian, Russian
Int Dial Code:	375
Map Page:	70

BELGIUM

Capital:	Brussels
Area:	30,528 km²
Population:	10,379,067
Currency:	Euro (EUR)
Main Religions:	Roman Catholic 75%, Protestant or other 25%
Main Languages:	Dutch 60%, French 40% legally bilingual (Dutch and French)
Int Dial Code:	32
Map Page:	55

BELIZE

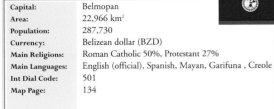

Capital:	Belmopan
Area:	22,966 km²
Population:	287,730
Currency:	Belizean dollar (BZD)
Main Religions:	Roman Catholic 50%, Protestant 27%
Main Languages:	English (official), Spanish, Mayan, Garifuna , Creole
Int Dial Code:	501
Map Page:	134

BENIN

Capital:	Porto-Novo
Area:	112,620 km²
Population:	7,862,944
Currency:	Communaute Financiere Africaine franc (XOF)
Main Religions:	Indigenous beliefs 50%, Christian 30%, Muslim 20%
Main Languages:	French (official), Fon and Yoruba, tribal languages
Int Dial Code:	229
Map Page:	105

BHUTAN

Capital:	Thimphu
Area:	47,000 km²
Population:	2,279,723
Currency:	Ngultrum (BTN); Indian rupee (INR)
Main Religions:	Lamaistic Buddhist 75%, Hinduism 25%
Main Languages:	Dzongkha (official), Bhotes speak various Tibetan dialects, Nepalese dialects
Int Dial Code:	975
Map Page:	88

BOLIVIA

Capital:	La Paz (seat of government); Sucre (legal capital and seat of judiciary)
Area:	1,098,580 km²
Population:	8,989,046
Currency:	Boliviano (BOB)
Main Religions:	Roman Catholic 95%, Protestant 5%
Main Languages:	Spanish (official), Quechua (official), Aymara
Int Dial Code:	591
Map Page:	140

BOSNIA AND HERZEGOVINA

Capital:	Sarajevo
Area:	51,129 km²
Population:	4,498,976
Currency:	Marka (BAM)
Main Religions:	Muslim 40%, Orthodox 31%, Roman Catholic 15%, Protestant 4%, other 14%
Main Languages:	Croatian, Serbian, Bosnian
Int Dial Code:	387
Map Page:	66

BOTSWANA

Capital:	Gaborone
Area:	600,370 km²
Population:	1,639,833
Currency:	Pula (BWP)
Main Religions:	Christian 72%, Badimo 6%
Main Languages:	Setswana, Kalanga, Sekgalagadi, English
Int Dial Code:	267
Map Page:	108

BRAZIL

Capital:	Brasilia
Area:	8,511,965 km²
Population:	188,078,227
Currency:	Real (BRL)
Main Religions:	Roman Catholic (nominal) 74%, Protestant 15%
Main Languages:	Portuguese (official), Spanish, English, French
Int Dial Code:	55
Map Page:	141

BRUNEI

Capital:	Bandar Seri Begawan
Area:	5,770 km²
Population:	379,444
Currency:	Bruneian dollar (BND)
Main Religions:	Muslim (official) 67%, Buddhist 13%, Christian 10%, indigenous beliefs and other 10%
Main Languages:	Malay (official), English, Chinese
Int Dial Code:	673
Map Page:	86

BULGARIA

Capital:	Sofia
Area:	110,910 km²
Population:	7,385,367
Currency:	Lev (BGL)
Main Religions:	Bulgarian Orthodox 82.6%, Muslim 13%, Roman Catholic 1.5%, Uniate Catholic 0.2%, Jewish 0.8%
Main Languages:	Bulgarian, Turkish
Int Dial Code:	359
Map Page:	67

BURKINA

Capital:	Ouagadougou
Area:	274,200 km²
Population:	13,902,972
Currency:	Communaute Financiere Africaine franc (XOF)
Main Religions:	Indigenous beliefs 40%, Muslim 50%, Christian 10%
Main Languages:	French (official), native African languages belonging to Sudanic family spoken by 90% of the population
Int Dial Code:	226
Map Page:	104

BURUNDI

Capital:	Bujumbura
Area:	27,830 km²
Population:	8,090,068
Currency:	Burundi franc (BIF)
Main Religions:	Christian 67% (Roman Catholic 62%, Protestant 5%), indigenous beliefs 23%, Muslim 10%
Main Languages:	Kirundi (official), French (official), Swahili
Int Dial Code:	257
Map Page:	106

CAMBODIA

Capital:	Phnom Penh
Area:	181,040 km²
Population:	13,881,427
Currency:	Riel (KHR)
Main Religions:	Theravada Buddhist 95%, other 5%
Main Languages:	Khmer (official) 95%, French, English
Int Dial Code:	855
Map Page:	84

CAMEROON

Capital:	Yaounde
Area:	475,440 km²
Population:	17,340,702
Currency:	Communaute Financiere Africaine franc (XAF)
Main Religions:	Indigenous beliefs 40%, Christian 40%, Muslim 20%
Main Languages:	24 major African language groups, English (official), French (official)
Int Dial Code:	237
Map Page:	105

CANADA

Capital:	Ottawa
Area:	9,984,670 km²
Population:	33,098,932
Currency:	Canadian dollar (CAD)
Main Religions:	Roman Catholic 42%, Protestant 23%, other 18%
Main Languages:	English 59.3% (official), French 23.2% (official), other 17.5%
Int Dial Code:	1
Map Page:	122

CAPE VERDE

Capital:	Praia
Area:	4,033 km²
Population:	420,979
Currency:	Cape Verdean escudo (CVE)
Main Religions:	Roman Catholic, Protestant
Main Languages:	Portuguese, Crioulo
Int Dial Code:	238
Map Page:	104

CENTRAL AFRICAN REPUBLIC

Capital:	Bangui
Area:	622,984 km²
Population:	4,303,356
Currency:	Communaute Financiere Africaine franc (XAF)
Main Religions:	Indigenous beliefs 35%, Protestant 25%, Roman Catholic 25%, Muslim 15%
Main Languages:	French (official), Sangho , Arabic, Hunsa, Swahili
Int Dial Code:	236
Map Page:	106

CHAD

Capital:	N'Djamena
Area:	1.284 million km²
Population:	9,944,201
Currency:	Communaute Financiere Africaine franc (XAF)
Main Religions:	Muslim 50%, Christian 35%
Main Languages:	French (official), Arabic (official), Sara and Sango, over 100 different languages and dialects
Int Dial Code:	235
Map Page:	100

CHILE

Capital:	Santiago
Area:	756,950 km²
Population:	16,134,219
Currency:	Chilean peso (CLP)
Main Religions:	Roman Catholic 89%, Protestant 11%
Main Languages:	Spanish
Int Dial Code:	56
Map Page:	142

CHINA

Capital:	Beijing
Area:	9,596,960 km²
Population:	1,313,973,713
Currency:	Yuan (CNY)
Main Religions:	Daoist (Taoist), Buddhist, Christian 3-4%, Muslim 1-2%
Main Languages:	Standard Chinese or Mandarin (Putonghua), Yue (Cantonese), Wu (Shanghaiese), Minbei (Fuzhou), Minnan (Hokkien-Taiwanese), Xiang, Gan, Hakka
Int Dial Code:	86
Map Page:	80

COLOMBIA

Capital:	Bogota
Area:	1,138,910 km²
Population:	43,593,035
Currency:	Colombian peso (COP)
Main Religions:	Roman Catholic 90%
Main Languages:	Spanish
Int Dial Code:	57
Map Page:	140

COMOROS

Capital:	Moroni
Area:	2,170 km²
Population:	690,948
Currency:	Comoran franc (KMF)
Main Religions:	Sunni Muslim 98%, Roman Catholic 2%
Main Languages:	Arabic (official), French (official), Comoran
Int Dial Code:	269
Map Page:	109

CONGO

Capital:	Brazzaville
Area:	342,000 km²
Population:	3,702,314
Currency:	Communaute Financiere Africaine franc (XAF)
Main Religions:	Christian 50%, Animist 48%, Muslim 2%
Main Languages:	French (official), Lingala and Monokutuba
Int Dial Code:	242
Map Page:	105

CONGO, DEM. REP. OF THE

Capital:	Kinshasa
Area:	2,345,410 km²
Population:	62,660,551
Currency:	Congolese franc (CDF)
Main Religions:	Roman Catholic 50%, Protestant 20%, Kimbanguist 10%, Muslim 10%, other 10%
Main Languages:	French (official), Lingala, Kingwana, Kikongo, Tshiluba
Int Dial Code:	243
Map Page:	106

COSTA RICA

Capital:	San José
Area:	51,100 km²
Population:	4,075,261
Currency:	Costa Rican colon (CRC)
Main Religions:	Roman Catholic 76.3%, Evangelical 13.7%, other Protestant 0.7%, Jehovah's Witnesses 1.3%,
Main Languages:	Spanish (official), English spoken around Puerto Limon
Int Dial Code:	506
Map Page:	135

COTE D'IVOIRE

Capital:	Yamoussoukro - capital since 1983, Abidjan is the administrative center
Area:	322,460 km²
Population:	17,654,843
Currency:	Communaute Financiere Africaine franc (XOF)
Main Religions:	Muslim 35%, Indigenous 25%, Christian 20%
Main Languages:	French (official), 60 native dialects
Int Dial Code:	225
Map Page:	104

CROATIA

Capital:	Zagreb
Area:	56,542 km²
Population:	4,494,749
Currency:	Kuna (HRK)
Main Religions:	Roman Catholic 87.8%, Orthodox 4.4%,
Main Languages:	Croatian 96%, other 4% (Italian, Hungarian, Czech)
Int Dial Code:	385
Map Page:	66

CUBA

Capital:	Havana
Area:	110,860 km²
Population:	11,382,820
Currency:	Cuban peso (CUP) and convertible Peso (CUC)
Main Religions:	Roman Catholic 85% , Protestants, Jehovah's Witnesses, Jews
Main Languages:	Spanish
Int Dial Code:	53
Map Page:	135

CYPRUS

Capital:	Nicosia
Area:	9,250 km² (3,355 km² in the Turkish Cypriot area)
Population:	784,301
Currency:	Cypriot pound (CYP); Turkish new lira (YTL)
Main Religions:	Greek Orthodox 78%, Muslim 18%,
Main Languages:	Greek, Turkish, English
Int Dial Code:	357
Map Page:	92

CZECH REPUBLIC

Capital:	Prague
Area:	78,866 km²
Population:	10,235,455
Currency:	Czech koruna (CZK)
Main Religions:	Roman Catholic 26.8%, Protestant 2.1%, Orthodox 3%
Main Languages:	Czech
Int Dial Code:	420
Map Page:	51

DENMARK

Capital:	Copenhagen
Area:	43,094 km²
Population:	5,450,661
Currency:	Danish krone (DKK)
Main Religions:	Evangelical Lutheran 95%, other Protestant and Roman Catholic 3%, Muslims 2%
Main Languages:	Danish, Faroese, Greenlandic, German, English
Int Dial Code:	45
Map Page:	49

DJIBOUTI

Capital:	Djibouti
Area:	23,000 km²
Population:	486,530
Currency:	Djiboutian franc (DJF)
Main Religions:	Muslim 94%, Christian 6%
Main Languages:	French (official), Arabic (official), Somali, Afar
Int Dial Code:	253
Map Page:	101

DOMINICA

Capital:	Roseau
Area:	754 km²
Population:	68,910
Currency:	East Caribbean dollar (XCD)
Main Religions:	Roman Catholic 77%, Protestant 15% (Methodist 5%, Pentecostal 3%, Seventh-Day Adventist 3%, Baptist 2%, other 2%), none 2%, other 6%
Main Languages:	English (official), French patois
Int Dial Code:	1 + 767
Map Page:	135

DOMINICAN REPUBLIC

Capital:	Santo Domingo
Area:	48,730 km²
Population:	9,183,984
Currency:	Dominican peso (DOP)
Main Religions:	Roman Catholic 95%
Main Languages:	Spanish
Int Dial Code:	1 + 809
Map Page:	135

EAST TIMOR

Capital:	Dili
Area:	15,007 km²
Population:	1,062,777
Currency:	US dollar
Main Religions:	Roman Catholic, Muslim
Main Languages:	Tetum, Portugese, Indonesian, English
Int Dial Code:	670
Map Page:	87

ECUADOR

Capital:	Quito
Area:	283,560 km²
Population:	13,547,510
Currency:	US dollar (USD)
Main Religions:	Roman Catholic 95%
Main Languages:	Spanish (official), Amerindian languages (especially Quechua)
Int Dial Code:	593
Map Page:	140

EGYPT

Capital:	Cairo
Area:	1,001,450 km²
Population:	78,887,007
Currency:	Egyptian pound (EGP)
Main Religions:	Muslim (mostly Sunni) 90%, Coptic Christian and other 6%
Main Languages:	Arabic (official), English and French
Int Dial Code:	20
Map Page:	100

EL SALVADOR

Capital:	San Salvador
Area:	21,040 km²
Population:	6,822,378
Currency:	Salvadoran colon (SVC); US dollar (USD)
Main Religions:	Roman Catholic 83%
Main Languages:	Spanish, Nahua
Int Dial Code:	503
Map Page:	134

EQUATORIAL GUINEA

Capital:	Malabo
Area:	28,051 km²
Population:	540,109
Currency:	Communaute Financiere Africaine franc (XAF)
Main Religions:	Christian (predominantly Roman Catholic)
Main Languages:	Spanish (official), French (official), Pidgin English, Fang, Bubi, Ibo
Int Dial Code:	240
Map Page:	105

ERITREA

Capital:	Asmara
Area:	121,320 km²
Population:	4,786,994
Currency:	Nakfa (ERN)
Main Religions:	Muslim, Coptic Christian, Roman Catholic, Protestant
Main Languages:	Afar, Amharic, Arabic, Tigre and Kunama, Tigrinya, other Cushitic languages
Int Dial Code:	291
Map Page:	101

ESTONIA

Capital:	Tallinn
Area:	45,226 km²
Population:	1,324,333
Currency:	Estonian kroon (EEK)
Main Religions:	Evangelical Lutheran, Russian Orthodox, Estonian Orthodox, Baptist, Methodist, Seventh-Day Adventist
Main Languages:	Estonian (official), Russian, Ukrainian, English, Finnish
Int Dial Code:	372
Map Page:	49

ETHIOPIA

Capital:	Addis Ababa
Area:	1,127,127 km2
Population:	74,777,981
Currency:	Birr (ETB)
Main Religions:	Muslim 45%-50%, Ethiopian Orthodox 35%-40%, animist 12%, other 3%-8%
Main Languages:	Amharic, Tigrinya, Oromigna, Guaragigna, Somali, Arabic, English
Int Dial Code:	251
Map Page:	107

FIJI

Capital:	Suva
Area:	18,270 km²
Population:	905,949
Currency:	Fijian dollar (FJD)
Main Religions:	Christian 52% (Methodist 37%, Roman Catholic 9%), Hindu 38%, Muslim 8%, other 2%
Main Languages:	English (official), Fijian, Hindustani
Int Dial Code:	679
Map Page:	112

FINLAND

Capital:	Helsinki
Area:	338,145 km²
Population:	5,231,372
Currency:	Euro (EUR)
Main Religions:	Evangelical Lutheran 89%, Greek Orthodox 1%, none 9%, other 1%
Main Languages:	Finnish 93.4% (official), Swedish 5.9% (official), small Lapp- and Russian-speaking minorities
Int Dial Code:	358
Map Page:	48

FRANCE

Capital:	Paris
Area:	547,030 km²
Population:	60,876,136
Currency:	Euro (EUR)
Main Religions:	Roman Catholic 90%, Protestant 2%, Jewish 1%, Muslim 3%, unaffiliated 4%
Main Languages:	French 100%, Provencal, Breton, Alsatian, Corsican, Catalan, Basque, Flemish
Int Dial Code:	33
Map Page:	58

GABON

Capital:	Libreville
Area:	267,667 km²
Population:	1,424,906
Currency:	Communaute Financiere Africaine franc (XAF)
Main Religions:	Christian 55%-75%, Animist, Muslim less than 1%
Main Languages:	French (official), Fang, Myene, Bapounou/Eschira, Bandjabi
Int Dial Code:	241
Map Page:	105

GAMBIA, THE

Capital:	Banjul
Area:	11,300 km²
Population:	1,641,564
Currency:	Dalasi (GMD)
Main Religions:	Muslim 90%, Christian 9%, Indigenous beliefs 1%
Main Languages:	English (official), Mandinka, Wolof, Fula
Int Dial Code:	220
Map Page:	104

GEORGIA

Capital:	T'bilisi
Area:	69,700 km²
Population:	4,661,473
Currency:	Lari (GEL)
Main Religions:	Georgian Orthodox 65%, Muslim 11%, Russian Orthodox 10%, Armenian Apostolic 8%
Main Languages:	Georgian 71% (official), Russian 9%, Armenian 7%,
Int Dial Code:	995
Map Page:	93

GERMANY

Capital:	Berlin
Area:	357,021 km²
Population:	82,422,299
Currency:	Euro (EUR)
Main Religions:	Protestant 34%, Roman Catholic 34%, Muslim 3.7%, unaffiliated or other 28.3%
Main Languages:	German
Int Dial Code:	49
Map Page:	52

GHANA

Capital:	Accra
Area:	239,460 km²
Population:	22,409,572
Currency:	Cedi (GHC)
Main Religions:	Indigenous beliefs 38%, Muslim 30%, Christian 24%, other 8%
Main Languages:	English (official), African languages (Akan, Moshi-Dagomba, Ewe, and Ga)
Int Dial Code:	233
Map Page:	104

GREECE

Capital:	Athens
Area:	131,940 km²
Population:	10,688,058
Currency:	Euro (EUR)
Main Religions:	Greek Orthodox 98%, Muslim 1.3%, other 0.7%
Main Languages:	Greek 99% (official), English, French
Int Dial Code:	30
Map Page:	68

GRENADA

Capital:	Saint George's
Area:	344 km²
Population:	89,703
Currency:	East Caribbean dollar (XCD)
Main Religions:	Roman Catholic 53%, Anglican 13.8%, other Protestant 33.2%
Main Languages:	English (official), French patois
Int Dial Code:	1 + 473
Map Page:	135

GUATEMALA

Capital:	Guatemala
Area:	108,890 km²
Population:	12,293,545
Currency:	Quetzal (GTQ), US dollar (USD), others allowed
Main Religions:	Roman Catholic, Protestant, Indigenous Mayan beliefs
Main Languages:	Spanish 60%, Amerindian languages 40%
Int Dial Code:	502
Map Page:	134

GUINEA

Capital:	Conakry
Area:	245,857 km²
Population:	9,690,222
Currency:	Guinean franc (GNF)
Main Religions:	Muslim 85%, Christian 8%, Indigenous beliefs 7%
Main Languages:	French (official), each ethnic group has its own language
Int Dial Code:	224
Map Page:	104

GUINEA-BISSAU

Capital:	Bissau
Area:	36,120 km²
Population:	1,442,029
Currency:	Communaute Financiere Africaine franc (XOF)
Main Religions:	Indigenous beliefs 50%, Muslim 45%, Christian 5%
Main Languages:	Portuguese (official), Crioulo, African languages
Int Dial Code:	245
Map Page:	104

GUYANA

Capital:	Georgetown
Area:	214,970 km²
Population:	767,245
Currency:	Guyanese dollar (GYD)
Main Religions:	Christian 50%, Hindu 35%, Muslim 10%, other 5%
Main Languages:	English, Amerindian dialects, Creole, Hindi, Urdu
Int Dial Code:	592
Map Page:	141

HAITI

Capital:	Port-au-Prince
Area:	27,750 km²
Population:	8,308,504
Currency:	Gourde (HTG)
Main Religions:	Roman Catholic 80%, Protestant 16% (Baptist 10%, Pentecostal 4%, Adventist 1%, other 1%)
Main Languages:	French (official), Creole (official)
Int Dial Code:	509
Map Page:	135

HONDURAS

Capital:	Tegucigalpa
Area:	112,090 km²
Population:	7,326,496
Currency:	Lempira (HNL)
Main Religions:	Roman Catholic 97%, Protestant
Main Languages:	Spanish, Amerindian dialects
Int Dial Code:	504
Map Page:	134

HUNGARY

Capital:	Budapest
Area:	93,030 km²
Population:	9,981,334
Currency:	Forint (HUF)
Main Languages:	Hungarian 98.2%, other 1.8%
Int Dial Code:	36
Map Page:	66

ICELAND

Capital:	Reykjavik
Area:	103,000 km²
Population:	299,388
Currency:	Icelandic krona (ISK)
Main Languages:	Icelandic
Int Dial Code:	354
Map Page:	48

INDIA

Capital:	New Delhi
Area:	3,287,590 km²
Population:	1,095,351,995
Currency:	Indian rupee (INR)
Main Religions:	Hindu 80.5%, Muslim 13.4%, Christian 2.3%, Sikh 1.9%,Buddhist, Jain, Parsi 2.5%
Main Languages:	English, Hindi 30%, Bengali, Telugu, Marathi, Tamil, Urdu, Gujarati, Malayalam, Kannada, Oriya, Punjabi
Int Dial Code:	91
Map Page:	88

INDONESIA

Capital:	Jakarta
Area:	1,919,440 km²
Population:	245,452,739
Currency:	Indonesian rupiah (IDR)
Main Religions:	Muslim 88%, Protestant 5%, Roman Catholic 3%, Hindu 2%, Buddhist 1%, other 1%
Main Languages:	Bahasa Indonesia (official), English, Dutch, local dialects
Int Dial Code:	62
Map Page:	86

IRAN

Capital:	Tehran
Area:	1.648 million km²
Population:	68,688,433
Currency:	Iranian rial (IRR)
Main Religions:	Shi'a Muslim 89%, Sunni Muslim 10%, Zoroastrian, Jewish, Christian, Baha'i 1%
Main Languages:	Persian and Persian dialects 58%, Turkic and Turkic dialects 26%, Kurdish 9%, Luri 2%, Balochi 1%
Int Dial Code:	98
Map Page:	90

IRAQ

Capital:	Baghdad
Area:	437,072 km²
Population:	26,783,383
Currency:	New Iraqi dinar (NID)
Main Religions:	Muslim 97% (Shi'a 60%-65%, Sunni 32%-37%), Christian or other 3%
Main Languages:	Arabic, Kurdish, Assyrian, Armenian
Int Dial Code:	964
Map Page:	90

IRELAND

Capital:	Dublin
Area:	70,280 km²
Population:	4,062,235
Currency:	Euro (EUR)
Main Religions:	Roman Catholic 88.4%, Church of Ireland 3%
Main Languages:	English, Irish (Gaelic)
Int Dial Code:	353
Map Page:	57

ISRAEL

Capital:	Jerusalem
Area:	20,770 km²
Population:	6,352,117
Currency:	New Israeli shekel (ILS or NIS)
Main Religions:	Jewish 76.5%, Muslim 15.9%, Arab Christian 1.7%
Main Languages:	Hebrew (official), Arabic, English
Int Dial Code:	972
Map Page:	94

ITALY

Capital:	Rome
Area:	301,230 km²
Population:	58,133,509
Currency:	Euro (EUR)
Main Religions:	predominately Roman Catholic, Protestant, Jewish and Muslim
Main Languages:	Italian (official), German, French, Slovene
Int Dial Code:	39
Map Page:	64

JAMAICA

Capital:	Kingston
Area:	10,990 km²
Population:	2,758,124
Currency:	Jamaican dollar (JMD)
Main Religions:	Protestant 61.3%, Roman Catholic 4%, other 34.7%
Main Languages:	English, Creole
Int Dial Code:	1 + 876
Map Page:	135

JAPAN

Capital:	Tokyo
Area:	377,835 km²
Population:	127,463,611
Currency:	Yen (JPY)
Main Religions:	Shinto and Buddhist 84%, other 16% (including Christian 0.7%)
Main Languages:	Japanese
Int Dial Code:	81
Map Page:	83

JORDAN

Capital:	Amman
Area:	92,300 km²
Population:	5,906,760
Currency:	Jordanian dinar (JOD)
Main Religions:	Sunni Muslim 92%, Christian 6% (majority Greek Orthodox), other 2%
Main Languages:	Arabic (official), English
Int Dial Code:	962
Map Page:	94

KAZAKHSTAN

Capital:	Astana
Area:	2,717,300 km²
Population:	15,233,244
Currency:	Tenge (KZT)
Main Religions:	Muslim 47%, Russian Orthodox 44%, Protestant 2%, other 7%
Main Languages:	Kazakh (Qazaq, state language), Russian (official)
Int Dial Code:	7
Map Page:	77

KENYA

Capital:	Nairobi
Area:	582,650 km²
Population:	34,707,817
Currency:	Kenyan shilling (KES)
Main Religions:	Protestant 45%, Roman Catholic 33%, indigenous beliefs 10%, Muslim 10%
Main Languages:	English (official), Kiswahili (official)
Int Dial Code:	254
Map Page:	107

KIRIBATI

Capital:	Tarawa
Area:	811 km²
Population:	105,432
Currency:	Australian dollar (AUD)
Main Religions:	Roman Catholic 54%, Protestant (Congregational) 30%, Seventh-Day Adventist, Baha'i, Latter-day Saints and Church of God
Main Languages:	English (official), I-Kiribati
Int Dial Code:	686
Map Page:	113

KUWAIT

Capital:	Kuwait
Area:	17,820 km²
Population:	2,418,393
Currency:	Kuwaiti dinar (KD)
Main Religions:	Muslim 85% (Sunni 70%, Shi'a 30%), Christian, Hindu, Parsi, and other 15%
Main Languages:	Arabic (official), English
Int Dial Code:	965
Map Page:	95

KYRGYZSTAN

Capital:	Bishkek
Area:	198,500 km²
Population:	5,213,898
Currency:	Kyrgyzstani som (KGS)
Main Religions:	Muslim 75%, Russian Orthodox 20%, other 5%
Main Languages:	Kirghiz (Kyrgyz) - official, Russian (official)
Int Dial Code:	996
Map Page:	77

LAOS

Capital:	Vientiane
Area:	236,800 km²
Population:	6,368,481
Currency:	Kip (LAK)
Main Religions:	Buddhist 60%, Animist and other 40%
Main Languages:	Lao (official), French, English
Int Dial Code:	856
Map Page:	84

LATVIA

Capital:	Riga
Area:	64,589 km²
Population:	2,274,735
Currency:	Latvian lat (LVL)
Main Religions:	Lutheran, Roman Catholic, Russian Orthodox
Main Languages:	Latvian or Lettish (official), Lithuanian, Russian
Int Dial Code:	371
Map Page:	49

LEBANON

Capital:	Beirut
Area:	10,400 km²
Population:	3,874,050
Currency:	Lebanese pound (LBP)
Main Religions:	Muslim 59.7% (including Shi'a, Sunni, Druze, Isma'ilite, Alawite or Nusayri), Christian 39% (including Orthodox Christian, Catholic, Protestant)
Main Languages:	Arabic (official), French, English, Armenian
Int Dial Code:	961
Map Page:	94

LESOTHO

Capital:	Maseru
Area:	30,355 km²
Population:	2,022,331
Currency:	Loti (LSL); South African Rand (ZAR)
Main Religions:	Christian 80%, Indigenous beliefs 20%
Main Languages:	Sesotho (southern Sotho), English (official), Zulu, Xhosa
Int Dial Code:	266
Map Page:	108

LIBERIA

Capital:	Monrovia
Area:	111,370 km²
Population:	3,042,004
Currency:	Liberian dollar (LRD)
Main Religions:	Indigenous beliefs 40%, Christian 40%, Muslim 20%
Main Languages:	English 20% (official), ethnic group languages
Int Dial Code:	231
Map Page:	104

LIBYA

Capital:	Tripoli
Area:	1,759,540 km²
Population:	5,900,754
Currency:	Libyan dinar (LYD)
Main Religions:	Sunni Muslim 97%
Main Languages:	Arabic, Italian, English
Int Dial Code:	218
Map Page:	100

LIECHTENSTEIN

Capital:	Vaduz
Area:	160 km²
Population:	33,987
Currency:	Swiss franc (CHF)
Main Religions:	Roman Catholic 80%, Protestant 7.4%, unknown 7.7%, other 4.9%
Main Languages:	German (official), Alemannic dialect
Int Dial Code:	423
Map Page:	62

LITHUANIA

Capital:	Vilnius
Area:	65,200 km²
Population:	3,585,906
Currency:	Litas (LTL)
Main Religions:	Roman Catholic (primarily), Lutheran, Russian Orthodox, Protestant, Evangelical Christian Baptist, Muslim, Jewish
Main Languages:	Lithuanian (official), Polish, Russian
Int Dial Code:	370
Map Page:	49

LUXEMBOURG

Capital:	Luxembourg
Area:	2,586 km²
Population:	474,413
Currency:	Euro (EUR)
Main Religions:	Roman Catholic with Protestants, Jews, and Muslims
Main Languages:	Luxembourgish (national language), German (administrative language), French
Int Dial Code:	352
Map Page:	55

MACEDONIA

Capital:	Skopje
Area:	25,333 km²
Population:	2,050,554
Currency:	Macedonian denar (MKD)
Main Religions:	Macedonian Orthodox 67%, Muslim 30%, other 3%
Main Languages:	Macedonian 70%, Albanian 21%, Turkish 3%, Serbo-Croatian 3%, other 3%
Int Dial Code:	389
Map Page:	68

MADAGASCAR

Capital:	Antananarivo
Area:	587,040 km²
Population:	18,595,469
Currency:	Madagascar Ariary (MGA)
Main Religions:	Indigenous beliefs 52%, Christian 41%, Muslim 7%
Main Languages:	French (official), Malagasy (official)
Int Dial Code:	261
Map Page:	109

MALAWI

Capital:	Lilongwe
Area:	118,480 km²
Population:	13,013,926
Currency:	Malawian kwacha (MWK)
Main Religions:	Christian 79.9%, Muslim 12.8%
Main Languages:	English (official), Chichewa (official)
Int Dial Code:	265
Map Page:	109

MALAYSIA

Capital:	Kuala Lumpur; Putrajaya is the federal government administration centre
Area:	329,750 km²
Population:	24,385,858
Currency:	Ringgit (MYR)
Main Religions:	Muslim, Budhist, Duoist, Hindu, Christian, Sikh, Shamanism
Main Languages:	Bahasa Melayu (official), English, Chinese dialects (Cantonese, Mandarin, Hokkien, Hakka, Hainan, Foochow), Tamil, Telugu, Malayalam, Panjabi, Thai
Int Dial Code:	60
Map Page:	86

MALDIVES

Capital:	Male
Area:	300 km²
Population:	359,008
Currency:	Rufiyaa (MVR)
Main Religions:	Sunni Muslim
Main Languages:	Maldivian Dhivehi (dialect of Sinhala, script derived from Arabic), English
Int Dial Code:	960
Map Page:	89

MALI

Capital:	Bamako
Area:	1.24 million km²
Population:	11,716,829
Currency:	Communaute Financiere Africaine franc (XOF)
Main Religions:	Muslim 90%, Indigenous beliefs 9%, Christian 1%
Main Languages:	French (official), Bambara 80%, numerous African languages
Int Dial Code:	223
Map Page:	102

MALTA

Capital:	Valletta
Area:	316 km²
Population:	400,214
Currency:	Maltese lira (MTL)
Main Religions:	Roman Catholic 98%
Main Languages:	Maltese (official), English (official)
Int Dial Code:	356
Map Page:	65

MARSHALL ISLANDS

Capital:	Majuro
Area:	181 km²
Population:	60,422
Currency:	US dollar (USD)
Main Religions:	Christian (mostly Protestant)
Main Languages:	English (official), two major Marshallese dialects from the Malayo-Polynesian family, Japanese
Int Dial Code:	692
Map Page:	112

MAURITANIA

Capital:	Nouakchott
Area:	1,030,700 km²
Population:	3,177,388
Currency:	Ouguiya (MRO)
Main Religions:	Muslim 100%
Main Languages:	Hasaniya Arabic (official), Pulaar, Soninke, Wolof, French
Int Dial Code:	222
Map Page:	102

MAURITIUS

Capital:	Port Louis
Area:	2,040 km²
Population:	1,240,827
Currency:	Mauritian rupee (MUR)
Main Religions:	Hindu 48%, Roman Catholic 23.6%, Muslim 16.6%, other christian 8.6%
Main Languages:	English (official), Creole, French, Hindi, Urdu, Hakka, Bojpoori
Int Dial Code:	230
Map Page:	109

MEXICO

Capital:	Mexico
Area:	1,972,550 km²
Population:	107,449,525
Currency:	Mexican peso (MXN):
Main Religions:	Nominally Roman Catholic 89%, Protestant 6%, other 5%
Main Languages:	Spanish, Mayan, Nahuatl
Int Dial Code:	52
Map Page:	134

MICRONESIA, FED. STATES OF

Capital:	Palikir
Area:	702 km²
Population:	108,004
Currency:	US dollar (USD)
Main Religions:	Roman Catholic 50%, Protestant 47%, other 3%
Main Languages:	English (official), Trukese, Pohnpeian, Yapese, Kosrean
Int Dial Code:	691
Map Page:	112

MOLDOVA

Capital:	Chisinau
Area:	33,843 km²
Population:	4,466,706
Currency:	Moldovan leu (MDL)
Main Religions:	Eastern Orthodox 98.5%, Jewish 1.5%, Baptist
Main Languages:	Moldovan (official), Russian, Gagauz (a Turkish dialect)
Int Dial Code:	373
Map Page:	67

MONACO

Capital:	Monaco
Area:	1.95 km²
Population:	32,543
Currency:	Euro (EUR)
Main Religions:	Roman Catholic 90%
Main Languages:	French (official), English, Italian, Monegasque
Int Dial Code:	377
Map Page:	62

MONGOLIA

Capital:	Ulaanbaatar
Area:	1.565 million km²
Population:	2,832,224
Currency:	Togrog/tugrik (MNT)
Main Religions:	Buddhist Lamaism 50%, Muslim, Shamanism, and Christian
Main Languages:	Khalkha Mongol 90%, Turkic, Russian
Int Dial Code:	976
Map Page:	75

MONTENEGRO

Capital:	Podgorica
Area:	14,026 km²
Population:	630,548
Currency:	Euro (EUR)
Main Religions:	Orthodox, Muslim, Roman Catholic
Main Languages:	Serbian, Montenegrin
Int Dial Code:	381 (shared with Serbia - new code expected)
Map Page:	66

MOROCCO

Capital:	Rabat
Area:	446,550 km²
Population:	33,241,259
Currency:	Moroccan dirham (MAD)
Main Religions:	Muslim 98.7%, Christian 1.1%, Jewish 0.2%
Main Languages:	Arabic (official), Berber dialects, French
Int Dial Code:	212
Map Page:	102

MOZAMBIQUE

Capital:	Maputo
Area:	801,590 km²
Population:	19,686,505
Currency:	Metical (MZM)
Main Religions:	Catholic 23.8%, Muslim 17.8%, Zionist Christian 17.5%
Main Languages:	Portuguese (official), indigenous dialects
Int Dial Code:	258
Map Page:	109

MYANMAR (BURMA)

Capital:	Naypyidaw
Area:	678,500 km²
Population:	47,382,633
Currency:	Kyat (MMK)
Main Religions:	Buddhist 89%, Christian 4% (Baptist 3%, Roman Catholic 1%), Muslim 4%, Animist 1%, other 2%
Main Languages:	Burmese
Int Dial Code:	95
Map Page:	84

NAMIBIA

Capital:	Windhoek
Area:	825,418 km²
Population:	2,044,147
Currency:	Namibian dollar (NAD); South African rand (ZAR)
Main Religions:	Christian 80% - 90% (Lutheran 50%), Indigenous beliefs 10%-20%
Main Languages:	English 7% (official), Afrikaans, German 32%, indigenous languages: Oshivambo, Herero, Nama
Int Dial Code:	264
Map Page:	108

NAURU

Capital:	no official capital; government offices in Yaren District
Area:	21 km²
Population:	13,287
Currency:	Australian dollar (AUD)
Main Religions:	Christian (66% Protestant, 33% Roman Catholic)
Main Languages:	Nauruan (official), English
Int Dial Code:	674
Map Page:	112

NEPAL

Capital:	Kathmandu
Area:	147,181 km²
Population:	28,287,147
Currency:	Nepalese rupee (NPR)
Main Religions:	Hinduism 80.6%, Buddhism 10.7%, Muslim 4.2%
Main Languages:	Nepali (official; spoken by 90% of the population), 30 major dialects, English
Int Dial Code:	977
Map Page:	88

NETHERLANDS

Capital:	Amsterdam; The Hague is the seat of government
Area:	41,526 km²
Population:	16,491,461
Currency:	Euro (EUR)
Main Religions:	Roman Catholic 31%, Protestant 21%, Muslim 4.4%, other 3.6%, unaffiliated 40%
Main Languages:	Dutch
Int Dial Code:	31
Map Page:	55

NEW ZEALAND

Capital:	Wellington
Area:	268,680 km²
Population:	4,076,140
Currency:	New Zealand dollar (NZD)
Main Religions:	Anglican 14.9%, Roman Catholic 12.4%, Presbyterian 10.9%, Methodist 2.9%,
Main Languages:	English (official), Maori (official)
Int Dial Code:	64
Map Page:	116

NICARAGUA

Capital:	Managua
Area:	129,494 km²
Population:	5,570,129
Currency:	Gold cordoba (NIO)
Main Religions:	Roman Catholic 72.9%, Evangelical 15.1%
Main Languages:	Spanish (official)
Int Dial Code:	505
Map Page:	135

NIGER

Capital:	Niamey
Area:	1.267 million km²
Population:	12,525,094
Currency:	Communaute Financiere Africaine franc (XOF)
Main Religions:	Muslim 80%, Indigenous beliefs and Christians
Main Languages:	French (official), Hausa, Djerma
Int Dial Code:	227
Map Page:	103

NIGERIA

Capital:	Abuja
Area:	923,768 km²
Population:	131,859,731
Currency:	Naira (NGN)
Main Religions:	Muslim 50%, Christian 40%, Indigenous beliefs 10%
Main Languages:	English (official), Hausa, Yoruba, Igbo (Ibo), Fulani
Int Dial Code:	234
Map Page:	105

NORTH KOREA

Capital:	P'yongyang
Area:	120,540 km²
Population:	23,113,019
Currency:	North Korean won (KPW)
Main Religions:	Buddhist and Confucianist, some Christian and syncretic Chondogyo (Religion of the Heavenly Way)
Main Languages:	Korean
Int Dial Code:	850
Map Page:	82

NORWAY

Capital:	Oslo
Area:	324,220 km²
Population:	4,610,820
Currency:	Norwegian krone (NOK)
Main Religions:	Church of Norway 85.7%, Roman Catholic 2.4%, Muslim 1.8%, Pentecostal 1%, other christian 2.4%
Main Languages:	Norwegian (official)
Int Dial Code:	47
Map Page:	48

OMAN

Capital:	Muscat
Area:	212,460 km²
Population:	3,102,229
Currency:	Omani rial (OMR)
Main Religions:	Ibadhi Muslim 75%, Sunni Muslim, Shi'a Muslim, Hindu
Main Languages:	Arabic (official), English, Baluchi, Urdu, Indian dialects
Int Dial Code:	968
Map Page:	91

PAKISTAN

Capital:	Islamabad
Area:	803,940 km²
Population:	165,803,560
Currency:	Pakistani rupee (PKR)
Main Religions:	Muslim 97% (Sunni 77%, Shi'a 20%)
Main Languages:	Punjabi 48%, Sindhi 12%, Siraiki 10%, Pashtu 8%, Urdu 8%, Balochi 3%, Hindko 2%, Brahui 1%
Int Dial Code:	92
Map Page:	91

PALAU

Capital:	Koror
Area:	458 km²
Population:	20,579
Currency:	US dollar (USD)
Main Religions:	Christian (Catholics, Seventh-Day Adventists, Jehovah's Witnesses, Assembly of God, the Liebenzell Mission, and Latter-Day Saints), Modekngei 33%
Main Languages:	English and Palauan, Tobi and Angaur
Int Dial Code:	680
Map Page:	112

PANAMA

Capital:	Panama
Area:	78,200 km²
Population:	3,191,319
Currency:	Balboa (PAB); US dollar (USD)
Main Religions:	Roman Catholic 85%, Protestant 15%
Main Languages:	Spanish (official), English 14%
Int Dial Code:	507
Map Page:	135

PAPUA NEW GUINEA

Capital:	Port Moresby
Area:	462,840 km²
Population:	5,670,544
Currency:	Kina (PGK)
Main Religions:	Roman Catholic 22%, Lutheran 16%, Presbyterian/Methodist/London Missionary Society 8%, Anglican 5%, Protestant 10%, Indigenous beliefs 34%
Main Languages:	English, Pidgin English, Motu
Int Dial Code:	675
Map Page:	112

PARAGUAY

Capital:	Asuncion
Area:	406,750 km²
Population:	6,506,464
Currency:	Guarani (PYG)
Main Religions:	Roman Catholic 90%, Mennonite, and other Protestant
Main Languages:	Spanish (official), Guarani (official)
Int Dial Code:	595
Map Page:	142

PERU

Capital:	Lima
Area:	1,285,220 km²
Population:	28,302,603
Currency:	Nuevo sol (PEN)
Main Religions:	Roman Catholic 90%
Main Languages:	Spanish (official), Quechua (official), Aymara
Int Dial Code:	51
Map Page:	140

PHILIPPINES

Capital:	Manila
Area:	300,000 km²
Population:	89,468,677
Currency:	Philippine peso (PHP)
Main Religions:	Roman Catholic 83%, Protestant 9%, Muslim 5%
Main Languages:	Filipino, English, eight major dialects including Tagalog, Cebuano, Ilocan, Hiligaynon or Ilonggo and Bicol
Int Dial Code:	63
Map Page:	85

POLAND

Capital:	Warsaw
Area:	312,685 km²
Population:	38,536,869
Currency:	Zloty (PLN)
Main Religions:	Roman Catholic 95%, Eastern Orthodox, Protestant, and other 5%
Main Languages:	Polish
Int Dial Code:	48
Map Page:	50

PORTUGAL

Capital:	Lisbon
Area:	92,391 km²
Population:	10,605,870
Currency:	Euro (EUR)
Main Religions:	Roman Catholic 94%, Protestant
Main Languages:	Portuguese, Mirandese
Int Dial Code:	351
Map Page:	60

QATAR

Capital:	Doha
Area:	11,437 km²
Population:	885,359
Currency:	Qatari rial (QAR)
Main Religions:	Muslim 95%
Main Languages:	Arabic (official), English
Int Dial Code:	974
Map Page:	95

ROMANIA

Capital:	Bucharest
Area:	237,500 km²
Population:	22,303,552
Currency:	Leu (RON)
Main Religions:	Eastern Orthodox 86.8%, Protestant 7.5%, Roman Catholic 4.7%
Main Languages:	Romanian, Hungarian, German
Int Dial Code:	40
Map Page:	67

RUSSIAN FEDERATION

Capital:	Moscow
Area:	17,075,200 km²
Population:	142,893,540
Currency:	Russian ruble (RUR)
Main Religions:	Russian Orthodox, Muslim
Main Languages:	Russian
Int Dial Code:	7
Map Page:	74

RWANDA

Capital:	Kigali
Area:	26,338 km²
Population:	8,648,248
Currency:	Rwandan franc (RWF):
Main Religions:	Roman Catholic 52.7%, Protestant 24%, Adventist 10.4%, Muslim 1.9%, Indigenous beliefs 6.5%
Main Languages:	Kinyarwanda, Bantu vernacular, French, English
Int Dial Code:	250
Map Page:	106

SAINT KITTS AND NEVIS

Capital:	Basseterre
Area:	261 km² (Saint Kitts 168 km²; Nevis 93 km²)
Population:	39,129
Currency:	East Caribbean dollar (XCD)
Main Religions:	Anglican, other Protestant, Roman Catholic
Main Languages:	English
Int Dial Code:	1 + 869
Map Page:	135

SAINT LUCIA

Capital:	Castries
Area:	616 km²
Population:	168,458
Currency:	East Caribbean dollar (XCD)
Main Religions:	Roman Catholic 67.5%, Seventh Day Adventist 8.5%, Pentecostal 5.7%, Anglican 2%, Evangelical 2%
Main Languages:	English (official), French patois
Int Dial Code:	1 + 758
Map Page:	135

SAINT VINCENT & THE GRENADINES

Capital:	Kingstown
Area:	389 km² (Saint Vincent 344 km²)
Population:	117,848
Currency:	East Caribbean dollar (XCD)
Main Religions:	Anglican 47%, Methodist 28%, Roman Catholic 13%, Seventh-Day Adventist, Hindu, other Protestant
Main Languages:	English, French patois
Int Dial Code:	1 + 784
Map Page:	135

SAMOA

Capital:	Apia
Area:	2,944 km²
Population:	176,908
Currency:	Tala (SAT)
Main Religions:	Christian 99.7% (London Missionary Society; includes Congregational, Roman Catholic, Methodist, Latter-Day Saints, Seventh-Day Adventist)
Main Languages:	Samoan (Polynesian), English
Int Dial Code:	685
Map Page:	113

SAN MARINO

Capital:	San Marino
Area:	61.2 km²
Population:	29,251
Currency:	Euro (EUR)
Main Religions:	Roman Catholic
Main Languages:	Italian
Int Dial Code:	378
Map Page:	63

SÃO TOMÉ AND PRÍNCIPE

Capital:	São Tomé
Area:	1,001 km²
Population:	193,413
Currency:	Dobra (STD)
Main Religions:	Christian 80% (Roman Catholic, Evangelical Protestant, Seventh-Day Adventist)
Main Languages:	Portuguese (official)
Int Dial Code:	239
Map Page:	105

SAUDI ARABIA

Capital:	Riyadh
Area:	1,960,582 km²
Population:	27,019,731
Currency:	Saudi riyal (SAR)
Main Religions:	Muslim 100%
Main Languages:	Arabic
Int Dial Code:	966
Map Page:	90

SENEGAL

Capital:	Dakar
Area:	196,190 km²
Population:	11,987,121
Currency:	Communaute Financiere Africaine franc (XOF)
Main Religions:	Muslim 92%, Indigenous beliefs 6%, Christian 2% (mostly Roman Catholic)
Main Languages:	French (official), Wolof, Pulaar, Jola, Mandinka
Int Dial Code:	221
Map Page:	104

SERBIA

Capital:	Belgrade
Area:	88,361 km²
Population:	9,396,411
Currency:	New Yugoslav dinar (YUM)
Main Religions:	Serbian Orthodox, Muslim, Roman Catholic, Protestant
Main Languages:	Serbian (official), Romanian, Hungarian, Slovak, Croatian, Albania
Int Dial Code:	381
Map Page:	66

SEYCHELLES

Capital	Victoria
Area:	455 km²
Population:	81,541
Currency:	Seychelles rupee (SCR)
Main Religions:	Roman Catholic 90%, Anglican 8%, other 2%
Main Languages:	English (official), French (official), Creole
Int Dial Code:	248
Map Page:	109

SIERRA LEONE

Capital:	Freetown
Area:	71,740 km²
Population:	6,005,250
Currency:	Leone (SLL)
Main Religions:	Muslim 60%, indigenous beliefs 30%, Christian 10%
Main Languages:	English (official), Mende, Temne, Krio (English-based Creole)
Int Dial Code:	232
Map Page:	104

SINGAPORE

Capital:	Singapore
Area:	692.7 km²
Population:	4,492,150
Currency:	Singapore dollar (SGD)
Main Religions:	Buddhist (Chinese), Muslim (Malays), Christian, Hindu, Sikh, Taoist, Confucianist
Main Languages:	Chinese (official), Malay (official and national), Tamil (official), English (official)
Int Dial Code:	65
Map Page:	86

SLOVAKIA

Capital:	Bratislava
Area:	48,845 km²
Population:	5,439,448
Currency:	Slovak koruna (SKK)
Main Religions:	Roman Catholic 60.3%, Atheist 9.7%, Protestant 8.4%, Orthodox 4.1%, other 17.5%
Main Languages:	Slovak (official), Hungarian
Int Dial Code:	421
Map Page:	51

SLOVENIA

Capital:	Ljubljana
Area:	20,273 km²
Population:	2,010,347
Currency:	Tolar (SIT)
Main Religions:	Catholic 57.8%, Muslim 2.4%, Orthodox 2.3%, other christian 0.9%
Main Languages:	Slovenian 91%, Serbo-Croatian 6%, other 3%
Int Dial Code:	386
Map Page:	63

SOLOMON ISLANDS

Capital:	Honiara
Area:	28,450 km²
Population:	552,438
Currency:	Solomon Islands dollar (SBD)
Main Religions:	Church of Melanesia 32.8%, Roman Catholic 19%, South Sea Evangelical 17%, Seventh Day Adventist 11.2%, United Church 10.3%, Christian Fellowship Church 2.4%, other christian 4.4%
Int Dial Code:	677
Map Page:	112

SOMALIA

Capital:	Mogadishu
Area:	637,657 km²
Population:	8,863,338
Currency:	Somali shilling (SOS)
Main Religions:	Sunni Muslim
Main Languages:	Somali (official), Arabic, Italian, English
Int Dial Code:	252
Map Page:	107

SOUTH AFRICA, REPUBLIC OF

Capital:	Pretoria (executive); Bloemfontein (judicial); Cape Town (legislative)
Area:	1,219,912 km²
Population:	44,187,637
Currency:	Rand (ZAR)
Main Religions:	Christian 68%, Muslim 2%, Hindu 1.5%, Indigenous beliefs and Animist 28.5%
Main Languages:	IsiZulu, IsiXhosa, Afrikaans, Sepedi, English, Setswana, Sesotho, Xitsonga
Int Dial Code:	27
Map Page:	108

SOUTH KOREA

Capital:	Seoul
Area:	98,480 km²
Population:	48,846,823
Currency:	South Korean Won (KRW)
Main Religions:	Christian 26%, Buddhist 26%, Confucianist 1%
Main Languages:	Korean, English
Int Dial Code:	82
Map Page:	82

SPAIN

Capital:	Madrid
Area:	504,782 km²
Population:	40,397,842
Currency:	Euro (EUR)
Main Religions:	Roman Catholic 94%, other 6%
Main Languages:	Castilian Spanish (official) 74%, Catalan 17%, Galician 7%, Basque 2%
Int Dial Code:	34
Map Page:	60

SRI LANKA

Capital:	Sri Jayewardenepura Kotte
Area:	65,610 km²
Population:	20,222,240
Currency:	Sri Lankan rupee (LKR)
Main Religions:	Buddhist 70%, Hindu 15%, Christian 8%, Muslim 7%
Main Languages:	Sinhala 74%, Tamil 18%, other 8%
Int Dial Code:	94
Map Page:	89

SUDAN

Capital:	Khartoum
Area:	2,505,810 km²
Population:	41,236,378
Currency:	Sudanese dinar (SDD)
Main Religions:	Sunni Muslim 70%, indigenous beliefs 25%, Christian 5%
Main Languages:	Arabic, Nubian, Ta Bedawie, diverse dialects of Nilotic, Nilo-Hamitic, Sudanic languages, English
Int Dial Code:	249
Map Page:	100

SURINAME

Capital:	Paramaribo
Area:	163,270 km²
Population:	439,117
Currency:	Surinamese guilder (SRG)
Main Religions:	Hindu 27.4%, Muslim 19.6%, Roman Catholic 22.8%, Protestant 25.2%, Indigenous beliefs 5%
Main Languages:	Dutch (official), English, Sranang Tongo, Hindustani, Javanese
Int Dial Code:	597
Map Page:	141

SWAZILAND

Capital:	Mbabane; Lobamba is the royal and legislative capital
Area:	17,363 km²
Population:	1,136,334
Currency:	Lilangeni (SZL)
Main Religions:	Zionist 40%, Roman Catholic 20%, Muslim 10%, Anglican, Bahai, Methodist, Mormon, Jewish
Main Languages:	English (official), Swati (official)
Int Dial Code:	268
Map Page:	109

SWEDEN

Capital:	Stockholm
Area:	449,964 km²
Population:	9,016,596
Currency:	Swedish krona (SEK)
Main Religions:	Lutheran 87%, Roman Catholic, Orthodox, Baptist, Muslim, Jewish, Buddhist
Main Languages:	Swedish
Int Dial Code:	46
Map Page:	48

SWITZERLAND

Capital:	Bern
Area:	41,290 km²
Population:	7,523,934
Currency:	Swiss franc (CHF)
Main Religions:	Roman Catholic 41.8%, Protestant 35.3%
Main Languages:	German (official) 63.7%, French (official) 19.2%, Italian (official) 7.6%, Romansch (official) 0.6%, other 8.9%
Int Dial Code:	41
Map Page:	62

SYRIA

Capital:	Damascus
Area:	185,180 km²
Population:	18,881,361
Currency:	Syrian pound (SYP)
Main Religions:	Sunni Muslim 74%, Alawite, Druze, and other Muslim sects 16%, Christian 10%, Jewish
Main Languages:	Arabic (official); Kurdish, Armenian, Aramaic, Circassian, French, English
Int Dial Code:	963
Map Page:	90

TAIWAN

Capital:	Taipei
Area:	35,980 km²
Population:	23,036,087
Currency:	Taiwan dollar (TWD)
Main Religions:	Buddhist, Confucian, and Taoist 93%, Christian 4.5%, other 2.5%
Main Languages:	Mandarin Chinese (official), Taiwanese (Min), Hakka dialects
Int Dial Code:	886
Map Page:	85

TAJIKISTAN

Capital:	Dushanbe
Area:	143,100 km²
Population:	7,320,815
Currency:	Somoni (SM)
Main Religions:	Sunni Muslim 85%, Shi'a Muslim 5%
Main Languages:	Tajik (official), Russian
Int Dial Code:	992
Map Page:	91

TANZANIA

Capital:	Dodoma
Area:	945,087 km²
Population:	37,445,392
Currency:	Tanzanian shilling (TZS)
Main Religions:	Christian 45%, Muslim 35%, indigenous beliefs 20%; Zanzibar - more than 99% Muslim
Main Languages:	Kiswahili or Swahili, Kiunguju, English, Arabic
Int Dial Code:	255
Map Page:	107

THAILAND

Capital:	Bangkok
Area:	514,000 km²
Population:	64,631,595
Currency:	Baht (THB)
Main Religions:	Buddhism 95%, Muslim 3.8%, Christianity 0.5%, Hinduism 0.1%, other 0.6%
Main Languages:	Thai, English, ethnic and regional dialects
Int Dial Code:	66
Map Page:	84

TOGO

Capital:	Lome
Area:	56,785 km²
Population:	5,548,702
Currency:	Communaute Financiere Africaine franc (XOF)
Main Religions:	Indigenous beliefs 59%, Christian 29%, Muslim 12%
Main Languages:	French (official), Ewe and Mina, Kabye and Dagomba
Int Dial Code:	228
Map Page:	104

TONGA

Capital:	Nuku'alofa
Area:	748 km²
Population:	114,689
Currency:	Pa'anga (TOP)
Main Religions:	Christian (Free Wesleyan Church claims over 30,000 adherents)
Main Languages:	Tongan, English
Int Dial Code:	676
Map Page:	113

TRINIDAD AND TOBAGO

Capital:	Port-of-Spain
Area:	5,128 km²
Population:	1,065,842
Currency:	Trinidad and Tobago dollar (TTD)
Main Religions:	Roman Catholic 29.4%, Hindu 23.8%, Anglican 10.9%, Muslim 5.8%, Presbyterian 3.4%, other 26.7%
Main Languages:	English (official), Hindi, French, Spanish, Chinese
Int Dial Code:	1 + 868
Map Page:	135

TUNISIA

Capital:	Tunis
Area:	163,610 km²
Population:	10,175,014
Currency:	Tunisian dinar (TND)
Main Religions:	Muslim 98%, Christian 1%, Jewish and other 1%
Main Languages:	Arabic (official), French (commerce)
Int Dial Code:	216
Map Page:	103

TURKEY

Capital:	Ankara
Area:	780,580 km²
Population:	70,413,958
Currency:	Turkish lira (YTL)
Main Religions:	Muslim 99.8% (mostly Sunni), other 0.2% (Christian and Jews)
Main Languages:	Turkish (official), Kurdish, Arabic, Armenian, Greek
Int Dial Code:	90
Map Page:	92

TURKMENISTAN

Capital:	Ashgabat
Area:	488,100 km²
Population:	5,042,920
Currency:	Turkmen manat (TMM)
Main Religions:	Muslim 89%, Eastern Orthodox 9%, unknown 2%
Main Languages:	Turkmen 72%, Russian 12%, Uzbek 9%, other 7%
Int Dial Code:	993
Map Page:	91

TUVALU

Capital:	Funafuti
Area:	26 km²
Population:	11,810
Currency:	Australian dollar (AUD); also a Tuvaluan dollar
Main Religions:	Church of Tuvalu (Congregationalist) 97%, Seventh-Day Adventist 1.4%, Baha'i 1%, other 0.6%
Main Languages:	Tuvaluan, English
Int Dial Code:	688
Map Page:	112

UGANDA

Capital:	Kampala
Area:	236,040 km²
Population:	28,195,754
Currency:	Ugandan shilling (UGX)
Main Religions:	Roman Catholic 33%, Protestant 33%, Muslim 16%, Indigenous beliefs 18%
Main Languages:	English, Ganda or Luganda, other Niger-Congo languages, Nilo-Saharan languages, Swahili, Arabic
Int Dial Code:	256
Map Page:	106

UKRAINE

Capital:	Kiev (Kyiv)
Area:	603,700 km²
Population:	46,710,816
Currency:	Hryvnia (UAH)
Main Religions:	Ukrainian Orthodox - Moscow Patriarchate, Ukrainian Orthodox - Kiev Patriarchate
Main Languages:	Ukrainian, Russian, Romanian, Polish, Hungarian
Int Dial Code:	380
Map Page:	70

UNITED ARAB EMIRATES

Capital:	Abu Dhabi
Area:	82,880 km²
Population:	2,602,713
Currency:	Emirati dirham (AED)
Main Religions:	Muslim 96% (Shi'a 16%), Christian, Hindu, and other 4%
Main Languages:	Arabic (official), Persian, English, Hindi, Urdu
Int Dial Code:	971
Map Page:	90

VATICAN CITY

Capital:	Vatican City
Area:	0.44 km²
Population:	932
Currency:	Euro (EUR)
Main Religions:	Roman Catholic
Main Languages:	Italian, Latin, French
Int Dial Code:	39
Map Page:	64

UNITED KINGDOM

Capital:	London
Area:	244,820 km²
Population:	60,609,153
Currency:	British pound (GBP)
Main Religions:	Christian 71.6%, Muslim 2.7%, Hindu 1%
Main Languages:	English, Welsh, Scottish form of Gaelic
Int Dial Code:	44
Map Page:	56

VENEZUELA

Capital:	Caracas
Area:	912,050 km²
Population:	25,730,435
Currency:	Bolivar (VEB)
Main Religions:	Roman Catholic 96%, Protestant 2%, other 2%
Main Languages:	Spanish (official), numerous indigenous dialects
Int Dial Code:	58
Map Page:	140

UNITED STATES

Capital:	Washington, D.C.
Area:	9,631,420 km²
Population:	298,444,215
Currency:	US dollar (USD)
Main Religions:	Protestant 52%, Roman Catholic 24%, Jewish 1%, Muslim 1%
Main Languages:	English, Spanish
Int Dial Code:	1
Map Page:	124

VIETNAM

Capital:	Hanoi
Area:	329,560 km²
Population:	84,402,966
Currency:	Dong (VND)
Main Religions:	Buddhist, Hoa Hao, Cao Dai, Christian (Roman Catholic, some Protestant), Indigenous beliefs, Muslim
Main Languages:	Vietnamese, English, French, Chinese, and Khmer
Int Dial Code:	84
Map Page:	84

URUGUAY

Capital:	Montevideo
Area:	176,220 km²
Population:	3,431,932
Currency:	Uruguayan peso (UYU)
Main Religions:	Roman Catholic 66%, Protestant 2%, Jewish 1%, nonprofessing or other 31%
Main Languages:	Spanish, Portunol, or Brazilero
Int Dial Code:	598
Map Page:	143

YEMEN

Capital:	Sanaa
Area:	527,970 km²
Population:	21,456,188
Currency:	Yemeni rial (YER)
Main Religions:	Muslim including Shaf'i (Sunni) and Zaydi (Shi'a), Jewish, Christian, and Hindu
Main Languages:	Arabic
Int Dial Code:	967
Map Page:	90

UZBEKISTAN

Capital:	Toshkent (Tashkent)
Area:	447,400 km²
Population:	27,307,134
Currency:	Uzbekistani sum (UZS)
Main Religions:	Muslim 88% (mostly Sunnis), Eastern Orthodox 9%, other 3%
Main Languages:	Uzbek 74.3%, Russian 14.2%, Tajik 4.4%, other 7.1%
Int Dial Code:	998
Map Page:	77

ZAMBIA

Capital:	Lusaka
Area:	752,614 km²
Population:	11,502,010
Currency:	Zambian kwacha (ZMK)
Main Religions:	Christian 50%-75%, Muslim and Hindu 24%-49%, Indigenous beliefs 1%
Main Languages:	English (official), Bemba, Kaonda, Lozi, Lunda, Luvale, Nyanja, Tonga, 70 other indigenous languages
Int Dial Code:	260
Map Page:	108

VANUATU

Capital:	Port-Vila
Area:	12,200 km²
Population:	208,869
Currency:	Vatu (VUV)
Main Religions:	Presbyterian 31.4%, Anglican 13.4%, Roman Catholic 13.1%, indigenous beliefs 5.6%
Main Languages:	English, French, Pidgin
Int Dial Code:	678
Map Page:	112

ZIMBABWE

Capital:	Harare
Area:	390,580 km²
Population:	12,236,805
Currency:	Zimbabwean dollar (ZWD)
Main Religions:	Syncretic (part Christian, part indigenous beliefs) 50%, Christian 25%, indigenous beliefs 24%, Muslim and other 1%
Main Languages:	English (official), Shona, Sindebele, tribal dialects
Int Dial Code:	263
Map Page:	108

KEY TO MAP SYMBOLS

Political Regions

CANADA   country

ONTARIO   state or province

━━━━━━━   international boundary

━━━━━━━   state or province boundary

▪━▪━▪━▪━▪   undefined/disputed boundary or ceasefire/demarcation line

Communications

━━━━━━━   motorway

━━━━━━━   main road

- - - - - - -   other road or track

━━━━━━━   railway

✈   international airport

Hydrographic Features

river, canal

seasonal river

Niagara Falls Kariba Dam   waterfall, dam

lake, seasonal lake

salt lake, seasonal salt lake

ice cap or glacier

Cities, Towns & Capitals

▪ **CHICAGO**   over 3 million

▪ **HAMBURG**   1 – 3 million

● **Bulawayo**   250 000 – 1 million

● Antofagasta   100 000 – 250 000

◦ Ajaccio   25 000 – 100 000

▪ Indian Springs   under 25 000

LONDON   country capital

Columbia   state or province capital

   urban area

Cultural Features

.₊ Persepolis   ancient site or ruin

▪▪▪▪▪▪▪▪▪▪▪▪   ancient wall

Topographic Features

▲ Mount Ziel
1510   elevation above sea level (in metres)

▾ 133   elevation of land below sea level (in metres)

⌓ Khyber Pass
1080   mountain pass (height in metres)

Each page also features a guide to relief colours

The World in

Maps

Political

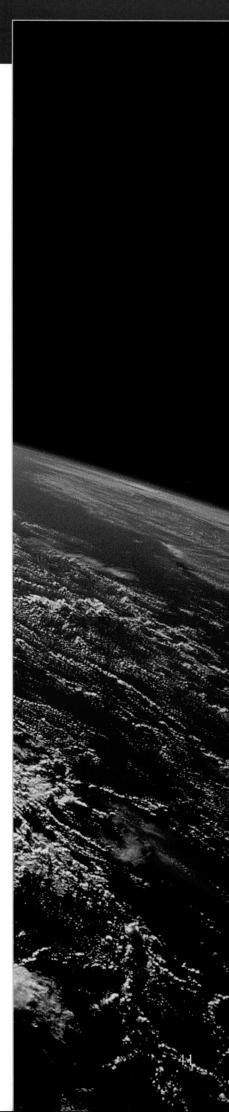

Physical

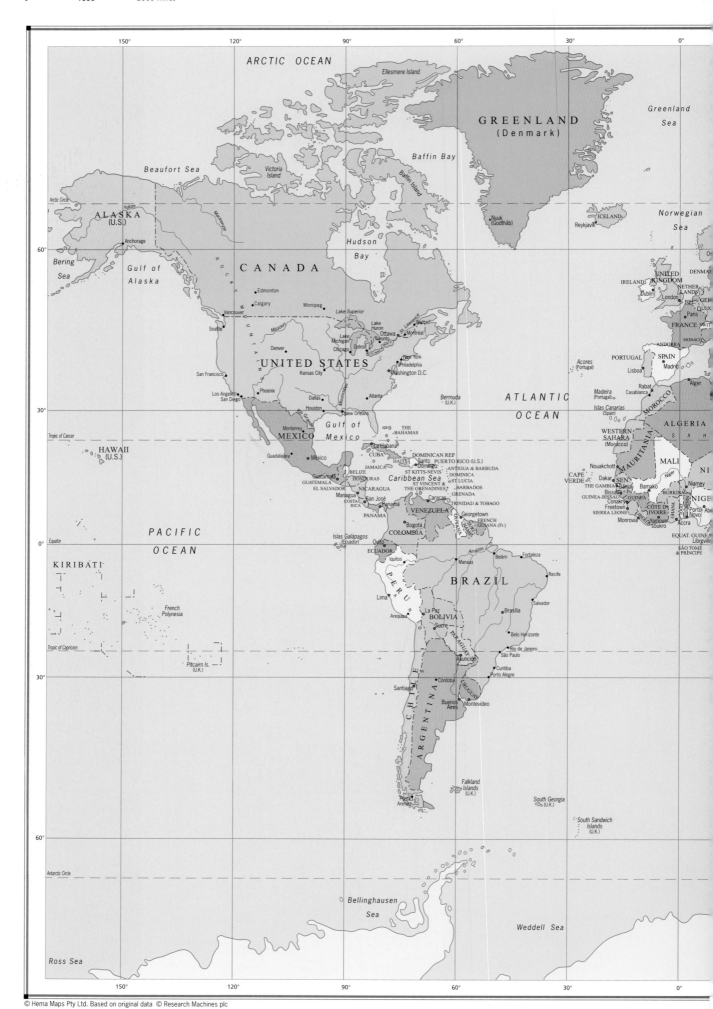

0   1000   2000   3000   4000 km

0   1000   2000 miles

150°   120°   90°   60°   30°   0°

ARCTIC OCEAN

Ellesmere Island

GREENLAND
(Denmark)

Greenland
Sea

Baffin Bay

Baffin Island

ICELAND

Norwegian
Sea

Beaufort Sea

Victoria
Island

Reykjavik

Arctic Circle

Yukon

ALASKA
(U.S.)

Nuuk
(Godthåb)

Anchorage

Hudson
Bay

60°

Bering
Sea

Gulf of
Alaska

Mackenzie

CANADA

UNITED
KINGDOM

DENMARK

IRELAND

GER

NETHER-
LANDS

Edmonton

Dublin

London

BEL
LUX

Calgary

Winnipeg

Vancouver

Lake Superior

Québec

Paris

FRANCE SWI

MONACO

Seattle

Lake
Huron

Ottawa Montréal

ANDORRA

ROCKY MOUNTAINS

Missouri

Lake
Michigan

Toronto

Detroit

New York

Acores
(Portugal)

PORTUGAL

SPAIN

Madrid

Tur

Denver

Chicago

Philadelphia

Lisboa

San Francisco

UNITED STATES

Kansas City

Washington D.C.

Rabat

Casablanca

MOROCCO

Los Angeles
San Diego

Phoenix

Dallas

Atlanta

Bermuda
(U.K.)

ATLANTIC
OCEAN

Madeira
(Portugal)

ALGERIA

30°

Tropic of Cancer

Mississippi

Houston

New Orleans

WESTERN
SAHARA
(Morocco)

Islas Canarias
(Spain)

SAH

HAWAII
(U.S.)

MEXICO

Gulf of
Mexico

THE
BAHAMAS

Nouakchott

MAURITANIA

MALI

Monterrey

CUBA

La Habana

CAPE
VERDE

Dakar

SEN

NI

Guadalajara

México

JAMAICA

DOMINICAN REP

PUERTO RICO (U.S.)

THE GAMBIA

Bamako

BURKINA

Santo

Banjul

BELIZE

Domingo

ANTIGUA & BARBUDA

GUINEA-BISSAU

Bissau

GUINEA

NIGE

Guatemala

HAITI

DOMINICA

Conakry

GUATEMALA

HONDURAS

Caribbean Sea

ST KITTS-NEVIS

SIERRA LEONE

Freetown

CÔTE D'

EL SALVADOR

NICARAGUA

ST LUCIA

ST VINCENT &
THE GRENADINES

BARBADOS

Monrovia

IVOIRE

GHANA

Porto

Accra

Novo

Abu

Managua

Yamous-
soukro

Abi

San José

COSTA
RICA

Panamá

GRENADA

TRINIDAD & TOBAGO

LIBERIA

EQUAT. GUINEA

PANAMA

Caracas

VENEZUELA

Libreville

Georgetown

FRENCH
GUIANA (Fr.)

SÃO TOMÉ
& PRÍNCIPE

PACIFIC

Bogotá

COLOMBIA

GUYANA

SURINAME

0°

Equator

Islas Galápagos
(Ecuador)

Quito

ECUADOR

Amazon

Belém

Fortaleza

OCEAN

Iquitos

Manaus

Recife

KIRIBATI

PERU

BRAZIL

Lima

Salvador

French
Polynesia

La Paz

BOLIVIA

Brasília

Arequipa

Sucre

Belo Horizonte

PARAGUAY

Rio de Janeiro

Tropic of Capricorn

Pitcairn Is.
(U.K.)

São Paulo

Asunción

Curitiba

Porto Alegre

URUGUAY

30°

Córdoba

ANDES

Santiago

CHILE

Buenos
Aires

Montevideo

ARGENTINA

Falkland
Islands
(U.K.)

South Georgia
(U.K.)

Punta
Arenas

South Sandwich
Islands
(U.K.)

60°

Bellinghausen
Sea

Antarctic Circle

Weddell Sea

Ross Sea

150°   120°   90°   60°   30°   0°

Mt. Everest, China/Nepal : 8,848 m or 29,029 ft	**Arica, Chile : 0.08 cm or 0.03 in**	**Nile, Egypt : 6,690 km or 4,160 mi**
Dead Sea, Israel/Jordan : 400 m or 1312 ft	**Mawsynram, India : 1187.2 cm or 467.4 in**	**Caspian Sea : 371,000 km² or 143,240 sq mi**

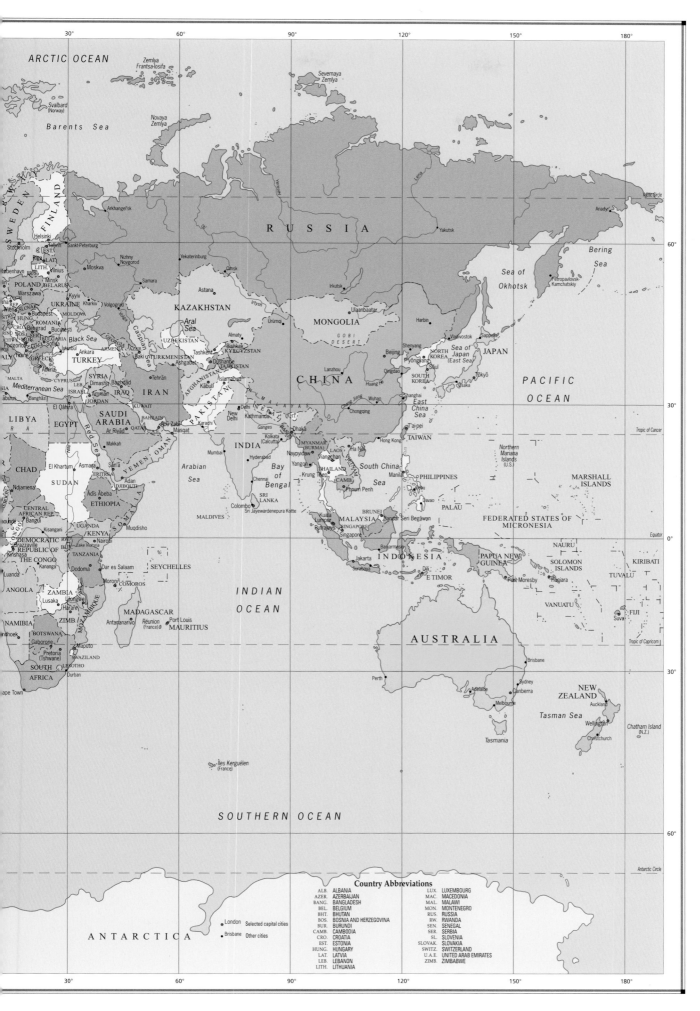

Scale 1 : 20 200 000

```
0      250     500     750    1000 km
0   100  200  300  400  500 miles
```

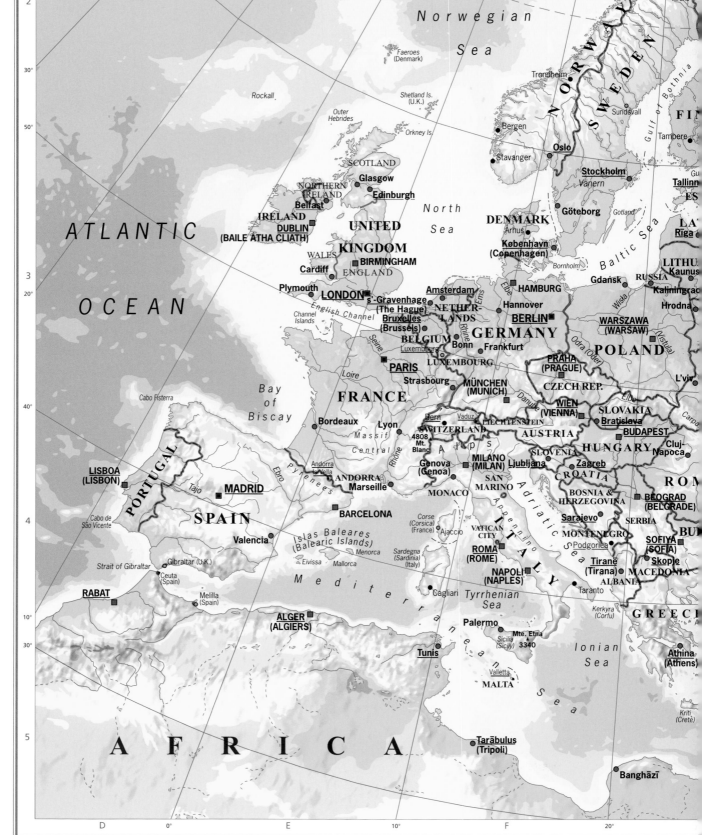

60° N A   1   30° W   B   20°   C   70° 10°   D   0°   E   10°   F   20°

Norwegian Sea

ICELAND

Reykjavik

Arctic Circle

Faeroes (Denmark)

Rockall

Shetland Is. (U.K.)

Tromsø

Kiruna

Trondheim

NORWAY

SWEDEN

Sundsvall

Gulf of Bothnia

FI

Bergen

Oslo

Stavanger

Tampere

ATLANTIC OCEAN

Outer Hebrides

Orkney Is

SCOTLAND

Glasgow

Edinburgh

NORTHERN IRELAND

Belfast

IRELAND

DUBLIN (BAILE ÁTHA CLIATH)

UNITED KINGDOM

WALES

ENGLAND

Cardiff

BIRMINGHAM

Plymouth

LONDON

North Sea

DENMARK

Århus

København (Copenhagen)

Bornholm

Göteborg

Gotland

Stockholm

Vänern

Tallinn

ES

LA

Rīga

LITHU-

Kaunas

RUSSIA

Kaliningrad

Hrodna

Stavanger

Amsterdam

s-Gravenhage (The Hague)

Bruxelles (Brussels)

NETHER-LANDS

BELGIUM

Elbe

HAMBURG

Hannover

BERLIN

Gdansk

Wisla

WARSZAWA (WARSAW)

Bonn

Frankfurt

GERMANY

Odra (Oder)

PRAHA (PRAGUE)

POLAND

L'viv

English Channel

Channel Islands

Seine

LUXEMBOURG

Luxembourg

PARIS

Loire

FRANCE

Strasbourg

Rhine

MÜNCHEN (MUNICH)

Danube

CZECH REP.

WIEN (VIENNA)

Elbe

SLOVAKIA

Bratislava

Carpa

Bay of Biscay

Cabo Fisterra

Bordeaux

Lyon

Massif Central

Rhône

Bern

SWITZERLAND

Vaduz

LIECHTENSTEIN

4808 Mt. Blanc

Alps

AUSTRIA

SLOVENIA

Ljubljana

BUDAPEST

HUNGARY

Cluj-Napoca

PORTUGAL

LISBOA (LISBON)

Tajo

MADRID

Ebro

Pyrenees

Andorra la Vella

ANDORRA

Marseille

Genova (Genoa)

MILANO (MILAN)

Zagreb

CROATIA

ROM

Cabo de São Vicente

SPAIN

BARCELONA

Valencia

Islas Baleares (Balearic Islands)

Menorca

MONACO

Corse (Corsica) (France)

Ajaccio

SAN MARINO

Apennines

BOSNIA & HERZEGOVINA

Sarajevo

SERBIA

MONTENEGRO

Podgorica

BEOGRAD (BELGRADE)

BU

SOFIYA (SOFIA)

Strait of Gibraltar

Gibraltar (U.K.)

Ceuta (Spain)

Eivissa

Mallorca

Sardegna (Sardinia) (Italy)

VATICAN CITY

ROMA (ROME)

ITALY

Adriatic Sea

Skopje

MACEDONIA

Tiranë (Tirana)

ALBANIA

GREECE

RABAT

Melilla (Spain)

Mediterranean

NAPOLI (NAPLES)

Taranto

Kerkyra (Corfu)

metres feet

8000 26250
6000 19690
4000 13120
2000 6560
1000 3280
500 1640
200 656
0   0

ALGER (ALGIERS)

Cagliari

Palermo

Sicilia (Sicily)

Mte. Etna 3340

Tyrrhenian Sea

Ionian Sea

Athina (Athens)

Tunis

Valletta

MALTA

656 200
3280 1000
6560 2000
13120 4000
19690 6000
26250 8000

feet metres

AFRICA

Tarābulus (Tripoli)

Kriti (Crete)

Banghāzī

A   1   30° W   B   0°   E   10°   F   20°

© Hema Maps Pty Ltd. Based on original data © Research Machines plc

44

 Elbrus, Russia : 5,642 m or 18,510 ft

Caspian Sea : 29 m or 84 ft

Astrakhan, Russia : 16.3 cm or 6.4 in

Crkvica, Bosnia-Herzegovina : 465 cm or 183 in

Volga, Russia : 3,531 km or 2,194 mi

Caspian Sea : 371,000 km² or 143,240 sq mi

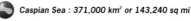

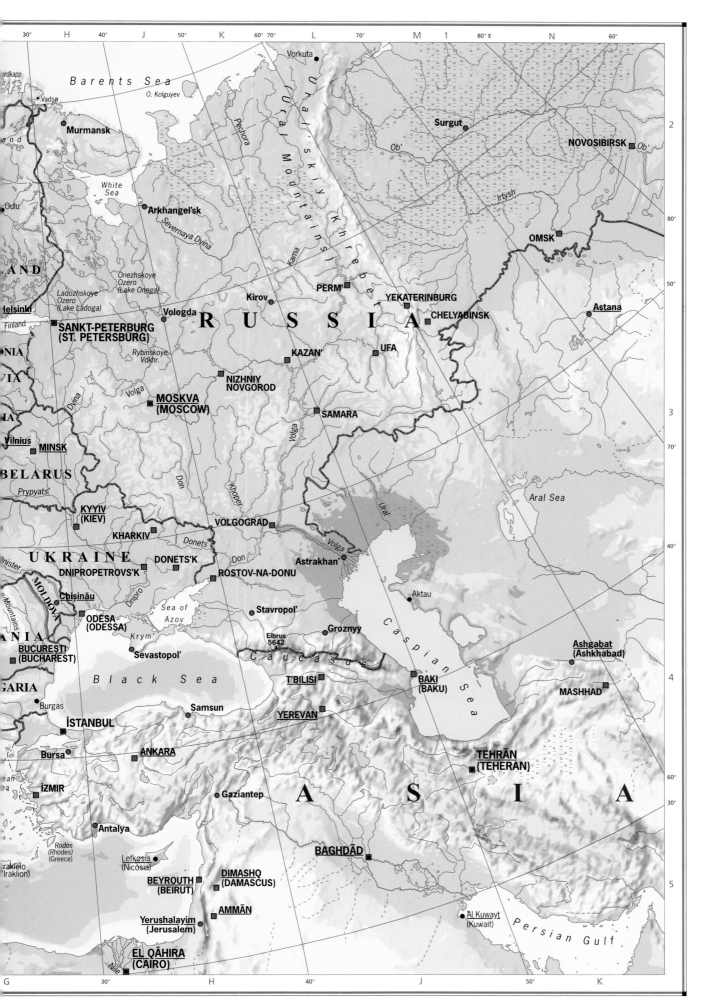

Barents Sea

Nordkapp
• Vadsø
• Murmansk

O. Kolguyev

Vorkuta •

White Sea

• Arkhangel'sk

Oulu

Severnaya Dvina

Surgut •

Ob'

NOVOSIBIRSK • *Ob'*

Irtysh

OMSK •

Onezhskoye
Ozero
(Lake Onega)

Ladozhskoye
Ozero
(Lake Ladoga)

Helsinki
Finland

Vologda

Kirov •

PERM' •

YEKATERINBURG •

CHELYABINSK •

Astana •

SANKT-PETERBURG
(ST. PETERSBURG)

R U S S I A

ONIA
VIA

Rybinskoye
Vdkhr.

KAZAN' •

UFA •

IA

Dvina

Volga

NIZHNIY
NOVGOROD •

Vilnius
MINSK

MOSKVA
(MOSCOW)

SAMARA •

BELARUS

Prypyats

Don

Khoper

Volga

KYYIV
(KIEV)

VOLGOGRAD •

Aral Sea

Ural

KHARKIV •

Donets

Ural

Volga

U K R A I N E

DONETS'K •

Don

Astrakhan' •

DNIPROPETROVS'K •

ROSTOV-NA-DONU •

Aktau •

MOLDOVA

Dnipro

Chişinău

ODESA
(ODESSA) •

Sea of
Azov

Stavropol' •

Caspian

ANIA

Mountains

Dnister

Krym'

Elbrus
5642 ▲

Groznyy •

Ashgabat
(Ashkhabad) •

BUCUREŞTI
(BUCHAREST)

Sevastopol'

C a u c a s u s

T'BILISI •

BAKI
(BAKU) •

Sea

GARIA

Black Sea

Burgas •

Samsun •

YEREVAN •

MASHHAD •

İSTANBUL

Bursa •

ANKARA •

TEHRĀN
(TEHERAN) •

İZMIR •

A S I A

ean
ea

Gaziantep •

A S I A

• Antalya

Rodos
(Rhodes)
(Greece)

Lefkoşa
(Nicosia) •

BAGHDĀD •

rakleio
(Iraklion)

DIMASHQ
(DAMASCUS)

BEYROUTH
(BEIRUT)

AMMĀN

Yerushalayim
(Jerusalem)

Al Kuwayt •
(Kuwait)

P e r s i a n   G u l f

EL QĀHIRA
(CAIRO)

Nile

Ust'-Shchugor, Russia : -55 °C or -67 °F

Seville, Spain : 50 °C or 122 °F

699,644,000

68 per km² or 177 per sq mi

10,245,000 km² or 3,956,000 sq mi

43

45

ATLANTIC

OCEAN

ICELAND

Reykjavik

Norwegian

Sea

Faeroes
(Denmark)

Rockall

Shetland Is.
(U.K.)

Outer
Hebrides

Orkney Is.

NORWAY

SWEDEN

FIN

Trondheim

Bergen

Stavanger

Oslo

Göteborg

Stockholm

Vänern

Gotland

Tallinn

ES

LA

Riga

North

Sea

DENMARK

Arhus

København
(Copenhagen)

Bornholm

Baltic Sea

Gdańsk

RUSSIA

Kaliningrad

LITHU

Kaunas

Hrodna

SCOTLAND

Glasgow

Edinburgh

NORTHERN
IRELAND

Belfast

IRELAND

DUBLIN
(BAILE ÁTHA CLIATH)

UNITED

KINGDOM

WALES

BIRMINGHAM

Cardiff

ENGLAND

Plymouth

LONDON

English Channel

Channel
Islands

Amsterdam

s-Gravenhage
(The Hague)

NETHER-
LANDS

Hannover

HAMBURG

BERLIN

Elbe

Ems

WARSZAWA
(WARSAW)

POLAND

L'viv

Wisła

Odra (Oder)

Vistula

Bruxelles
(Brussels)

BELGIUM

Bonn

Frankfurt

GERMANY

Rhine

Luxembourg

LUXEMBOURG

PARIS

Strasbourg

MÜNCHEN
(MUNICH)

PRAHA
(PRAGUE)

CZECH REP.

WIEN
(VIENNA)

Elbe

SLOVAKIA

Bratislava

BUDAPEST

Cluj-
Napoca

R O M

Seine

FRANCE

Loire

Bay

of

Biscay

Cabo Fisterra

Bordeaux

Lyon

Massif

Central

Rhône

Danube

Bern

Vaduz

LIECHTENSTEIN

SWITZERLAND

4808
Mt.
Blanc

Alps

AUSTRIA

HUNGARY

SLOVENIA

Ljubljana

Zagreb

CROATIA

MILANO
(MILAN)

Genova
(Genoa)

PORTUGAL

LISBOA
(LISBON)

MADRID

Tajo

Ebro

Pyrenees

Andorra
la Vella

ANDORRA

Marseille

MONACO

SAN
MARINO

Corse
(Corsica)
(France)

Ajaccio

VATICAN
CITY

ROMA
(ROME)

Apennines

Adriatic

Sea

BOSNIA &
HERZEGOVINA

Sarajevo

MONTENEGRO

Podgorica

BEOGRAD
(BELGRADE)

SERBIA

SOFIYA
(SOFIA)

BU

Cabo de
São Vicente

SPAIN

Valencia

BARCELONA

Islas Baleares
(Balearic Islands)

Menorca

Mallorca

Eivissa

Sardegna
(Sardinia)
(Italy)

ITALY

NAPOLI
(NAPLES)

Taranto

Tirane
(Tirana)

MACEDONIA

ALBANIA

Skopje

Strait of Gibraltar

Gibraltar (U.K.)

Ceuta
(Spain)

Melilla
(Spain)

RABAT

ALGER
(ALGIERS)

Mediterranean

Cagliari

Palermo

Sicilia
(Sicily)

Mte. Etna
3340

Tyrrhenian
Sea

Kerkyra
(Corfu)

GREEC

Ionian

Sea

Athina
(Athens)

Tunis

Sea

Valletta

MALTA

Sea

Kriti
(Crete)

A F R I C A

Tarābulus
(Tripoli)

Banghāzī

Elbrus, Russia : 5,642 m or 18,510 ft

Caspian Sea : 29 m or 84 ft

Astrakhan, Russia : 16.3 cm or 6.4 in

Crkvica, Bosnia-Herzegovina : 465 cm or 183 in

Volga, Russia : 3,531 km or 2,194 mi

Caspian Sea : 371,000 km² or 143,240 sq mi

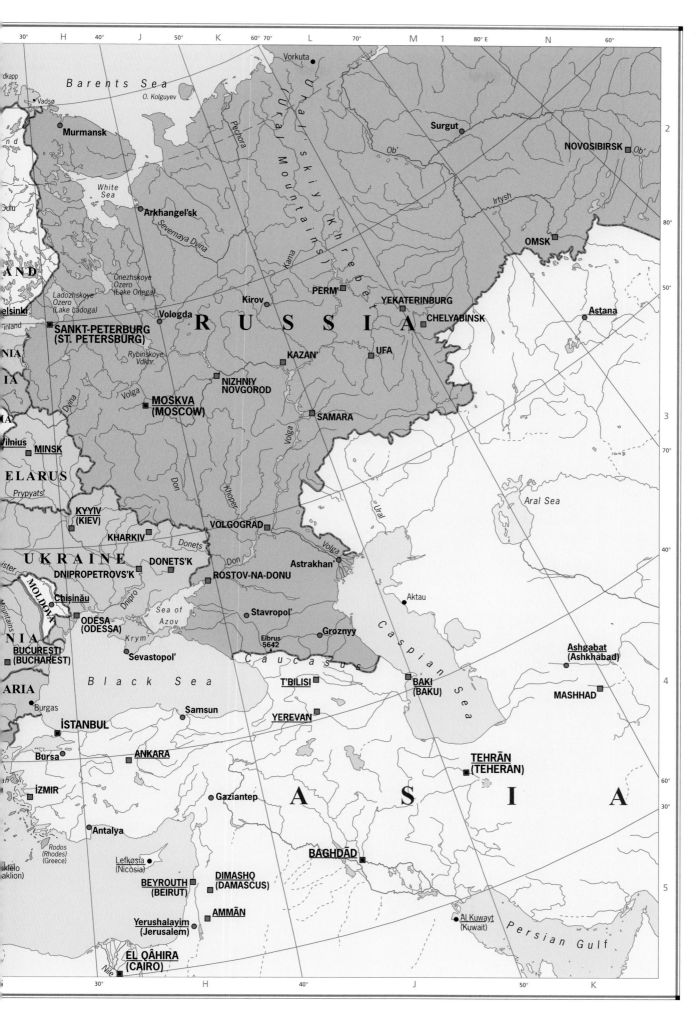

Barents Sea

Vadsø

O. Kolguyev

Murmansk

Vorkuta

Surgut

NOVOSIBIRSK   Ob'

White Sea

Arkhangel'sk

Severnaya Dvina

Pechora

Ural'skiy Khrebet (Ural Mountains)

Ob'

Irtysh

OMSK

Onezhskoye Ozero (Lake Onega)

Ladozhskoye Ozero (Lake Ladoga)

Vologda

Kirov

PERM'

Kama

YEKATERINBURG

CHELYABINSK

Astana

Helsinki

Finland

SANKT-PETERBURG (ST. PETERSBURG)

R U S S I A

KAZAN'

UFA

Rybinskoye Vdkhr.

NIA

IA

IA

NIZHNIY NOVGOROD

Duina

Volga

MOSKVA (MOSCOW)

SAMARA

Vilnius

MINSK

Volga

Don

ELARUS

Prypyats'

Khoper

KYYIV (KIEV)

KHARKIV

Donets

VOLGOGRAD

Ural

Aral Sea

Dnipro

Don

Ural

Volga

Astrakhan'

U K R A I N E

DONETS'K

DNIPROPETROVS'K

ROSTOV-NA-DONU

MOLDOVA

Chişinău

Dnipro

Sea of Azov

Stavropol'

Aktau

NIA

ODESA (ODESSA)

Krym'

Groznyy

Caspian Sea

Ashgabat (Ashkhabad)

BUCUREŞTI (BUCHAREST)

Sevastopol'

Elbrus 5642

C a u c a s u s

Dnister

Mountains

ARIA

B l a c k   S e a

T'BILISI

BAKI (BAKU)

MASHHAD

Burgas

Samsun

YEREVAN

İSTANBUL

Bursa

ANKARA

TEHRĀN (TEHERAN)

İZMIR

Gaziantep

A S I A

Antalya

Rodos (Rhodes) (Greece)

Lefkosia (Nicosia)

BAGHDĀD

aklio

aklion)

BEYROUTH (BEIRUT)

DIMASHQ (DAMASCUS)

AMMĀN

Yerushalayim (Jerusalem)

Al Kuwayt (Kuwait)

P e r s i a n   G u l f

EL QÂHIRA (CAIRO)

Nile

 Ust'-Shchugor, Russia : -55 °C or -67 °F

 Seville, Spain : 50 °C or 122 °F

 699,644,000

 68 per km² or 177 per sq mi

 10,245,000 km² or 3,956,000 sq mi

 43

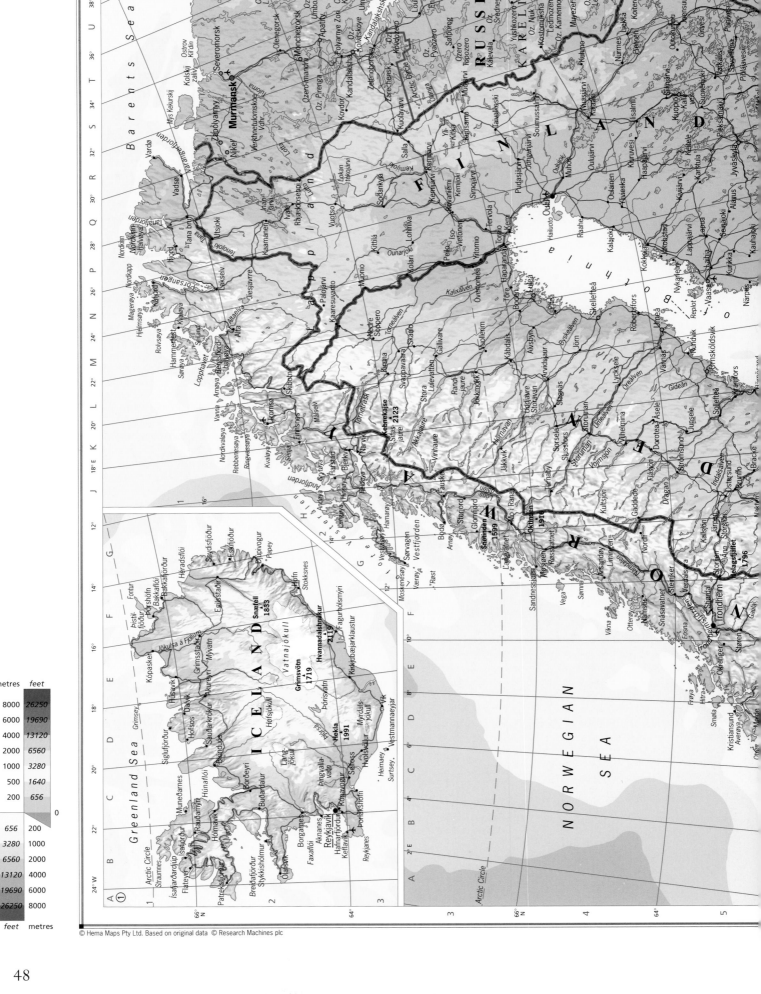

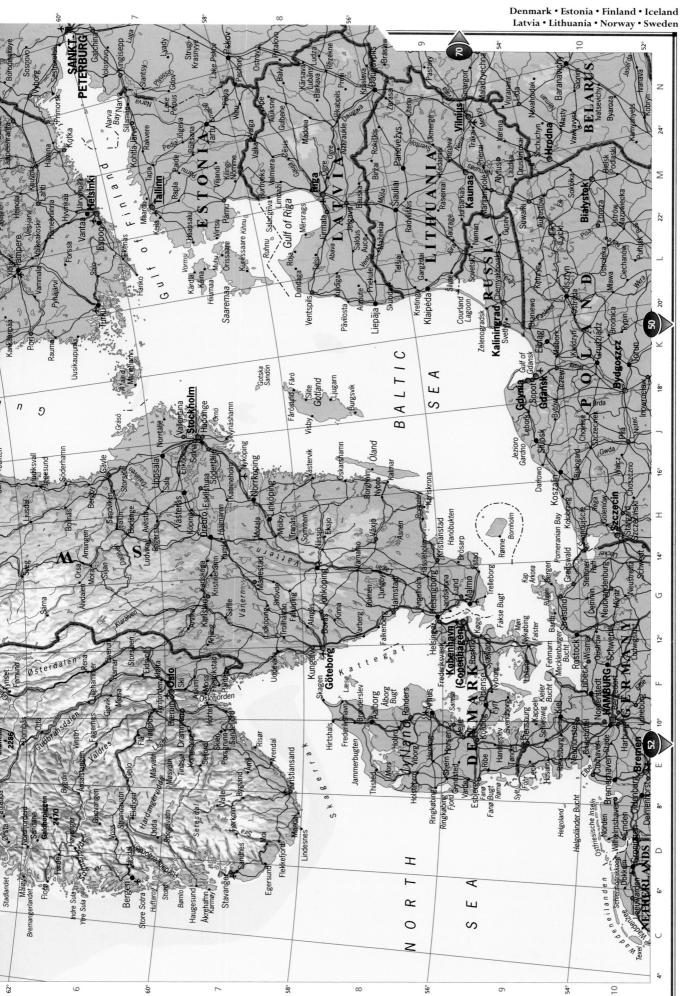

■ over 3 million
● 100 000 – 250 000
—— country capital underline

▣ 1 – 3 million
● 25 000 – 100 000

◉ 250 000 – 1 million
• under 25 000

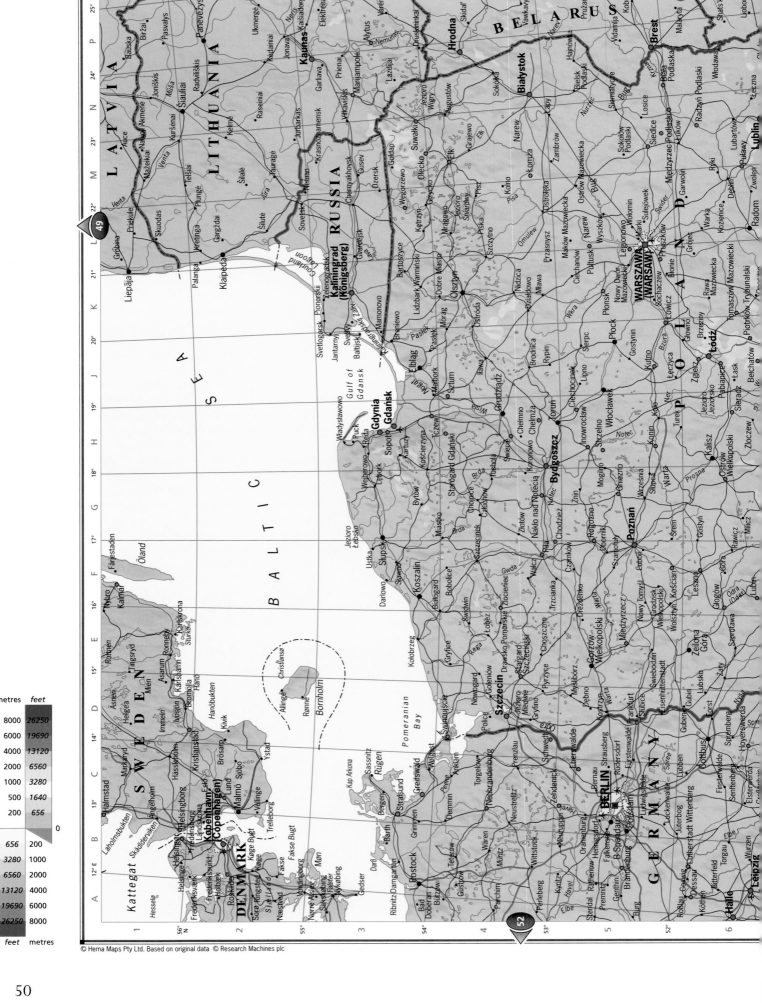

Scale 1 : 3 450 000

metres	feet
8000	26250
6000	19690
4000	13120
2000	6560
1000	3280
500	1640
200	656

feet	metres
656	200
3280	1000
6560	2000
13120	4000
19690	6000
26250	8000

© Hema Maps Pty Ltd. Based on original data © Research Machines plc

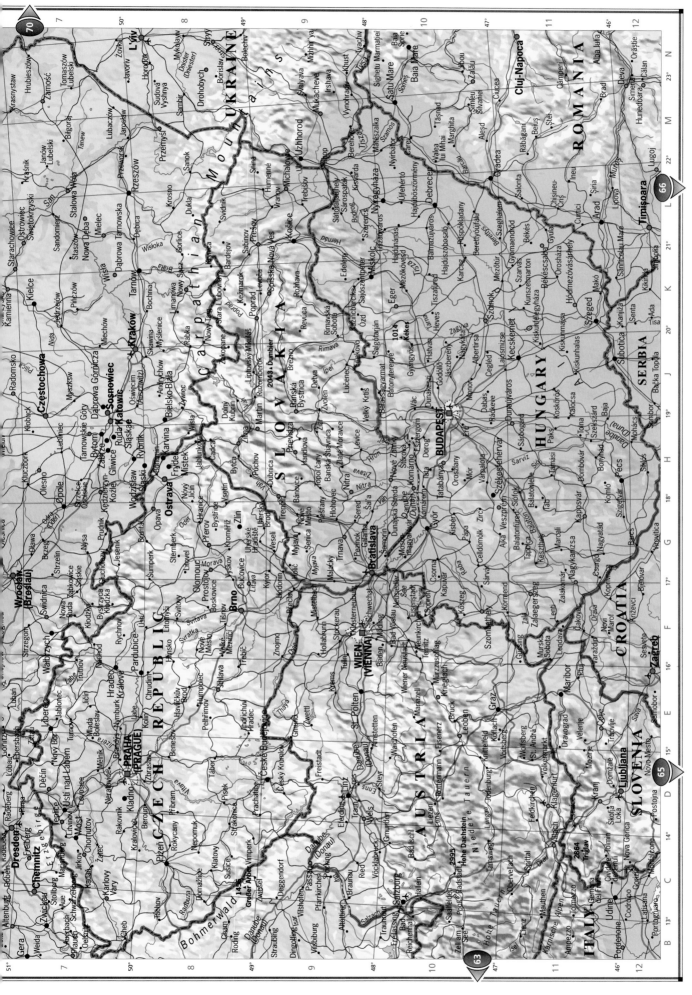

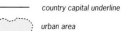

■ over 3 million	● 100 000 – 250 000	—— country capital underline
▢ 1 – 3 million	○ 25 000 – 100 000	urban area
● 250 000 – 1 million	• under 25 000	

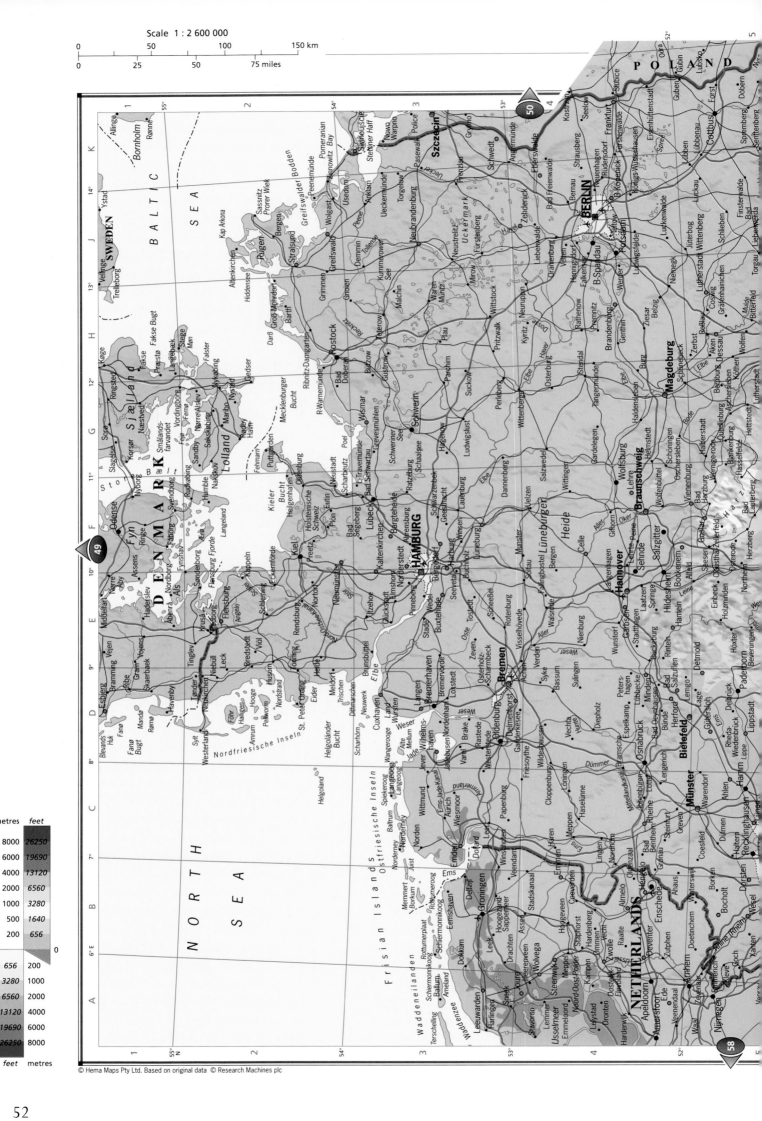

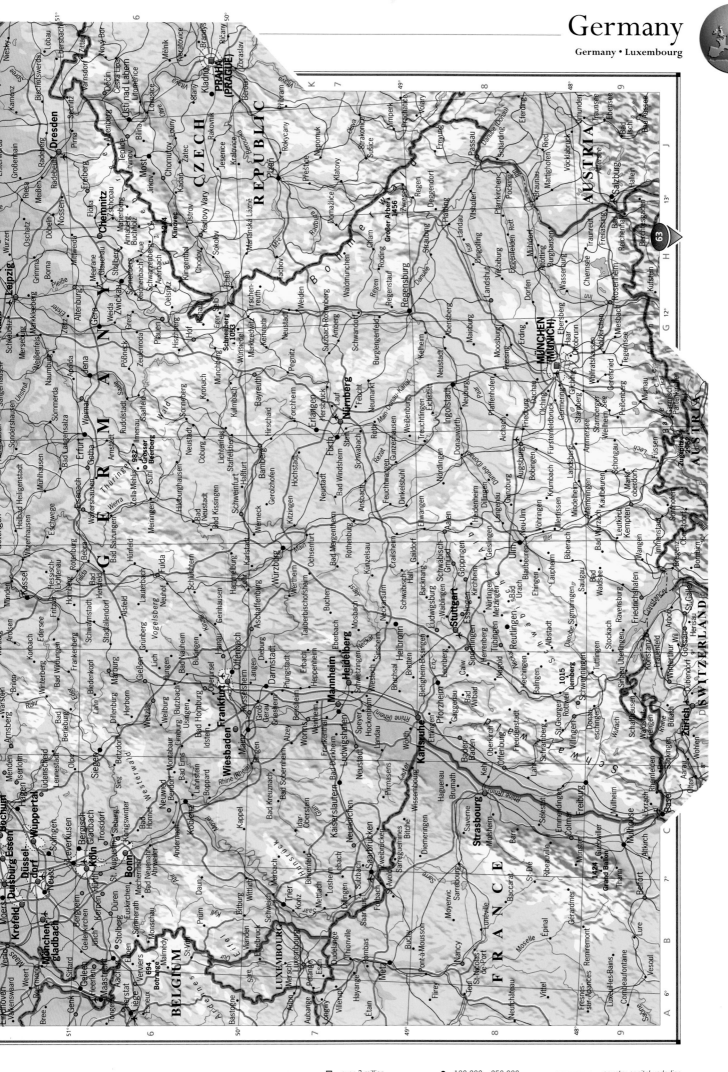

Legend:

- ■ over 3 million
- ▣ 1 – 3 million
- ● 250 000 – 1 million
- ● 100 000 – 250 000
- ● 25 000 – 100 000
- • under 25 000
- —— country capital underline
- urban area

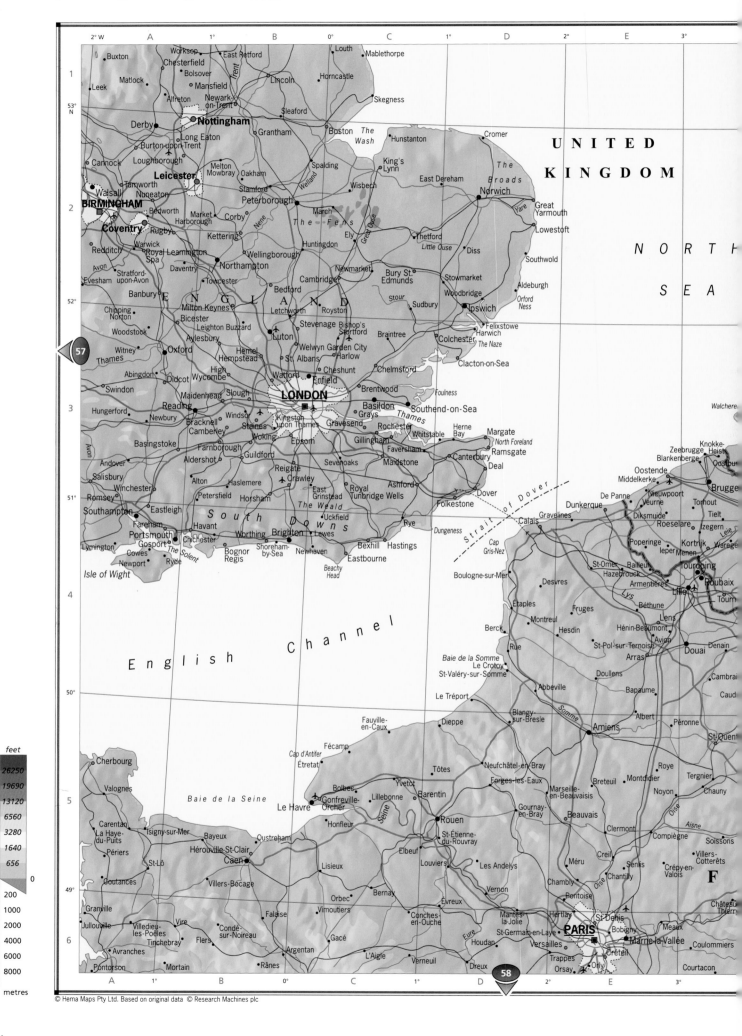

UNITED

KINGDOM

NORTH

SEA

N O R T H

S E A

E N G L A N D

English Channel

Isle of Wight

South Downs

The Weald

Strait of Dover

Baie de la Seine

Thames

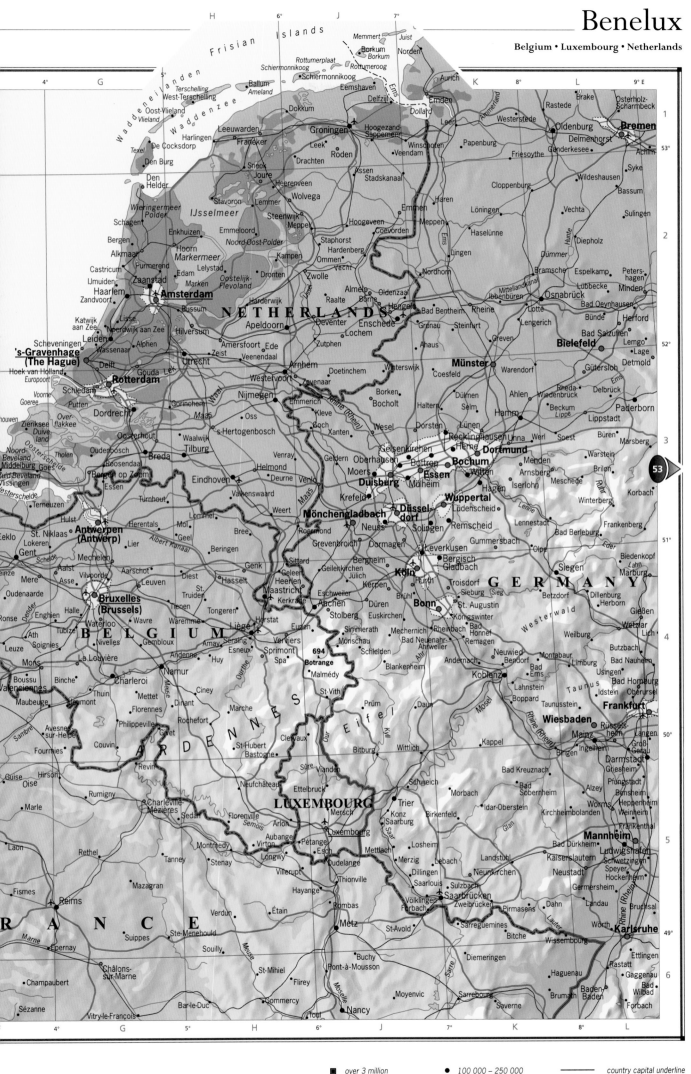

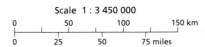

Scale 1 : 3 450 000

```
0        50        100       150 km
|----|----|----|----|----|----|
0     25        50      75 miles
```

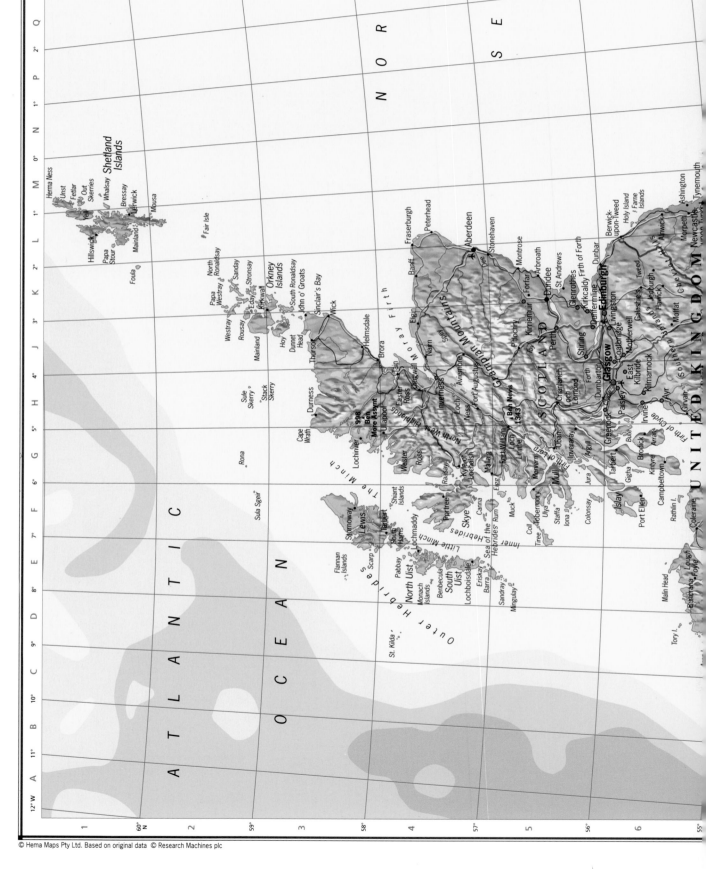

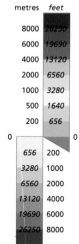

metres	feet
8000	26250
6000	19690
4000	13120
2000	6560
1000	3280
500	1640
200	656
0	0
656	200
3280	1000
6560	2000
13120	4000
19690	6000
26250	8000
feet	metres

ATLANTIC OCEAN

NORTH SEA

Shetland Islands

Orkney Islands

SCOTLAND

UNITED KINGDOM

© Hema Maps Pty Ltd. Based on original data © Research Machines plc

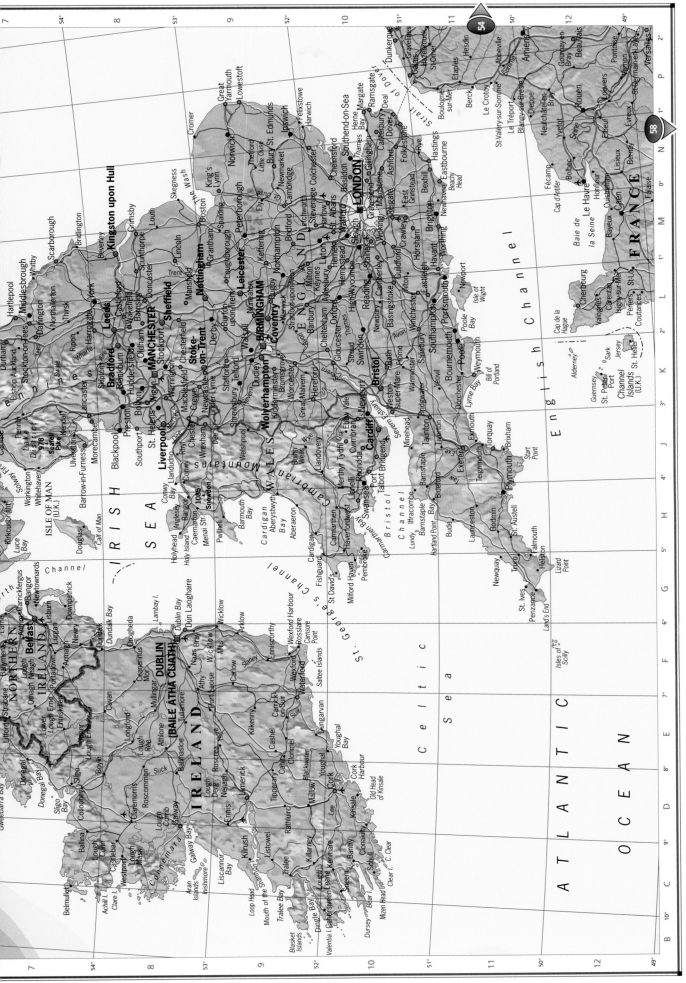

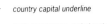

■ over 3 million	● 100 000 – 250 000	—— country capital underline
▣ 1 – 3 million	◉ 25 000 – 100 000	—— state or province capital underline
◉ 250 000 – 1 million	• under 25 000	urban area

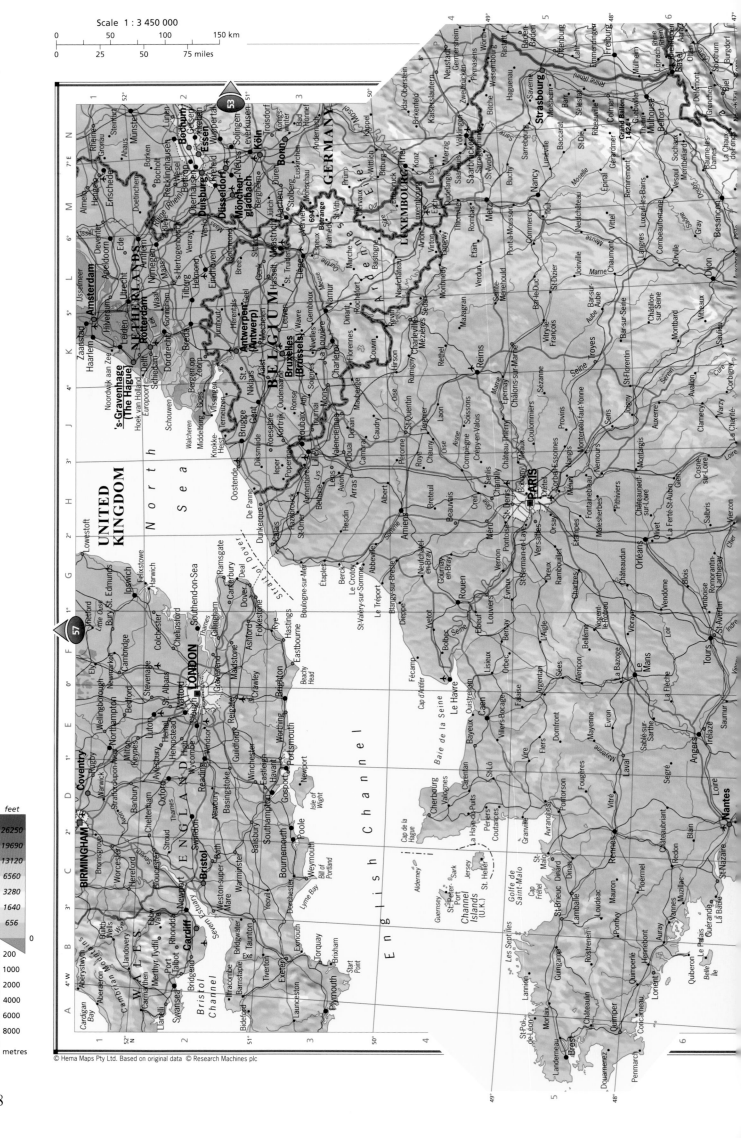

France

Andorra • Channel Islands • France • Monaco

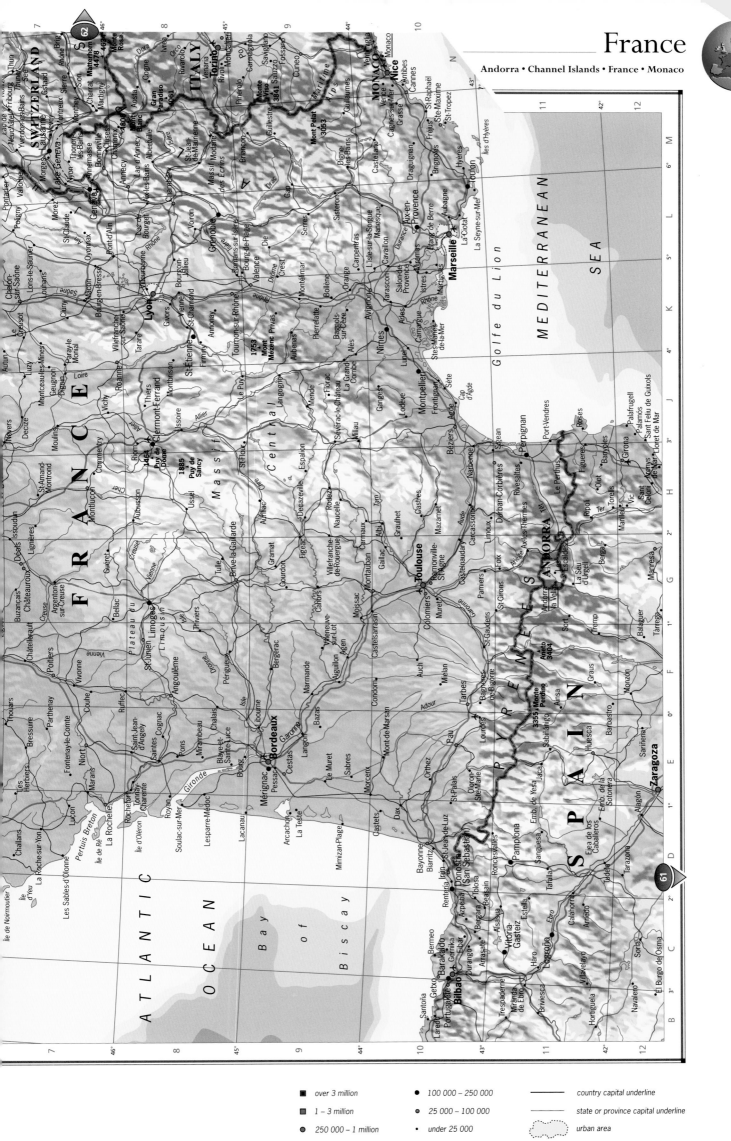

■	over 3 million	●	100 000 – 250 000	———	country capital underline	
▣	1 – 3 million	●	25 000 – 100 000	———	state or province capital underline	
●	250 000 – 1 million	•	under 25 000	⌁	urban area	

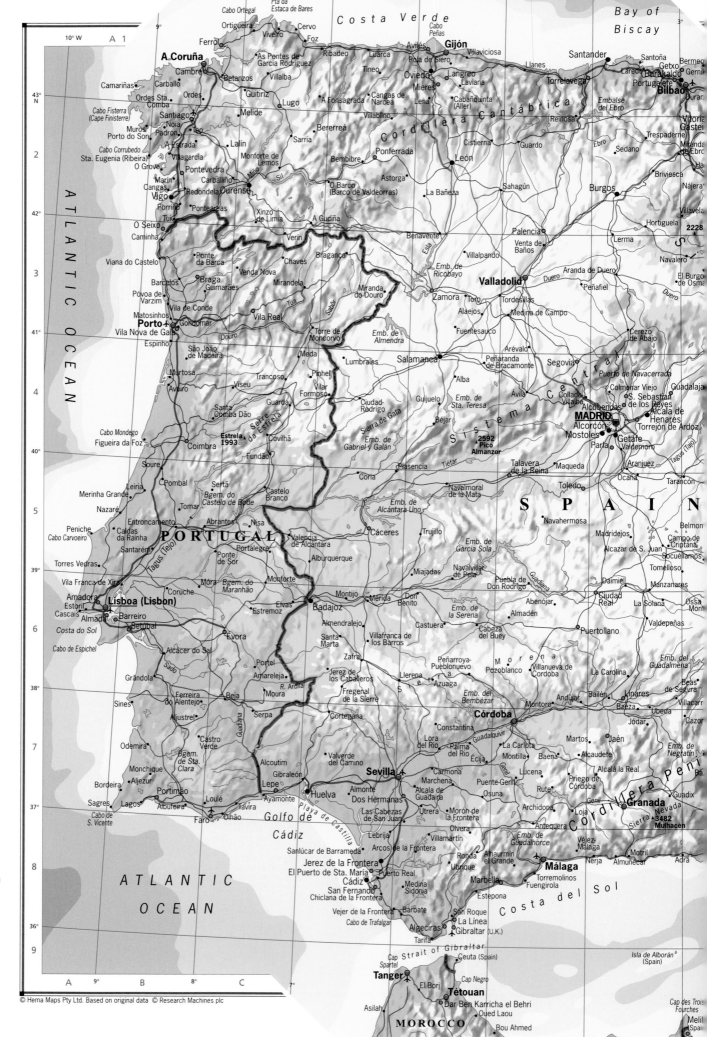

Scale 1 : 3 450 000

© Hema Maps Pty Ltd. Based on original data © Research Machines plc

■	over 3 million	
◼	1 – 3 million	
⬤	250 000 – 1 million	

●	100 000 – 250 000	
◦	25 000 – 100 000	
•	under 25 000	

——	country capital underline
⬡	urban area

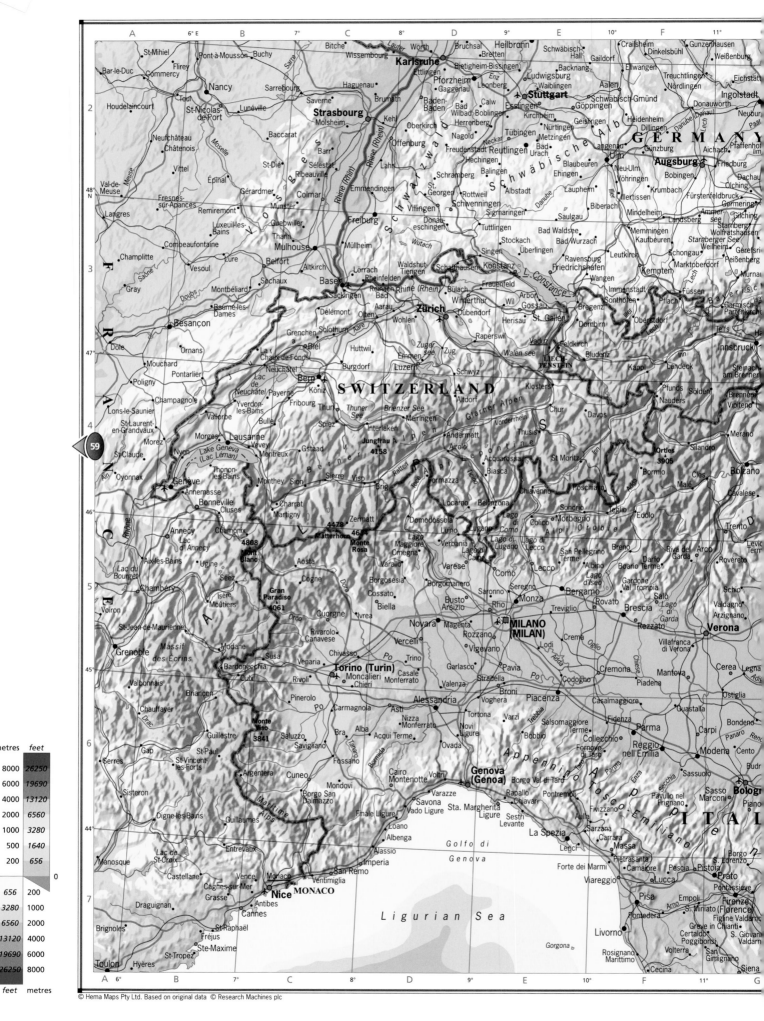

0   50   100   150 km

0   25   50   75 miles

© Hema Maps Pty Ltd. Based on original data   © Research Machines plc

metres	feet
8000	26250
6000	19690
4000	13120
2000	6560
1000	3280
500	1640
200	656
0	0
656	200
3280	1000
6560	2000
13120	4000
19690	6000
26250	8000
feet	metres

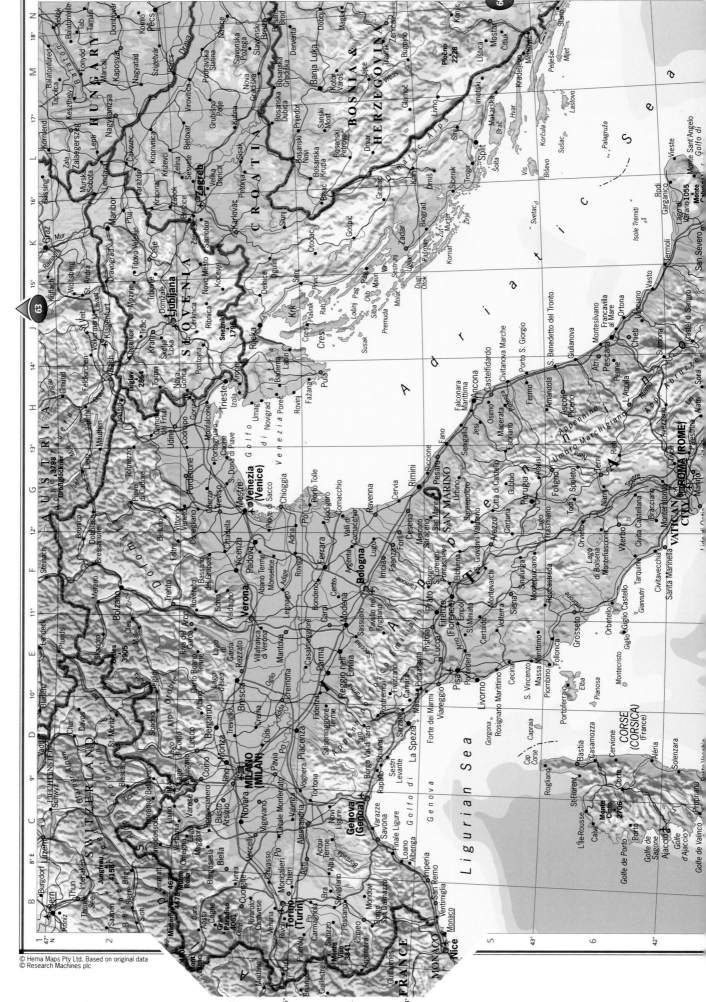

0   50   100   150 km

0   25   50   75 miles

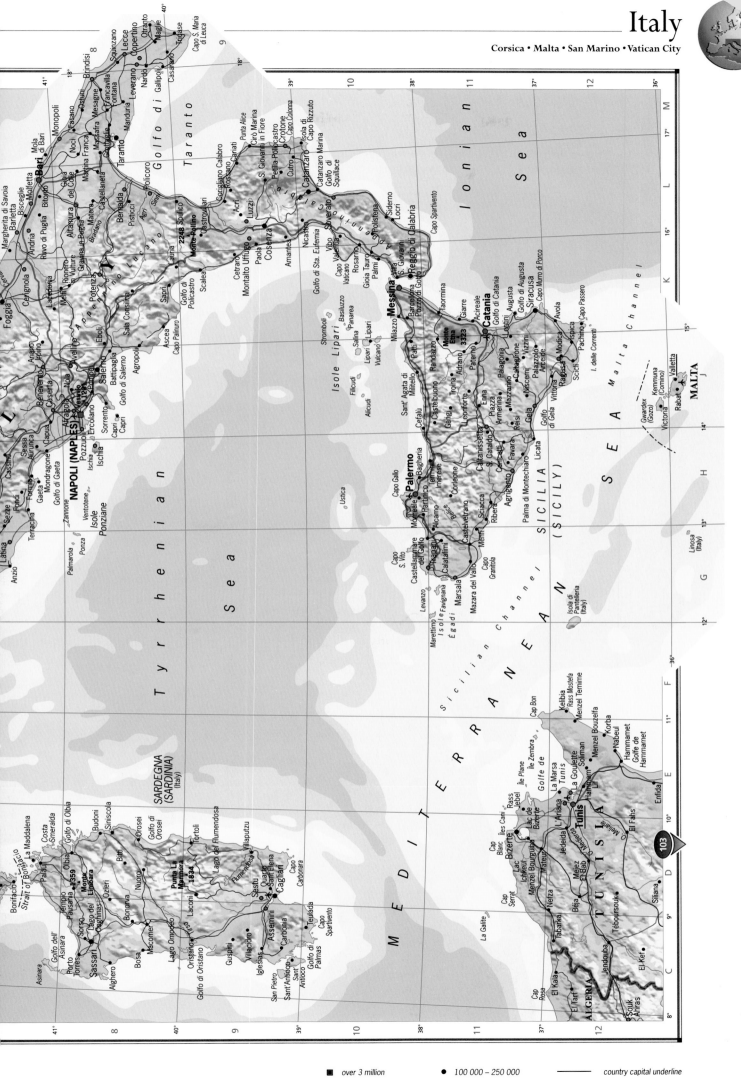

■ over 3 million	● 100 000 – 250 000	—— country capital underline
▣ 1 – 3 million	● 25 000 – 100 000	urban area
● 250 000 – 1 million	• under 25 000	

Scale 1 : 3 450 000

| 0 | 50 | 100 | 150 km |
| 0 | 25 | 50 | 75 miles |

Countries: SLOVAKIA, AUSTRIA, HUNGARY, SLOVENIA, CROATIA, BOSNIA & HERZEGOVINA, SERBIA, MONTENEGRO, ALBANIA, MACED(ONIA), ITALY, VOJVODINA, KOSOVO, ISTRA

Seas: ADRIATIC SEA

Capitals / major cities: WIEN (VIENNA), Bratislava, BUDAPEST, Ljubljana, Zagreb, Sarajevo, BEOGRAD (BELGRADE), Podgorica, Tiranë (Tirana), Skopje

Other places (selection): Wels, Linz, St. Pölten, Klosterneuburg, Tulln, Trnava, Nitra, Zlaté Moravce, Amstetten, Steyr, Waidhofen an der Ybbs, Mödling, Baden, Schwechat, Pezinok, Senec, Galanta, Sered, Šurany, Nové Zámky, Levice, Šahy, Velký Krtíš, Lučenec, Rimavská Sobota, Edelény, Košice, Trebišov, Michalovce, Vranov nad Toplou, Rožňava, Sátoraljaújhely, Chiméc, Encs, Sárospatak, Szerencs, Kazincbarcika, Ózd, Miskolc

Mariazell, Neunkirchen, Wiener Neustadt, Eisenstadt, Neusiedler See, Sopron, Mosonmagyaróvár, Győr, Komárno, Komárom, Esztergom, Dorog, Vác, Dunakeszi, Gödöllő, Hatvan, Gyöngyös, Pásztó, Kékes 1014, Eger, Mezőkövesd, Tiszaújváros, Nyíregyháza, Nagykálló, Újfehértó, Hajdúböszörmény, Balmazújváros, Debrecen

Rottenmann, Eisenerz, Krieglach, Mürzzuschlag, Kapuvár, Csorna, Tata, Tatabánya, Szentendre, Érd, Vecsés, Dabas, Monor, Cegléd, Nagykőrös, Kecskemét, Szolnok, Jászberény, Karcag, Berettyóújfalu, Nagyvárad (Oradea)

Fohnsdorf, Judenburg, Knittelfeld, Köflach, Voitsberg, Graz, Leoben, Bruck an der Mur, Köszeg, Szombathely, Sárvár, Celldömölk, Pápa, Zirc, Mór, Várpalota, Veszprém, Székesfehérvár, Ajka, Balatonfüred, Siófok, Dunaújváros, Sárbogárd, Kiskőrös, Kalocsa, Szentes, Békéscsaba, Gyula, Sarkad, Mezőberény, Gyomaendrőd, Szeghalom, Salonta

Villach, Feldkirchen, St. Veit an der Glan, St. Andrä, Wolfsberg, Völkermarkt, Klagenfurt, Jesenice, Triglav 2864, Kranj, Škofja Loka, Domžale, Tržič, Celje, Velenje, Maribor, Ptuj, Dravograd, Mozirje, Murska Sobota, Lendava, Lenti, Zalalövő, Zalaegerszeg, Keszthely, Nagykanizsa, Zalakomár, Fonyód, Mardali, Tab, Tamási, Paks, Tolna, Szekszárd, Bonyhád, Mohács, Baja, Kiskunhalas, Kiskunfélegyháza, Kiskunmajsa, Szeged, Makó, Hódmezővásárhely, Orosháza, Subotica, Senta, Kikinda, Jimbolia, Biled, Sânnicolau Mare, Kanjiža, Curtici, Arad, Ineu, Lipova, Mureş

Tolmin, Nova Gorica, Trieste, Postojna, Ribnica, Kočevje, Novo Mesto, Brežice, Samobor, Zaprešić, Sesvete, Zelina, Bjelovar, Koprivnica, Križevci, Varaždin, Čakovec, Novi Marof, Durmanec, Zabok, Csurgó, Nagyatád, Kaposvár, Dombóvár, Komló, Pécs, Szigetvár, Barcs, Siklós, Sombor, Bačka Topola, Crvenka, Vrbas, Srbobran, Bečej, Novi Bečej, Temerin, Zrenjanin, Deta, Reşiţa, Bošca, Oravita

Koper, Snežnik 1796, Delnice, Ogulin, Karlovac, Petrinja, Sisak, Kutina, Virovitica, Grubišno Polje, Podravska Slatina, Našice, Beli Manastir, Osijek, Đakovo, Vukovar, Vinkovci, Apatin, Bačka Palanka, Odžaci, Futog, Novi Sad, Titel, Ruma, Stara Pazova, Nova Pazova, Pančevo, Bela Crkva, Kovin, Smederevo, Moldova Nouă, Požarevac

Pula, Rijeka, Labin, Baderna, Cres, Krk, Senj, Otočac, Slunj, Bihać, Bosanska Krupa, Bosanski Novi, Bosanska Dubica, Bosanska Gradiška, Prijedor, Sanski Most, Banja Luka, Derventa, Modriča, Bosanski Brod, Slavonski Brod, Nova Gradiška, Slavonska Požega, Đurđevac, Žabalj, Šid, Županja, Brčko, Bijeljina, Šabac, Loznica, Mladenovac, Velika Plana

Rab, Prvić, Losinj, Silba, Olib, Vir, Premuda, Molat, Zadar, Biograd, Pašman, Ugljan, Dugi Otok, Kornat, Žirje, Šibenik, Trogir, Drniš, Knin, Drvar, Bosanski Petrovac, Gospić, Kotor Varoš, Doboj, Gračanica, Maglaj, Tešanj, Zavidovići, Zvornik, Kladanj, Bratunac, Srebrenica, Gornji Milanovac, Kragujevac, Arandjelovac, Topola, Petrovac, Kučevo

Svetac, Vis, Brač, Hvar, Šolta, Supetar, Makarska, Imotski, Sinj, Split, Omiš, Livno, Glamoč, Bugojno, Travnik, Vitez, Zenica, Visoko, Tuzla, Lukavac, Zavidovići, Užice, Čačak, Požega, Kraljevo, Trstenik, Kruševac, Aleksinac

Biševo, Vela Luka, Korčula, Lastovo, Mljet, Sušac, Palagruža, Čitluk, Mostar, Nevesinje, Gacko, Foča, Ulog, Goražde, Pljevlja, Prijepolje, Sjenica, Raška, Novi Pazar, Sjenica, Kuršumlija, Lešak, Leskovac, Prokuplje, Niš

Metković, Ploče, Kradeljevo, Čapljina, Stolac, Bileća, Blečko Jez, Trebinje, Nikšić, Kolašin, Ivangrad, Bijelo Polje, Durmitor 2522, Dubrovnik, Cavtat, Herceg-Novi, Slano, Kosovska Mitrovica, Vučitrn, Priština, Vranje, Gnjilane

Cetinje, Budva, Bar, Ulcinj, Lake Scutari, Koplik, Shkodër, Bajram Curri, Liq. Komanit, Liq. i Fierzës, Kukës, Gjakova, Orahovac, Uroševac, Prizren, Preševo, Kumanovo, Bujanov

Termoli, Lago di Verano, Rodi Garganico, Vieste, Monte Sant'Angelo, Monte Calvo 1055, San Severo, Lucera, Golfo di Manfredonia, Manfredonia, Margherita di Savoia, Foggia, Ariano Irpino, Cerignola, Andria, Barletta, Bisceglie, Molfetta, Ruvo di Puglia, Bitonto, Bari, Mola di Bari, Monopoli

Lezhë, Rrëshen, Peshkopi, Burrel, Laç, Krujë, Tiranë (Tirana), Durrës, Kavajë, Elbasan, Cërrik, Lushnjë, Pogradec, L. Ohrid, L. Prespa, Bitola, Resen, Ohrid, Struga, Debar, Kičevo, Debrešte, Prilep, Gostivar, Tetovo, Veles, Kavadarci, Negotino

Eboli, Potenza, Rionero in Vulture, Melfi, Lacedonia, Lavello, Gravina in Puglia, Altamura, Noci, Fasano, Gioia del Colle

Rivers / water features: Danube (Donau), Danube (Duna), Drava, Sava, Tisza, Drina, Bosna, Vrbas, Morava, Ibar, Mur, Raba, Balaton

Elevation legend:

metres	feet
8000	26250
6000	19690
4000	13120
2000	6560
1000	3280
500	1640
200	656
0	0
656	200
3280	1000
6560	2000
13120	4000
19690	6000
26250	8000
feet	metres

The Balkans

Bosnia-Herzegovina • Bulgaria • Croatia
• Moldova • Romania • Serbia • Montenegro

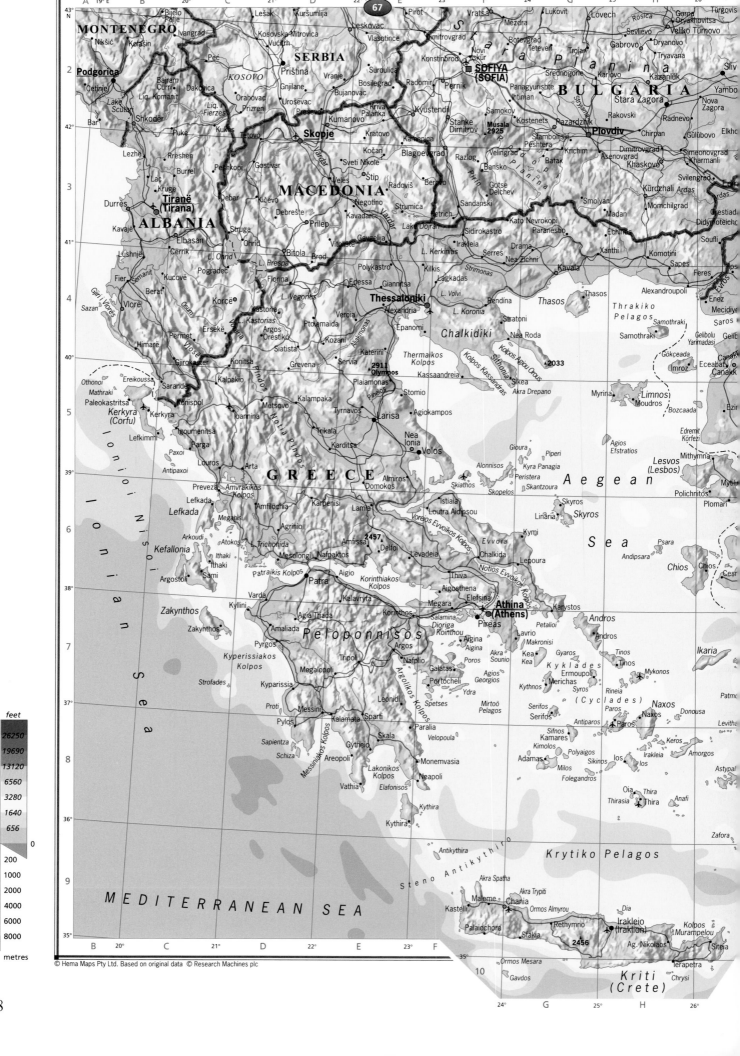

Scale 1 : 3 450 000

metres	feet
8000	26250
6000	19690
4000	13120
2000	6560
1000	3280
500	1640
200	656
0	0
656	200
3280	1000
6560	2000
13120	4000
19690	6000
26250	8000
feet	metres

© Hema Maps Pty Ltd. Based on original data © Research Machines plc

BLACK SEA

Varna

Provadiya
Devnya
Staro
Oryakhovo
Byala
Aytos
Nos Emine
Nesebŭr
Pomorie
Karnobat
Sozopol
Burgas
Burgaski Zaliv
Grudovo
Michurin
Malko
Tŭrnovo
Resovo
Igneada

Kerempe
Burnu
Inebolu
Cide
Azdavay
Taşköprü
Bartin
Kastamonu
Zonguldak
Çaycuma
Safranbolu
Kozlu
Ereğli
Akçakoca
Karabük
Tosya
Kursunlu

Yıldız Dağları
Kırklareli
Kıyıköy
Vize
Karacaköy
Pınarhisar
Saray
Lüleburgaz
Çerkezköy
İstanbul Boğazı (Bosporus)
Şile
Ağva
Kandıra
Karasu
Gerede
Çankırı

Babaeski
Hayrabolu
Muratlı
Çorlu
Silivri
İSTANBUL
Sarıyer
Beykoz
Kartal
Gebze
Büyükçekmece
Yeşilköy
Pendik
Hendek
Düzce
Bolu
Çerkes Dağları
Köroğlu Dağları
Kızılcahamam
Çubuk

esan
Kumbağ
Tekirdağ
Büyükada
İzmit
Sapanca
Karamürsel
Sakarya
Mudurnu
Köroğlu Tepesi 2400
Nallıhan
Beypazarı
Çerikli

Şarköy
Marmara Adası
Sea of Marmara
Marmara Denizi
Yalova
İznik Gölü
İznik
Geyve
Sakarya
ANKARA
Elmadağ
Kırıkkale

Türkeli Adası
Paşalimanı Adası
Erdek
Bandırma
Mudanya
Gemlik
Gemlik Körfezi
Bilecik
Beypazarı
Bala
Kaman
Kırşehir

Biga
Gönen
Karacabey
Bursa
İnegöl
Sakarya
Bozüyük
Eskişehir
Polatlı
Sivrihisar
Kulu
Mucur

Can
Susurluk
Ulubat Gölü
Mustafakemalpaşa
Tavşanlı
Kaymaz
Kaman
Gülşehir

Bayramiç
Balıkesir
Dursunbey
Kütahya
Şereflikoçhisar
Nevşehir

Edremit
Burhaniye
Bigadiç
Simav
T U R K E Y
Emirdağ
Yunak
Tuz Gölü
Cihanbeyli

Ayvalık
Savaştepe
Gölcük
Gediz
Afyon
Bolvadin
Sarayönü
Aksaray

Bergama
Soma
Demirci
A N A T O L I A
Banaz
Çay
Akşehir
Sultanhanı

Dikili
Kınık
Kırkağaç
Uşak
Sandıklı
İlgın
Kadınhanı

Akhisar
Saruhanlı
Gölmarmara
Kula
Dinar
Keçiborlu
Konya
Karapınar

Aliağa
Manisa
Salihli
Gediz
Eğridir Gölü
Akşehir
Niğde

Foça
Menemen
Turgutlu
Alaşehir
Sarıköy
Acı Göl
Isparta
Eğridir
Beyşehir
Çumra
Ereğli

Karsıyaka
İzmir
Kemalpaşa
Nazilli
Denizli
Bucak
Beyşehir Gölü
Beyşehir

Urla
Bayındır
Ödemiş
2528 Esler Dağ
Burdur
Burdur Gölü
Seydişehir

Seferihisar
Torbalı
Tire
Kale
Boz Dağ 2419
Kızılkaya
Bozkır
Karaman

Selçuk
Germencik
Aydın
İncirliova
Çine
Muğla
Köyceğiz
Korkuteli
Cevizli
Akseki

Kuşadası
Ortaklar
Söke
Koçarlı
Yatağan
Gölhisar
Serik
Geyik Dağ 2877
Ermenek
Mut
Silifke

Camiçigölü
Milas
Ören
Bodrum
Gökova Körfezi
Toros Dağları
Karacal T. 2339

Yenihisar
Dalaman
Fethiye
Elmalı
Kemer
Antalya
Manavgat
Alanya
Gazipaşa
Anamur
Aydıncık

Kara Ada
Datça
Marmaris
3073
Antalya Körfezi
Kumluca
Ovacık

İçel (Mersin)
Erdemli

Rodos (Rhodes)
Megisti (Greece)
Kemer
Kalkan
Finike
Yardımcı Burnu

Lindos
MEDITERRANEAN SEA
Keryneia
Aigialousa

Karpathos
Morfou
Lefkosia (Nicosia)
Ammochostos (Famagusta)

Kasós
C. Arnaoutis
Polis
CYPRUS
Cape Greko

Troodos
Olympus 1952
Larnaka

Pafos
Episkopi
Lemesos (Limassol)

92

■ over 3 million
● 100 000 – 250 000
— country capital underline

■ 1 – 3 million
○ 25 000 – 100 000
— state or province capital underline

● 250 000 – 1 million
• under 25 000
urban area

0   200   400   600 km
0   100   200   300 miles

10° E 65° N   15°   20°   25°   30°   35°   40°

A   B   C   D   1   E   F   G   H

Norwegian Sea

NORWAY
SWEDEN

2470 Galdhøpiggen
1796 Helagsfjället

Namsos
Kristiansund
Verdalsøra
Molde
Trondheim
Gäddede
Dombås
Røros
Fagernes
Lillehammer
Mjøsa
Hamar
Hønefoss
Oslo
Moss
Arvika
Skien
Fredrikstad
Karlstad
Vänern
Örebro
Västerås
Uppsala
Skövde
Motala
Eskilstuna
Borås
Norrköping
Södertälje
Jönköping
Vättern
Linköping
Nyköping
Stockholm
Värnamo
Västervik
Växjö
Öland
Kalmar
Karlskrona

Tärnaby
Storuman
Vilhelmina
Åsele
Lycksele
Strömsund
Östersund
Ånge
Kramfors
Härnösand
Sundsvall
Hudiksvall
Ljusdal
Mora
Falun
Ludvika
Gävle

Jokkmokk
Arvidsjaur
Piteå
Boden
Luleå
Skellefteå
Umeå
Örnsköldsvik
Vaasa
Kokkola
Jakobstad

Arctic Circle

Gulf of Bothnia

Pella
Sodankylä
Kemijärvi
Salla
Rovaniemi
Kemi
Tornio
Oulu
Kuusamo
Pudasjärvi
Suomussalmi
Kajaani
Nurmes
Iisalmi

FINLAND
KARELIYA

Seinäjoki
Jyväskylä
Kuopio
Joensuu
Sortavala
Pori
Tampere
Parainen
Hämeenlinna
Lahti
Mikkeli
Savonlinna
Imatra
Lappeenranta
Kotka
Turku
Vantaa
Espoo
Helsinki
Hanko

Monchegorsk
Apatity
Kandalaksha
Zelenoborsky
Oz. Pyaozero
Loukhi
Kalevala
Belomorsk
Segezha
Kondopoga
Onega
Petrozavodsk

Kolskiy Poluostrov
Barents Sea
Umba
Kuzomen'
Ponoy
Kuya
Intsy
Mezen'
Beloye More (White Sea)
Severodvinsk
Arkhangel'sk
Novodvinsk

BALTIC SEA

Gotland
Öland

Gulf of Finland
Tallinn
ESTONIA
Pärnu
Haapsalu
Rakvere
Narva
Hiiumaa
Saaremaa

Sankt-Peterburg (St Petersburg)
Pushkin
Gatchina
Kirishi
Volkhov
Tikhvin

LATVIA
Riga
Ventspils
Liepāja
Jūrmala
Jelgava
Talsi
Valmiera
Gulf of Riga

Cherepovets
Vologda
Rybinsk
Yaroslavl'
Kostroma

LITHUANIA
Klaipėda
Šiauliai
Panevėžys
Daugavpils
Kaunas
Vilnius

RUSSIA
Gdynia
Gdańsk
Kaliningrad
Chernyakhovsk

POLAND
Bydgoszcz
Olsztyn
Suwałki
Grudziądz
Toruń
Włocławek
Płock
Kalisz
Łódź
WARSZAWA (WARSAW)
Białystok
Hrodna
Lida
Vitsyebsk
Smolensk
Tver'
Ivanovo
Vladimir
MOSKVA (MOSCOW)
Dzerzhinsk
NIZHNIY NOVGOROD

Minsk
BELARUS
Baranavichy
Brest
Pinsk
Mahilyow
Homyel'
Bryansk
Kaluga
Tula
Ryazan'
Orel

Częstochowa
Katowice
Kraków
Kielce
Radom
Lublin

SLOVAKIA
Košice
Prešov

HUNGARY
Nyíregyháza
Debrecen

L'viv
Ternopil'
UKRAINE
Chernihiv
Sumy
Kursk
Voronezh
Belgorod
KHARKIV
Zhytomyr
KYYIV (KIEV)
Cherkasy
Poltava
Bila Tserkva

ROMANIA
Cluj-Napoca
Oradea
Baia Mare
Satu Mare
Suceava
Iaşi
MOLDOVA
Chişinău
Tiraspol
ODESA (ODESSA)
Mykolaiv
Kherson
DNIPROPETROVS'K
Kryvyy Rih
Zaporizhzhya
DONETS'K
Makiyivka
Luhans'k
Mariupol'
Taganrog
ROSTOV-NA-DONU
VOLGOGRAD

BUCUREŞTI (BUCHAREST)
BULGARIA
Constanţa
Sea of Azov
Krym
Simferopol'
Sevastopol'
Yalta
Black Sea
Krasnodar
Novorossiysk
Stavropol'
KALMY

metres	feet
8000	26250
6000	19690
4000	13120
2000	6560
1000	3280
500	1640
200	656
0	0
656	200
3280	1000
6560	2000
13120	4000
19690	6000
26250	8000

feet   metres

25°   30°   35°   40°   45°

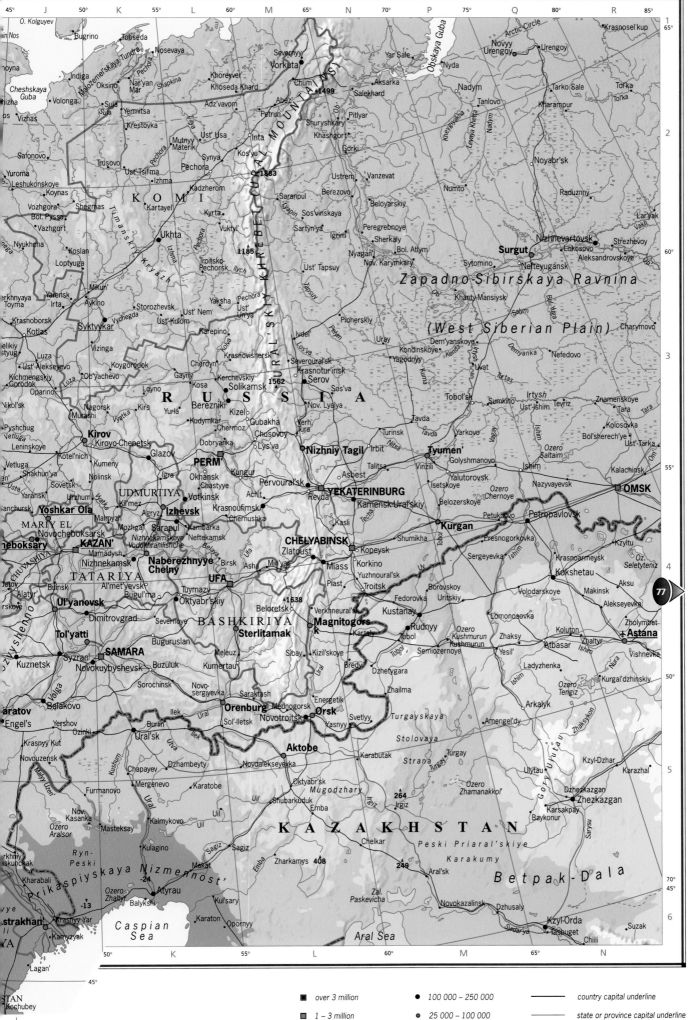

■ over 3 million	● 100 000 – 250 000	—— country capital underline
■ 1 – 3 million	● 25 000 – 100 000	—— state or province capital underline
● 250 000 – 1 million	• under 25 000	

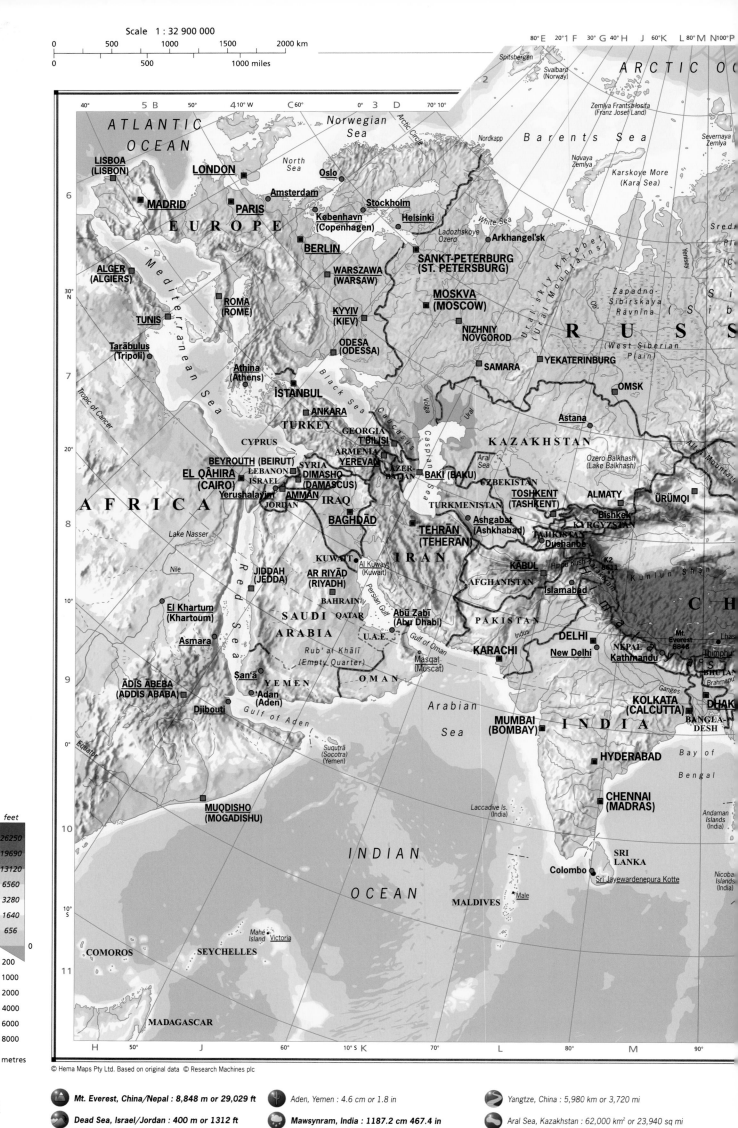

80°E 20°1 F 30°G H J 60°K L 80°M N100°P

500   1000   1500   2000 km

500   1000 miles

ATLANTIC
OCEAN

Norwegian
Sea

Arctic Circle

Spitsbergen

Svalbard
(Norway)

ARCTIC O

Barents Sea

Zemlya Frantsa-Iosifa
(Franz Josef Land)

Nordkapp

Novaya
Zemlya

Severnaya
Zemlya

Sredr

North
Sea

Karskoye More
(Kara Sea)

LISBOA
(LISBON)

LONDON

Oslo

Amsterdam

MADRID

PARIS

Stockholm

København
(Copenhagen)

Helsinki

EUROPE

BERLIN

White Sea

Ladozhskoye
Ozero

Arkhangel'sk

Zapadno-
Sibirskaya
Ravnina (Sib

(West Siberian
Plain)

R U S S

Ob'

Yenisey

IC

Pl

Ural'skiy Khrebet
(Ural Mountains)

ALGER
(ALGIERS)

WARSZAWA
(WARSAW)

SANKT-PETERBURG
(ST. PETERSBURG)

ROMA
(ROME)

TUNIS

KYYIV
(KIEV)

MOSKVA
(MOSCOW)

NIZHNIY
NOVGOROD

YEKATERINBURG

Mediterranean Sea

Tarābulus
(Tripoli)

ODESA
(ODESSA)

SAMARA

OMSK

Tropic of Cancer

Athina
(Athens)

İSTANBUL

Black Sea

Volga

Ural

Astana

KAZAKHSTAN

Altai Mountains

ANKARA

TURKEY

GEORGIA
T'BILISI

Caucasus

Caspian Sea

Aral
Sea

Ozero Balkhash
(Lake Balkhash)

CYPRUS

ARMENIA
YEREVAN

AZER-
BAIJAN

BAKI (BAKU)

UZBEKISTAN

ÜRÜMQI

BEYROUTH (BEIRUT)

SYRIA
DIMASHQ
(DAMASCUS)

LEBANON
Israel

TOSHKENT
(TASHKENT)

ALMATY

EL QÂHIRA
(CAIRO)

Yerushalayim

AMMAN

IRAQ

TURKMENISTAN

Ashgabat
(Ashkhabad)

Bishkek

KYRGYZSTAN

AFRICA

JORDAN

BAGHDĀD

TEHRĀN
(TEHERAN)

TAJIKISTAN
Dushanbe

K2
8611

Kunlun Shan

C

Lake Nasser

Nile

KUWAIT

Al Kuwayt
(Kuwait)

IRAN

KĀBUL

Hindu Kush

Islamabad

H

JIDDAH
(JEDDA)

AR RIYĀD
(RIYADH)

BAHRAIN

AFGHANISTAN

El Khartum
(Khartoum)

QATAR

Persian Gulf

Abū Ẓabī
(Abu Dhabi)

PAKISTAN

Indus

DELHI

Mt.
Everest
8848

Lhas

Asmara

SAUDI
ARABIA

U.A.E.

Gulf of Oman

KARACHI

New Delhi

NEPAL
Kathmandu

Thimphu

ĀDĪS ĀBEBA
(ADDIS ABABA)

Rub' al Khālī
(Empty Quarter)

Masqaṭ
(Muscat)

Ganges

BHUTAN

S

Brahmapu

Djibouti

Ṣan'ā

YEMEN

OMAN

KOLKATA
(CALCUTTA)

DHAK

ʿAdan
(Aden)

Gulf of Aden

Arabian
Sea

MUMBAI
(BOMBAY)

INDIA

BANGLA-
DESH

Equator

Suquṭrā
(Socotra)
(Yemen)

HYDERABAD

Bay of
Bengal

MUQDISHO
(MOGADISHU)

Laccadive Is.
(India)

CHENNAI
(MADRAS)

Andaman
Islands
(India)

INDIAN
OCEAN

SRI
LANKA

Colombo

Nicobar
Islands
(India)

Sri Jayewardenepura Kotte

MALDIVES

Male

COMOROS

Mahé
Island

Victoria

SEYCHELLES

MADAGASCAR

metres	feet
8000	26250
6000	19690
4000	13120
2000	6560
1000	3280
500	1640
200	656
0	0
656	200
3280	1000
6560	2000
13120	4000
19690	6000
26250	8000
feet	metres

Mt. Everest, China/Nepal : 8,848 m or 29,029 ft

Aden, Yemen : 4.6 cm or 1.8 in

Yangtze, China : 5,980 km or 3,720 mi

Dead Sea, Israel/Jordan : 400 m or 1312 ft

Mawsynram, India : 1187.2 cm 467.4 in

Aral Sea, Kazakhstan : 62,000 km² or 23,940 sq mi

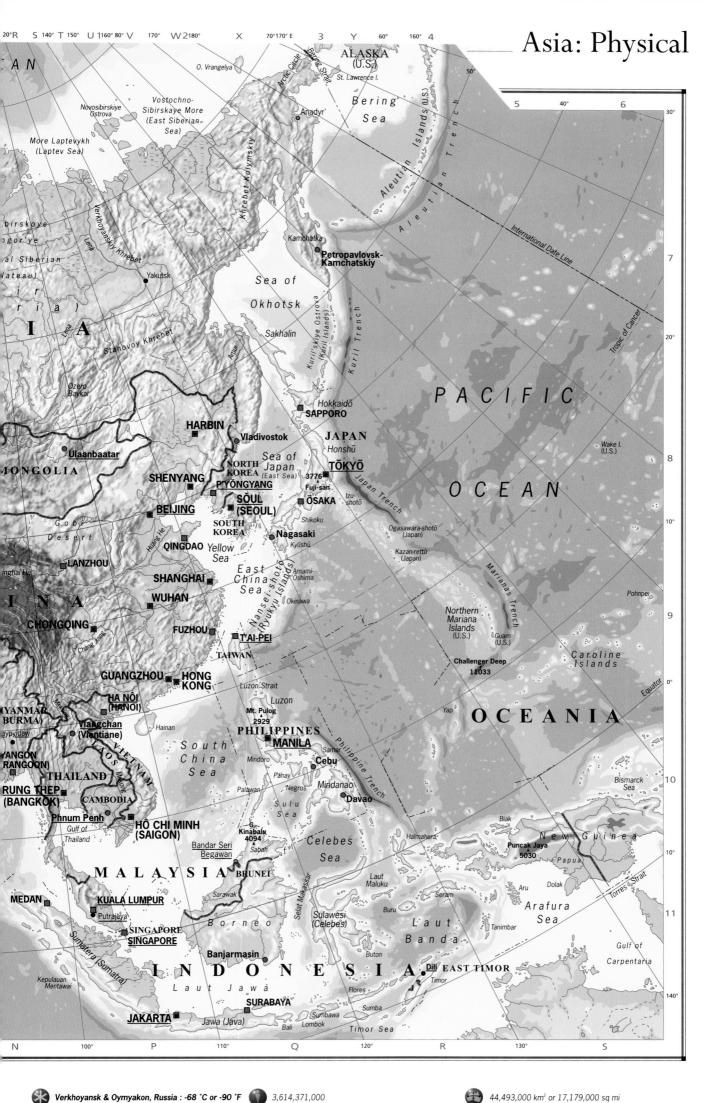

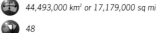

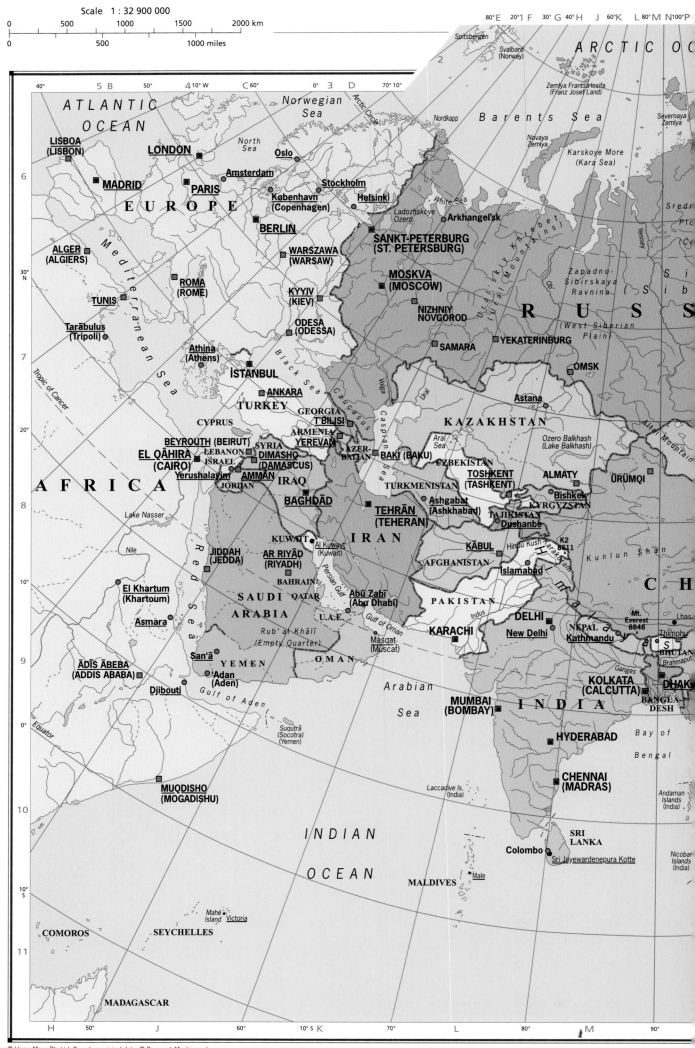

Scale 1 : 32 900 000

| 0 | | 500 | | 1000 | | 1500 | | 2000 km |
| 0 | | | 500 | | | 1000 miles |

ATLANTIC OCEAN

Norwegian Sea

ARCTIC OC

Spitsbergen

Svalbard (Norway)

Zemlya Frantsa-Iosifa (Franz Josef Land)

Barents Sea

Nordkapp

Novaya Zemlya

Severnaya Zemlya

Karskoye More (Kara Sea)

Zemlya

LISBOA (LISBON)

LONDON

Oslo

North Sea

Arctic Circle

EUROPE

MADRID

PARIS

Amsterdam

Stockholm

København (Copenhagen)

Helsinki

BERLIN

ALGER (ALGIERS)

WARSZAWA (WARSAW)

ROMA (ROME)

KYYIV (KIEV)

TUNIS

ODESA (ODESSA)

Tarābulus (Tripoli)

Athina (Athens)

İSTANBUL

ANKARA

Black Sea

Mediterranean Sea

Tropic of Cancer

TURKEY

CYPRUS

GEORGIA

T'BILISI

ARMENIA

YEREVAN

BEYROUTH (BEIRUT)

Lebanon

SYRIA

DIMASHQ (DAMASCUS)

AZER-BAIJAN

BAKI (BAKU)

White Sea

Ladozhskoye Ozero

Arkhangel'sk

SANKT-PETERBURG (ST. PETERSBURG)

MOSKVA (MOSCOW)

NIZHNIY NOVGOROD

SAMARA

YEKATERINBURG

RUSS

Zapadno-Sibirskaya Ravnina (Si

(West Siberian Plain)

Ob'

OMSK

Astana

KAZAKHSTAN

Ozero Balkhash (Lake Balkhash)

Aral Sea

UZBEKISTAN

TOSHKENT (TASHKENT)

ALMATY

ÜRÜMQI

Altai Mountain

S

Yenisey

Sredr

PTO

Ce

Si

EL QÂHIRA (CAIRO)

Yerushalayim

Israel

AMMAN

IRAQ

Jordan

BAGHDĀD

AFRICA

Lake Nasser

Nile

TEHRĀN (TEHERAN)

TURKMENISTAN

Ashgabat (Ashkhabad)

Caspian Sea

Volga

Ural

Caucasus

KUWAIT

Al Kuwayt (Kuwait)

IRAN

AR RIYĀD (RIYADH)

JIDDAH (JEDDA)

BAHRAIN

QATAR

SAUDI ARABIA

El Khartum (Khartoum)

Asmara

Red Sea

Persian Gulf

ABŪ ẒABĪ (Abu Dhabi)

U.A.E.

Rub' al Khālī (Empty Quarter)

Gulf of Oman

Masqat (Muscat)

KĀBUL

Hindu Kush

AFGHANISTAN

Islamabad

TAJIKISTAN

Dushanbe

Bishkek

KYRGYZSTAN

K2 8611

Karakoram

Kunlun Shan

KARACHI

PAKISTAN

Indus

DELHI

New Delhi

NEPAL

Kathmandu

Mt. Everest 8848

Himalaya

Lha

Thimphu

BHUTAN

Brahmaput

CH

ĀDĪS ĀBEBA (ADDIS ABABA)

Djibouti

San'ā

Adan (Aden)

YEMEN

Gulf of Aden

OMAN

Arabian Sea

MUMBAI (BOMBAY)

INDIA

HYDERABAD

KOLKATA (CALCUTTA)

DHAK

BANGLA-DESH

Ganges

Bay of Bengal

Suquṭrā (Socotra) (Yemen)

MUQDISHO (MOGADISHU)

CHENNAI (MADRAS)

Laccadive Is. (India)

Andaman Islands (India)

INDIAN OCEAN

SRI LANKA

Colombo

Sri Jayewardenepura Kotte

Nicobar Islands (India)

MALDIVES

Male

COMOROS

Mahé Island

Victoria

SEYCHELLES

MADAGASCAR

80°E 20° F 30° G 40° H J 60° K L 80° M N100° P

40° 5 B 50° 4 10° W C 60° 0° 3 D 70° 10°

H J 60° 10° S K 70° L 80° M 90°

6

30°N

7

20°

8

10°

9

0°

10°S

10

11

 Mt. Everest, China/Nepal : 8,848 m or 29,029 ft

 Dead Sea, Israel/Jordan : 400 m or 1312 ft

 Aden, Yemen : 4.6 cm or 1.8 in

 Mawsynram, India : 1187.2 cm 467.4 in

Yangtze, China : 5,980 km or 3,720 mi

Aral Sea, Kazakhstan : 62,000 km² or 23,940 sq mi

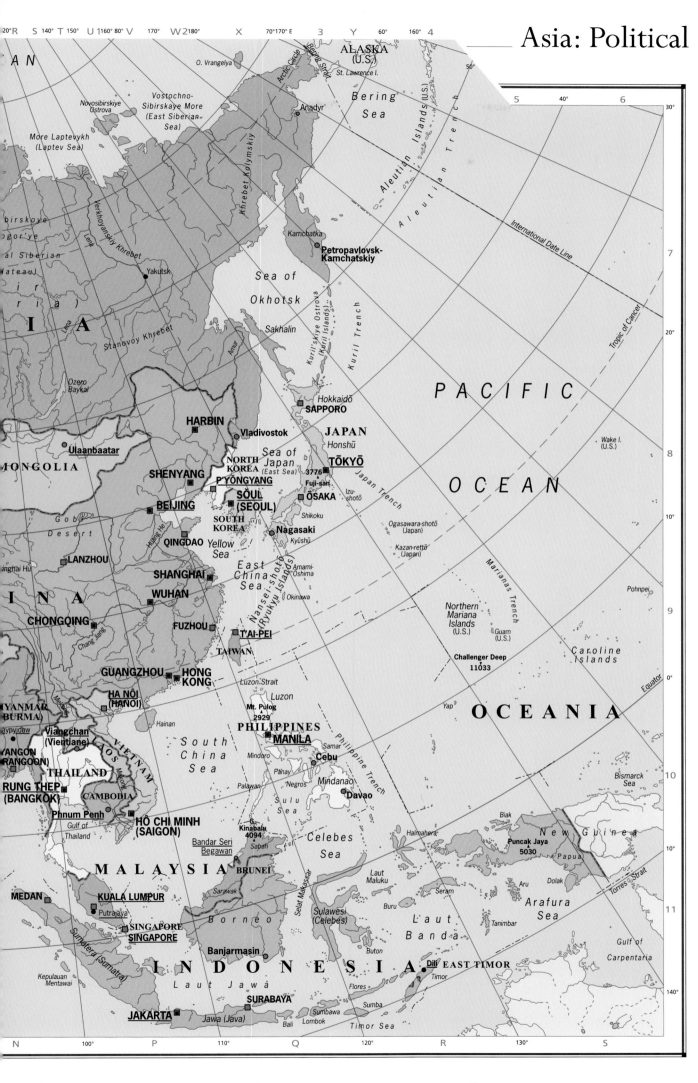

Verkhoyansk & Oymyakon, Russia : -68 ˚C or -90 ˚F
Tirat Tsevi, Israel : 54 ˚C or 129 ˚F

3,614,371,000
81 per km² or 210 per sq mi

44,493,000 km² or 17,179,000 sq mi
48

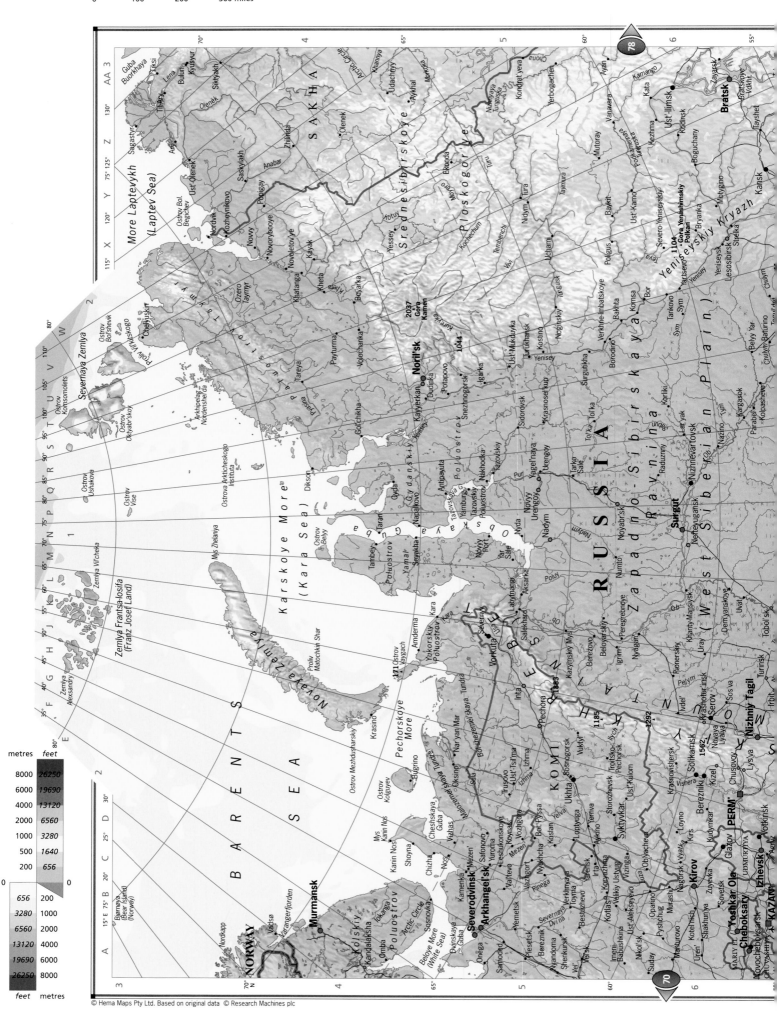

metres feet

8000	26250
6000	19690
4000	13120
2000	6560
1000	3280
500	1640
200	656

0

656	200
3280	1000
6560	2000
13120	4000
19690	6000
26250	8000

feet metres

■	over 3 million	●	100 000 – 250 000	——	country capital underline
▣	1 – 3 million	●	25 000 – 100 000	——	state or province capital underline
●	250 000 – 1 million	•	under 25 000		

77

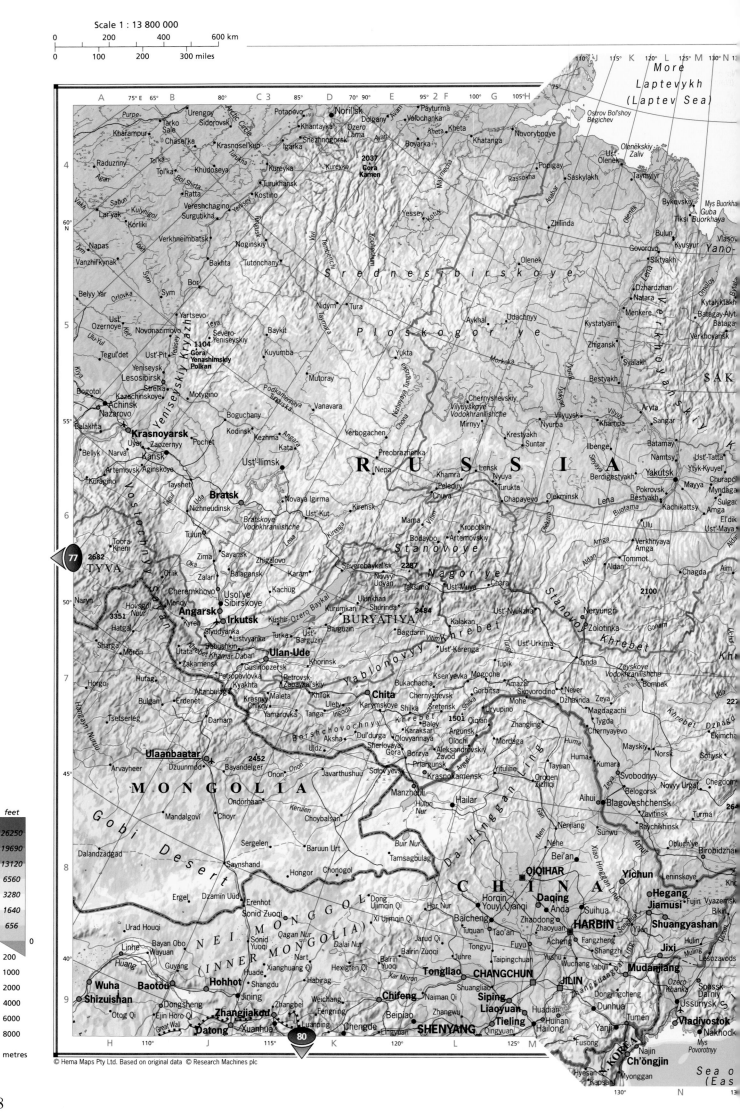

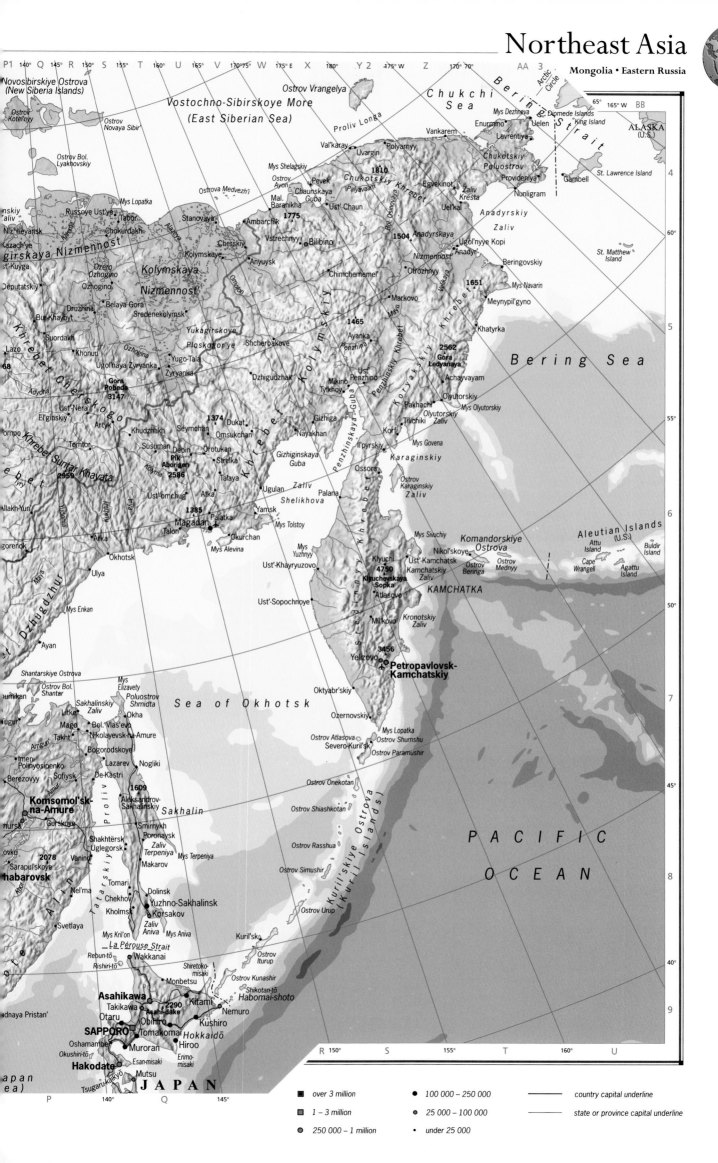

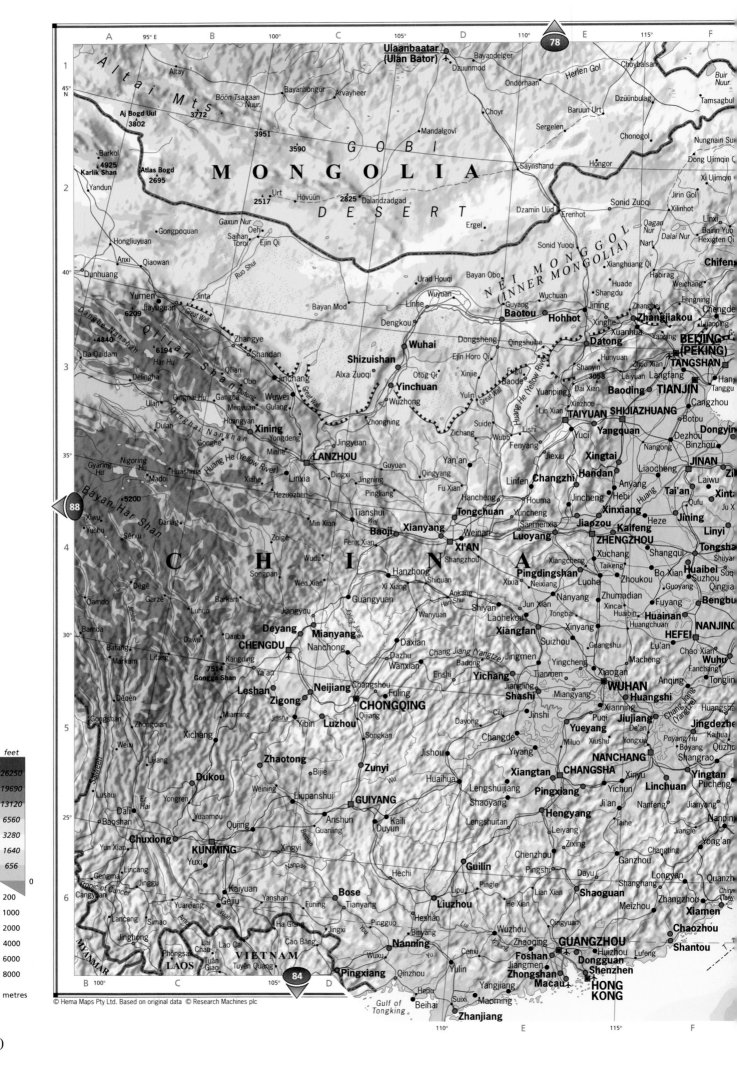

SEA OF
JAPAN
(East Sea)

YELLOW
SEA

NORTH
KOREA

SOUTH
KOREA

HOKKAIDŌ

HONSHŪ

JAPAN

SHIKOKU

KYŪSHŪ

EAST
CHINA SEA

PACIFIC

OCEAN

Nansei-shotō
(Ryukyu Islands)

TAIWAN

Tropic of Cancer

■ over 3 million	● 100 000 – 250 000	—— country capital underline
▪ 1 – 3 million	○ 25 000 – 100 000	
● 250 000 – 1 million	• under 25 000	

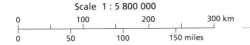

Japan and Korea

Japan • North Korea • South Korea

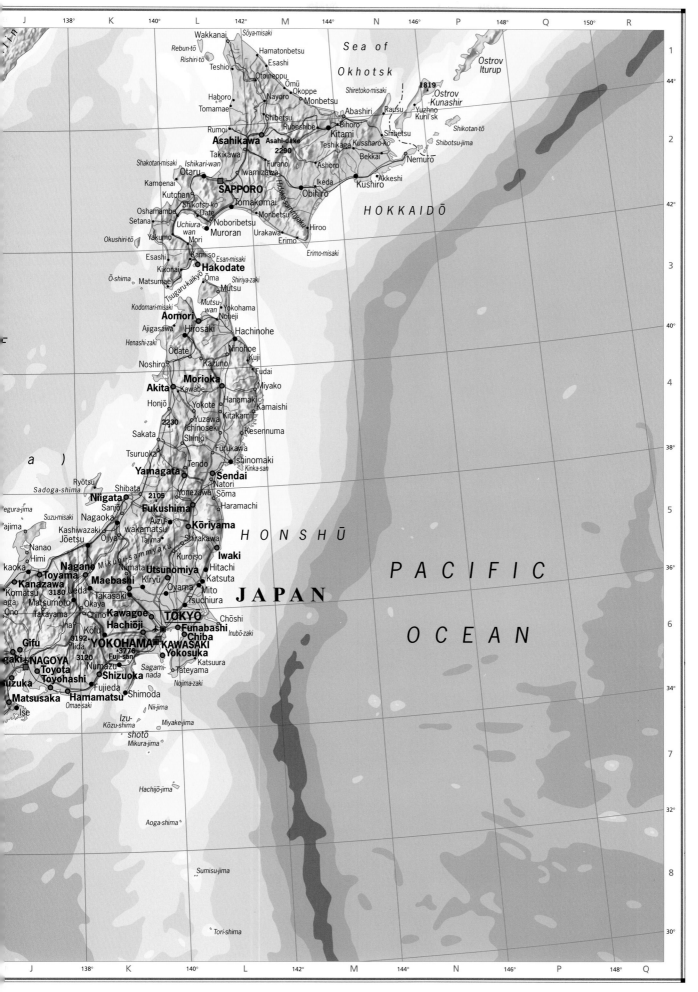

J 138° K 140° L 142° M 144° N 146° P 148° Q 150° R

Sea of Okhotsk

Wakkanai
Sōya-misaki
Rebun-tō
Rishiri-tō
Hamatonbetsu
Teshio
Esashi
Otoineppu
Haboro
Ōmu
Nayoro
Okoppe
Monbetsu
Tomamae
Shiretoko-misaki
1819
Ostrov Iturup
Rumoi
Shibetsu
Abashiri
Rausu
Ostrov Kunashir
Yuzhno Kuril'sk
Asahikawa
Asahi-dake
2290
Turano
Bihoro
Shibetsu
Takikawa
Teshikaga
Kussharo-ko
Shikotan-tō
Kitami
Shakotan-misaki
Ishikari-wan
Iwamizawa
Ashoro
Bekkai
Nemuro
Shibotsu-jima
Kamoenai
Otaru
Ikeda
Akkeshi
SAPPORO
Tomakomai
Obihiro
Kushiro
Kutchan
Shikotsu-ko
Kamiso
Hidaka-sammyaku
HOKKAIDŌ
Oshamamba
Date
Noboribetsu
Setana
Yakumo
Uchiura-wan
Muroran
Hiroo
Okushiri-tō
Mori
Urakawa
Erimo
Esashi
Kikonai
Kamiso
Esan-misaki
Erimo-misaki
Ō-shima
Matsumae
Hakodate
Ōma
Shiriya-zaki
Matsumae
Tsugaru-kaikyō
Mutsu
Kodomari-misaki
Mutsu-wan
Yokohama
Noheji
Aomori
Ajigasawa
Hirosaki
Hachinohe
Henashi-zaki
Ōdate
Ninohe
Noshiro
Kazuno
Kuji
Morioka
Fudai
Kawabe
Miyako
Akita
Yokote
Hanamaki
Kamaishi
Honjō
Yuzawa
Kitakami
2230
Ichinoseki
Kesennuma
Sakata
Shinjō
Tsuruoka
Furukawa
Ishinomaki
Tendo
Kinka-san
Yamagata
Sendai
Ryōtsu
Natori
Sadoga-shima
Shibata
Yonezawa
Sōma
Niigata
Sanjō
2105
Haramachi
Fukushima
Nagaoka
Suzu-misaki
Kashiwazaki
Aizu-wakamatsu
Kōriyama
Jōetsu
Ojiya
Tajima
Shirakawa
HONSHŪ
Nanao
Kuroiso
Iwaki
Himi
Mikuni-sammyaku
Numata
Hitachi
Nagano
Utsunomiya
Katsuta
kaoka
Toyama
Maebashi
Kiryū
Mito
PACIFIC
Kanazawa
3180 Ueda
Takasaki
Oyama
Tsuchiura
Komatsu
Matsumoto
Okaya
JAPAN
aga
Takayama
Chino
Kawagoe
Chōshi
Ono
Kōfu
Hachiōji
Inubō-zaki
Gifu
3192 Iida
TOKYO
OCEAN
YOKOHAMA
Funabashi
gaki
3776
KAWASAKI
Chiba
NAGOYA
Fuji-san
Yokosuka
uzuka
Toyota
Numazu
Katsuura
Toyohashi
Sagami-nada
Tateyama
Matsusaka
Shizuoka
Fujieda
Hamamatsu
Nojima-zaki
Ise
Omaesaki
Shimoda
Nii-jima
Izu-Kōzu-shima
Miyake-jima
shotō
Mikura-jima
Hachijō-jima
Aoga-shima
Sumisu-jima
Tori-shima

44°
42°
40°
38°
36°
34°
32°
30°

J 138° K 140° L 142° M 144° N 146° P 148° Q

■	over 3 million	●	100 000 – 250 000	———	country capital underline
■	1 – 3 million	○	25 000 – 100 000		
●	250 000 – 1 million	·	under 25 000		

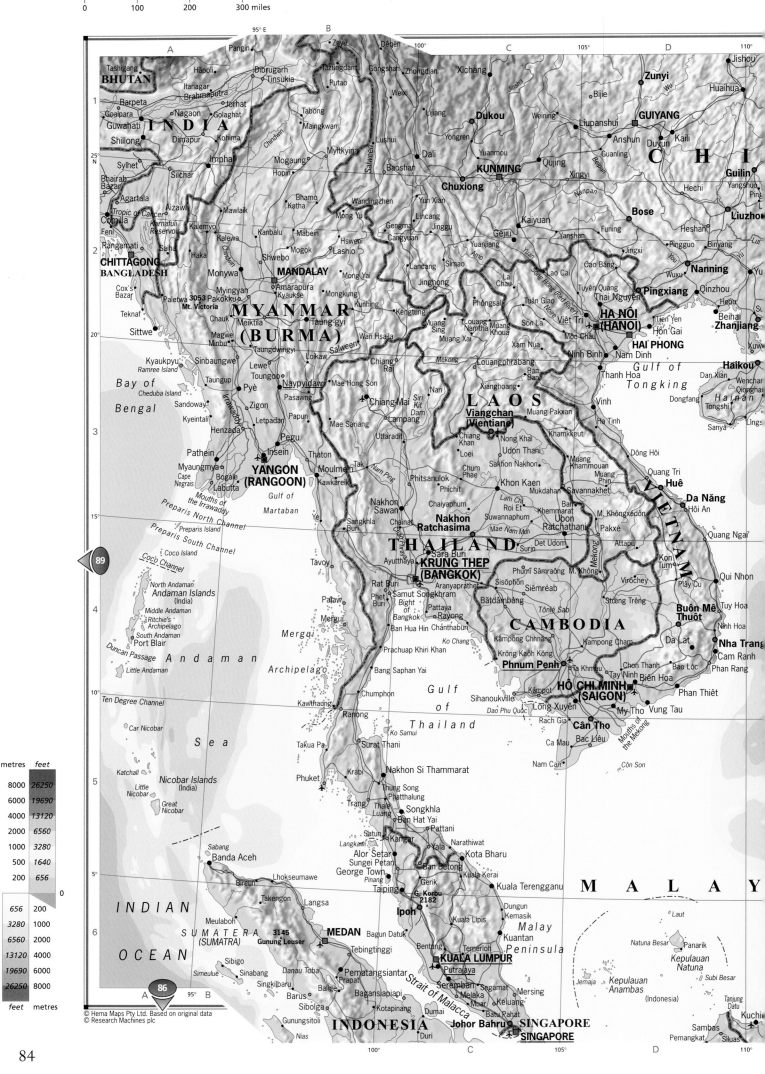

0   200   400   600 km

0   100   200   300 miles

95° E   B   100°   C   105°   D   110°

A

BHUTAN
Tashigang
Itanagar
Hápoli
Pangin
Zayul
Dêtⁿ̂en
Jishou
Barpeta   Nagaon   Dibrugarh   Tazungdam   Gongshan   Zhongdian   Xichang   Zunyi
25° N   Guwahati   Golaghat   Tinsukia   Putao   Weixi   Lijiang   Bijie   Huaihua   GUIYANG
I N D I A   Dimapur   Jorhat   Tabong   Maingkwan   Myitkyina   Lushui   Yongren   Liupanshui   Anshun   Duyun   Kaili
Shillong   Kohima   Mogaung   Baoshan   Dali   Yuanmou   **KUNMING**   Qujing   Guanling   **C H I**
Sylhet   Silchar   Imphal   Hopin   **Chuxiong**   Xichang   Guilin
Bhairab   Mawlaik   Katha   Wandingzhen   Yun Xian   Lincang   Gengma   Kaiyuan   Yanshan   Hechi   Yangshuo
Bazar   Agartala   Aizawl   Bhamo   Mong Yu   Jinggu   Arno   Funing   Ringguo   Binyang   **Liuzho**
CHITTAGONG   Kalemyo   Kanbalu   Mabein   Mong Yai   Lashio   Lancang   Simao   Yuanjiang   Jingxi   **Nanning**   Yu
BANGLADESH   Monywa   Mogok   Hsweni   Mongkung   Kengtung   Jinghong   Lao Cai   Cao Bằng   Wuxu   Qinzhou
Cox's   Haka   Shwebo   Kunhing   Muang   Louang   Tuyên Quang   Thai Nguyen   **Pingxiang**   Hepu   **Zhanjiang**
Bazar   Myingyan   **MANDALAY**   Sing   Namtha   Muang   Khoua   Viêt Tri   **HA NÔI**   Tiên Yen   Beihai

E 115° F 120° G 125° H 130° J

EAST CHINA
SEA

Nago • Okinawa
• Okinawa
JAPAN • Naha

Shangrao

Xiangtan Lianyuan □ **CHANGSHA** Xinyu • **Linchuan** Pucheng • Wenzhou
Lengshuijiang Yichun Ji'an Nanping Ningde
iaoyang **Pingxiang** Taihe Jiangle Fuding
Hengyang Lengshuitan Changting Yong'an **FUZHOU**
Leiyang Zixing Ganzhou Putian Matsu (Taiwan)
Lian Xian **Shaoguan** Meizhou Longyan Quanzhou Chinmen (Taiwan)
Chenzhou Hsin-chu **T'ao-** **Chi-lung**
Wuzhou **Xiamen** Zhangzhou **yuan** **T'AI-PEI**
Qingyuan 3884
GUANGZHOU Huizhou **Chaozhou** Hsueh-Shan
Zhaoqing **Dongguan** Lufeng **Shantou** Chang-hua **T'ai-chung**
enxi Jiangmen **Foshan Shenzhen** Shanwei **Chia-i** 3950
Zhongshan **Macau HONG KONG** Yu Shan **TAIWAN**
aoming Yangjiang **T'ai-nan** T'ai-tung
KAO-HSIUNG P'ing-tung

Tropic of Cancer

Oluan-pi

Luzon

Dongsha Qundao (Pratas) (China) Strait Batan Islands
• Basco

PACIFIC

Balintang Channel

Babuyan Islands

Bangui Claveria San Vicente
Laoag Kabugao Aparri
Vigan Bangued Lal-lo **OCEAN**
Santa Cruz Tuguegarao Palanan
San Fernando Bontoc Ilagan
Baguio Mt. Pulog Santiago
2929 Casiguran
Paracel Islands Alaminos Dagupan
Lingayen San Carlos Baler

SOUTH Tarlac Cabanatuan
Angeles Gapan
Olongapo **QUEZON CITY** Polillo Is.
CHINA **MANILA** Calauag Is. Cantanduanes
Pasig San Pablo Daet Pandan
Nasugbu Calauag Virac
Batangas Lucena Lopez Naga
SEA Mamburao Calapan Pascual Legaspi
Mindoro Boac Sorsogon
2488 Pinamalayan Bulan Catarman
Mount Baco Masbate Allen Samar
San Pedro Masbate Calbayog
Calamian Nabas Catbalogan
Group Coron Placer Borongan
San Jose de Kalibo Roxas Tacloban
El Nido Buenavista **Iloilo** Bogo Ormoc
Panay Bago Cebu Leyte Sogod Libjo
Roxas **Bacolod** Carcar **Cebu** Maasin Dinagat
Cauayan Bais Bohol Tagbilaran Surigao Dapa
Palawan Negros Dumaguete Butuan Madrid
Puerto Princesa Tandag
Sulu Sea **PHILIPPINES** Prosperidad
Quezon Dipolog **Cagayan de Oro** Bislig
Brooke's Point Manukan 2560 Malaybalay Tagum
Liloy Iligan **Mindanao**
Bugsuk Sibuco Pagadian Davao
Balabac Kudat Zamboanga Cotabato 2954 Mati
Balabac Langkon Kota Belud Isabela Tacurong Mt. Apo Cape San Agustin
Strait 4094 Ranau Jolo Polomoloc **General Santos**
Kota Kinabalu G. Kinabalu Sandakan Palimbang Glan
Beaufort Tungku Pangutaran Basilan Moro Gulf
SABAH Lahad Datu Group Jolo Sulu Archipelago Sarangani Is.
Bintulu Tawitawi Kepulauan
Bongao Nanusa
BRUNEI Gunung Mulu Kalabakan Celebes Beo Kepulauan
Bandar Seri Begawan 2371 Tawau Tahuna **INDONESIA** Karkaralong
Seria Bareo Semporna Sea Kepulauan
2499 Talaud
Bintulu Tarakan Kepulauan
Belaga **SARAWAK** Tanjungselor Sangir Morotai
Sibu Sarikei Kapit 2988 Tanjungredeb **INDONESIA** Laut Maluku Daruba
imanggang **KALIMANTAN** Sepinang
Muarawahau Sangkulirang
Muara Sangkulirang

E 115° F 120° G 125° H

N
A

S
I
A

G 87

■ over 3 million ● 100 000 – 250 000 —— country capital underline

■ 1 – 3 million ○ 25 000 – 100 000

● 250 000 – 1 million • under 25 000

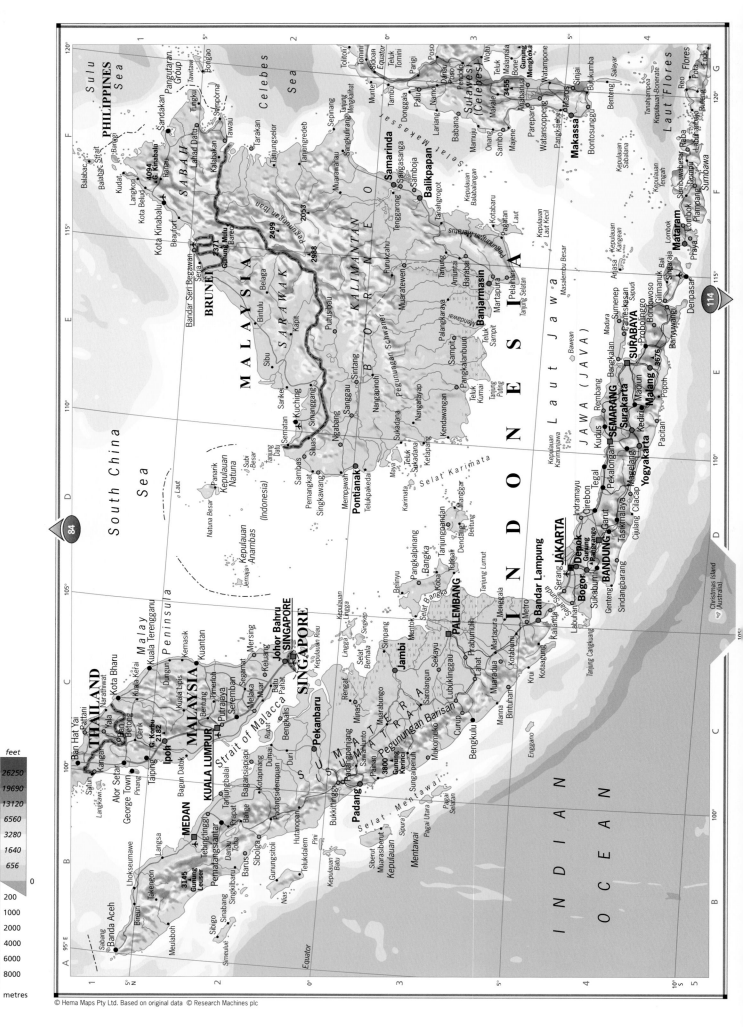

0   200   400   600 km
0   100   200   300 miles

metres	feet
8000	26250
6000	19690
4000	13120
2000	6560
1000	3280
500	1640
200	656
0	0
656	200
3280	1000
6560	2000
13120	4000
19690	6000
26250	8000

feet   metres

© Hema Maps Pty Ltd. Based on original data © Research Machines plc

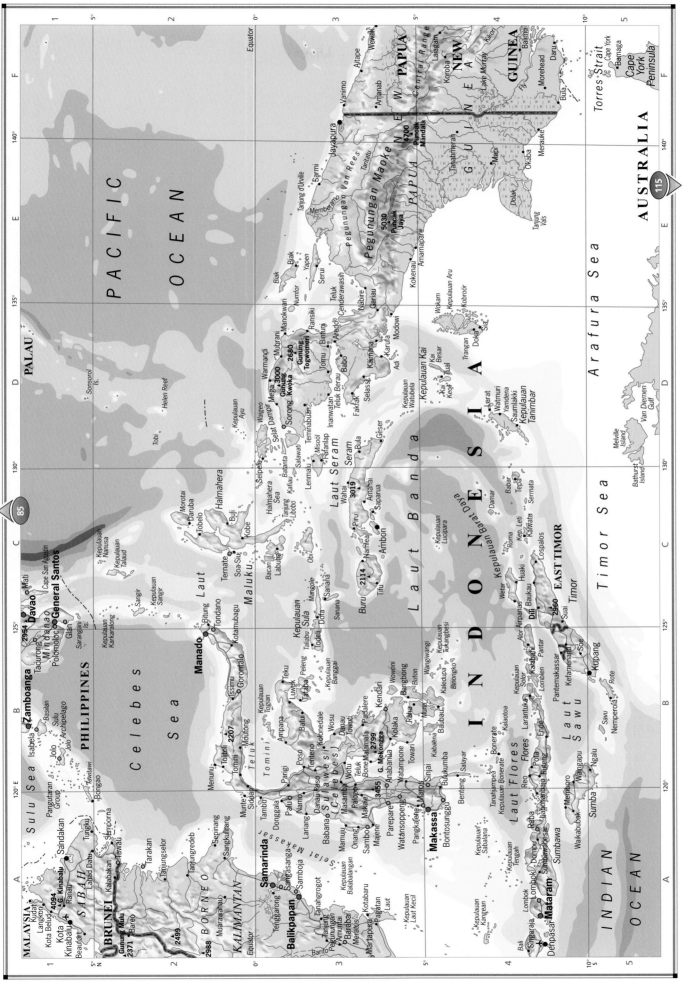

Symbol	Population
■ (black square)	over 3 million
▣ (grey square)	1 – 3 million
⬤ (large circle)	250 000 – 1 million
●	100 000 – 250 000
◎	25 000 – 100 000
•	under 25 000
——	country capital underline

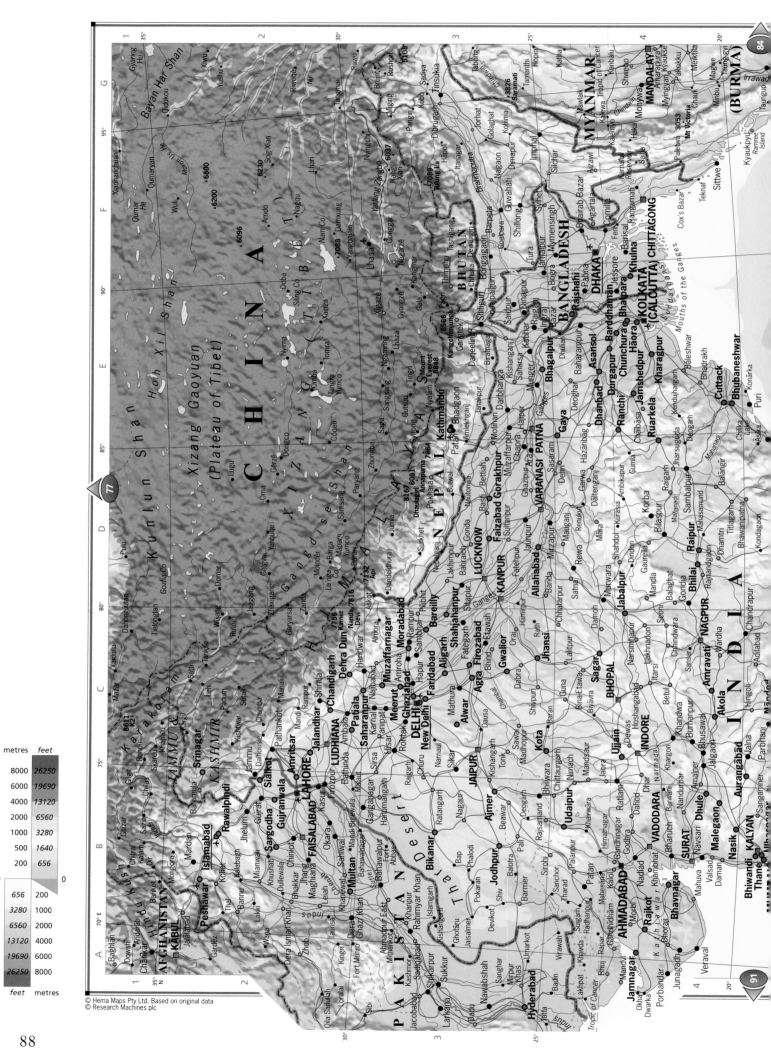

0   200   400   600 km
0   100   200   300 miles

© Hema Maps Pty Ltd. Based on original data
© Research Machines plc

■ over 3 million	● 100 000 – 250 000	—— country capital underline
■ 1 – 3 million	● 25 000 – 100 000	
● 250 000 – 1 million	• under 25 000	

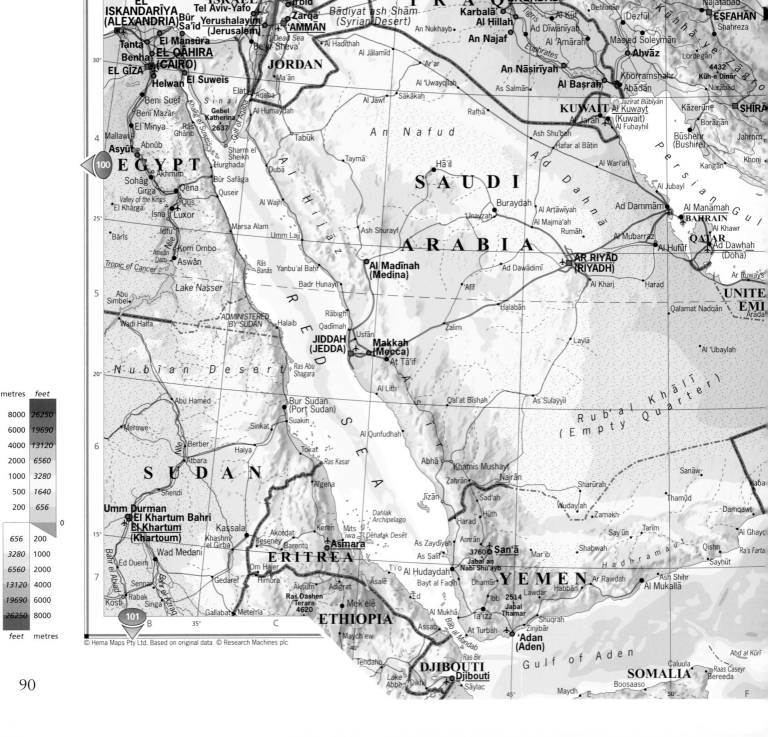

Scale 1 : 12 700 000

0	200	400	600 km	
0	100	200	300 miles	

A 30° E **B** 35° **C** 40° **D** 45° E **E** 50° **F**

1

İSTANBUL
Marmara
Denizi
Gebze
İzmit
Bursa
Balıkesir
Eskişehir
Zonguldak
Ereğli
Düzce
Bolu
Sakarya
Bartın
Kastamonu
İnebolu
İnce Burun
Sinop

Black Sea

Och'amch'ire
Zugdidi
Bat'umi
Samtredia
Samsun

K'ut'aisi
GEORGIA
T'BILISI
Rust'avi
Vanadzor

RUSSIA
Vachi
Izberbash
Derbent

Caspian

KAZAK

Fetisovo

2

40°
N

Bursa
Simav
Uşak
Denizli
Muğla
Antalya
Fethiye
Elmalı

Kütahya
Afyon
Salihli
Sandıklı
Dinar
Isparta
Burdur
Bucak
Bozkır

ANKARA
Polatlı
Balâ
Kırıkkale
Kırşehir
Konya
Karaman
Aksaray
Niğde

Çankırı
Çorum
Sungurlu
Yozgat

Amasya
Turhal
Tokat

Ordu
Trabzon
Rize

Gümüşhane
Artvin
Oltu
Kars
Horasan

Ardahan
Ardanuç

3549
Erzurum
Ağrı

Gyumri
YEREVAN
ARMENIA
Mt. Ararat
5165

Vanadzor
AZER
Naxçıvan
Maku

Gäncä
Mingäçevir
AZERBAIJAN
3724

BAKI
(BAKU)

Xaçmaz
Quba
Siyäzän
Sumqayıt

TURKEY

Sivas
Kayseri
Gürün

Darende

Divriği
Tunceli

Bingöl
Muş
Suphan Dağı

Patnos
Murat 4434

Van
Tatvan

Baskale
Hakkâri

Qotur
Khvoy

Jolfa
Marand
Ahar

4810 Ardabil
3710

Miäneh

Astara

Länkäran

Sea

Ostrov
Ogurchinskiy

Okarem

3

35°

Antalya
Anamur
Silifke
Ermenek
C. Andreas
Lefkosia
(Nicosia)
Pafos
Lemesos
(Limassol)

İçel
Tarsus
Mersin
Osmaniye
Antakya

ADANA
İskenderun

Al
Lādhiqīyah

Al Qāmishlī
Al Ḥasakah

Sinjar

Tall
'Afar

Zākho
Dahūk
Al Mawṣil
Arbīl
As Sulaymānīyah

Mahābād
3107
Kirk
Bülāg Dāgh

Saqqez
Bāneh

Marivān
Bijār

Orūmīyeh
Maragheh

Takestān

Tonkābon
Now
Shahr

Rasht

Bandar-e Anzalī
Lāhījān

5671 Qolleh-ye
Damāvand

Gazan Kuli

Bandar-e

Cyprus

C. Arnaoutis

Mediterranean

HALAB
(ALEPPO)

Idlib

Manbij
Ar Raqqah

Dayr az Zawr

Kirkūk

Sanandaj

Zanjān

Qazvīn

Karaj
Eslāmshahr
Takestān

TEHRĀN
(TEHERAN)
Varāmīn

Das

Sea

Ḥamāh
Ḥimṣ
(Homs)

Tadmur

Al Bū Kamāl

'Ānah

Bāji
Tikrīt

Paveh

Kermānshāh
Īlām
Mehrān

Hamadān
Malāyer
Borūjerd

Arāk
Qom

4

Lebanon
BEYROUTH (BEIRUT)
Trâblous
Zahlé
DIMASHQ
(DAMASCUS)

SYRIA

Ar Rutba

Ba'qūbah

BAGHDAD

Dehlorān

Khorramābād

ESFAHĀN

Hefa
(Haifa)
ISRAEL
Tel Aviv-Yafo
Yerushalayim
(Jerusalem)

EL
ISKANDARÎYA
(ALEXANDRIA)
Bûr Sa'îd
Tanta
El Mansûra
Benha
EL QÂHIRA
(CAIRO)
EL GÎZA
Helwan

Irbid
Zarqā'
AMMĀN
Be'ér Sheva'

JORDAN

Ma'ān

Al Ḥadīthah

An Nukhayb

Ar Ramādī
Karbalā'
Al Ḥillah

Al Jālāmīd

Najafābād
Shahreza

Ad Dīwānīyah
Al 'Amārah
Masjed Soleymān

Ahvāz

Dezfūl

4432
Kūh-e Dīnār
Nūrābād

Lordegān

An Najaf

An Nāṣirīyah
Al Kūt

Al Ḥarīthah

5

El Suweis
Helwan
Beni Suef
Beni Mazâr
El Minya
Mallawi
Asyût
Abnûb
Sohâg
Akhmîm
Girga
Qena
Qus
Luxor
Idfu
El Khârga
Esna
Kom Ombo
Aswân
Aswân Dam

EGYPT

Elat
Aqaba
Gebel
Katherîna
2637
Sinai
Khalîg el Suweis
Râs Ghârib
Hurghada
Bûr Safâga
Sharm el
Sheikh

Al Ḥumaydah
Tabūk
Duba
Al Wajh

Taymā'

An Nafud

Ḥā'il

Buraydah
'Unayzah

Ar Rafhā'
Sākākah
Al Jawf
'Ar'ar
Al 'Uwayqilah

Ar Artāwīyah
Al Majma'ah
Rumāh

Ad Dawādimī

AR RIYĀD
(RIYADH)

Al Kharj

SAUDI
ARABIA

KUWAIT
Al Kuwayt
(Kuwait)
Al Jarah
Al Fuḥayḥil
Ash Shu'bah
Ḥafar al Bāṭin
Ash Sha'bah

Al Wārī'ah

Al Jubayl

Ad Dammām
Al Manāmah
BAHRAIN
Al Khawr
QATAR
Al Mubarraz
Al Hufūf
Ad Dawhah
(Doha)
Ar Ruways

Jazīrat Būbīyān

SHIRĀ

Būshehr
(Bushire)

Kangān

Borāzjān
Kāzerūn
Jahrom
Khonj

Persian Gulf

UNITE
EMI
Arada

Qalamat Nadqān

6

25°

Abu
Simbel
Wadi Halfa
ADMINISTERED
BY SUDAN
Halaib

Ras Banâs
Marsa Alam
Umm Lajj
Yanbu'al Bahr

Badr Ḥunayn
Rābigh
Qadīmah

Al Madīnah
(Medina)

'Afīf

Ad Dawādimī
Halabān

Zalim

Layla

Harad

Qal'at Bīshah

As Sulayyil

Rub' al Khālī
(Empty Quarter)

Al 'Ubaylah

Tropic of Cancer

Lake Nasser

Nubian Desert

Ras Abu
Shagara

JIDDAH
(JEDDA)
Makkah
(Mecca)

Usfān
At Ṭā'if

Al Lith

Abu Hamed
Merowe
Berber

Bur Sudan
(Port Sudan)
Suakin
Sinkat

Al Qunfudhah

7

SUDAN

Atbara
Haiya
Tokar
Ras Kasar

Abhā
Khamis Mushayt
Zahrān
Najrān

Jīzān

Sad'ah

Ḥūth

Wuday'ah
Zamakh
Thamūd

Sharūrah

Sanāw

Nabā

Ras Fartak

20°

Umm Durman
El Khartum Bahri
El Khartum
(Khartoum)
Kassala
Khashm
el Girba
Wad Medani

Kosti
Rabak
Singa
Ed Dueim
Sennar
Gedaref

Shendi
Berber
Haiya
Âlgena

Tessenei
Barentu
Teseney

Keren
Akordat
Mits'iwa
(Massawa)

Asmara
ERITREA

Dahlak
Archipelago
Dahlak Desēt

As Zaydīyah
As Ṣalīf
Al Hudaydah

Dhamār
Al Mukhā
Ta'izz

Amrān
San'ā
3760
Jabal an
Nabi Shu'ayb

Mar'ib
Shabwah

Say'ūn
Tarīm

Ḥadramaut

Qishn

Al Ghayḍ

Damqawt

Ed Damer

B
35°
C

Om Hajer
Gallabat
Metema
Ras Dashen
Terara
4620
Mek'elē

ETHIOPIA

Al Mukhā
Zinjibār
Shuqrah
'Adan
(Aden)

Lawdar
Ḥabbān
Al Mukallā
'Ash Shiḥr

YEMEN

2514
Jabal
Thamar
Ibb

Gulf of Aden

Abd al Kūrī

SOMALIA

Boosaaso
Bereeda

Ras Caseyr
Caluula

© Hema Maps Pty Ltd. Based on original data © Research Machines plc

Maych'ew
Adīgrat
Aksum

Ti'o
Al Ḥudaydah
Bayt al Faqīh
Dhamār

Ar Rawdah

Mayḍi

DJIBOUTI
Djibouti
Dikhil
Lake
Abbe
Ṣaylac

Tendaho

90

metres / feet

metres	feet
8000	26250
6000	19690
4000	13120
2000	6560
1000	3280
500	1640
200	656

0

feet	metres
656	200
3280	1000
6560	2000
13120	4000
19690	6000
26250	8000

feet metres

100

101

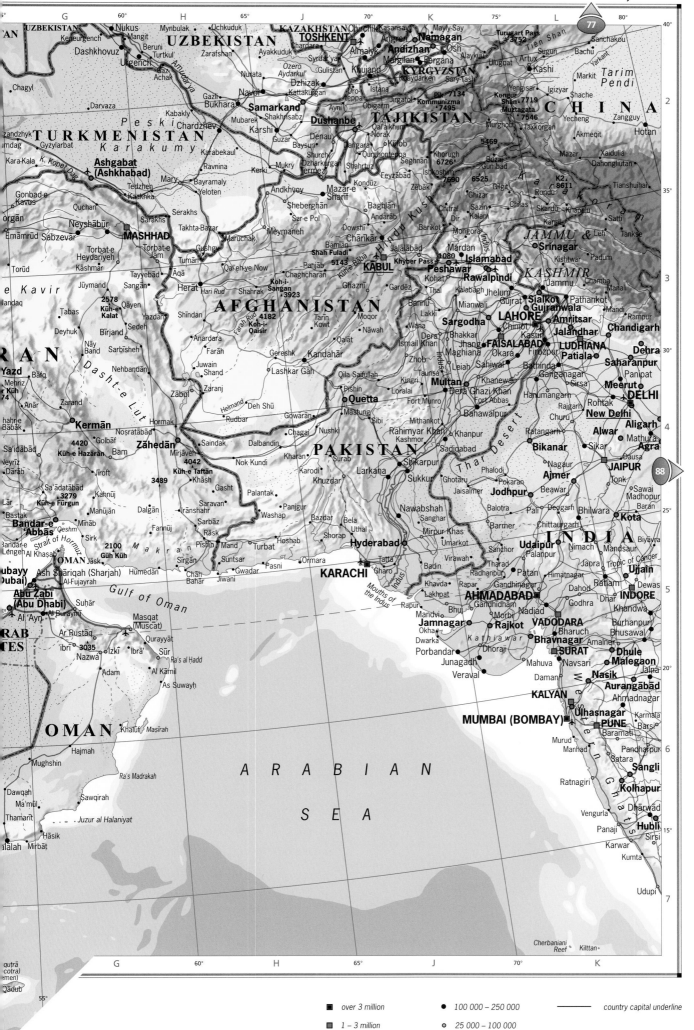

■ over 3 million	● 100 000 – 250 000	——— country capital underline
■ 1 – 3 million	○ 25 000 – 100 000	
● 250 000 – 1 million	• under 25 000	

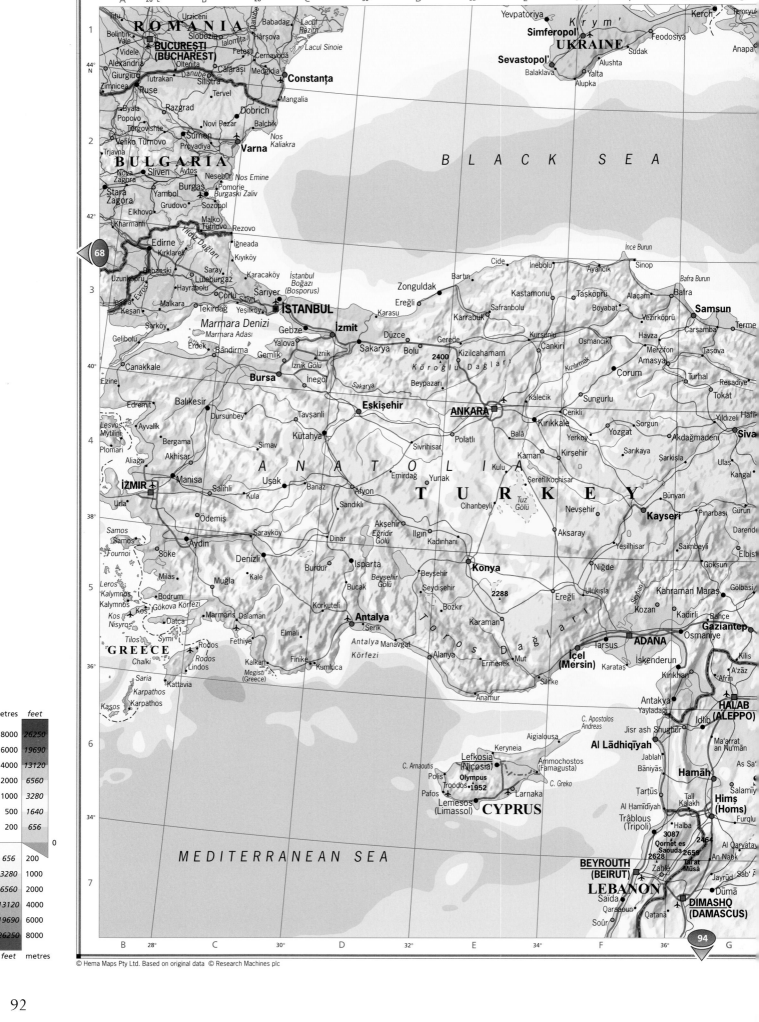

RUSSIA

KALMYKIYA

Krasnodar

Stavropol'

Novorossiysk

Sochi

ADYGEYA

KARACHAYEVO-
CHERKESIYA

KABARDINO-
BALKARIYA

5642
Elbrus

5203

Vladikavkaz

SEVERNAYA
OSETIYA

CHECHNYA

Groznyy

DAGESTAN

Makhachkala

CASPIAN

SEA

C   a   u   c   a   s   u   s

4494
4276
Diklosmta

4131

GEORGIA

T'BILISI

Rust'avi

4466
Gora
Bazardyuzu

Sumqayıt

BAKI
(BAKU)

AZERBAIJAN

Erzurum

ARMENIA
YEREVAN

Mt.
Ararat
5165

3724

Gäncä

Tabrīz

AZER.

Naxçıvan

Qazangöldag
3829

4810

Ardabīl

Astara

Rasht

Elazığ

Malatya

Diyarbakır

Batman

IRAN

3710
Kuh-e
Sahand

Orūmīyeh

Zanjān

Şanlıurfa

Al Mawşil

Arbīl

Kirk
Bulāg D.
3107

Sanandaj

As Sulaymānīyah

Kirkūk

Kermānshāh

S Y R I A

M E S O P O T A M I A

I R A Q

Dayr az Zawr

Bādiyat ash Shām
(Syrian Desert)

BAGHDĀD

Ar Ramādī

70

90

101

■ over 3 million	● 100 000 – 250 000	── country capital underline
■ 1 – 3 million	◦ 25 000 – 100 000	── state or province capital underline
● 250 000 – 1 million	• under 25 000	

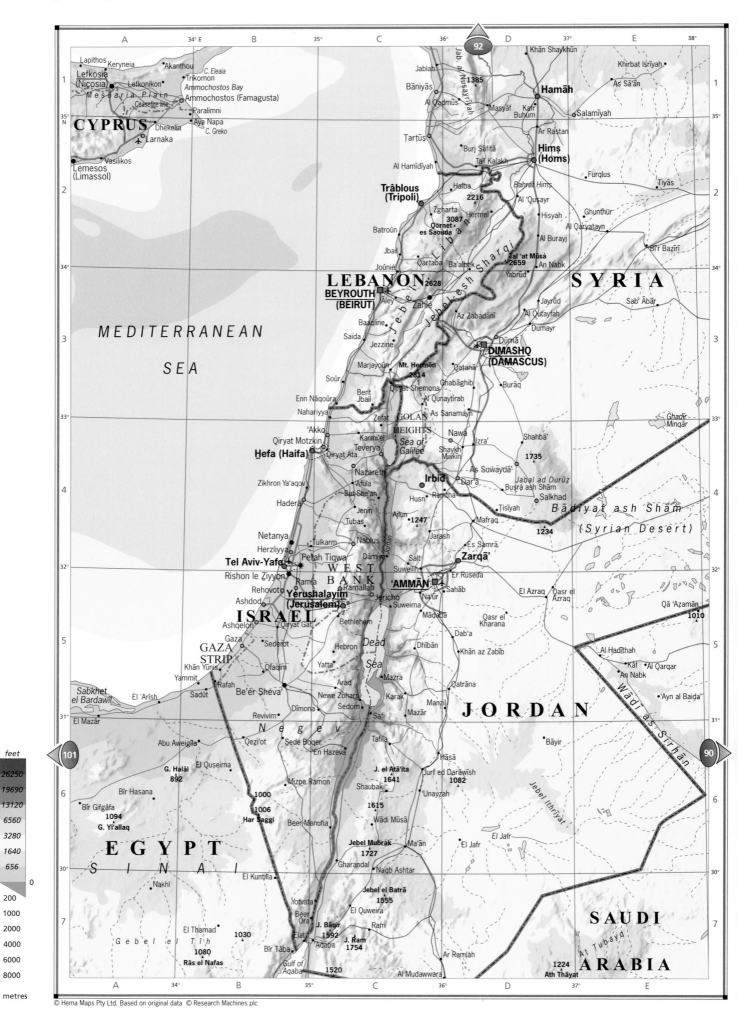

Scale 1 : 2 850 000

| Scale bar (km) | 0 | 50 | 100 | 150 km |
| Scale bar (miles) | 0 | 25 | 50 | 75 miles |

A 34° E **B** 35° **C** 36° **D** 37° **E** 38°

CYPRUS

Lapithos Keryneia Akanthou
Lefkosía (Nicosia) Lefkonikon C. Eleaia
Trikomon Ammochostos Bay
Mesoaria Plain Ceasefire line Ammochostos (Famagusta)
Paralimni
Aya Napa
Dhekelia C. Greko
Larnaka

Vasilikos
Lemesos (Limassol)

35° N

MEDITERRANEAN

SEA

34°

33°

32°

31°

LEBANON
BEYROUTH (BEIRUT)

Trâblous (Tripoli)

Khán Shaykhún
Jablah
Bániyás 1385
Al Qadmús
Masyáf Kafr Buhum Hamāh
Tartús
Burj Sáfíta Tall Kalakh Hims (Homs)
Al Hamídíyah Halba
Zgharta Hermel Bahrat Hims
2216 Al 'Qusayr
3087 Hisyah
Qornet es Saouda
Batroûn Al Burayj
Jbail Qartaba Ba'albek Yabrûd An Nabk
Joûnié Tal 'at Músá
2628 2659
Áley Zahlé Az Zabadání Al Qutayfah
Baaqline Jayrûd Dumayr
Saïda DIMASHQ (DAMASCUS)
Dûmá
Jezzine Qatana Burāq
Marjayoûn Mt. Hermōn Ghabághib
2814 Al Qunaytirah As Sanamáyn
Soûr Bent Jbail Qiryat Shemona Nawá Izra' Shahbá'
Enn Nâqoûra Al Qunaytirah Shaykh Miskin 1735
Nahariyya Zefat GOLAN HEIGHTS Dar'a
'Akko Karmi'el Sea of Galilee As Suwaydá'
Qiryat Motzkin Teverya Irbid Jabal ad Durúz
Hefa (Haifa) Qiryat Ata Husn Busrá ash Sham Salkhad
Zikhron Ya'aqov Nazareth Ramtha
Afula Ajlun Tisíyah
Bet-She'an 1247
Hadera Jenin Mafraq 1234
Tubas Jarash
Netanya Tulkarm Nablus Es Samrá'
Herzliyya Dámiya Zarqā'
Petah Tiqwa Salt
Tel Aviv-Yafo Suweilih 'AMMĀN Er Ruseifa
Rishon le Ziyyon Ramallah Saháb
Ramla Jericho Na'úr
Rehovot Suweima El Azraq Qasr el Ázraq
Ashdod Yerushalayim (Jerusalem) Mádaba
Bethlehem Qasr el Kharana
Ashqelon Qiryat Gat Dab'a Qā 'Azamān
Hebron 1010
Gaza Khān az Zabíb
GAZA STRIP Sederot Dead Sea Dhíbán
Khān Yúnis Ofaqim Yatta Mazra'
Yammit Rafah Arad Karak Qatrána Manzil
Sadût Newe Zohars Mazár
Revivim Sedom Safi

SYRIA

As Sā'ān
Salamíyah
Furqlus
Ghunthûr Tiyás
Al Qaryatayn Bîr Bazírî
Sab' Ábár

Bādiyat ash Sham
(Syrian Desert)

JORDAN

Al Hadíthah
Káf Al Qarqar
An Nabk

ISRAEL

Be'ér Shéva'
Dímona

N e g e v

Abu Aweigîla Qezi'ot Sede Boqer Tafila Báyir
'En Hazeva
El Quseima
Mizpe Ramon J. el Atá'ita Jurf ed Daráwîsh Hāsā
G. Halál 1641 1082
892 1000 Shaubak
Bîr Hasana 1006 1615 'Unayzah
Bîr Gifgâfa Har Saggi Wādi Músā
1094 Beer Menuha
G. Yi'allaq Jebel Mubrāk Ma'ān El Jafr
1727 El Jafr
Gharandal Naqb Ashtar

EGYPT

S I N A I

Nakhl El Kuntilla
Jebel el Batrã
1555
Yotvata El Quweira
Beer Ora Ram
El Thamad J. Bágir 1030
Elat 1592 J. Ram
Ras el Nafas 1080 Aqaba 1754
Bîr Tâba
Gulf of Aqaba 1520
Al Mudawwara

SAUDI

'Ayn al Baida

Wādi as Sirhān
Jebel Ithríyat

Ghadîr Minqâr

1224
Ath Tháyat **ARABIA**

Ar Ramlah

metres feet
8000 26250
6000 19690
4000 13120
2000 6560
1000 3280
500 1640
200 656
0 0
656 200
3280 1000
6560 2000
13120 4000
19690 6000
26250 8000
feet metres

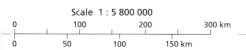
Bahrain • Israel • Jordan • Kuwait
Lebanon • Qatar • United Arab Emirates

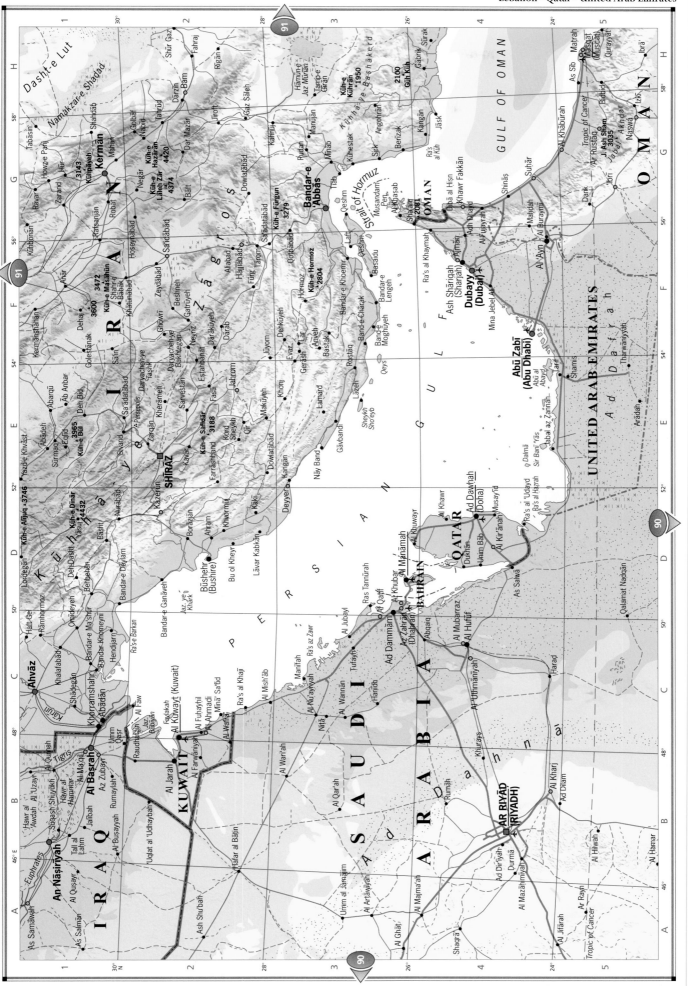

■ over 3 million
■ 1 – 3 million
● 250 000 – 1 million
● 100 000 – 250 000
○ 25 000 – 100 000
• under 25 000
— country capital underline
⬭ urban area

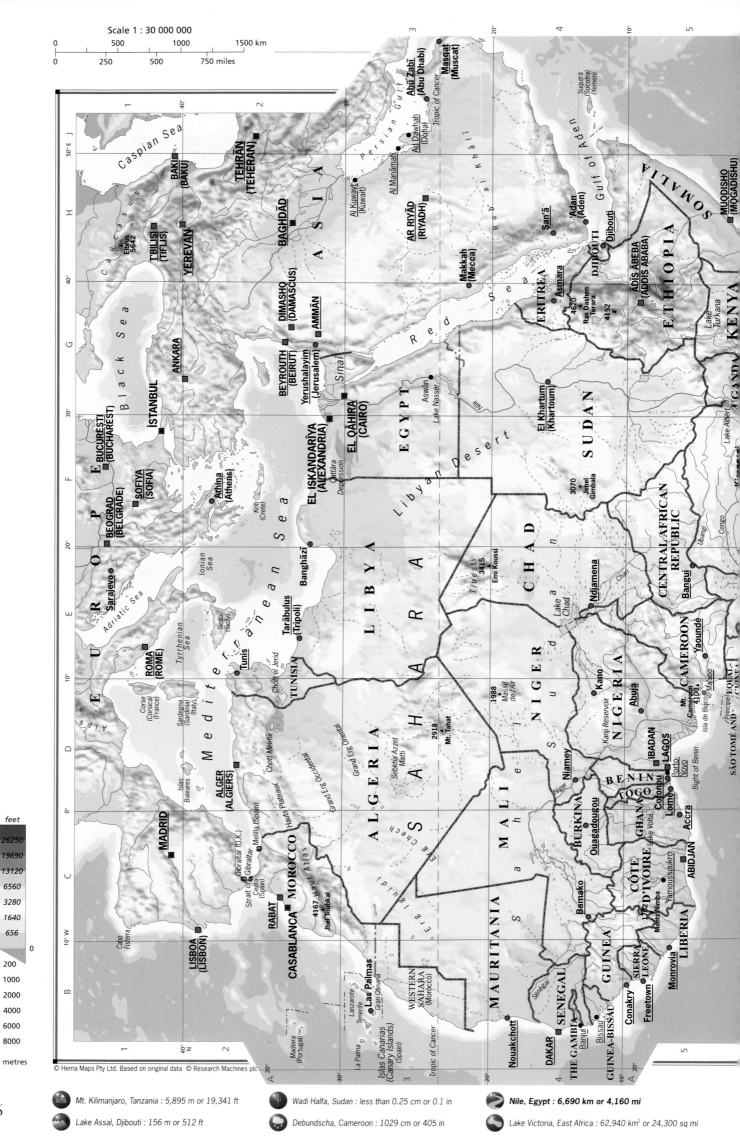

Scale 1 : 30 000 000

| 0 | 500 | 1000 | 1500 km |
| 0 | 250 | 500 | 750 miles |

metres feet
8000 26250
6000 19690
4000 13120
2000 6560
1000 3280
500 1640
200 656
0 0
656 200
3280 1000
6560 2000
13120 4000
19690 6000
26250 8000
feet metres

© Hema Maps Pty Ltd. Based on original data © Research Machines plc

Mt. Kilimanjaro, Tanzania : 5,895 m or 19,341 ft

Lake Assal, Djibouti : 156 m or 512 ft

Wadi Halfa, Sudan : less than 0.25 cm or 0.1 in

Debundscha, Cameroon : 1029 cm or 405 in

Nile, Egypt : 6,690 km or 4,160 mi

Lake Victoria, East Africa : 62,940 km² or 24,300 sq mi

Equator

6
10°

INDIAN OCEAN

Seychelles Is.
Coetivy I.
Amirante Is.
Agalega Is. (Mauritius)

SEYCHELLES

Cosmoledo Group
Glorieuses (France)

COMOROS
Njazidja
Mayotte (France)

Juan de Nova (France)

MADAGASCAR
ANTANANARIVO
Tanjona Bobaomby

Tanjona Vohimena

Tropic of Capricorn

Mombasa
NAIROBI
5199
5895
Mt. Kilimanjaro

DAR ES SALAAM
Pemba I.
Zanzibar I.

TANZANIA
Dodoma

Lake Victoria
Lake Nyasa

RWANDA
BURUNDI
Bujumbura
Lake Kivu
Lake Tanganyika

Mozambique Channel

MOZAMBIQUE

Beira

MALAWI
Lilongwe
3002
Mt. Mulanje

HARARE
Lago de Cahora Bassa

ZIMBABWE
Bulawayo
Limpopo

Maputo
SWAZILAND
Mbabane
Lobamba
DURBAN

Drakensberg

REPUBLIC OF THE CONGO
KINSHASA
Kananga
Lubumbashi
Lake Mweru

ZAMBIA
Ndola
Lusaka
Lake Kariba
Zambezi
Kasai
Kwango
Lomami

ANGOLA
LUANDA
CABINDA (Angola)

Brazzaville
GABON
Annobon (Pagalu) (Equatorial Guinea)

Okavango Delta
Makgadikgadi

BOTSWANA
Kalahari Desert
Gaborone

Pretoria (Tshwane)
Johannesburg
Vaal

LESOTHO
Maseru
2430

SOUTH AFRICA
Port Elizabeth
Cape Agulhas

Etosha Pan

NAMIBIA
Windhoek
Brandberg
2574
Cunene
Cuanza

Namib Desert
Walvis Bay

Orange
St. Helena Bay
CAPE TOWN
Cape of Good Hope

Gulf of Guinea

ATLANTIC OCEAN

St. Helena (U.K.)
Ascension (U.K.)

Tristan da Cunha (U.K.)
Gough I. (U.K.)

Tropic of Capricorn

Prince Edward Island (South Africa)

Îles Crozet (France)

Equator

Ifrane, Morocco : -24 °C or -11 °F	748,927,000	30,293,000 km² or 11,696,000 sq mi	
Al Aziziyah, Libya : 58 °C or 136 °F	25 per km² or 64 per sq mi	53	

97

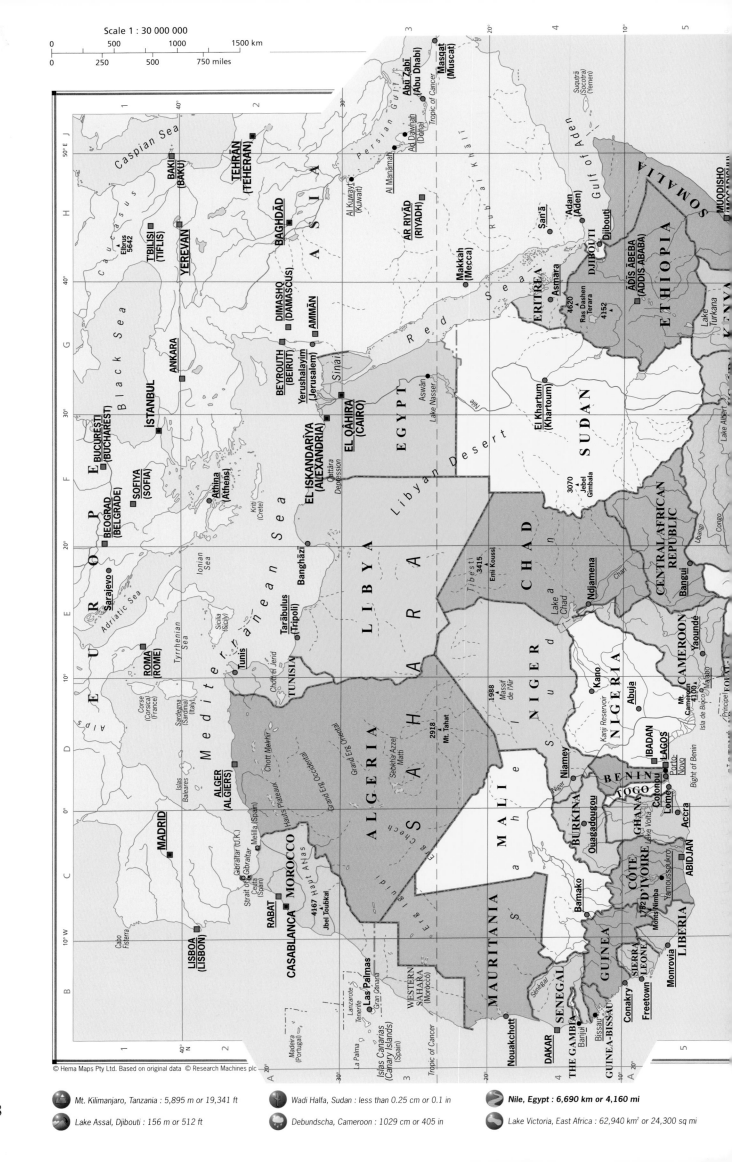

Scale 1 : 30 000 000

0   500   1000   1500 km

0   250   500   750 miles

98

Mt. Kilimanjaro, Tanzania : 5,895 m or 19,341 ft

Lake Assal, Djibouti : 156 m or 512 ft

Wadi Halfa, Sudan : less than 0.25 cm or 0.1 in

Debundscha, Cameroon : 1029 cm or 405 in

Nile, Egypt : 6,690 km or 4,160 mi

Lake Victoria, East Africa : 62,940 km² or 24,300 sq mi

© Hema Maps Pty Ltd. Based on original data © Research Machines plc

 Ifrane, Morocco : -24 ˚C or -11 ˚F

Al Aziziyah, Libya : 58 ˚C or 136 ˚F

 748,927,000

25 per km² or 64 per sq mi

 30,293,000 km² or 11,696,000 sq mi

53

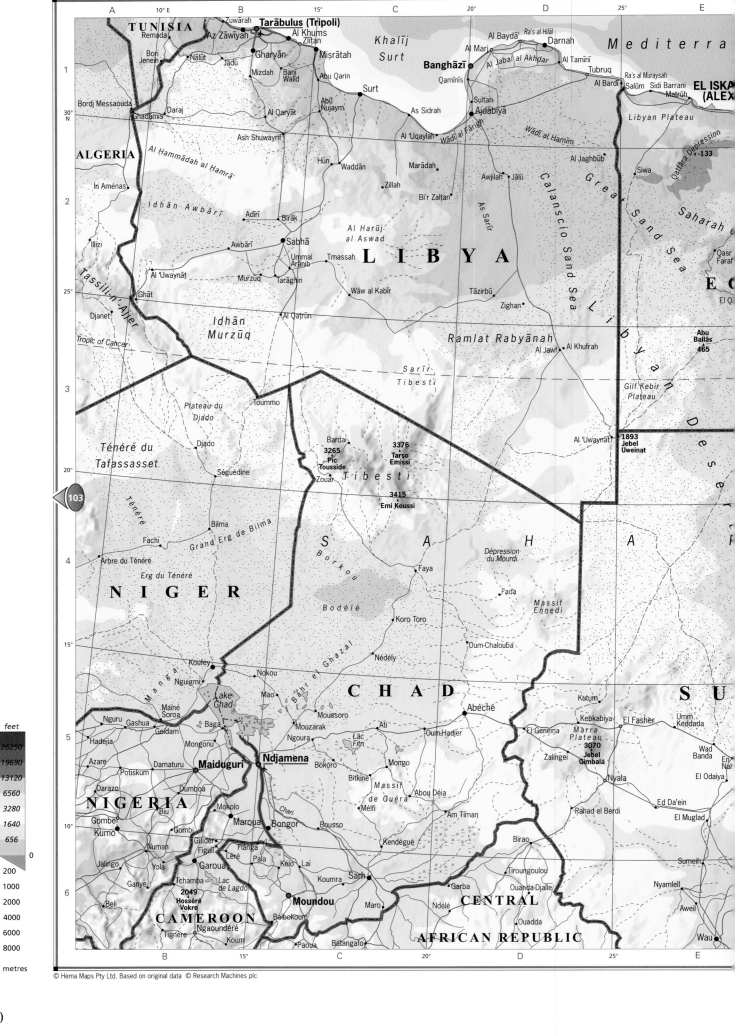

TUNISIA
Remada
Bordj
Jenien
Nālūt
Zuwārah
Az Zāwiyah
Al Khums
Zlītan
Tarābulus (Tripoli)
Gharyān
Jādū
Mizdah
Banī
Walīd
Mişrātah
Abu Qarin
Khalīj
Surt
Al Bayḍā'
Ra's al Hilāl
Darnah
Al Marj
Al Jabal al Akhdar
Al Tamīnī
Tubruq
Ra's al Muraysah
Mediterra
Al Bardī
Salûm
Sidi Barrani
Matrûh
**EL ISKA
(ALEX**

Banghāzī
Qamīnīs
Surt
Daraj
Ghadāmis
Bori
Messaouda
Al Qaryāt
Abū
Nujaym
As Sidrah
Ajdābiyā
Sultan
Al 'Uqaylah
Wādī al Fārigh
Wādī al Hamīm
Libyan Plateau

ALGERIA
In Aménas
Ghadāmis
Al Hammādah al Hamrā'
Ash Shuwayrif
Hūn
Waddān
Marādah
Zillah
Bi'r Zaltan
Awjilah
Jālū
Al Jaghbūb
Siwa
Qattara Depression
-133

Illizi
Idhān Awbārī
Adīrī
Bīrāk
*Al Harūj
al Aswad*
As Sarīr
Calanscio Sand Sea
Great Sand Sea
Saharah
E
Qasr
Faraf

Awbārī
Sabhā
Ummal
Arānib
Tmassah
L I B Y A
Tāzirbū
Zighan
El Q

Al 'Uwaynāt
Murzuq
Tarāghin
Wāw al Kabīr
Tassilin-n' Ajjer
Ghāt
*Idhān
Murzūq*
Al Qatrūn
Ramlat Rabyānah
Al Jawf
Al Khufrah
Libyan De
**Abu
Ballâs**
465

Djanet
Tropic of Cancer
*Sarīr
Tibesti*
*Gilf Kebir
Plateau*

Toummo
Bardai
**3265
Pic
Tousside**
**3376
Tarso
Emissi**
Al 'Uwaynāt
**1893
Jebel
Uweinat**

*Plateau du
Djado*
Djado
Zouar
Tibesti
**3415
Emi Koussi**

*Ténéré du
Tafassasset*
Séguédine

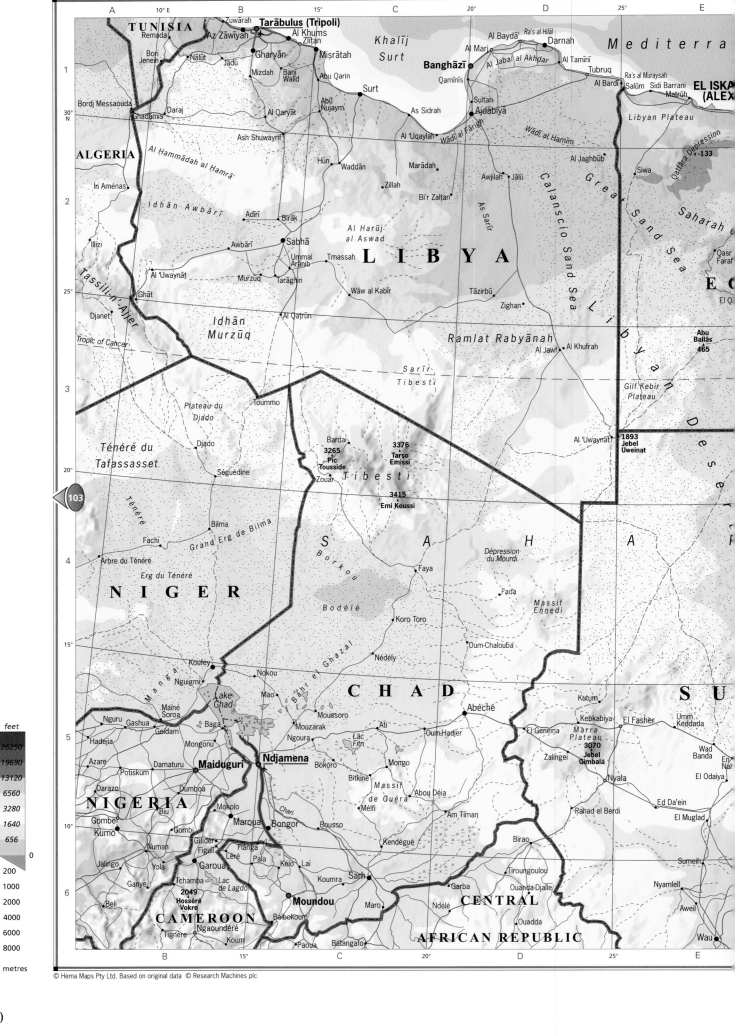
103

Ténéré
Bilma
Grand Erg de Bilma
S   A   H   A
Fachi
Arbre du Ténéré
Erg du Ténéré
Borkou
Faya
*Dépression
du Mourdi*
*Massif
Ennedi*

N I G E R
Bodélé
Fada
Koro Toro
Oum-Chalouba

Koufey
Nédély
Kutum
S U
Nguigmi
Nokou
C H A D
Abéché
Kebkabiya
El Fasher
Umm
Keddada
Maïné
Soroa
Lake
Chad
Mao
Moussoro
*Marra
Plateau*
**3070
Jebel
Gimbala**
Wad
Banda
En
Nal

Nguru
Gashua
Geidam
Baga
Mouzarak
Ngoura
Ati
Lāc
Fitri
Oum-Hadjer
Mongo
Zalingei
Nyala
Ed Da'ein

Hadejia
Azare
Damaturu
Mongonu
Ndjamena
Bokoro
Bitkine
*Massif
de Guéra*
Abou Déia
Am Tīman
Rahad el Berdi
El Odaiya

Potiskum
Maiduguri
Dumboa
Mokolo
Chari
Mélfi
Rahad el Berdi
El Muglad

Darazo
NIGERIA
Biu
Maroua
Bongor
Bousso
Kendégué
Birao
Sumeih

Gombe
Kumo
Numan
Gombi
Guider
Figuil
Lére
Pala
Kélo
Laï
Sarh
Tiroungoulou
Ouanda-Djalle
Nyamlell

Jalingo
Yola
Garoua
Tchamba
*Lac
de Lagdo*
Koumra
Maro
Ndélé
Garba
CENTRAL
Aweil

Beli
**2049
Hosséré
Vokre**
Bābokoum
Moundou
CAMEROON
Ngaoundéré
Koum
Tignère
Paoua
Batangafo
Ouadda
AFRICAN REPUBLIC
Wau

metres	feet
8000	26250
6000	19690
4000	13120
2000	6560
1000	3280
500	1640
200	656
0	0
656	200
3280	1000
6560	2000
13120	4000
19690	6000
26250	8000

feet | metres

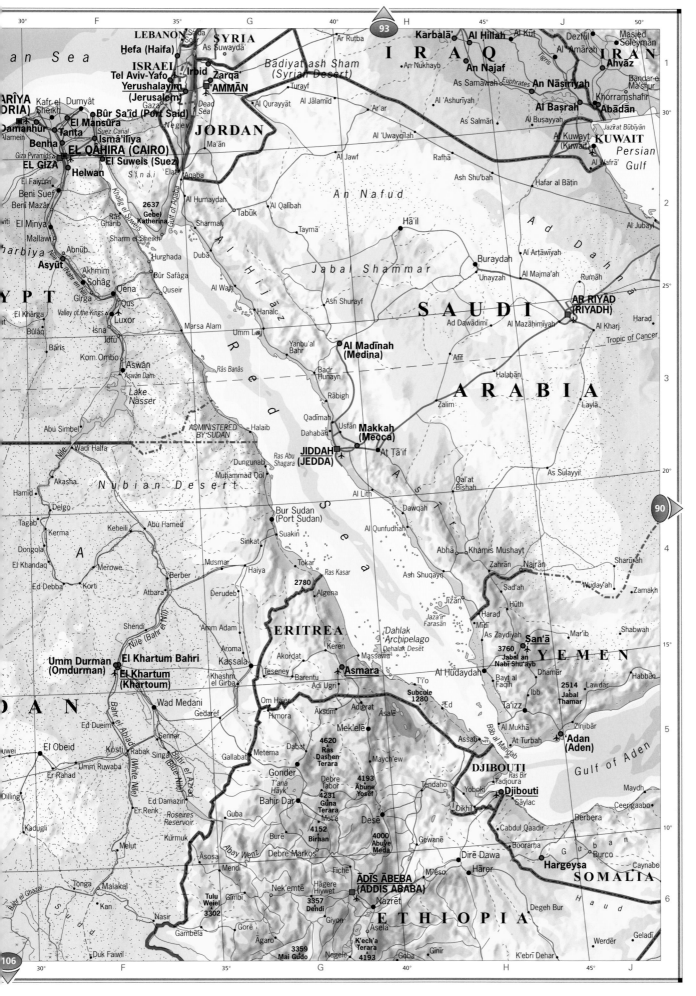

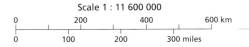

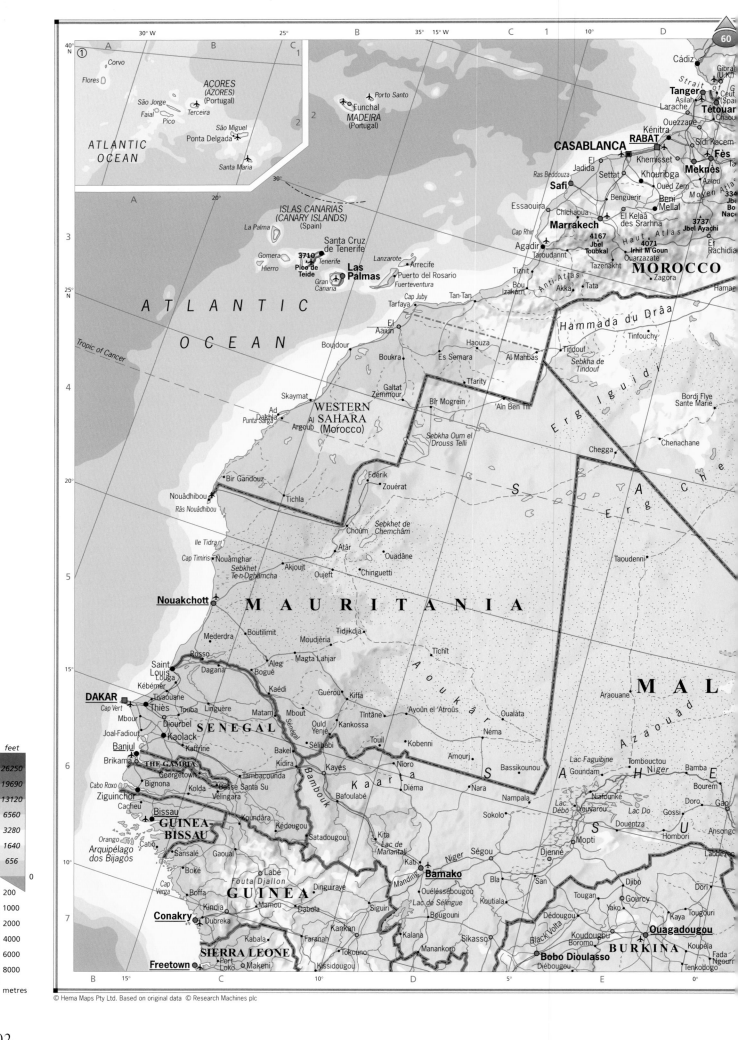

60

ATLANTIC OCEAN

ACORES
(AZORES)
(Portugal)

Corvo
Flores
São Jorge
Faial · Pico
Terceira
São Miguel
Ponta Delgada
Santa Maria

Porto Santo
Funchal
MADEIRA
(Portugal)

Cádiz
Strait of G
Tanger   Gibral (U.K.)
Asilah   Ceut (Spai
Larache   **Tétouar**
Ouezzane   Chaou

CASABLANCA   **RABAT**
Khemisset   Sidi Kacem
El   Settat   Khouribga   **Meknès**   **Fès**
Jadida   Azrou   Ta
Safi   Oued Zem   Beni   Moyen   334
Ras Beddouza   Benguerir   Mellal   Atlas   **Jbe**
Essaouira   Chichaoua   El Kelaâ   **Bo**
Cap Rhir   **Marrakech**   des Srarhna   3737   **Nac**
4167   Irhil M'Goun   **Jbel Ayachi**
Agadir   4071   **Jbel**   El
Taroudannt   **Toubkal**   Ouarzazate   Rachidia
Tiznit   Anti-Atlas   Tazenakht   Zagora
MOROCCO
Bou   Akka   Tata   Hamag
Izakarn

ISLAS CANARIAS
(CANARY ISLANDS)
(Spain)

La Palma
Gomera   3710   Tenerife   Lanzarote
Hierro   Pico de   Arrecife
Teide   **Las**   Puerto del Rosario
Gran   **Palmas**   Fuerteventura
Canaria
Cap Juby   Tan-Tan   Hammada du Drâa
Tarfaya   Tinfouchy
El   Haouza   Tindouf
Aaiún   Boujdour   Es Semara   Al Mahbas   Sebkha de
Boukra   Tindouf
Tfarity   Erg Iguidi

Tropic of Cancer

Skaymat   Galtat   'Ain Ben Tili   Bordj Flye
Zemmour   Bîr Mogrein   Sante Marie
WESTERN   Punta Sarga   Ad   Chenachane
SAHARA   Dakhla   Argoub   Sebkha Oum el
(Morocco)   Drouss Telli   Chegga
Bir Gandouz   Fdérik   Erg Chche
Tichla   Zouérat   S
Nouâdhibou   A
Râs Nouâdhibou   Choûm   Sebkhet de   Ergg   G
Ile Tidra   Atâr   Chemchâm
Ouadâne   Taoudenni
Cap Timiris · Nouâmghar   Akjoujt   Chinguetti
Sebkhet   Oujeft
Te-n-Dghamcha
Nouakchott   **M A U R I T A N I A**
Boutilimit   Tidjikdja
Mederdra   Moudjèria   Tichît   Araouane
Rosso   Magta Lahjar   Araouane
Saint   Aleg   **M A L**
Louis   Dagana   Bogué   Kaédi   Kiffa   Aoukâr   Nema
Louga   Guérou   'Ayoûn el 'Atroûs   Oualàta
Kébémèr   Touba   Matam   Mbout   Tîntâne   Kankossa
DAKAR   Tivaouane   Linguère   Ould   Nema   Nampala   Tombouctou
Cap Vert   **Thiès**   Yenjé   Kobenni   Lac Faguibine   Bamba
Mbour   Diourbel   **SENEGAL**   Séibabi   Touil   Amourj   Goundam   Niger   Bourem
Joal-Fadiout   **Kaolack**   Bakel   Kayes   Nioro   Bassikounou   **Lac**   Gao
Banjul   Kaffrine   Kidira   Diéma   Nara   Débo   Niafounké   Doro   Ansongo
Brikama   Diouloulou   **THE GAMBIA**   Georgetown   Tambacounda   **K a a r t a**   Nampala   Lac   Douentza   Hombori   **S**
Cabo Roxo   Bignona   Basse Santa Su   Bafoulabé   Sokolo   Débo
Ziguinchor   Vélingara   Diéma   Lac   **U**
Cacheu   Kolda   Koundâra   Kédougou   Kati   Labbéz
Bissau   Satadougou   Kita   Séqou   Djenné
GUINEA-   Lac de   Djibo
BISSAU   Orango   Sansalé   Gaoual   Mananfali   Niger   Mopti
Arquipélago   Catió   Boké   Labé   Lac de   Sikasso   **BURKINA**
dos Bijagós   Cap   Boffa   **Fouta Djallon**   Sélingue   **Bamako**   Bla   San
Verga   Dinguiraye   Mandimg   Ouéléssébougou   Koutiala   Tougan   Yako
GUINEA   Kindia   Dabola   Siguiri   Bougouni   Dédougou
Conakry   Mamou   Kankan   Kalana   Koudougou   Kaya   **Ouagadougou**
Dubreka   Kabala   Faranah   Sikasso   Boromo   Koupéla
SIERRA LEONE   Kissidougou   Tokouno   Manankoro   Black Volta   Diébougou   Tenkodogo

Freetown   Port   Makeni   Fada
Loko   Ngourr

© Hema Maps Pty Ltd. Based on original data © Research Machines plc

metres	feet
8000	26250
6000	19690
4000	13120
2000	6560
1000	3280
500	1640
200	656
0	0
656	200
3280	1000
6560	2000
13120	4000
19690	6000
26250	8000
feet	metres

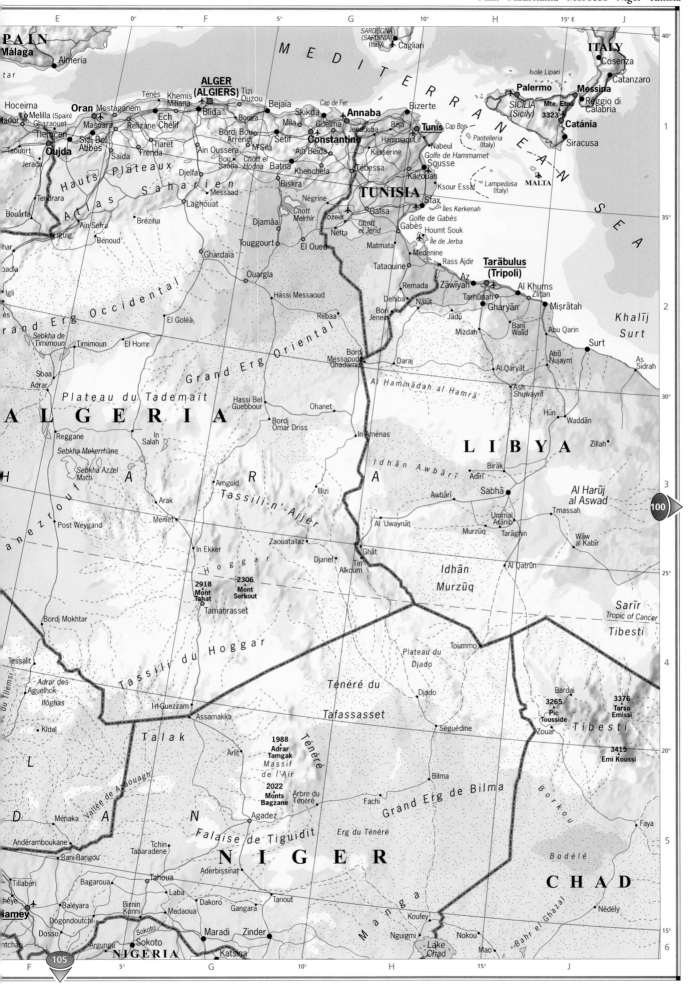

Symbol	Population
■	over 3 million
■	1 – 3 million
●	250 000 – 1 million
●	100 000 – 250 000
●	25 000 – 100 000
•	under 25 000
——	country capital underline

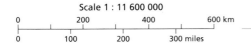

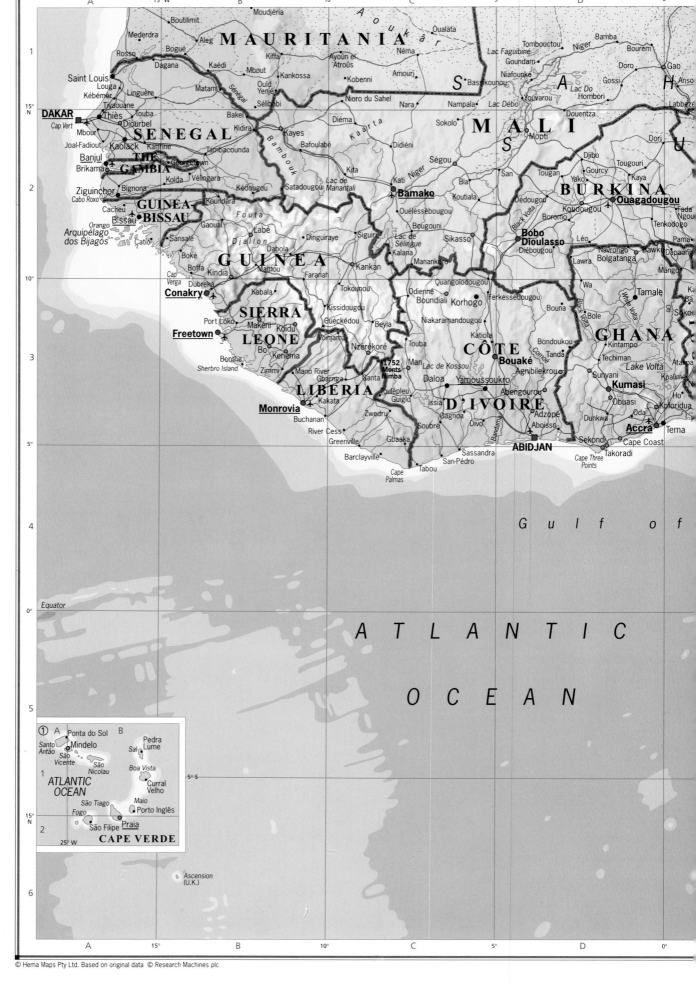

Benin • Burkina • Cameroon • Cape Verde • Congo • Côte d'Ivoire • Equatorial Guinea • Gabon • The Gambia
• Ghana • Guinea • Guinea-Bissau • Liberia • Nigeria • São Tomé & Príncipe • Senegal • Sierra Leone • Togo

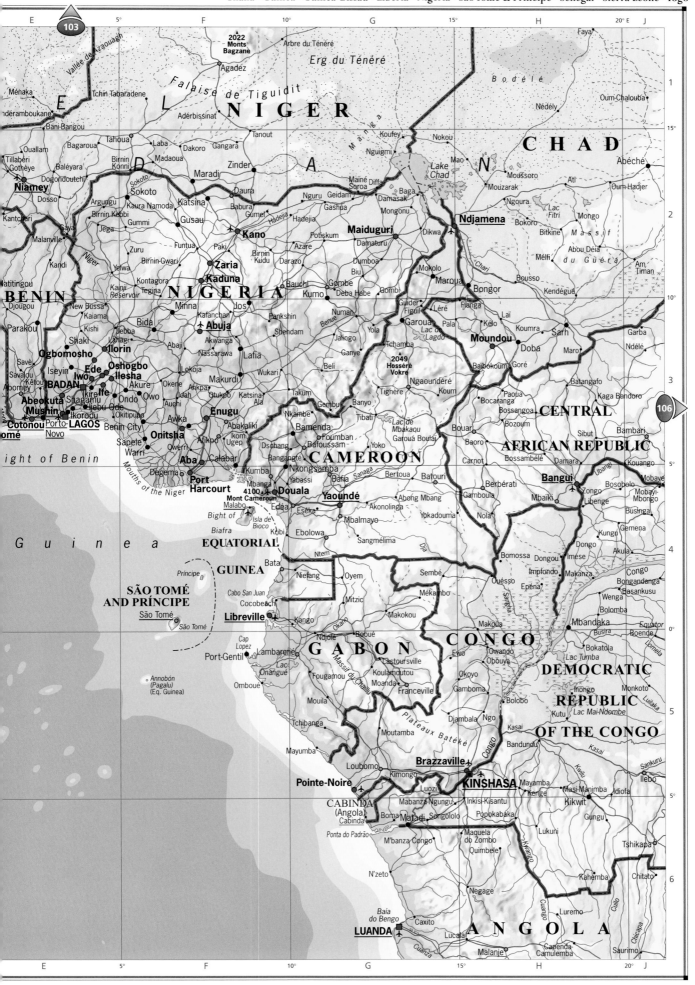

over 3 million	100 000 – 250 000	country capital underline
1 – 3 million	25 000 – 100 000	state or province capital underline
250 000 – 1 million	under 25 000	

0   200   400   600 km

0   100   200   300 miles

metres	feet
8000	26250
6000	19690
4000	13120
2000	6560
1000	3280
500	1640
200	656
0	0
656	200
3280	1000
6560	2000
13120	4000
19690	6000
26250	8000
feet	metres

NIGERIA

CHAD

CENTRAL
AFRICAN REPUBLIC

SUDAN

CAMEROON

CONGO

GABON

DEMOCRATIC REPUBLIC
OF THE CONGO

RWANDA

BURUNDI

ATLANTIC
OCEAN

ANGOLA

ZAMBIA

Great Rift Valley

Lake Tanganyika

Central Africa

Angola • Burundi • Central African Republic • The Democratic Republic of Congo
Djibouti • Ethiopia • Kenya • Rwanda • Somalia • Tanzania • Uganda

■ over 3 million	● 100 000 – 250 000	—— country capital underline
■ 1 – 3 million	○ 25 000 – 100 000	
● 250 000 – 1 million	• under 25 000	

107

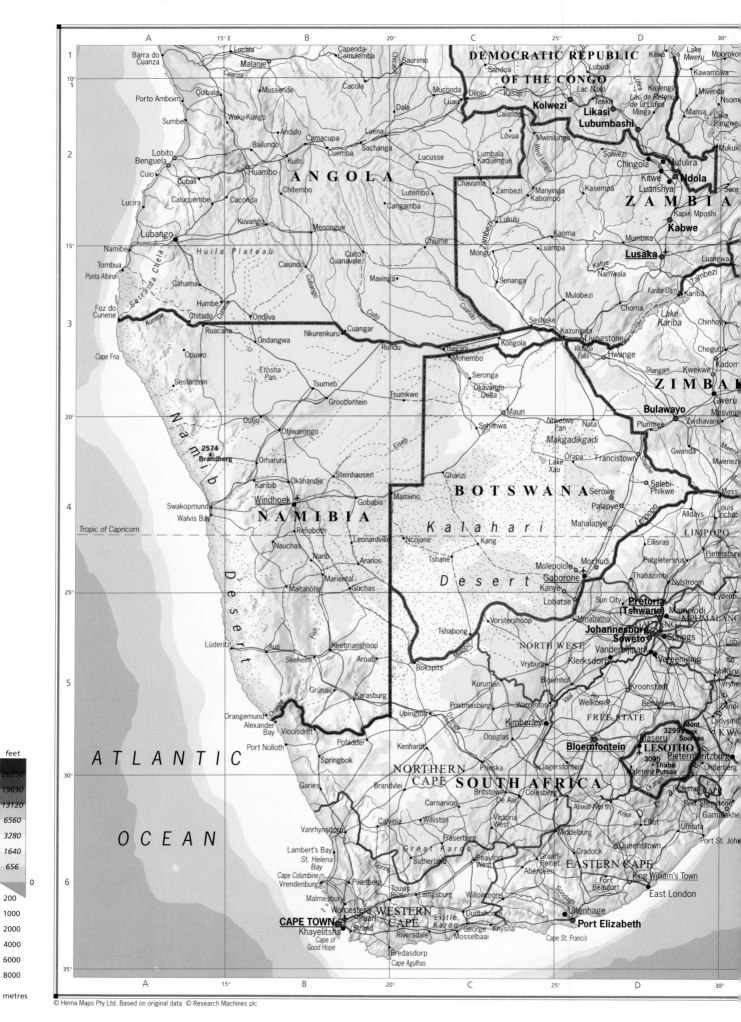

Scale 1 : 11 600 000

| 0 | 200 | 400 | 600 km |

| 0 | 100 | 200 | 300 miles |

A   15° E   B   20°   C   25°   D   30°

DEMOCRATIC REPUBLIC
OF THE CONGO

ANGOLA

ZAMBIA

Lubango

Huila Plateau

NAMIBIA

BOTSWANA

Kalahari

Desert

Windhoek

Tropic of Capricorn

ZIMBABWE

Bulawayo

metres	feet
8000	26250
6000	19690
4000	13120
2000	6560
1000	3280
500	1640
200	656
0	0
656	200
3280	1000
6560	2000
13120	4000
19690	6000
26250	8000
feet	metres

ATLANTIC

OCEAN

SOUTH AFRICA

NORTHERN
CAPE

EASTERN CAPE

LESOTHO

FREE STATE

NORTH WEST

Johannesburg
Soweto
Pretoria
(Tshwane)

Bloemfontein

WESTERN
CAPE

CAPE TOWN
Cape of
Good Hope

Port Elizabeth

A   15°   B   20°   C   25°   D   30°

© Hema Maps Pty Ltd. Based on original data © Research Machines plc

Southern Africa

Botswana • Comoros • Lesotho • Madagascar • Malawi • Mauritius
Mozambique • Namibia • Seychelles • South Africa • Swaziland • Zambia • Zimbabwe

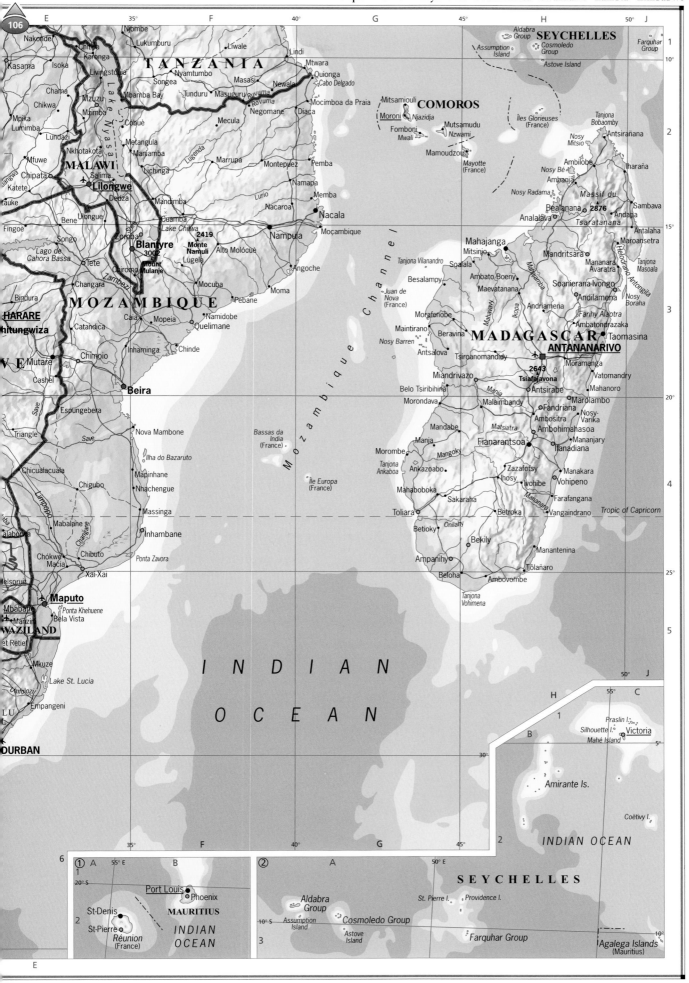

E 35° **F** 40° **G** 45° **H** 50° **J**

SEYCHELLES

Aldabra Group
Assumption Island
Cosmoledo Group
Astove Island
Farquhar Group

Nakonde
Chipa
Karonga
Livingstonia
Mbamba Bay
Songea
Nyamtumbo
Masasi
Newala
Njombe
Lukumburu
Liwale
Lindi
Mtwara
Quionga
Cabo Delgado

TANZANIA

Kasama
Isoka
Chama
Chikwa
Mpika
Lumimba
Lundazi
Mfuwe
Chipata
Katete
Tauke
Fingoè
Mzuzu
Mzimba
Cobuè
Metangula
Mandimba
Nichinga
Montepuez
Pemba

MALAWI
Salima
Lilongwe
Dedza

Tunduru
Masuguru
Rovuma
Negomane
Diaca
Mocímboa da Praia

Mitsamiouli
Moroni
Njazidja
Fomboni
Mwali
Mutsamudu
Nzwani
COMOROS
Mamoudzou
Mayotte (France)

Îles Glorieuses (France)

Nosy Mitsio
Tanjona Bobaomby
Antsirañana
Ambilobe
Iharaña
Nosy Bé
Ambanja
Nosy Radama
Massif du Tsaratanana
2876
Bealanana
Analalava
Andapa
Sambava
Antalaha
Maroansetra
Tanjona Masoala

HARARE
htungwiza
Mutare
Cashel

MOZAMBIQUE

Bene
Songo
Lago de Cahora Bassa
Tete
Changara
Bindura
Blantyre
Monte Namuli 3002
Mount Mulanje
Chiromo
Lugela
Alto Molócuè
Mandimba
Lake Chilwa
Cuamba
2419
Lúrio
Nacaroa
Namapa
Memba
Nampula
Nacala
Moçambique
Angoche

Juan de Nova (France)
Besalampy
Soalala
Mitsinjo
Mahajanga
Ambato Boeny
Maevatanana
Mananara Avaratra
Andilamena
Soanierana-Ivongo
Farihy Alaotra
Ambatondrazaka
Taomasina
Nosy Boraha

MADAGASCAR
ANTANANARIVO
2643
Tsiafajavona
Moramanga
Vatomandry
Mahanoro

Morafenobe
Maintirano
Beravina
Antsalova
Nosy Barren
Tsiroanomandidy
Miandrivazo
Andriamena

HARARE
Chinhoyi
Mutare
Cashel
Chimoio
Beira
Espungabera
Nova Mambone

Nosy Radama

VE
Mutare
Cashel

Belo Tsiribihina
Morondava
Mandabe
Morombe
Manja
Mangoky
Ankazoabo
Mahaboboka
Sakaraha
Toliara
Betioky
Onilahy
Ampanihy
Beloha

Malaimbandy
Antsirabe
Fandriana
Ambositra
Ambohimahasoa
Fianarantsoa
Ilanadiana
Zazafotsy
Ihosy
Ivohibe
Vohipeno
Manakara
Farafangana
Vangaindrano
Tanjona Vohimena

Nosy-Varika
Mananjary
Ambovombe
Manantenina
Tôlañaro
Bekily

Marolambo

Matsiatra

Triangle
Save
Chicualacuala
Chigubo
Mapinhane
Nhachengue
Massinga
Inhambane
Ponta Zavora
Ilha do Bazaruto

Bassas da India (France)
Île Europa (France)

Tropic of Capricorn

Limpopo
Mabalane
Chókwè
Macia
Xai-Xai
Chibuto

INDIAN

elspruit
Maputo
Ponta Khehuene
Bela Vista
Mbabane
WAZILAND
et Retief
Manzini

OCEAN

Mkuze
Lake St. Lucia
ntolozi
Empangeni
LU
DURBAN

30°

INDIAN OCEAN

H 55° **C**
55°
Praslin I.
Silhouette I.
Mahé Island
Victoria
5°

Amirante Is.

Coëtivy I.

SEYCHELLES

St. Pierre I.
Providence I.

Aldabra Group
Assumption Island
Cosmoledo Group
Astove Island
Farquhar Group
Agalega Islands (Mauritius)

F 35° **G** 40° **50° E**

① **A** 55° E **B**
20° S
Port Louis
Phoenix
MAURITIUS
St-Denis
St-Pierre
Réunion (France)
INDIAN OCEAN

② **A** 50° E
10° S

● over 3 million
● 1 – 3 million
● 250 000 – 1 million

● 100 000 – 250 000
○ 25 000 – 100 000
• under 25 000

———— country capital underline
———— state or province capital underline

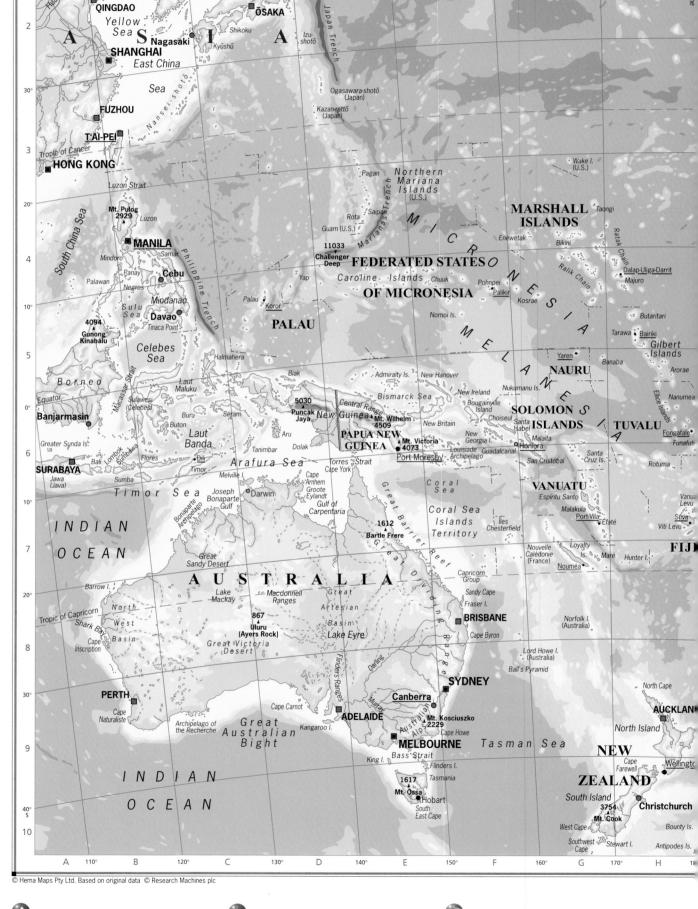

Scale 1 : 40 500 000

0	500	1000	1500	2000 km	
0	250	500	750	1000 miles	

metres	feet
8000	26250
6000	19690
4000	13120
2000	6560
1000	3280
500	1640
200	656
0	0
656	200
3280	1000
6560	2000
13120	4000
19690	6000
26250	8000
feet	metres

© Hema Maps Pty Ltd. Based on original data © Research Machines plc

110

Mt. Wilhelm, Papua New Guinea : 4,509 m or 14,793 ft

Lake Eyre, Australia : 15 m or 49 ft

Mulka, Australia : 10.3 cm or 4.05 in

Mt. Waialeale, Hawaii : 1168 cm or 460 in

Murray-Darling, Australia : 3,750 km² or 2,330 sq mi

Lake Eyre, Australia : 8,800 km² or 3,400 sq mi

 Charlotte Pass, Australia : -23 °C or -9.4 °F

Cloncurry, Australia : 53 °C or 128 °F

 29,642,000

3.3 per km² or 8.6 per sq mi

 8,945,000 km² or 3,454,000 sq mi

14

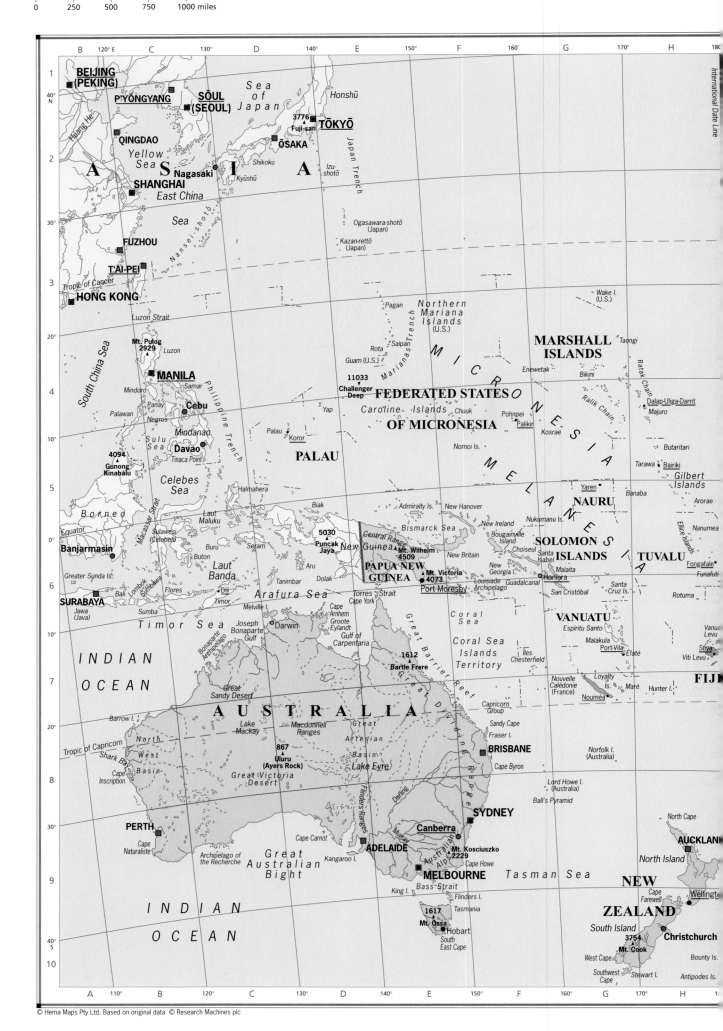

Scale 1 : 40 500 000

0   500   1000   1500   2000 km
0   250   500   750   1000 miles

BEIJING (PEKING)

P'YŎNGYANG

SŎUL (SEOUL)

Sea of Japan

Honshū

Huang He

40° N

QINGDAO

Yellow Sea

3776
Fuji-san

TŌKYŌ

ŌSAKA

A S I A

SHANGHAI

East China Sea

Nagasaki

Shikoku

Kyūshū

Izu-shotō

Japan Trench

30°

FUZHOU

Nansei-shotō

Ogasawara-shotō (Japan)

Kazan-rettō (Japan)

Tropic of Cancer

T'AI-PEI

Wake I. (U.S.)

HONG KONG

Luzon Strait

Pagan

Northern Mariana Islands (U.S.)

3°

20°

South China Sea

Mt. Pulog
2929

Luzon

M I C R O N E S I A

Rota   Saipan

Guam (U.S.)

MARSHALL ISLANDS

Taongi

Enewetak

Bikini

Ratak Chain

11033
Challenger Deep

FEDERATED STATES

Caroline Islands   Chuuk

Pohnpei

Palikir

Kosrae

Ralik Chain

Dalap-Uliga-Darrit

Majuro

MANILA

Mindoro   Samar

Yap

Palau

OF MICRONESIA

Nomoi Is.

Butaritari

Tarawa   Bairiki

Gilbert Islands

Cebu

Panay

Negros

PALAU

Koror

Cebu

Palawan

Mindanao

Sulu Sea

4094

Gunong Kinabalu

Davao

Tinaca Point

Celebes Sea

Halmahera

Biak

Admiralty Is.

New Hanover

New Ireland

Nukumanu Is.

NAURU

Yaren

Banaba

Arorae

Nanumea

Borneo

Macassar Strait

Sulawesi (Celebes)

Laut Maluku

Buru

Seram

5030
Puncak Jaya

New Guinea

Central Range

Bismarck Sea

Bougainville Island

New Britain

Choiseul

Santa Isabel

SOLOMON ISLANDS

Malaita

Honiara

TUVALU

Fongafale

Funafuti

Equator

Banjarmasin

Greater Sunda Is.

Bali

Lombok

Sumbawa

Flores

Dili

Timor

Buton

Laut Banda

Tanimbar

Aru

Dolak

PAPUA NEW GUINEA

Mt. Wilhelm
4509

Mt. Victoria
4073

Port Moresby

Louisiade Archipelago

New Georgia I.

Guadalcanal

San Cristóbal

Santa Cruz Is.

Rotuma

VANUATU

Vanua Levu

SURABAYA

Jawa (Java)

Sumba

Cape Arnhem

Torres Strait

Cape York

Coral Sea

Espíritu Santo

Malakula

Viti Levu

Port-Vila   Efaté

FIJI

Timor Sea

Melville I.

Groote Eylandt

Gulf of Carpentaria

Great Barrier Reef

Coral Sea Islands Territory

Îles Chesterfield

INDIAN

Joseph Bonaparte Gulf

Bonaparte Archipelago

Darwin

Cape

10°

OCEAN

Barrow I.

Great Sandy Desert

1612
Bartle Frere

Nouvelle Calédonie (France)

Loyalty Is.

Maré

Hunter I.

Noumea

AUSTRALIA

Great Dividing Range

Capricorn Group

Sandy Cape

Fraser I.

Tropic of Capricorn

North West Basin

Shark Bay

Lake Mackay

Macdonnell Ranges

Great

Artesian

Basin

Lake Eyre

Sandy Cape

BRISBANE

Cape Byron

Norfolk I. (Australia)

Cape Inscription

867
Uluru (Ayers Rock)

Great Victoria Desert

Lord Howe I. (Australia)

Ball's Pyramid

PERTH

Cape Naturaliste

Cape Carnot

Flinders Ranges

SYDNEY

Canberra

North Cape

AUCKLAND

North Island

Archipelago of the Recherche

Great Australian Bight

Kangaroo I.

ADELAIDE

Murray

Australian Alps

Mt. Kosciuszko
2229

Cape Howe

MELBOURNE

King I.

Bass Strait

Flinders I.

Tasman Sea

NEW

Cape Farewell

INDIAN

1617
Mt. Ossa

Tasmania

ZEALAND

South Island

Wellington

OCEAN

South East Cape

West Cape

3754
Mt. Cook

Christchurch

40° S

Southwest Cape

Stewart I.

Antipodes Is.

Bounty Is.

A   110°   B   120°   C   130°   D   140°   E   150°   F   160°   G   170°   H

Mt. Wilhelm, Papua New Guinea : 4,509 m or 14,793 ft

Mulka, Australia : 10.3 cm or 4.05 in

Murray-Darling, Australia : 3,750 km² or 2,330 sq mi

Lake Eyre, Australia : 15 m or 49 ft

Mt. Waialeale, Hawaii : 1168 cm or 460 in

Lake Eyre, Australia : 8,800 km² or 3,400 sq mi

J 170° K 160° L 150° M 140° N 130° P 120° W Q

NORTH AMERICA

40°

LOS ANGELES ■

SAN DIEGO ■

2

Kure I.
dway Is.

P A C I F I C

Laysan I.
Necker I.

HAWAII
(U.S.)

Guadalupe
(Mexico)

30°

Kauai Oahu
Honolulu Maui

Tropic of Cancer

3

Hawaii

Johnston I.
(U.S.)

N. W. Christmas Island Ridge

20°

Is. Revillagigedo
(Mexico)

4

O C E A N

Palmyra I.
(U.S.)

10°

Tabuaeran
Kiritimati

Howland (U.S.)
Baker (U.S.)

Jarvis
(U.S.)

5

Phoenix Islands

Birnie   Rawaki
Orona   Manra

KIRIBATI

Malden I.

Equator

0°

Starbuck I.

O L Y N E S I A

Atafu   Tokelau
Nukunonu   (New Zealand)

Tongareva

Marquesas Islands

6

Swains I.   Danger Is.
Nassau

Manihiki

Vostok I.   Caroline I.

Nuku Hiva

Hiva Oa

llis et
tuna
ance)   **SAMOA** American
Samoa
Hoorn Is.   Savaii Apia   Tutuila
(France)   Upolu

Flint I.

Îles
Désappointement

Tafahi

Rose I.

Cook Islands

Suvorov I.

Îles Palliser

Archipel des Tuamotu

Pukapuka

10°

Raroia

Motu One

TONGA   Niue   Palmerston I.
(New Zealand)

Aitutaki

Arch.
de la Société   Tahiti

Hao

Îles Duc de
Gloucester

uku alofa
Ata

Rarotonga

F r e n c h
P o l y n e s i a

7

Horizon Depth
10882
efs

Mangaia   Îles
Maria   Rurutu

Groupe Actéon

Tubuai   Mururoa

Morane   Gambier
Is.

Raevavae

T u b u a i   I s l a n d s

Mangareva

ermadec Islands
(New Zealand)

Rapa

Marotiri

Oeno

Henderson I.

Pitcairn Is.
(U.K.)   Ducie I.

Tropic of Capricorn

20°

8

Easter I.
(Chile)

S o u t h   W e s t

30°

P a c i f i c

B a s i n

9

ham Is.
Zealand)

40°

10

J 170° K 160° L 150° M 140° N 130° P 120° Q 110° R

 Charlotte Pass, Australia : -23 °C or -9.4 °F   29,642,000   8,945,000 km² or 3,454,000 sq mi

Cloncurry, Australia : 53 °C or 128 °F   3.3 per km² or 8.6 per sq mi   14

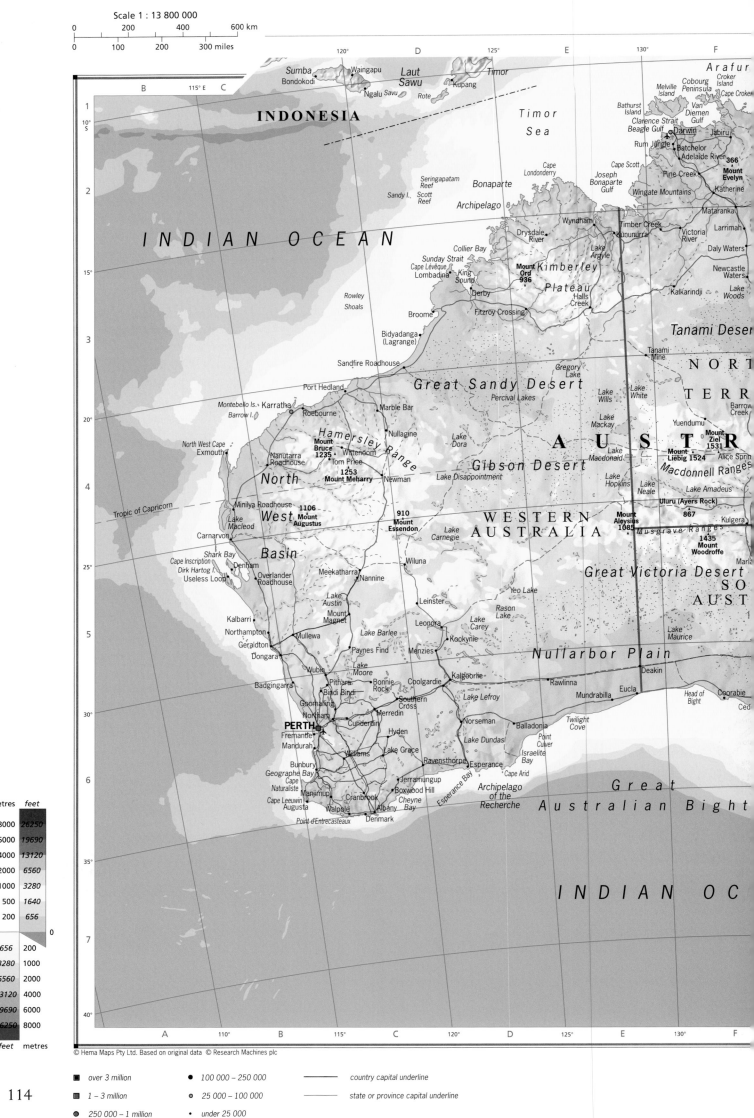

Scale 1 : 13 800 000

metres	feet
8000	26250
6000	19690
4000	13120
2000	6560
1000	3280
500	1640
200	656
0	0
656	200
3280	1000
6560	2000
13120	4000
19690	6000
26250	8000

feet metres

© Hema Maps Pty Ltd. Based on original data © Research Machines plc

- ■ over 3 million
- ■ 1 – 3 million
- ● 250 000 – 1 million
- ● 100 000 – 250 000
- ● 25 000 – 100 000
- • under 25 000
- ——— country capital underline
- ——— state or province capital underline

135°   G   140°   H   145°   J   150°

PAPUA
NEW GUINEA

Port
Moresby

D'Entrecasteaux
Islands

Alotau

K   155°   L

Louisiade
Archipelago

1

10°

Cape Wessel
Wessel Islands
Nangalala   Nhulunbuy
Cape Arnhem

Mulgrave I.   Moa (Banks Island)
Torres Strait
Prince of Wales
Island
Bamaga   Somerset

CORAL SEA ISLANDS

CORAL SEA

K   155°   L

2

Bickerton Island
Groote
Eylandt
Numbulwar
Roper Bar

Gulf of
Carpentaria

Duifken Point
Weipa   Cape
Albatross Bay York
Aurukun   Peninsula

Cape
Grenville
Cape
Direction

Princess Charlotte Bay

Osprey Reef
Shark Reef

T E R R I T O R Y
(Australia)

15°

Cape Crawford

Borroloola

Cape
Crawford

Sir Edward
Pellew Group

Mornington I.
Bentinck I.

Wellesley
Islands

Burketown   Normanton
Karumba

Coen

Cape Melville

Laura
Cooktown

Port Douglas
Mareeba   Cairns
1612 Mount Bartle Frere
Mount Garnet Innisfail

Bougainville Reef

Holmes Reefs   Diane Bank

Herald
Cays

Willis Group

Magdelaine Cays

Diamond Islets

Turtle I.
Tregosse Islets

Malay Reef

P A C I F I C

O C E A N

3

Barkly Tableland

Tennant Creek

Camooweal

Mount Isa
Cloncurry
McKinlay
Richmond

Croydon
Georgetown
Forsayth
Greenvale

Ingham
Mutarnee   Halifax Bay
Townsville
Ayr

Charters
Towers   Bowen   The
Dalrymple   Whitsundays
Lake   Proserpine
Repulse Bay
Mackay
Sarina

QUEENSLAND

Hughenden

Winton

Boulia

Muttaburra

Clermont

Nebo

Broad Sound
Clairview
Townshend I.

Swain
Reefs

20°

Simpson
Desert

Great

Artesian

Longreach
Barcaldine

Jundah
Blackall

Jericho
Emerald

Blackwater

Yeppoon
Rockhampton
Curtis I.

Springsure

Gladstone

Capricorn
Group

Cato I.

Tropic of Capricorn

4

Lake Eyre
Basin

Sturt Stony
Desert   Basin

Birdsville

Betoota

Windorah

Lake
Yamma
Yamma

Augathella
Charleville

Tambo

Banana
Taroom

Biloela

Bundaberg   Sandy Cape
Eidsvold   Hervey Bay
Gayndah Maryborough Fraser I.
Gympie

25°

Oodnadatta

Tirari
Desert

Coober Pedy
Lake Eyre
South

Marree

Quilpie

Thargomindah

Muckadilla

St
George

Roma

Miles

Glenmorgan

Moonie

Dalby

Kingaroy

Toowoomba

Caloundra

Moreton I.

BRISBANE

North Stradbroke I.

Leigh Creek
Glendambo

Lake
Blanche
Lake
Callabonna

Tibooburra
Wanaaring

Hungerford

Cunnamulla

Dirranbandi

Goondiwindi
Bungunya

Boggabilla

Casino

Mount
Roberts
1387

Beenleigh
Surfers Paradise
Gold
Coast
Cape Byron
Ballina

30°

Marree

Lake
Frome

White
Cliffs

Bourke

Brewarrina

Walgett

Moree

Narrabri

Tenterfield
Glen Innes

Grafton

Pimba
Lake
Torrens

Broken
Hill

Wilcannia

Louth
Coolabah

Cobar

Gunnedah

Armidale

Round
Mountain
1608

Coffs Harbour

Hawker

Menindee

Darling

Nyngan

Coonabarabran

Tamworth

Black
Sugarloaf
1494

Port Macquarie

Port Augusta
Orroroo

Ivanhoe
Roto

Condobolin

Gilgandra

Dubbo

Quirindi

Taree

Whyalla
Port Pirie
Burra
Morgan

Murray River

Goolgowi

Marsden
Hay

Bathurst

West Wyalong
Cowra

Orange

1274

Lithgow
Katoomba

Singleton

Cessnock

Newcastle

SYDNEY

Gawler Ranges

Murra

Renmark

Swan
Hill

Narrandera

Cootamundra

1204

Wollongong

6

ADELAIDE

Murray Bridge

Ouyen
Hopetoun

Deniliquin

Finley

Wagga Wagga

Canberra

Nowra

Victor
Harbor
Tailem Bend

Mildura
Balranald

Narrandera
Albury

Tumut
A.C.T.

Batemans Bay

Kingscote
Kangaroo I.

Bordertown

Big Desert
Little
Desert

VICTORIA

Swan
Hill

Shepparton

Omeo

2229
Mount
Kosciuszko

Cooma

35°

Robe

Horsham

Bendigo

Yea

GREA

Mount Bogong
1986

Bombala

Mount Gambier
Portland

Hamilton
Ballarat

MELBOURNE

Bairnsdale

Eden

Cape Howe

Geelong

Morwell

Sale

Warrnambool

Apollo
Bay

Korumburra
Walkerville

Port Albert
Wilson's Promontory
South East Point

116

7

King Island
Currie

Bass Strait

Flinders I.

Cape Grim   Stanley
Burnie
Devonport

Furneaux
Group
Whitemark
Cape Barren I.

T A S M A N   S E A

Banks Strait

George
Town   Launceston

1617
Mount
Ossa

TASMANIA

Queenstown
Lake Gordon

Swansea

Cape Forestier

A.C.T. = Australian Capital Territory

40°

Hobart

Dover

Port Arthur
Storm Bay

South West
Cape   South
East Cape

135°   G   140°   H   145°   J   150°

K   155°   L   M   8

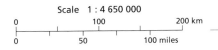

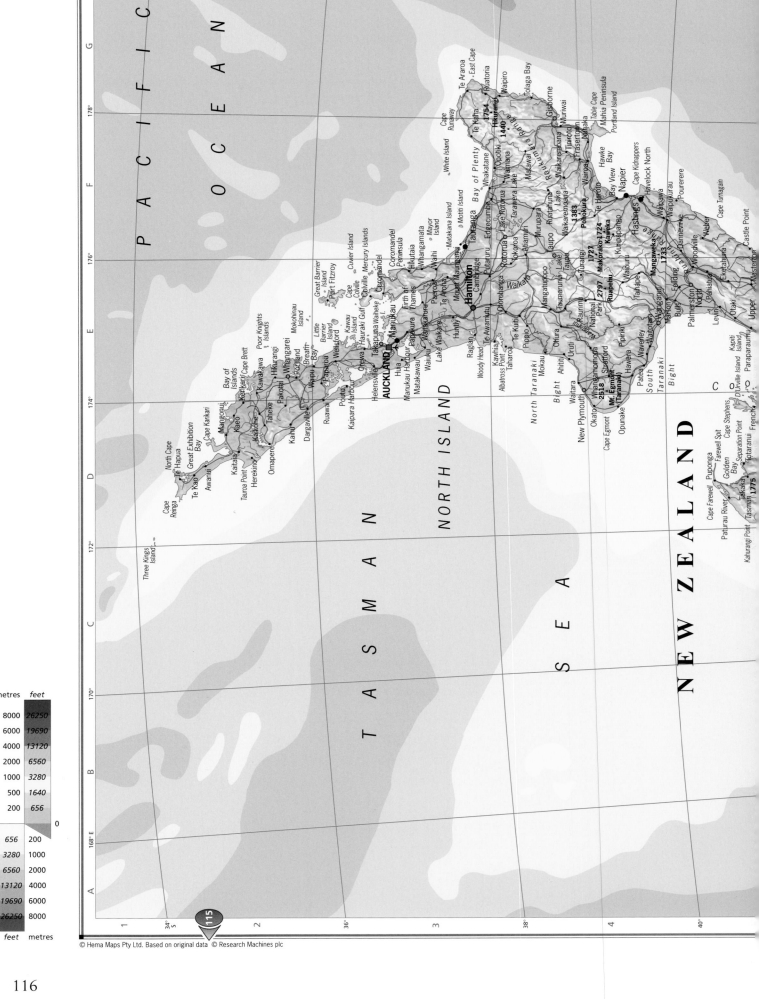

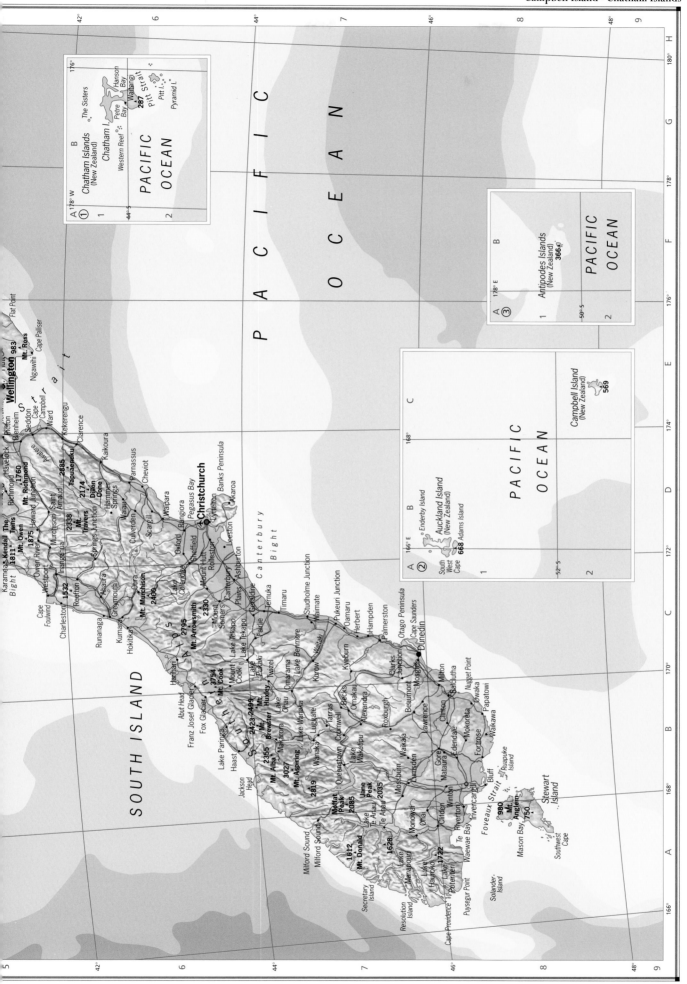

PACIFIC OCEAN

SOUTH ISLAND

Chatham Islands (New Zealand) ①
The Sisters
Western Reef
Hanson Bay
Petre Bay
Waitangi **287**
Pitt Strait
Pitt I.
Pyramid I.
Chatham I.

Antipodes Islands (New Zealand) ③
366
PACIFIC OCEAN

Auckland Island (New Zealand) ②
Enderby Island
Adams Island **668**
South West Cape
Campbell Island (New Zealand)
569
PACIFIC OCEAN

Wellington 983 Mt. Ross
Ngawihi
Cape Palliser
Flat Point
Cape Campbell
Ward
Seddon
Blenheim
Picton
Havelock
Kekerengu
Clarence
Kaikoura
Parnassus
Cheviot
Richmond
Mt. Richmond **1760**
2885 Tapuaenuku
2174 Dillon Cone
Murchison Saint Arnaud
Mt. Travers **2338**
Hanmer Springs
Springs Junction
Waiau
Culverden
Scargill
Waipara
Rangiora
Oxford
Sheffield
Christchurch
Lyttelton
Banks Peninsula
Akaroa
Pegasus Bay
Kendall The **983**
Mt. Owen **1875**
Inangahua
Owen River **1811**
Reefton
Murchison
Mt. Murchison **2400**
Lake Coleridge
Methven
Mount Hutt
Rolleston
Leeston
Ashburton
Karamea
Karamea Bight
Westport
Charleston **1532**
Cape Foulwind
Runanaga
Kumara
Greymouth
Hokitika
Harihari
Mt. Arrowsmith **2795**
Mount Somers **2330**
Geraldine
Temuka
Timaru
Pleasant Point
Fairlie
Canterbury Plains
Studholme Junction
Waimate
Pukeuri Junction
Oamaru
Herbert
Hampden
Palmerston
Cape Saunders
Otago Peninsula
Dunedin
Mosgiel
Abut Head
Franz Josef Glacier
Fox Glacier
3754 Mt. Cook
Mount Cook
Lake Tekapo
Lake Tekapo
Lake Pukaki
Twizel
Omarama
Lake Benmore
Kurow
Waitaki
Kyeburn
Becks
Clarks Junction
Lake Paringa
Haast
Jackson Head
2423 **2499** Mt. Huxley
Mt. Brewster
Mt. Aspiring **3027**
Lake Wanaka
Lake Hawea
Makarora
Ohau
Tarras
Luggate
Cromwell
Omakau
Alexandra
Roxburgh
Beaumont
Clydevale
Lawrence
Milton
Balclutha
Owaka
Nugget Point
Waikawa
Papatowai
Kaitangata
Stirling
Milford Sound
Milford Sound
1612 Mt. Donald
2355 Mt. Alba
2819
Moffat Peak **2085**
Jane Peak **2035**
Lake Wakatipu
Queenstown
Lake Te Anau
Te Anau
Mossburn
Lumsden
Waikaia
Gore
Mataura
Edendale
Fortrose
Mokoreta
Mt. Anglem **980**
750
Stewart Island
Ruapuke Island
Bluff
Invercargill
Riverton
Otautau
Winton
Clifden
Ohai
Monowai
Lake Manapouri
1628
1722
Lake Poteriteri
Lake Hauroko
Te Waewae Bay
Waewae Bay
Mason Bay
Southwest Cape
Secretary Island
Resolution Island
Cape Providence
Puysegur Point
Solander Island
Foveaux Strait
Te Anau

PACIFIC OCEAN

■ over 3 million
■ 1 – 3 million
● 250 000 – 1 million
● 100 000 – 250 000
◉ 25 000 – 100 000
· under 25 000
—— country capital underline

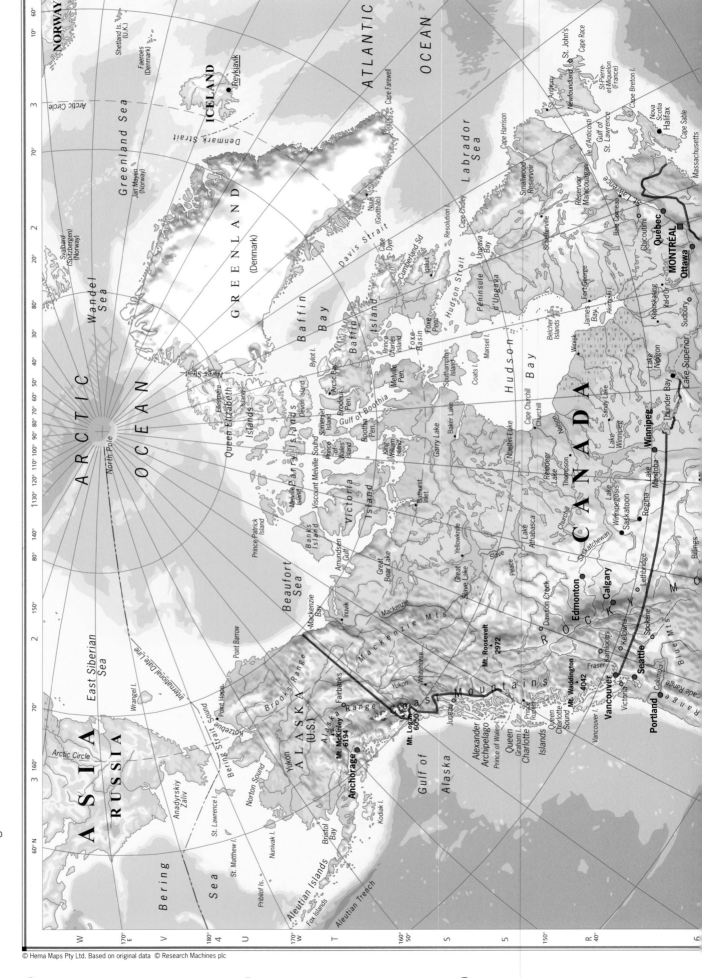

Scale 1 : 34 700 000

© Hema Maps Pty Ltd. Based on original data © Research Machines plc

118

Mt. McKinley, Alaska : 6,194 m or 20,322 ft

Death Valley, USA : 86 m or 282 ft

Bateques, Mexico : 3.0 cm or 1.2 in

Henderson Lake, Canada : 650 cm or 256 in

Mississippi-Missouri, USA : 6,020 km or 3,740 mi

Lake Superior, USA/Canada : 82,260 km² or 31,760 sq mi

 Northice, Greenland : -66 ˚C or -87 ˚F

Death Valley, USA : 57 ˚C or 134 ˚F

 475,525,000

19 per km² or 50 per sq mi

 24,454,000 km² or 9,442,000 sq mi

23

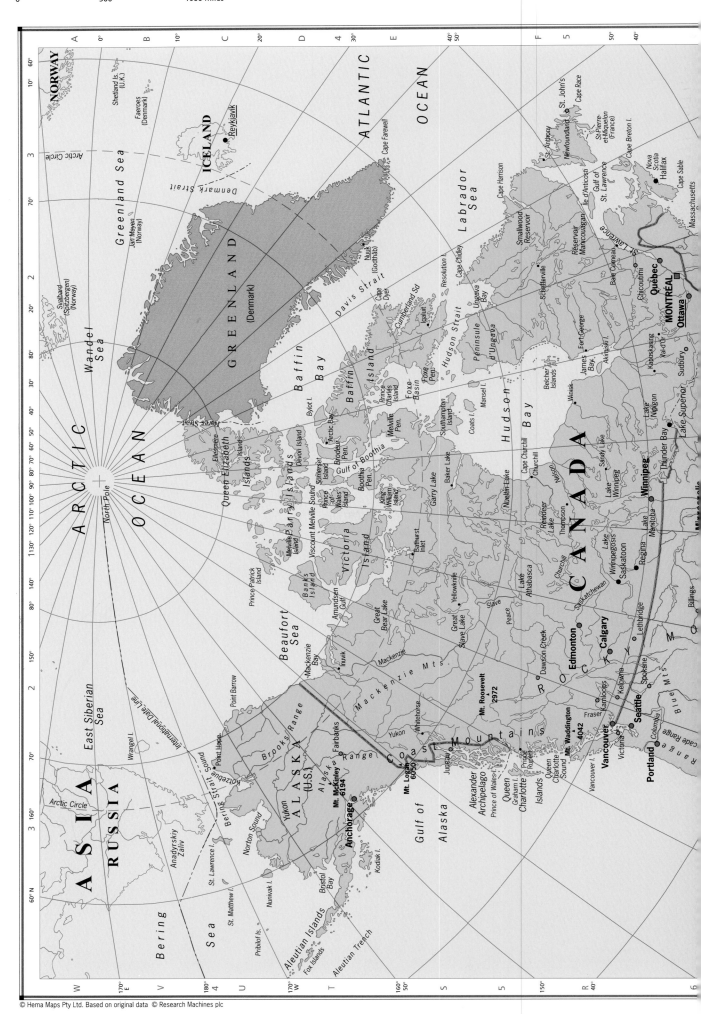

© Hema Maps Pty Ltd. Based on original data © Research Machines plc

Mt. McKinley, Alaska : 6,194 m or 20,322 ft

Death Valley, USA : 86 m or 282 ft

Bateques, Mexico : 3.0 cm or 1.2 in

Henderson Lake, Canada : 650 cm or 256 in

Mississippi-Missouri, USA : 6,020 km or 3,740 mi

Lake Superior, USA/Canada : 82,260 km² or 31,760 sq mi

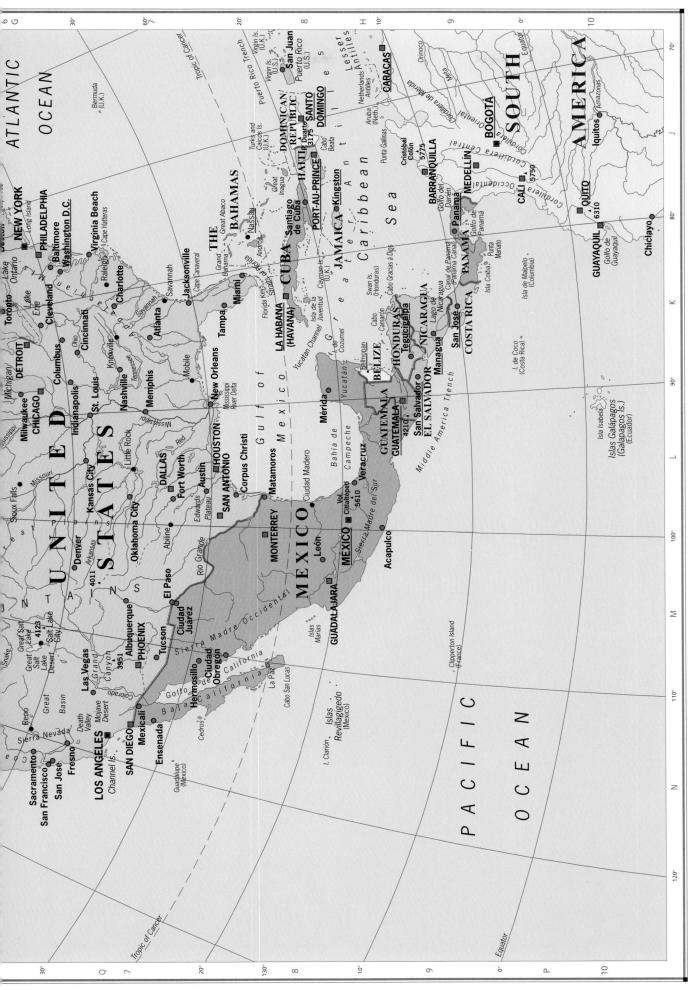

ATLANTIC OCEAN

Bermuda (U.K.)

NEW YORK
PHILADELPHIA
Baltimore
Washington D.C.
Virginia Beach
Long Island
Cape Hatteras
Raleigh
Charlotte
Knoxville
Cincinnati
Cleveland
Columbus
Indianapolis
St. Louis
Nashville
Memphis
Atlanta
Savannah
Jacksonville
Cape Canaveral
Tampa
Miami
Grand Bahama
Great Abaco
Nassau
THE BAHAMAS
Andros
Florida Keys
Straits of Florida

Toronto
Lake Ontario
Lake Erie
Detroit
Milwaukee
CHICAGO
Lake Michigan
Ohio
Kansas City
Little Rock
New Orleans
Mississippi River Delta
Red
Tennessee

UNITED STATES
Missouri
Sioux Falls
Denver
4011
Oklahoma City
DALLAS
Fort Worth
Austin
SAN ANTONIO
HOUSTON
Corpus Christi
Matamoros
Ciudad Madero
Great Plains
Edwards Plateau
Arkansas
Abilene
El Paso
Rio Grande
Ciudad Juárez

Reno
Sacramento
San Francisco
San Jose
Fresno
Sierra Nevada
Death Valley
Mojave Desert
LOS ANGELES
Channel Is.
SAN DIEGO
Mexicali
Ensenada
Las Vegas
Grand Canyon
3951
PHOENIX
Tucson
Albuquerque
Great Salt Lake
Salt Lake City
4123
Great Salt Lake Desert
Great Basin
Snake
Colorado

Gulf of Mexico
Mexico
MONTERREY
León
MÉXICO
GUADALAJARA
MEXICO
Acapulco
Veracruz
Vol. Citlaltepetl 5610
Sierra Madre del Sur
Sierra Madre Occidental
Bahía de Campeche
Mérida
Yucatán
Bahía de Campeche
Hermosillo
Ciudad Obregón
Baja California
La Paz
Cabo San Lucas
Cedros I.
Golfo de California
Guadalupe (Mexico)
Islas Marías
Islas Revillagigedo (Mexico)
I. Clarión
Tropic of Cancer

CUBA
LA HABANA (HAVANA)
Santiago de Cuba
Isla de la Juventud
Yucatán Channel
Cozumel
BELIZE
Belmopan
GUATEMALA
GUATEMALA
4210
SAN SALVADOR
San Salvador
EL SALVADOR
HONDURAS
Tegucigalpha
NICARAGUA
Managua
Lago de Nicaragua
COSTA RICA
San José
Cabo Camarón
Swan Is. (Honduras)
Cabo Gracias á Dios
Middle America Trench

Greater Antilles
HAITI
PORT-AU-PRINCE
DOMINICAN REPUBLIC
SANTO DOMINGO
Pico Duarte 3175
Cabo Beata
JAMAICA
Kingston
Cayman Is. (U.K.)
Puerto Rico Trench
San Juan
Puerto Rico (U.S.)
Virgin Is. (U.S.)
Virgin Is. (U.K.)
Turks and Caicos (U.K.)
Great Inagua
Lesser Antilles
Netherlands Antilles
Aruba (Neth.)
Punta Gallinas

Caribbean Sea

CARACAS
Orinoco
Meta
SOUTH AMERICA
Cordillera de Mérida
BOGOTÁ
BARRANQUILLA
MEDELLÍN
Golfo del Darién
Panama
PANAMA
Golfo de Panamá
Panama Canal (Canal de Panamá)
Punta Mariato
I. de Coco (Costa Rica)
Isla Coiba
Isla de Malpelo (Columbia)
CALI
5750
5775
Cristóbal Colón
Cordillera Oriental
Cordillera Central
Cordillera Occidental
QUITO
6310
GUAYAQUIL
Golfo de Guayaquil
Chiclayo
Iquitos
Amazonas
Equator

Islas Galápagos (Galapagos Is.) (Ecuador)
Isla Isabela
Clipperton Island (France)

PACIFIC OCEAN

Northice, Greenland : -66 °C or -87 °F
Death Valley, USA : 57 °C or 134 °F

475,525,000
19 per km² or 50 per sq mi

24,454,000 km² or 9,442,000 sq mi
23

Scale 1 : 13 800 000

```
0        200      400      600 km
0    100      200      300 miles
```

metres / feet

metres	feet
8000	26250
6000	19690
4000	13120
2000	6560
1000	3280
500	1640
200	656
0	0
656	200
3280	1000
6560	2000
13120	4000
19690	6000
26250	8000

feet / metres

■ over 3 million
■ 1 – 3 million
● 250 000 – 1 million
● 100 000 – 250 000
○ 25 000 – 100 000
• under 25 000

—— country capital underline
—— state or province capital underline

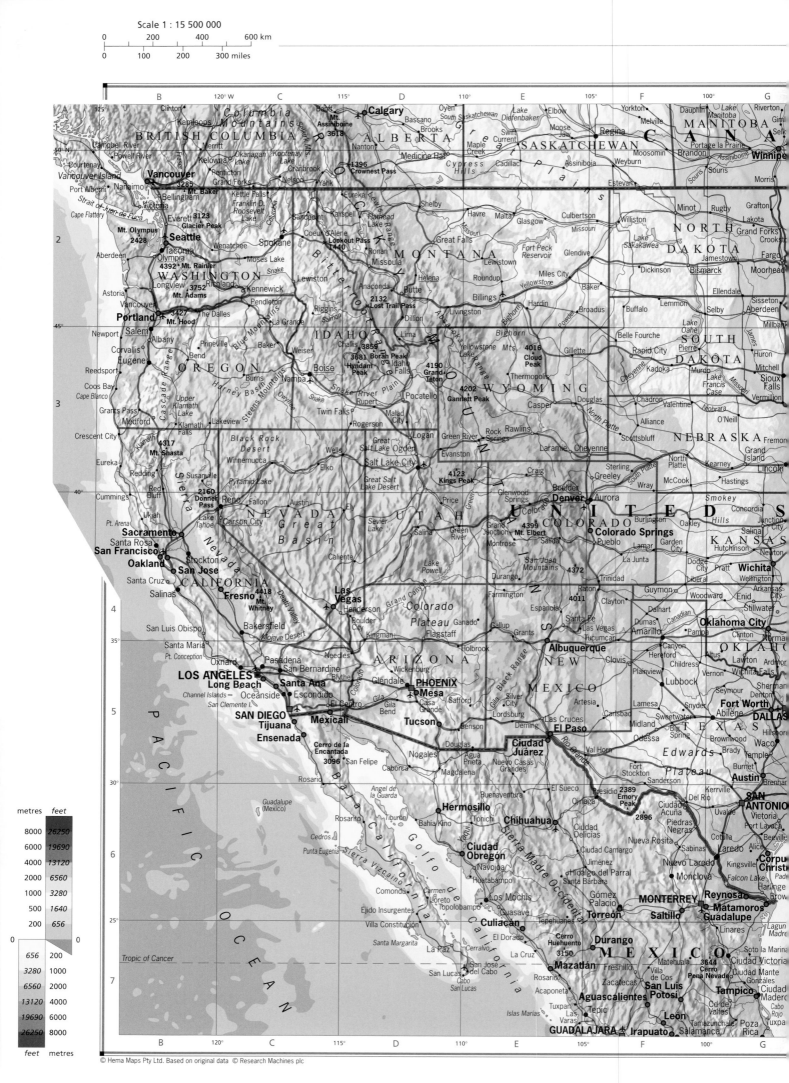

Scale 1 : 15 500 000

metres	feet
8000	26250
6000	19690
4000	13120
2000	6560
1000	3280
500	1640
200	656
0	0
656	200
3280	1000
6560	2000
13120	4000
19690	6000
26250	8000
feet	metres

© Hema Maps Pty Ltd. Based on original data © Research Machines plc

124

■ over 3 million	● 100 000 – 250 000
■ 1 – 3 million	○ 25 000 – 100 000
● 250 000 – 1 million	• under 25 000

country capital underline

state or province capital underline

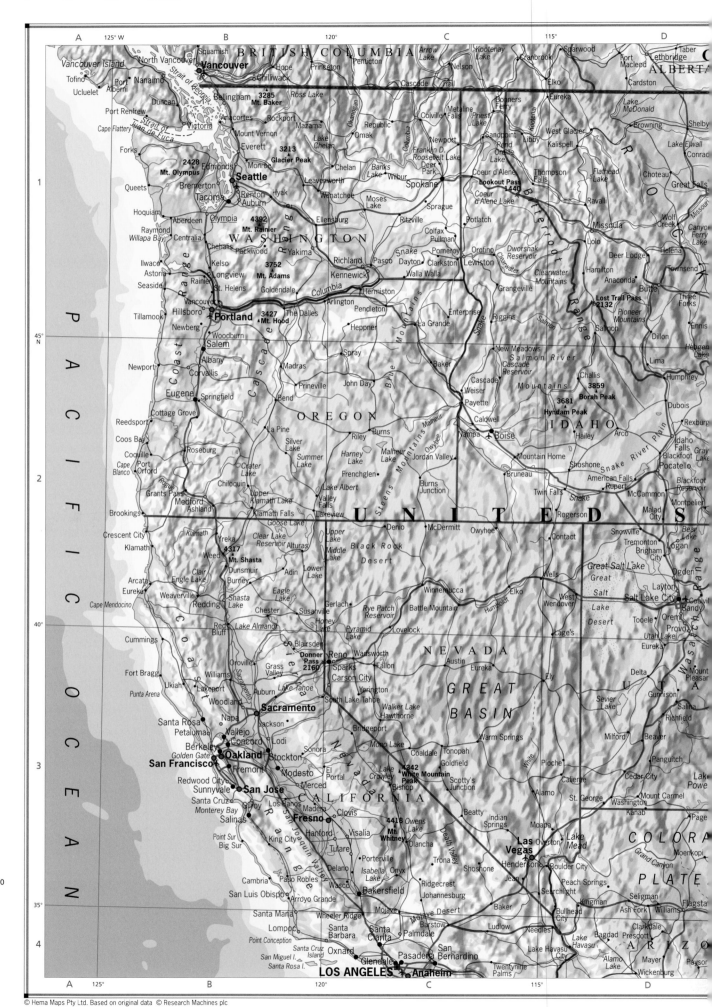

Scale 1 : 7 200 000

metres	feet
8000	26250
6000	19690
4000	13120
2000	6560
1000	3280
500	1640
200	656
0	0
656	200
3280	1000
6560	2000
13120	4000
19690	6000
26250	8000
feet	metres

© Hema Maps Pty Ltd. Based on original data © Research Machines plc

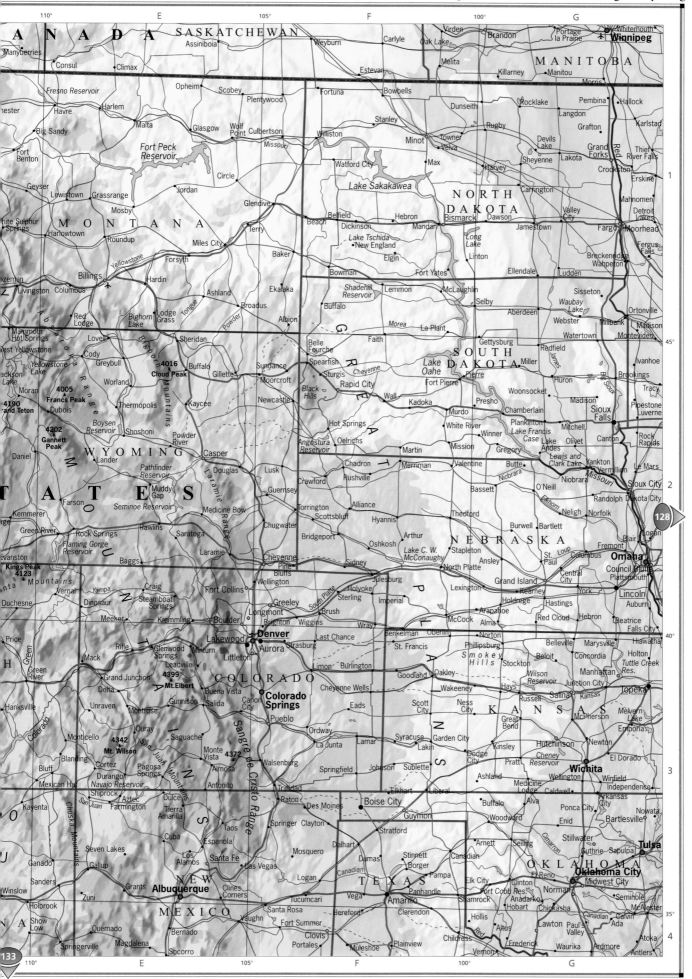

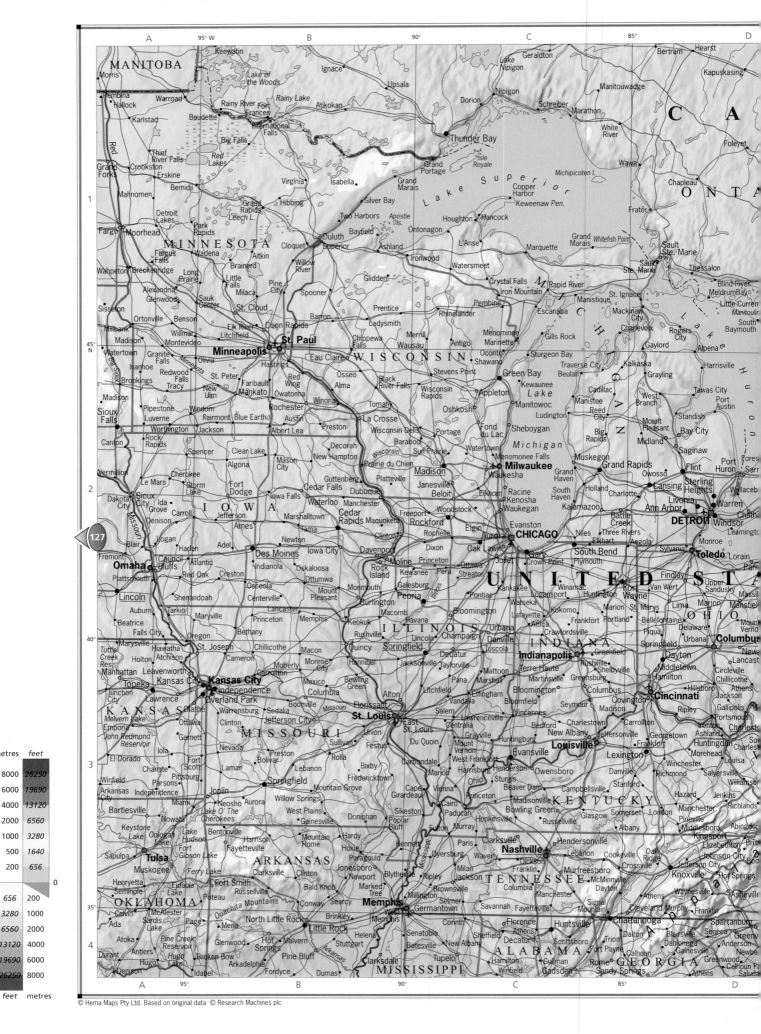

Northeast United States

Connecticut • Delaware • District of Columbia • Illinois • Indiana • Iowa • Maine • Maryland • Massachusetts • Michigan
Minnesota • New Hampshire • New Jersey • New York • Ohio • Pennsylvania • Rhode Island • Vermont • West Virginia • Wisconsin

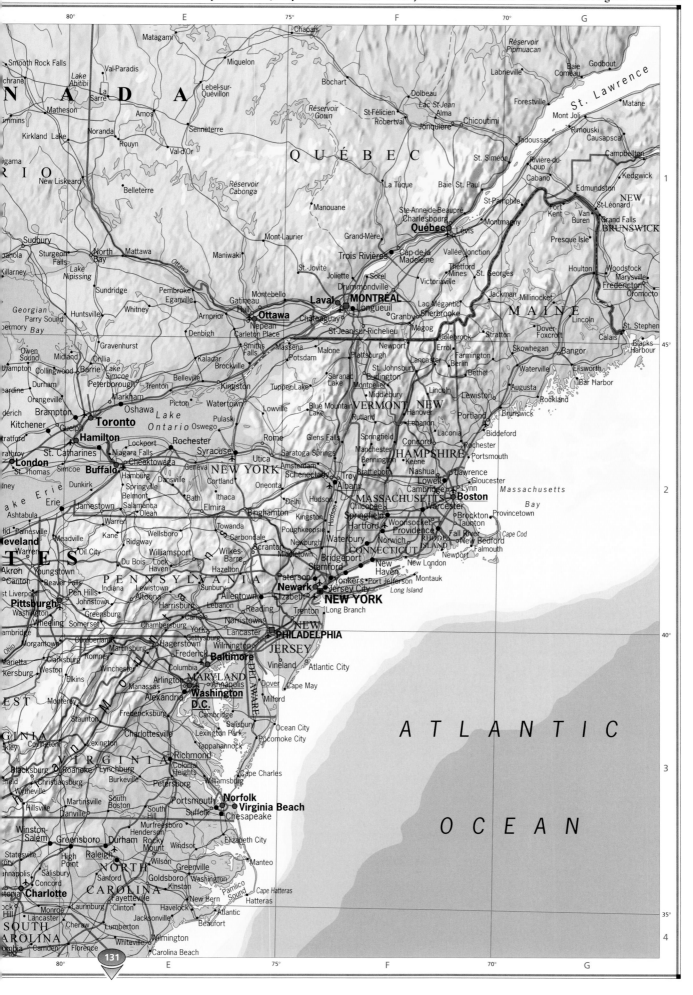

◼ over 3 million	● 100 000 – 250 000	——— country capital underline
◼ 1 – 3 million	◉ 25 000 – 100 000	——— state or province capital underline
● 250 000 – 1 million	• under 25 000	

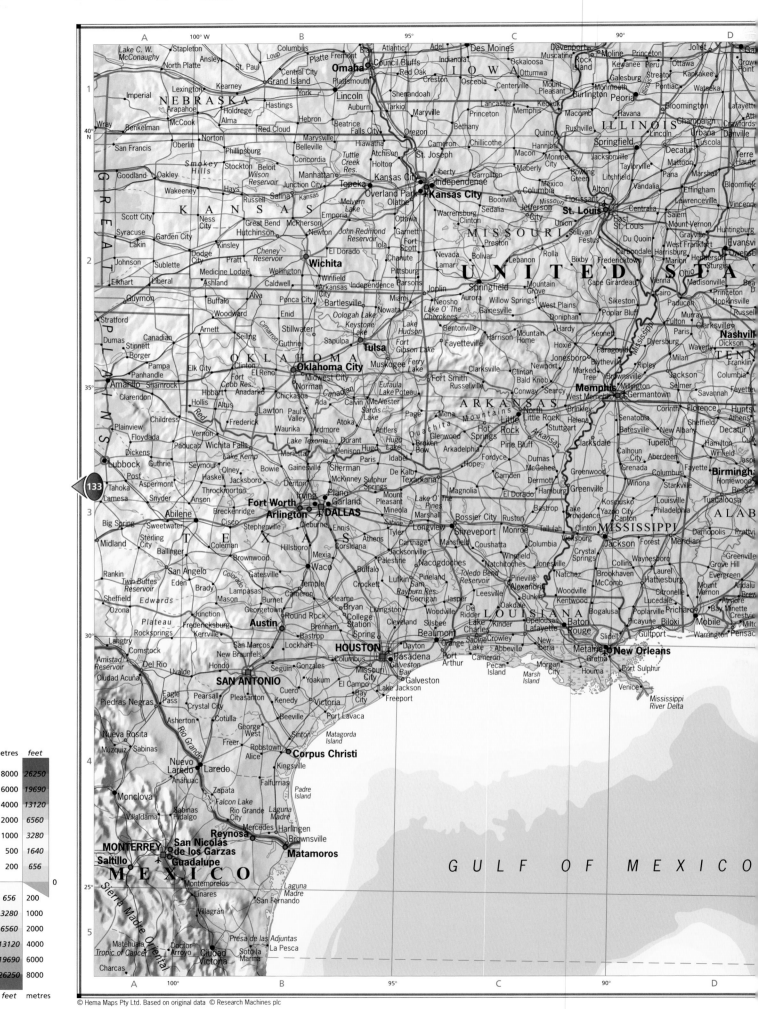

Scale 1 : 7 200 000

0   100   200   300 km
0   50   100   150 miles

© Hema Maps Pty Ltd. Based on original data © Research Machines plc

Southeast United States

**Alabama • Arkansas •The Bahamas • Florida • Georgia • Kentucky • Louisiana
Mississippi • Missouri • North Carolina • South Carolina • Tennessee •Texas • Virginia**

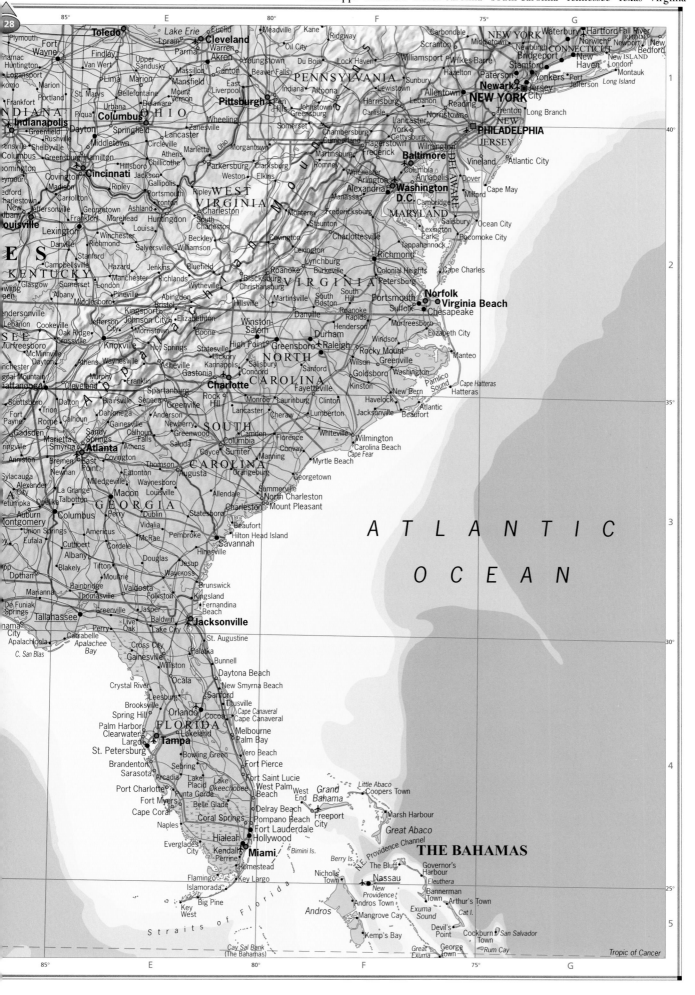

■ over 3 million
■ 1 – 3 million
● 250 000 – 1 million
● 100 000 – 250 000
◉ 25 000 – 100 000
• under 25 000

____ country capital underline
____ state or province capital underline

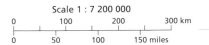

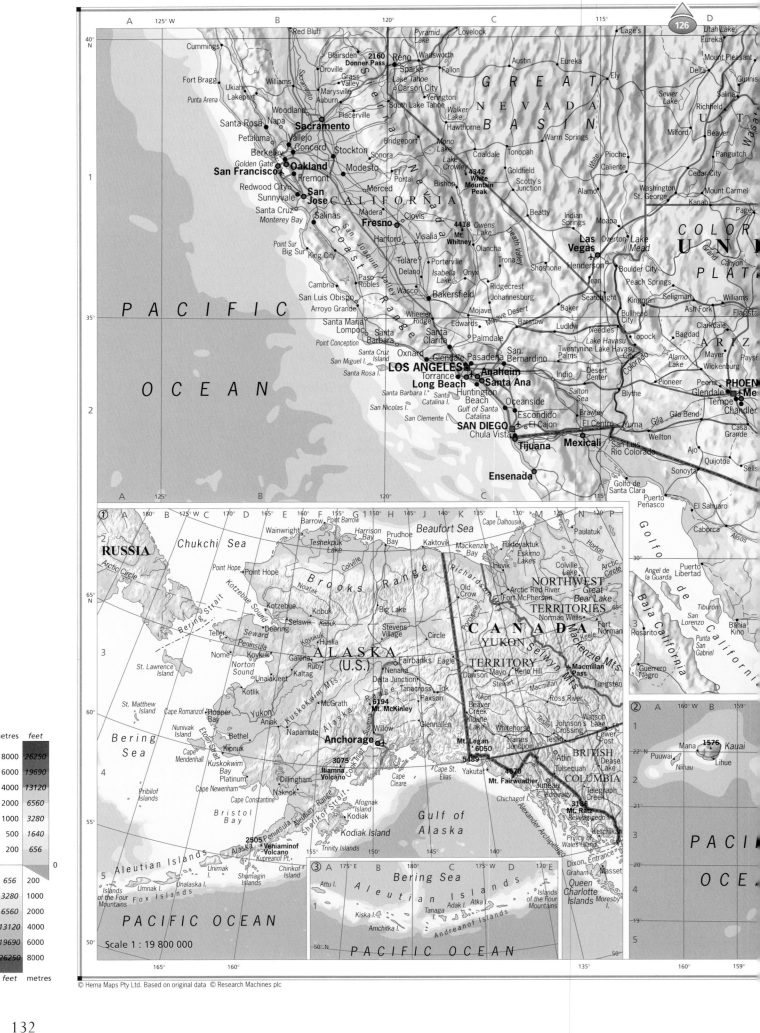

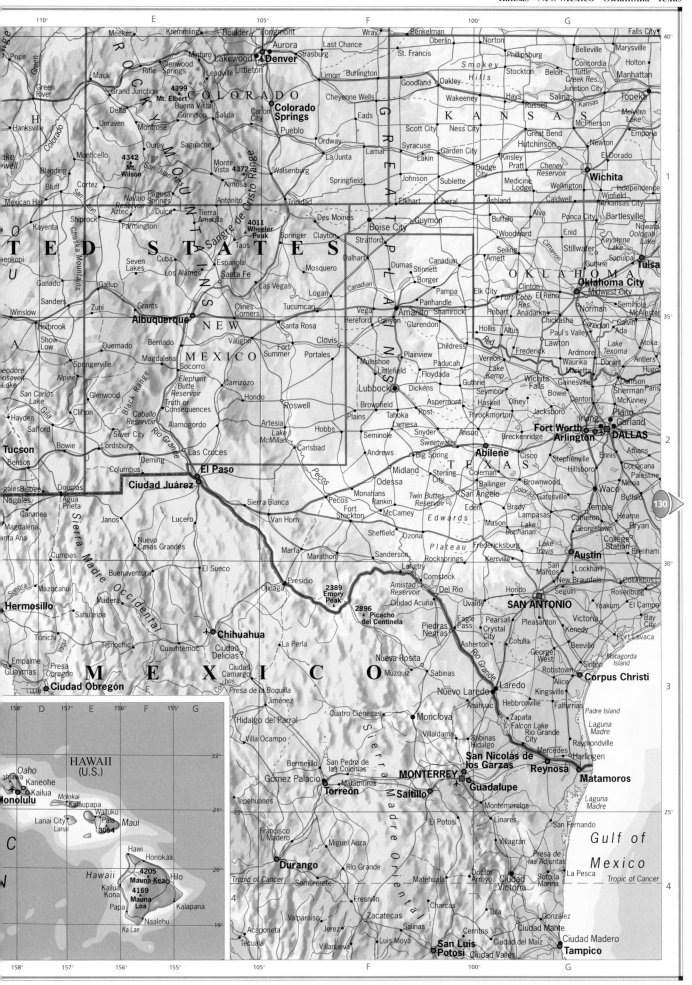

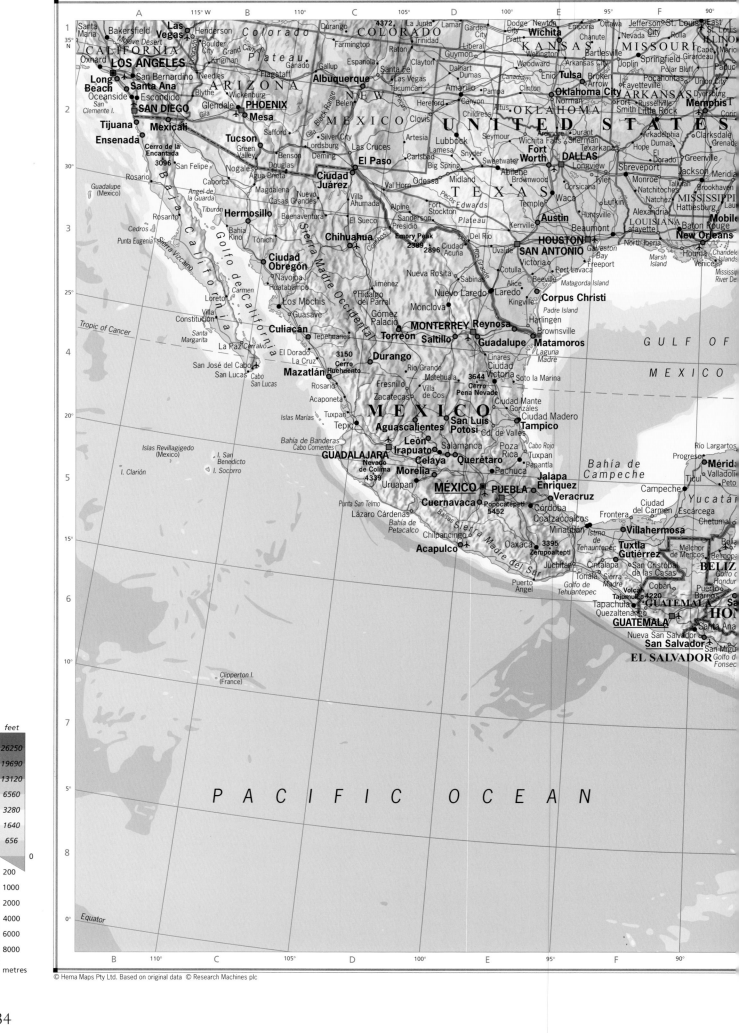

0   200   400   600 km
0   100   200   300 miles

metres	feet
8000	26250
6000	19690
4000	13120
2000	6560
1000	3280
500	1640
200	656
0	0
656	200
3280	1000
6560	2000
13120	4000
19690	6000
26250	8000
feet	metres

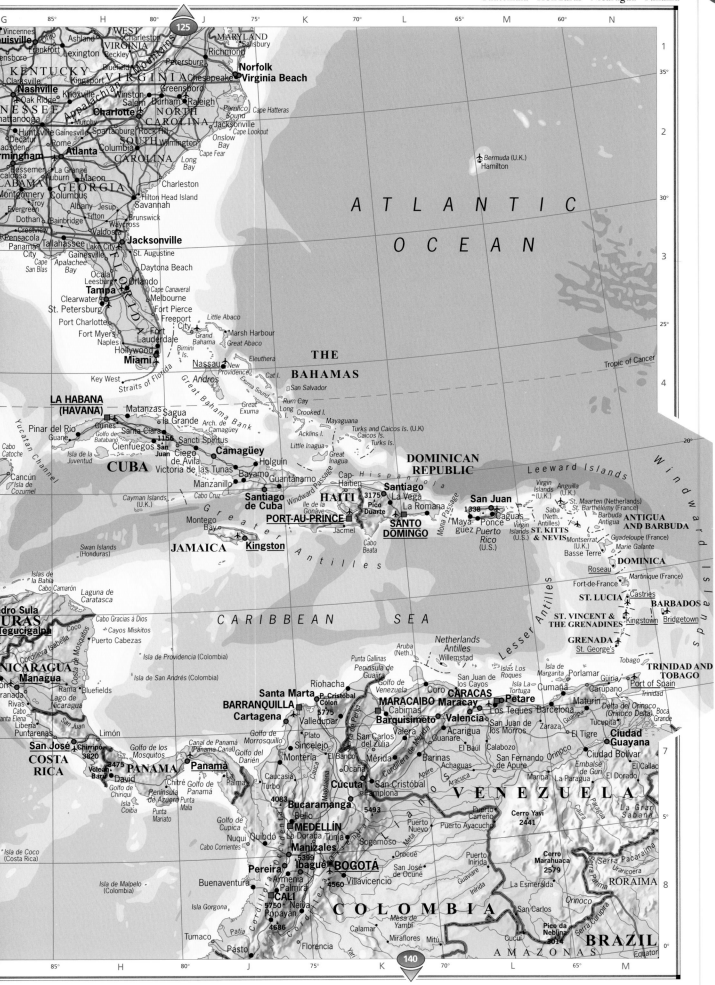

Central America and the Caribbean

Belize • Caribbean Islands • Costa Rica • El Salvador
Guatemala • Honduras • Nicaragua • Panama

125

ATLANTIC

OCEAN

WEST VIRGINIA
Vincennes
Ohio
Louisville
Ashland
Charleston
MARYLAND
Salisbury
Frankfort
Lexington
Beckley
Richmond
Greensboro
Bluefield
Petersburg
Norfolk
Virginia Beach
Chesapeake
Nashville
Knoxville
Winston
Durham
Raleigh
Oak Ridge
Salem
Greensboro
Charlotte
VIRGINIA
Pamlico Sound
Cape Hatteras
Murphy
NORTH CAROLINA
Jacksonville
Cape Lookout
Huntsville
Gainesville
Spartanburg
Rock Hill
Onslow Bay
Wilmington
SOUTH CAROLINA
Atlanta
Columbia
Cape Fear
Rome
GEORGIA
Charleston
Long Bay
Albany
Jesup
Savannah
Dothan
Tifton
Brunswick
Waycross
Crestview
Valdosta
Panama City
Tallahassee
Lake City
Jacksonville
Cape San Blas
Apalachee Bay
Gainesville
St. Augustine
Ocala
Leesburg
Daytona Beach
Tampa
Orlando
Cape Canaveral
Clearwater
Melbourne
St. Petersburg
Fort Pierce
Port Charlotte
Freeport
Fort Myers
Fort Lauderdale
Naples
Hollywood
Miami
Key West
Straits of Florida
FLORIDA
Little Abaco
Grand Bahama
Great Abaco
Marsh Harbour
Bimini Is.
Nassau
New Providence
Eleuthera
Andros
Cat I.
THE BAHAMAS
San Salvador
Rum Cay
Great Exuma
Long I.
Exuma Sound
Crooked I.
Mayaguana
Acklins I.
Turks and Caicos Is. (U.K)
Little Inagua
Caicos Is.
Great Inagua
Turks Is.
Tropic of Cancer

LA HABANA (HAVANA)
Matanzas
Pinar del Río
Güines
Sagua la Grande
Guane
Golfo de Batabanó
Santa Clara
Arch. de Camagüey
Cabo Catoche
Cienfuegos
San Juan
1155
Sancti Spíritus
Cancún
Isla de Cozumel
Isla de la Juventud
Ciego de Ávila
Camagüey
Holguín
Victoria de las Tunas
Bayamo
CUBA
Manzanillo
Guantánamo
Cabo Cruz
Cayman Islands (U.K.)
Santiago de Cuba
Windward Passage
Cap-Haïtien
Montego Bay
Greater Antilles
Île de la Gonâve
HAITI
3175 Pico Duarte
PORT-AU-PRINCE
Jacmel
Cabo Beata
JAMAICA
Kingston
Swan Islands (Honduras)
La Vega
Santiago
DOMINICAN REPUBLIC
SANTO DOMINGO
La Romana
Hispaniola
Mona Passage
Maya-güez
Ponce
1338
San Juan
Caguas
Puerto Rico (U.S.)
Virgin Islands (U.K.)
Virgin Islands (U.S.)
ST. KITTS & NEVIS
Anguilla (U.K.)
St. Maarten (Netherlands)
St. Barthélemy (France)
Saba (Neth.)
Antilles (Neth.)
Barbuda
Antigua
ANTIGUA AND BARBUDA
Montserrat (U.K.)
Guadeloupe (France)
Marie Galante
Basse Terre
DOMINICA
Roseau
Martinique (France)
Fort-de-France
ST. LUCIA
Castries
BARBADOS
Bridgetown
ST. VINCENT & THE GRENADINES
Kingstown
Lesser Antilles
GRENADA
St. George's
Leeward Islands
Windward Islands

CARIBBEAN SEA

Islas de la Bahía
Cabo Camarón
Laguna de Caratasca
Pedro Sula
HONDURAS
Tegucigalpa
Coco
Cabo Gracias á Dios
Cayos Miskitos
Cordillera Isabella
Puerto Cabezas
Isla de Providencia (Colombia)
NICARAGUA
Managua
Granada
Rama
Bluefields
Lago de Nicaragua
Rivas
Isla de San Andrés (Colombia)
Santa Elena
Liberia
Cabo
San Juan
Puntarenas
Limón
San José
COSTA RICA
Chirripó 3820
Volcán Barú 3475
David
Chitré
Golfo de Chiriquí
Isla Coiba
Punta Mariato
Península de Azuero
Punta Mala
Golfo de los Mosquitos
Canal de Panamá (Panama Canal)
PANAMA
Golfo del Darién
Panamá
La Palma
Golfo de San Miguel
Turbo

Isla de Coco (Costa Rica)
Isla de Malpelo (Colombia)

Aruba (Neth.)
Netherlands Antilles
Willemstad
Punta Gallinas
Península de Guajira
Golfo de Venezuela
Coro
Islas Los Roques
Isla de Margarita
Porlamar
Isla La Tortuga
San Juan de los Cayos
Isla de Margarita
Tobago
TRINIDAD AND TOBAGO
Port of Spain
Güiria
Carúpano
Maturín
Cumaná
Barcelona
Los Teques
Trinidad
Delta del Orinoco (Orinoco Delta)
Boca Grande
Tucupita
Riohacha
Santa Marta
P. Cristóbal Colón 5775
MARACAIBO
CARACAS
Maracay
Valencia
Petare
Barranquilla
Cabimas
Barquisimeto
Cartagena
Valledupar
Valera
Acarigua
El Tigre
Ciudad Guayana
Golfo de Morrosquillo
Plato
San Carlos del Zulia
Guanare
Zaraza
Guanipa
Sincelejo
El Banco
Mérida
Barinas
Calabozo
San Fernando de Apure
Orinoco
Montería
El Baúl
Achaguas
Ciudad Bolívar
Caucasia
Ocaña
San Cristóbal
Apure
Maripa
La Paragua
El Callao
Cúcuta
Pamplona
Arauca
Embalse de Guri
El Dorado
4083
Bucaramanga
5493
VENEZUELA
Bello
Puerto Carreño
Cerro Yaví 2441
MEDELLÍN
La Dorada
Tunja
Sogamoso
Puerto Nuevo
La Gran Sabana
Manizales
Orocué
Puerto Ayacucho
Serra Pacaraima
Quibdó
Nuquí
Cabo Corrientes
Pereira
5399
Ibagué
BOGOTÁ
Villavicencio
San José de Ocuné
Puerto Inírida
Cerro Marahuaca 2579
RORAIMA
Buenaventura
Armenia
Palmira
4560
Guaviare
La Esmeralda
Isla Gorgona
CALI
Neiva
COLOMBIA
5750
Popayán
Mesa de Yambí
Inírida
San Carlos
4686
Orinoco
Tumaco
Patía
Calamar
Florencia
Miraflores
Mitú
Cúcui
Pico da Neblina 3014
Serra Curupira
BRAZIL
Pasto
Yarí
AMAZONAS
Equator

140

Legend:

■ over 3 million	● 100 000 – 250 000	——— country capital underline
■ 1 – 3 million	● 25 000 – 100 000	——— state or province capital underline
● 250 000 – 1 million	• under 25 000	

135

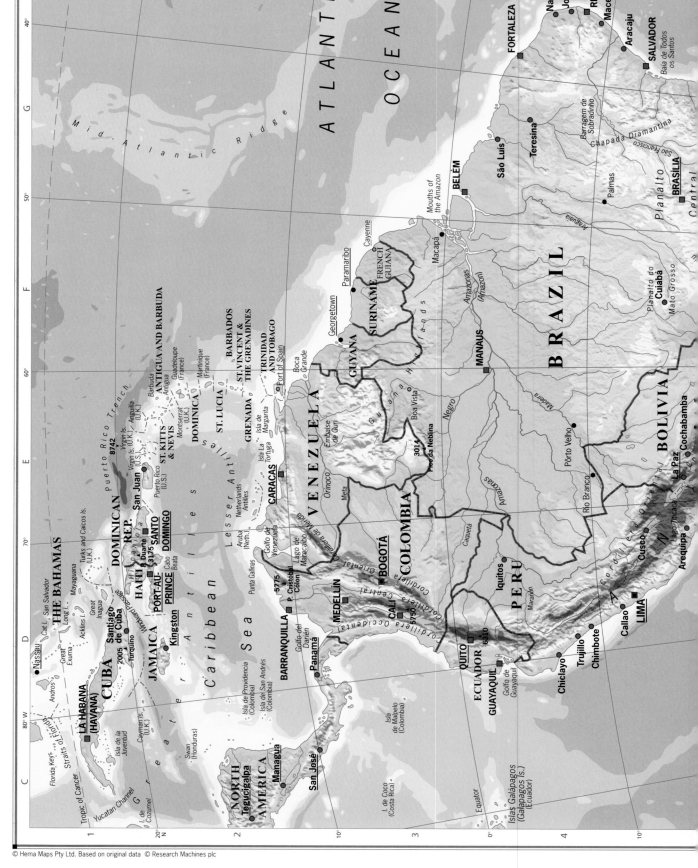

Scale 1 : 28 000 000

| 0 | 500 | 1000 | 1500 km |

| 0 | 250 | 500 | 750 miles |

H

Tropic of Cancer

ATLANTIC OCEAN

Mid Atlantic Ridge

G

F

E

D

C

THE BAHAMAS

CUBA
LA HABANA (HAVANA)

Santiago de Cuba
2005

JAMAICA
Kingston

HAITI
PORT-AU-PRINCE

DOMINICAN REP.
Duarte 3175
SANTO DOMINGO

San Juan
Puerto Rico (U.S.)

Puerto Rico Trench
8742

Turks and Caicos Is. (U.K.)

Lesser Antilles

ANTIGUA AND BARBUDA
Barbuda
Antigua

ST. KITTS & NEVIS
Montserrat (U.K.)
Guadeloupe (France)

DOMINICA

Martinique (France)

ST. LUCIA

BARBADOS

ST. VINCENT & THE GRENADINES

GRENADA

TRINIDAD AND TOBAGO
Port of Spain

Isla de Margarita

CARACAS

VENEZUELA

Orinoco

Meta

COLOMBIA
BOGOTÁ

MEDELLÍN

CALI

Caribbean Sea

BARRANQUILLA

Golfo del Darién

PANAMÁ

Panama

Lago de Maracaibo

Cristóbal Colón 5775

NORTH AMERICA

Managua

San José

Tegucigalpa

Isla de Providencia (Colombia)

Isla de San Andrés (Colombia)

Isla de Malpelo (Colombia)

I. de Coco (Costa Rica)

Islas Galápagos (Galápagos Is.) (Ecuador)

QUITO

ECUADOR
GUAYAQUIL

Golfo de Guayaquil

Chimborazo 6310

Chiclayo

Trujillo

Chimbote

PERU

Iquitos

Marañón

Callao

LIMA

Equator

Equator

Tropic of Cancer

BRAZIL

FORTALEZA

Natal
João Pessoa
RECIFE
Maceió

Aracaju

SALVADOR
Baía de Todos os Santos

Teresina

São Luís

BELÉM

Mouths of the Amazon

Macapá

Amazonas (Amazon)

Cayenne
FRENCH GUIANA

Paramaribo
SURINAME

Georgetown
GUYANA

Boca Grande

MANAUS

Boa Vista

Pico da Neblina 3014

Negro

Madeira

Pôrto Velho

Rio Branco

BOLIVIA
La Paz
Cochabamba

Cusco

Lago Titicaca

Arequipa

Barragem de Sobradinho

Chapada Diamantina

Palmas

BRASÍLIA

Planalto Central

Planalto do Mato Grosso

Guiana Highlands

metres	feet
8000	26250
6000	19690
4000	13120
2000	6560
1000	3280
500	1640
200	656
0	0
656	200
3280	1000
6560	2000
13120	4000
19690	6000
26250	8000
feet	metres

Aconcagua, Argentina : 6,959 m or 22,835 ft

Península Valdés, Argentina : 40 m or 131 ft

Arica, Chile : 0.08 cm or 0.03 in

Quibdo, Colombia : 899 cm or 354 in

Amazon-Ucayali, Brazil : 6,570 km or 4,080 mi

Lake Maracaibo, Venezuela : 13,010 km² or 5,020 sq mi

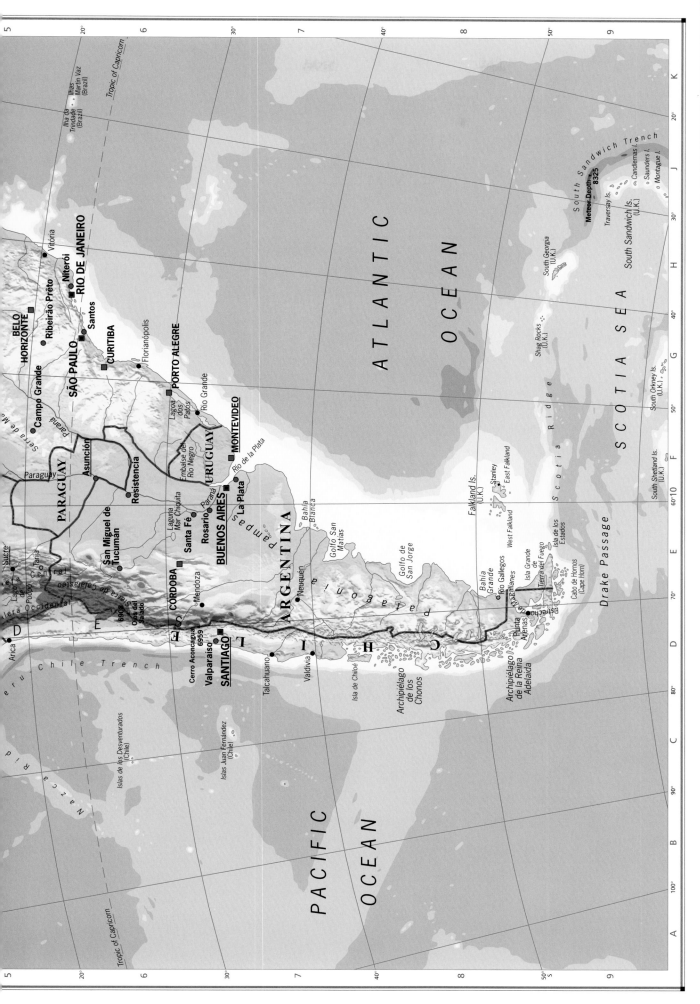

ATLANTIC OCEAN

PACIFIC OCEAN

SCOTIA SEA

South Sandwich Trench
Meteor Depth 8325

Drake Passage

Tropic of Capricorn

Ilhas Martin Vaz (Brazil)
Ilha da Trindade (Brazil)

Vitória
Niterói
RIO DE JANEIRO
Ribeirão Prêto
Santos
BELO HORIZONTE
CURITIBA
SÃO PAULO
Florianópolis
Campo Grande
PORTO ALEGRE
Lagoa dos Patos
Rio Grande
Asunción
PARAGUAY
Paraguay
Resistencia
URUGUAY
Embalse del Rio Negro
MONTEVIDEO
San Miguel de Tucumán
Laguna Mar Chiquita
Santa Fé
Rosario
Paraná
BUENOS AIRES
La Plata
Rio de la Plata
Sucre
Ojos del Salado 6908
CÓRDOBA
Mendoza
Cerro Aconcagua 6959
Valparaíso
SANTIAGO
Talcahuano
Valdivia
ARGENTINA
Bahía Blanca
Neuquén
Golfo San Matías
Golfo de San Jorge
Pampas
Patagonia
CHILE
Arica
Chile Trench
Isla de Chiloé
Archipiélago de los Chonos
Islas de los Desventurados (Chile)
Islas Juan Fernández (Chile)
Nazca Ridge
Peru-Chile Ridge
Cordillera Occidental
Cordillera Central
Sierra de Famatina
ANDES
Bahía Grande
Rio Gallegos
Estrecho de Magallanes
Punta Arenas
Isla Grande de Tierra del Fuego
Cabo de Hornos (Cape Horn)
Isla de los Estados
Archipiélago de la Reina Adelaida
Falkland Is. (U.K.)
Stanley
East Falkland
West Falkland
South Georgia (U.K.)
Shag Rocks (U.K.)
Scotia Ridge
South Orkney Is. (U.K.)
South Shetland Is. (U.K.)
Traversay Is.
Candlemas I.
Saunders I.
Montagu I.
South Sandwich Is. (U.K.)

Tropic of Capricorn

Sarmiento, Argentina : -33 °C or -27 °F

Rivadavia, Argentina : 49 °C or 120 °F

335,716,000

19 per km² or 49 per sq mi

17,838,000 km² or 6,887,000 sq mi

12

137

Scale 1 : 28 000 000

| 0 | 500 | 1000 | 1500 km |
| 0 | 250 | 500 | 750 miles |

H

G

F

E

D

C

ATLANTIC OCEAN

Mid-Atlantic Ridge

Tropic of Cancer

Equator

BRAZIL

FORTALEZA
Natal
João Pessoa
RECIFE
Maceió
Aracaju
SALVADOR
Baía de Todos
os Santos

Teresina
São Luís
Barragem de
Sobradinho
Chapada Diamantha
São Francisco

BELÉM
Mouths of
the Amazon
Macapá
Amazonas (Amazon)
Palmas
BRASÍLIA
Planalto Central

Cayenne
Paramaribo
FRENCH GUIANA
SURINAME
Georgetown
GUYANA
Boca Grande
Port of Spain

Planalto do
Mato Grosso

Guiana Highlands

Pico da Neblina
3014
Boa Vista
Negro
MANAUS
Madeira

Pôrto Velho

BOLIVIA
Cochabamba
La Paz
Lago Titicaca

Rio Branco

Cordillera Oriental

Cusco
Arequipa

VENEZUELA
Embalse
de Guri
Orinoco
Meta
Isla La
Tortuga
Isla de
Margarita

CARACAS
Netherlands
Antilles
Aruba
(Neth.)
Golfo de
Venezuela
Lago de
Maracaibo
Cordillera de Mérida

Punta Gallinas
5775
P. Cristóbal
Colón

BARRANQUILLA
Golfo del
Darién
Panamá

MEDELLÍN
CALI
5750
BOGOTÁ
COLOMBIA
Caquetá
Marañón
Caquetá

Iquitos
PERU
LIMA
Callao
Chimbote
Trujillo
Chiclayo

QUITO
6310
ECUADOR
GUAYAQUIL
Golfo de
Guayaquil

Islas Galápagos
(Galápagos Is.)
(Ecuador)

I. de Coco
(Costa Rica)

Isla
de Malpelo
(Colombia)

Isla de San Andrés
(Colombia)

Isla de Providencia
(Colombia)

NORTH
AMERICA

Tegucigalpa
Managua
San José

Caribbean Sea

Swan Is.
(Honduras)

Cayman Is.
(U.K.)

JAMAICA
Kingston

CUBA
LA HABANA
(HAVANA)
Santiago
de Cuba
2005
Turquino

Isla de la
Juventud

THE BAHAMAS
NASSAU
Cat I. San Salvador
Long I.
Great
Exuma
Acklins I.
Great
Inagua
Mayaguana

Turks and Caicos Is.
(U.K.)

HAITI
PORT-AU-
PRINCE
DOMINICAN
REP.
SANTO
DOMINGO
3175
Duarte
Cabo
Beata

Puerto Rico
(U.S.)
San Juan
Virgin Is. (U.K.)
Virgin Is.
(U.S.)
Anguilla
(U.K.)
ANTIGUA AND BARBUDA
Barbuda
Antigua
Guadeloupe
(France)
ST. KITTS
& NEVIS
Montserrat
(U.K.)
DOMINICA
Martinique
(France)
ST. LUCIA
BARBADOS
ST. VINCENT &
THE GRENADINES
GRENADA
TRINIDAD
AND TOBAGO

Lesser Antilles

Greater Antilles

Puerto Rico Trench
8742

Florida Keys
Straits of Florida
Andros I.

Yucatán Channel

I. de
Cozumel

Tropic of Cancer

Aconcagua, Argentina : 6,959 m or 22,835 ft

Península Valdés, Argentina : 40 m or 131 ft

Arica, Chile : 0.08 cm or 0.03 in

Quibdo, Colombia : 899 cm or 354 in

Amazon-Ucayali, Brazil : 6,570 km or 4,080 mi

Lake Maracaibo, Venezuela : 13,010 km² or 5,020 sq mi

© Hema Maps Pty Ltd. Based on original data © Research Machines plc

Sarmiento, Argentina : -33 °C or -27 °F

Rivadavia, Argentina : 49 °C or 120 °F

335,716,000

19 per km² or 49 per sq mi

17,838,000 km² or 6,887,000 sq mi

12

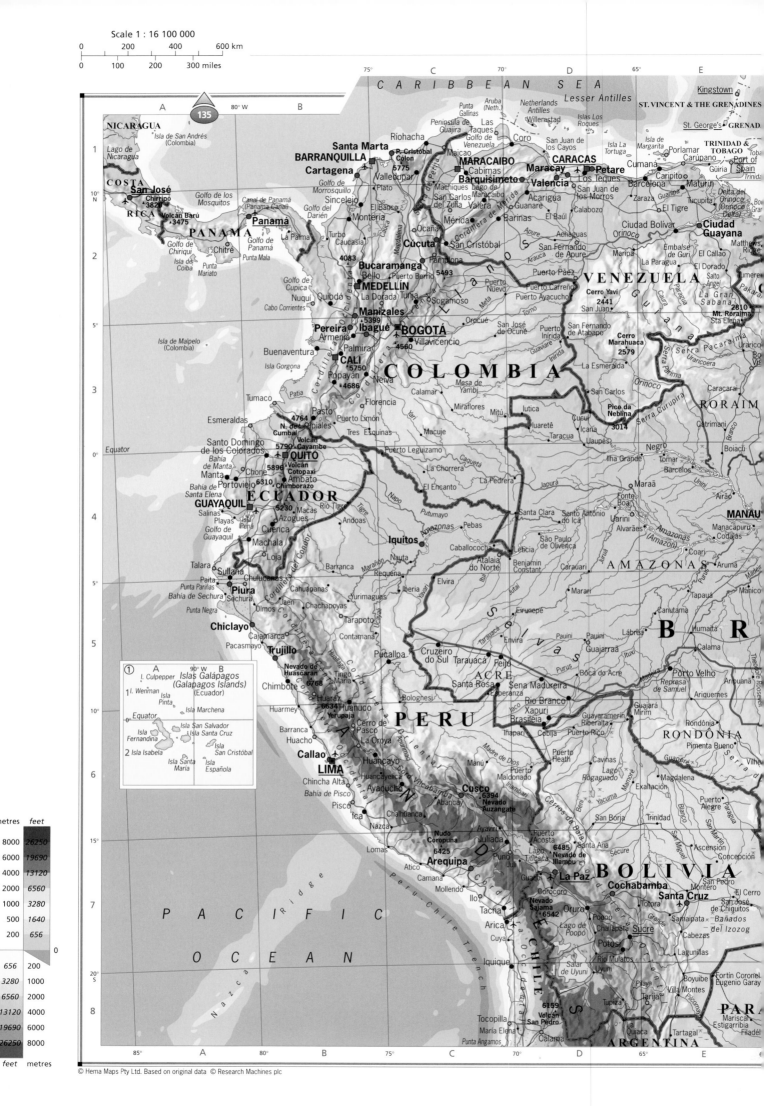

Scale 1 : 16 100 000

0	200	400	600 km	
0	100	200	300 miles	

CARIBBEAN SEA
Lesser Antilles
Kingstown
ST. VINCENT & THE GRENADINES
St. George's GRENAD
TRINIDAD & TOBAGO
Port of Spain

NICARAGUA
Isla de San Andrés (Colombia)
Lago de Nicaragua

COSTA
San José
RICA
Chirripó 3820
Volcán Barú 3475

PANAMA
Golfo de Chiriquí
Isla de Coiba
Punta Mariato
Chitré
Golfo de Panamá
Punta Mala
Panamá
Canal de Panamá (Panama Canal)
Golfo del Darién

Santa Marta
BARRANQUILLA
Cartagena
Golfo de Morrosquillo
Sincelejo
Montería
Turbo
Caucasia

Ríohacha
P. Cristóbal Colón 5775
Valledupar
El Banco
Plato

Punta Gallinas
Península de Guajira
Maicao
Machiques
Lago de Maracaibo

MARACAIBO
Cabimas
CARACAS
Maracay Petare
Barquisimeto
Valencia Los Teques
San Juan de los Morros

VENEZUELA

COLOMBIA

Quibdó
Nuquí
Cabo Corrientes
Golfo de Cupica

MEDELLÍN
Bello
La Dorada
4083
Bucaramanga
Puerto Berrío
5493
Tunja
Sogamoso

Manizales 5399
Pereira
Ibagué
Armenia
Palmira
BOGOTÁ
4560
Villavicencio

CALI 5750
Popayán
4686

Buenaventura
Isla Gorgona

PERU

© Hema Maps Pty Ltd. Based on original data © Research Machines plc

metres	feet
8000	26250
6000	19690
4000	13120
2000	6560
1000	3280
500	1640
200	656
0	0
656	200
3280	1000
6560	2000
13120	4000
19690	6000
26250	8000
feet	metres

Bolivia • Brazil • Colombia • Ecuador • French Guiana
Galapagos Islands • Guyana • Peru • Suriname • Venezuela

ATLANTIC OCEAN

BARBADOS
Bridgetown

GUYANA
Georgetown
New Amsterdam
Corriverton Paramaribo
Nieuw Nickerie Nieuw Amsterdam
Apoera Albina St. Laurent Kourou
Brokopondo W. J. van Iracoubo Cayenne
Embalse Blommestein-meer
Toekomstig Maroni
SURINAME FRENCH GUIANA
1230 Juliana Top
Oronoque
Highlands
Serra Acari
Serra Tumucumaque
AMAPÁ
Macapá

Mouths of the Amazon

BELÉM
São Luís
FORTALEZA
MARANHÃO
CEARÁ
Teresina Natal
PIAUÍ
RIO GRANDE DO NORTE
PARAÍBA João Pessoa
Campina Grande
Olinda
RECIFE
PERNAMBUCO
PARÁ
Maceió
ALAGOAS
BRAZIL
Aracaju
SERGIPE
TOCANTINS
Palmas
BAHIA
Feira de Santana
SALVADOR
MATO GROSSO
GOIÁS
Cuiabá
BRASÍLIA
DISTRITO FEDERAL
Goiânia
MINAS GERAIS
Uberlândia
MATO GROSSO DO SUL
Campo Grande
BELO HORIZONTE
ESPÍRITO SANTO
Ribeirão Prêto
Juiz de Fora
SÃO PAULO
RIO DE JANEIRO
Nova Iguaçu Niterói

Equator

Legend

Symbol	Population
■	over 3 million
■	1 – 3 million
●	250 000 – 1 million
●	100 000 – 250 000
○	25 000 – 100 000
•	under 25 000

———— country capital underline

———— state or province capital underline

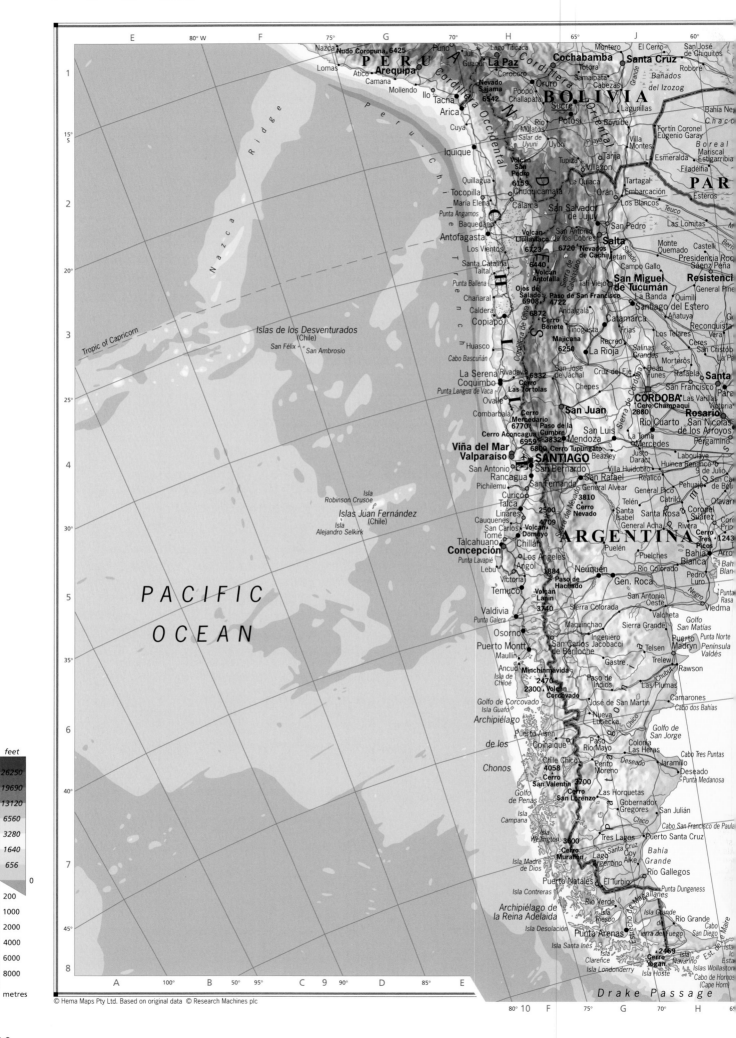

Scale 1 : 16 100 000

metres	feet
8000	26250
6000	19690
4000	13120
2000	6560
1000	3280
500	1640
200	656
0	0
656	200
3280	1000
6560	2000
13120	4000
19690	6000
26250	8000
feet	metres

© Hema Maps Pty Ltd. Based on original data © Research Machines plc

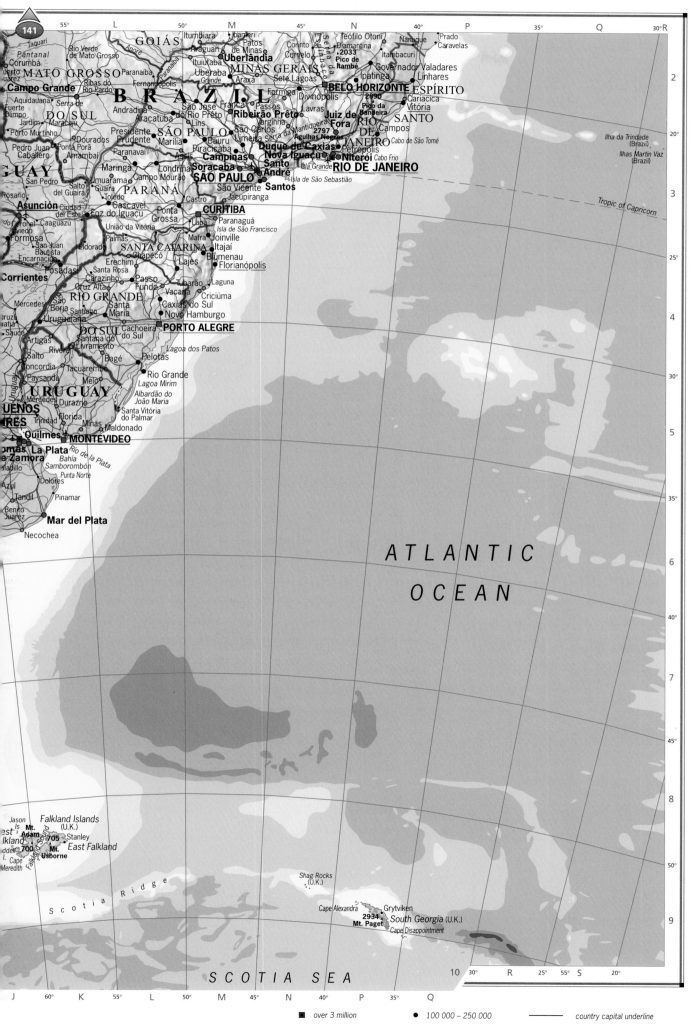

141

55° L 50° M 45° N 40° P 35° Q 30° R

GOIÁS
Itumbiara
Patos
de Minas
Teófilo Otoni
Nanuque
Prado
Caravelas
Taquari
Pântanal
Rio Verde
de Mato Grosso
Araguari
Araguari
Diamantina
Itambacuri
Corumbá
Paranaíba
2033
Pico de
Itambé
Uberlândia
Curvelo
Governador Valadares
Puerto
Juárez
MATO GROSSO
Ituiutaba
Uberaba
MINAS GERAIS
Sete Lagoas
Ipatinga
Linhares
Campo Grande
Ribas do
Rio Pardo
Araxá
BELO HORIZONTE
ESPÍRITO
Aquidauana
Serra de
B R A Z I L
Formiga
2890
Cariacica
Fuerte
Olimpo
DO SUL
Andradina
São José
do Rio Prêto
Franca
Passos
Divinópolis
Lavras
Pico da
Bandeira
Vitória
SANTO
Jardim
Maracaju
Presidente
Prudente
Ribeirão Prêto
Varginha
2797
Juiz de
Fora
Campos
Pôrto Murtinho
Dourados
Marília
São Carlos
Limeira Serra
RIO
DE
Pedro Juan
Caballero
Ponta Porã
Paranavaí
Piracicaba
Agulhas Negras
JANEIRO
Cabo de São Tomé
GUAY
Amambaí
Maringá
Campinas
Duque de Caxias
Petrópolis
San Pedro
Londrina
SÃO PAULO
Soracaba
Nova Iguaçu
Niterói
Cabo Frio
Umuarama
Campo Mourão
SÃO PAULO
Santo
RIO DE JANEIRO
Salto
del Guaíra
Guaíra
PARANÁ
São Vicente
André
Isla Grande
Asunciòn
Ciudad
del Este
Foz do Iguaçu
Ponta
Grossa
CURITIBA
Santos
Isla de São Sebastião
Coronel
Caaguazú
Jacupiranga
Oviedo
União da Vitória
Itajaí
Paranaguá
Formosa
Palmas
Mafra
Joinville
Isla de São Francisco
San Juan
Bautista
Eldorado
SANTA CATARINA
Itajaí
Encarnación
Chapecó
Blumenau
Posadas
Erechim
Lajes
Florianópolis
Corrientes
Santa Rosa
Cruz Alta
Passo
Fundo
Tubarão
Laguna
Carazinho
Vacaría
Criciúma
Mercedes
São
Borja
Santiago
Santa
Maria
Caxias do Sul
RIO GRANDE
Uruguaiana
Novo Hamburgo
Uruguaiana
DO SUL
Cachoeira
do Sul
PORTO ALEGRE
Artigas
Santana do
Livramento
Lagoa dos Patos
Salto
Rivera
Bagé
Pelotas
Concordia
Paysandú
Melo
Rio Grande
Sauce
Lagoa Mirim
URUGUAY
Albardão do
João Maria
Mercedes
Durazno
Santa Vitória
do Palmar
UENOS
Trinidad
Florida
Minas
IRES
Quilmes
MONTEVIDEO
Maldonado
La Plata
Rio de la Plata
adillo
Bahía
Samborombón
Zamora
Punta Norte
Azul
Dolores
Tandil
Pinamar
Benito
Juárez
Mar del Plata
Necochea

ATLANTIC

OCEAN

Tropic of Capricorn

Ilha da Trindade
(Brazil)
Ilhas Martin Vaz
(Brazil)

2°
20°
3°
25°
4°
30°
5°
35°
6°
40°
7°
45°
8°
50°
9°
10°

Jason
Is
Mt.
Adam
705 Stanley
est
Ikland
Mt.
700
Usborne
dden
East Falkland
I. Cape
Meredith

Falkland Islands
(U.K.)

Scotia Ridge

Scotia

Shag Rocks
(U.K.)

Cape Alexandra
Grytviken
2934
South Georgia (U.K.)
Mt. Paget
Cape Disappointment

SCOTIA SEA

J 60° K 55° L 50° M 45° N 40° P 35° Q
30° R 25° 55° S 20°

■ over 3 million	● 100 000 – 250 000
▪ 1 – 3 million	◉ 25 000 – 100 000
● 250 000 – 1 million	• under 25 000

——— country capital underline

——— state or province capital underline

143

Polar Regions

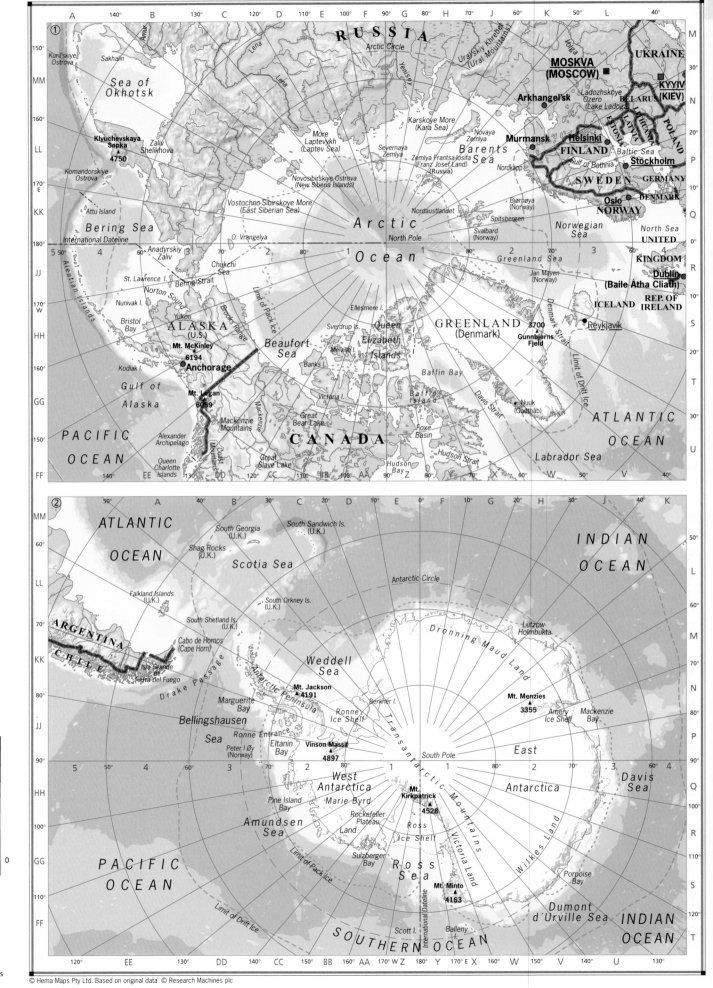

metres	feet
8000	26250
6000	19690
4000	13120
2000	6560
1000	3280
500	1640
200	656
0	0
656	200
3280	1000
6560	2000
13120	4000
19690	6000
26250	8000
feet	metres

■ over 3 million   ● 100 000 – 250 000   —— country capital underline

■ 1 – 3 million   ○ 25 000 – 100 000

● 250 000 – 1 million   · under 25 000

INDEX TO COUNTRY MAPS

GLOSSARY

This is an alphabetically arranged glossary of the geographical terms used on the maps and in this index. The first column shows the map form, the second the language of origin and the third the English translation.

A

açude	Portuguese	reservoir
adası	Turkish	island
akra	Greek	peninsula
alpen	German	mountains
alpes	French	mountains
alpi	Italian	mountains
älven	Swedish	river
archipiélago	Spanish	archipelago
arquipélago	Portuguese	archipelago

B

bab	Arabic	strait
bahía	Spanish	bay
bahir, bahr	Arabic	bay, lake, river
baía	Portuguese	bay
baie	French	bay
baja	Spanish	lower
bandar	Arabic, Somalian, Malay, Persian	harbour, port
baraji	Turkish	dam
barragem	Portuguese	reservoir
ben	Gaelic	mountain
Berg(e)	German	mountain(s)
boğazı	Turkish	strait
Bucht	German	bay
buèayrat	Arabic	lake
burnu, burun	Turkish	cape

C

cabo	Spanish	cape
canal	French, Spanish	canal, channel
canale	Italian	canal, channel
cerro	Spanish	mountain
chott	Arabic	marsh, salt lake
co	Tibetan	lake
collines	French	hills
cordillera	Spanish	range

D

dağ(ı)	Turkish	mountain
dağlar(ı)	Turkish	mountains
danau	Indonesian	lake
daryacheh	Persian	lake
dasht	Persian	desert
djebel	Arabic	mountain(s)
-do	Korean	island

E

embalse	Spanish	reservoir
erg	Arabic	sandy desert
estrecho	Spanish	strait

F

feng	Chinese	mountain
-fjördur	Icelandic	fjord
-flói	Icelandic	bay

G

Gebirge	German	range
golfe	French	bay, gulf
golfo	Italian, Portuguese, Spanish	bay, gulf
göl, gölü	Turkish	lake
gora	Russian	mountain
gory	Russian	mountains
gunong	Malay	mountain
gunung	Indonesian	mountain

H

hai	Chinese	lake, sea
hämün	Persian	lake, marsh
hawr	Arabic	lake
hu	Chinese	lake, reservoir

I

île(s)	French	island(s)
ilha(s)	Portuguese	island(s)
isla(s)	Spanish	island(s)

J

jabal	Arabic	mountain(s)
-järvi	Finnish	lake

jaza'ir	Arabic	islands
jazirat	Arabic	island
jbel	Arabic	mountain
jebel	Arabic	mountain
jezero	Serbo-Croatian	lake
jezioro	Polish	lake
jiang	Chinese	river
-jima	Japanese	island
-joki	Finnish	river
-jökull	Icelandic	glacier

K

kepulauan	Indonesian	islands
khrebet	Russian	mountain range
-ko	Japanese	lake
kolpos	Greek	bay, gulf
körfezi	Turkish	bay, gulf
kryazh	Russian	ridge
küh(ha)	Persian	mountain(s)

L

lac	French	lake
lacul	Romanian	lake
lago	Italian, Portuguese, Spanish	lake
lagoa	Portuguese	lagoon
laguna	Spanish	lagoon, lake
limni	Greek	lake
ling	Chinese	mountain(s), peak
liqeni	Albanian	lake
loch, lough	Gaelic	lake

M

massif	French	mountains
-meer	Dutch	lake, sea
mont	French	mount
monte	Italian, Portuguese, Spanish	mount
montes	Portuguese, Spanish	mountains
monts	French	mountains
muntii	Romanian	mountains
mys	Russian	cape

N

nafud	Arabic	desert
nevado	Spanish	snow-capped mountain
nuruu	Mongolian	mountains
nuur	Mongolian	lake

O

ostrov(a)	Russian	island(s)
ozero	Russian	lake

P

pegunungan	Indonesian	mountains
pelagos	Greek	sea
pendi	Chinese	basin
pesky	Russian	sandy desert
pic	French	peak
pico	Portuguese, Spanish	peak
planalto	Portuguese	plateau
planina	Bulgarian	mountains
poluostrov	Russian	peninsula
puerto	Spanish	harbour, port
puncak	Indonesian	peak
punta	Italian, Spanish	point
puy	French	peak

Q

qundao	Chinese	archipelago

R

ras, râs, ra's	Arabic	cape
represa	Portuguese	dam, reservoir
-rettō	Japanese	archipelago
rio	Portuguese	river
río	Spanish	river

S

sahra	Arabic	desert
salar	Spanish	salt flat
-san	Japanese, Korean	mountain
-sanmaek	Korean	mountains
sebkha	Arabic	salt flat
sebkhet	Arabic	salt marsh
See	German	lake
serra	Portuguese	range
severnaya, severo-	Russian	northern
shan	Chinese	mountain(s)
-shima	Japanese	island
-shotō	Japanese	islands
sierra	Spanish	range

T

tanjona	Malagasy	cape
tanjung	Indonesian	cape
teluk	Indonesian	bay, gulf
ténéré	Berber	desert
-tō	Japanese	island

V

vârful	Romanian	mountain
-vesi	Finnish	lake
vodokhranilishche	Russian	reservoir
volcán	Spanish	volcano

W

wādī	Arabic	watercourse
Wald	German	forest

Z

-zaki	Japanese	cape
zaliv	Russian	bay, gulf

Abbreviations

Ak.	Alaska
Al.	Alabama
Ariz.	Arizona
Ark.	Arkansas
B.C.	British Columbia
Calif.	California
Colo.	Colorado
Conn.	Connecticut
Del.	Delaware
Dem. Rep. of the Congo	Democratic Republic of the Congo
Eng.	England
Fla.	Florida
Ga.	Georgia
Ia.	Iowa
Id.	Idaho
Ill.	Illinois
Ind.	Indiana
Kans.	Kansas
Ky.	Kentucky
La.	Louisiana
Man.	Manitoba
Mass.	Massachusetts
Md.	Maryland
Me.	Maine
M.G.	Mato Grosso
Mich.	Michigan
Minn.	Minnesota
Miss.	Mississippi
Mo.	Missouri
Mont.	Montana
N.B.	New Brunswick
N.C.	North Carolina
N.D.	North Dakota
Nebr.	Nebraska
Nev.	Nevada
Nfld.	Newfoundland
N.H.	New Hampshire
N. Ire.	Northern Ireland
N.J.	New Jersey
N. Mex.	New Mexico
N.W.T.	Northwest Territories
N.Y.	New York
Oh.	Ohio
Okla.	Oklahoma
Ont.	Ontario
Oreg.	Oregon
Orkney Is.	Orkney Islands
Pa.	Pennsylvania
R.G.S.	Rio Grande do Sul
R.I.	Rhode Island
S.C.	South Carolina
Scot.	Scotland
S.D.	South Dakota
Shetland Is.	Shetland Islands
Tenn.	Tennessee
Tex.	Texas
UK	United Kingdom
US	United States
Ut.	Utah
Va.	Virginia
Vt.	Vermont
Wash.	Washington
Wis.	Wisconsin
W. Va.	West Virginia
Wyo.	Wyoming
Y.T.	Yukon Territory

How to use the index

This is an alphabetically arranged index of the places and features that can be found on the maps in this atlas. Each name is generally indexed to the largest scale map on which it appears. If that map covers a double page, the name will always be indexed by the left-hand page number.

Names composed of two or more words are alphabetised as if they were one word.

All names appear in full in the index, except for 'St.' and 'Ste.', which although abbreviated, are indexed as though spelled in full.

Where two or more places have the same name, they can be distinguished from each other by the country or province name which immediately follows the entry. These names are indexed in the alphabetical order of the country or province.

Alternative names, such as English translations, can also be found in the index and are cross-referenced to the map form by the '=' sign. In these cases the names also appear in brackets on the maps.

Settlements are indexed to the position of the symbol, all other features are indexed to the position of the name on the map.

Finding a name on the map

Each index entry contains the name, followed by a symbol indicating the feature type (for example, settlement, river), a page reference and a grid reference:

	Name	Sym	Page	Grid
Name →	Owosso	●	126	D2
	Owyhee	●	124	C2
	Owyhee	✓	124	C2
Symbol →	Oxford, *New Zealand*	●	112	D6
	Oxford, *United Kingdom*		40	A3
	Oxnard	●	130	C2
Page reference →	Oyama	●	72	K5
	Oyapock	✓	140	G3
	Oyem	●	98	G4
Grid reference →	Oyen	●	122	D1

The grid reference locates a place or feature within a rectangle formed by the network of lines of longitude and latitude. A name can be found by referring to the red letters and numbers placed around the maps. First find the letter, which appears along the top and bottom of the map, and then the number, down the sides. The name will be found within the rectangle uniquely defined by that letter and number. A number in brackets preceding the grid reference indicates that the name is to be found within an inset map.

Symbols

X Continent name	**●** Settlement	**✓** Lake, salt lake	**⚬⚬** Island or island group, rocky or coral reef
A Country name	**▲** Mountain, volcano, peak	**▨** Gulf, strait, bay	
a State or province name	**▟▟** Mountain range	**▬** Sea, ocean	**✳** Place of interest
■ Country capital	**▨** Physical region or feature	**▷** Cape, point	**ℋ** Historical or cultural region
□ State or province capital	**✓** River, canal		

Name	Page	Ref
Aïn Bessem	60	P8
Aïn el Hadjel	60	P9
Ain Oussera	102	F1
Ainsa	60	L2
Aïn Sefra	102	E2
Aïn Taya	60	P8
Aïn-Tédélès	60	L8
Aïn Témouchent	60	J9
Airão	140	E4
Aire	56	L8
Air Force Island	122	S3
Airolo	62	D4
Airpanas	87	C4
Aisne	54	F5
Aitape	87	F3
Aitkin	128	B1
Aitutaki	112	K7
Aiud	66	L3
Aix-en-Provence	58	L10
Aix-les-Bains	58	L8
Aizawl	88	F4
Aizkraukle	48	N8
Aizpute	48	L8
Aizu-wakamatsu	82	K5
Ajaccio	64	C7
Aj Bogd Uul	80	B2
Ajdābiyā	100	D1
Ajigasawa	82	L3
Ajka	50	G10
Ajlun	94	C4
Ajmān	95	F4
Ajmer	88	B3
Ajo	132	D2
Akanthou	94	A1
Akaroa	116	D6
Akasha	100	F3
Akashi	82	H6
Akbalyk	76	P8
Akbasty	76	L8
Akçakale	92	H5
Akçakoca	68	P3
Akdağmadeni	92	F4
Aken	52	H5
Aketi	106	C3
Akhalk'alak'i	92	K3
Akhisar	68	K6
Akhmîm	100	F2
Akhty	92	M3
Akimiski Island	122	Q6
Akita	82	L4
Akjoujt	102	C5
Akka	102	D3
Akkajaure	48	J3
Akkeshi	82	N2
'Akko	94	C4
Akmeqit	90	L2
Aknanes	48	(1)B2
Akobo	106	E2
Akola	88	C4
Akonolinga	104	G4
Akordat	100	G4
Akpatok Island	122	T4
Akra Drepano	68	G5
Akra Sounio	68	F7
Akra Spatha	68	F9
Akra Trypiti	68	G9
Åkrehamn	48	C7
Akron	128	D2
Aksaray	92	E4
Aksarka	76	M4
Akşehir	68	P6
Akseki	68	P7
Aksha	78	J6
Akshiy	76	P9
Aksu	76	Q9
Aksuat	76	Q8
Āksum	100	G5
Aktau, Kazakhstan	46	K3
Aktau, Kazakhstan	76	N7
Aktobe	70	L4
Aktogay, Kazakhstan	76	N8
Aktogay, Kazakhstan	76	P8
Aktuma	76	M8
Akula	106	C3
Akulivik	122	R4
Akune	82	F8
Akure	104	F3
Akureyri	48	(1)E2
Akwanga	104	F3
Alabama	130	D3
Alaçam	92	F3
Alaejos	60	E3
Alagoas	140	K5
Alagoinhas	140	K6
Alagón	60	J3
Al Ahmadi	95	C2
Al 'Amārah	90	E3
Alaminos	84	F3
Alamo	126	C3
Alamogordo	132	E2
Alamo Lake	132	D2
Åland	48	K6
Alanya	92	E5
Alappuzha	88	C7
Al Argoub	102	B4
Al Artāwīyah	90	E4
Alaşehir	68	L6
Al 'Ashurīyah	100	H1
Alaska	132	(1)F2
Alaska Peninsula	132	(1)E4
Alaska Range	132	(1)G3
Alassio	62	D6
Alatri	64	H7
Alatyr'	70	J4
Alavus	92	L3
Alaykuu	76	N9
Al 'Ayn	95	F4
Alazeya	78	S2
Alba, Italy	62	D6
Alba, Spain	60	E4
Albacete	60	J5
Alba Iulia	66	L3
Albania	68	B3
Albany	122	Q6
Albany, Australia	114	C6
Albany, Ga., US	130	E3
Albany, Ky., US	130	E2
Albany, N.Y., US	128	F2
Albany, Oreg., US	126	B2
Albardão do João Maria	142	L4
Al Bardī	100	D1
Al Başrah	90	E3
Albatross Bay	114	H2
Albatross Point	116	E4
Al Baydā'	100	D1
Albenga	62	D6
Albert	54	E4
Alberta	122	H6
Albertirsa	50	J10
Albert Kanaal	54	G3
Albert Lea	128	B2
Albert Nile	106	E3
Albi	58	H10
Albina	140	G2
Albino	62	E5
Albion	126	F1
Ålborg Bugt	48	F8
Albox	60	H7
Albstadt	52	E8
Albufeira	60	B7
Āl Bū Kamāl	92	J6
Albuquerque	132	E1
Al Burayj	94	D2
Al Buraymī	90	G5
Alburquerque	60	D5
Albury	114	J7
Al Buşayyah	95	B1
Alcácer do Sal	60	B6
Alcala de Guadaira	60	E7
Alcala de Henares	60	G4
Alcalá la Real	60	G7
Alcamo	64	G11
Alcañiz	60	K3
Alcantarilla	60	J7
Alcaraz	60	H6
Alcaudete	60	F7
Alcazar de San Juan	60	G5
Alcobendas	60	G4
Alcoi	60	K6
Alcolea del Pinar	60	H3
Alcorcón	60	G4
Alcoutim	60	C7
Aldabra Group	108	(2)A2
Aldan	78	M5
Aldan	78	N5
Aldeburgh	54	D2
Alderney	58	C4
Aldershot	54	B3
Aleg	102	C5
Aleksandrov-Sakhalinskiy	78	Q6
Aleksandrovskiy Zavod	78	K6
Aleksandrovskoye	70	Q2
Alekseyevka	76	N7
Aleksinac	66	J6
Alençon	58	F5
Aleppo = Halab	92	G5
Aléria	64	D6
Alès	58	K9
Aleşd	50	M10
Alessandria	62	D6
Ålesund	48	D5
Aleutian Islands	132	(3)B1
Aleutian Range	132	(1)F4
Aleutian Trench	74	W5
Alexander Archipelago	132	(1)K4
Alexander Bay	108	B5
Alexander City	130	D3
Alexandra	116	B7
Alexandreia	68	E4
Alexandria = El Iskandarîya, Egypt	100	E1
Alexandria, Romania	66	N6
Alexandria, La., US	130	C3
Alexandria, Minn., US	128	A1
Alexandria, Va., US	128	E3
Alexandroupoli	68	H4
Alexis Creek	122	G6
Aley	76	Q7
'Āley	94	C3
Aleysk	76	Q7
Al Farwānīyah	95	B2
Al Fāw	95	C2
Alfeld	52	E5
Alföld	66	H2
Alfonsine	62	H6
Alfreton	54	A1
Al Fuhayhil	95	C2
Al-Fujayrah	95	G4
Algeciras	60	E8
Algemes	60	K5
Algena	100	G4
Alger	102	F1
Algeria	102	E3
Al Ghāt	95	A3
Al Ghaydah	90	F6
Alghero	64	C8
Algiers = Alger	102	F1
Algona	128	B2
Al Hadīthah	94	E5
Alhama de Murcia	60	J7
Al Hamar	95	B5
Al Hamīdīyah	94	C2
Al Hammādah al Hamrā'	102	G3
Al Harūj al Aswad	100	C2
Al Hasakah	92	J5
Alhaurmín el Grande	60	F8
Al Hijāz	100	G2
Al Hillah	90	D3
Al Hilwah	95	B5
Al Hoceima	102	E1
Al Hudaydah	100	H5
Al Hufūf	95	C4
Al Humaydah	90	C4
Aliabad	95	F2
Aliağa	68	J6
Aliakmonas	68	E4
Āli Bayramlı	92	N4
Alicante	60	K6
Alice	130	B4
Alice Springs	114	F4
Alicudi	64	J10
Aligarh	88	C3
Alindao	106	C2
Alingås	48	G8
Alisos	132	D2
Aliwal North	108	D6
Al Jabal al Akhdar	100	D1
Al Jaghbūb	100	D2
Al Jālamīd	100	G1
Al Jarah	95	B2
Al Jawf, Libya	100	D3
Al Jawf, Saudi Arabia	100	G2
Aljezur	60	B7
Al Jifārah	95	A5
Al Jubayl	95	C3
Aljustrel	60	B7
Al Kāmil	90	G5
Al Khābūrah	95	G5
Al Khālis	92	L7
Al Kharj	95	B4
Al Khasab	95	G3
Al Khawr	95	D4
Al Khubar	95	D3
Al Khufrah	100	D3
Al Khums	102	H2
Al Khuwayr	95	D3
Al Kir'ānah	95	D4
Alkmaar	54	G2
Al Kūt	90	E3
Al Kuwayt	95	C2
Al Lādhiqīyah	92	F6
Allahabad	88	D3
Allakh-Yun'	78	P4
Alldays	108	D4
Allen	84	G4
Allendale	130	E3
Allentown	128	E2
Aller	52	E4
Aller = Cabañaquinta	60	E1
Alliance	126	F2
Allier	58	J8
Allinge	50	D2
Al Lith	100	H3
Alma, Canada	128	F1
Alma, Nebr., US	126	G2
Alma, Wis., US	128	B2
Almada	60	A6
Almadén	60	F6
Al Madīnah	100	G3
Al Mahbas	102	D3
Al Majma'ah	90	E4
Almalyk	76	M9
Al Manāmah	95	D3
Almansa	60	J6
Al Ma'qil	95	B1
Al Marj	100	D1
Almaty	76	P9
Al Mawşil	92	K5
Al Mazāhimīyah	95	B4
Almazán	60	H3
Almeirim	140	G4
Almelo	54	J2
Almendralejo	60	D6
Almería	60	H8
Al'met'yevsk	76	J7
Almiros	68	E5
Al Mish'āb	95	C2
Almonte	60	D7
Almora	88	C3
Almosa	126	E3
Al Mubarraz	95	C4
Al Mudawwara	94	D7
Al Mukallā	90	E7
Al Mukhā	100	H5
Almuñécar	60	G8
Al Muqdādīyah	92	L7
Al Nu'ayrīyah	95	C3
Alnwick	56	L6
Alonnisos	68	F5
Alor	87	B4
Alor Setar	84	C5
Alotau	114	K2
Alpena	128	D1
Alphen	54	G2
Alpi Lepontine	62	D4
Alpine	132	E2
Alpi Orobie	62	E4
Alps	62	B5
Al Qadmūs	94	D1
Al Qālibah	100	G2
Al Qāmishlī	92	J5
Al Qar'ah	95	B3
Al Qarqar	94	E5
Al Qaryāt	100	B1
Al Qaryatayn	94	E2
Al Qatif	95	C3
Al Qatrūn	100	B3
Al Qunaytirah	94	C3
Al Qunfudhah	100	H4
Al Qurayyāt	100	G1
Al Qurnah	95	B1
Al 'Quşayr, Iraq	95	A1
Al 'Quşayr, Syria	94	D2
Al Qutayfah	94	D3
Als	52	E1
Alsask	122	K6
Alsasua	60	H2
Alsfeld	52	E6
Alta	48	M2
Altaelva	48	M2
Altai Mountains	80	A1
Al Tamīnī	100	D1
Altamira	140	G4
Altamura	64	L8
Altanbulag	78	H6
Altay	76	R7
Altay, China	76	R8
Altay, Mongolia	80	B1
Altdorf	62	D4
Alte Mellum	52	D5
Altenberg	52	J6
Altenburg	52	H6
Altenkirchen	52	J2
Altkirch	62	C3
Alto Garças	140	G7
Alto Molócuè	108	F3
Alton, UK	54	B3
Alton, US	128	B3
Altoona	128	E2
Alto Parnaíba	140	H5
Altötting	62	H2
Altun Shan	76	S10
Alturas	126	B2
Altus	130	B3
Al 'Ubaylah	90	F5
Alūksne	48	P8
Alupka	92	E1
Al 'Uqaylah	100	C1
Alushta	92	F1
Al 'Uthmānīyah	95	C4
Al 'Uwaynāt, Libya	100	B2
Al 'Uwaynāt, Libya	100	D3
Al 'Uwayqīlah	100	H1
Al 'Uzayr	95	B1
Alva	130	B2
Alvarães	140	E4
Älvdalen	48	H6
Älvsbyn	48	L4
Al Wafrā'	95	B2
Al Wajh	100	G2
Al Wannān	95	C3
Alwar	88	C3
Al Wari'ah	95	B3
Alxa Zuoqi	80	D3
Alytus	50	P3
Alzey	52	D7
Alzira	60	K5
Amadi	106	E2
Amādīyah	92	K5
Amadjuak Lake	122	S4
Amadora	60	A6
Amahai	87	C3
Amakusa-Shimo-shima	82	E7
Amaliada	68	D7
Amalner	88	C4
Amamapare	87	E3
Amambaí	142	K3
Amami-Ōshima	74	S7
Amanab	87	F3
Amandola	64	H6
Amantea	64	L9
Amapá	140	G3
Amapá	140	G3
Amarante	140	J5
Amarapura	84	B2
Amareleja	60	C6
Amarillo	132	F1
Amasya	92	F3
Amay	54	H4
Amazar	78	L6
Amazon = Amazonas	138	D4
Amazonas	140	D4
Amazonas	140	E4
Ambala	88	C2
Ambanjä	108	H2
Ambarchik	78	U3
Ambato	140	B4
Ambato Boeny	108	H3
Ambatondrazaka	108	H3
Amberg	52	G7
Ambikapur	88	D4
Ambilobe	108	H2
Ambohimahasoa	108	H4
Amboise	58	G6
Ambon	87	C3
Ambositra	108	H4
Ambovombe	108	H5
Amchitka Island	132	(3)B1
Amderma	76	L4
Amdo	88	F2
Ameland	54	H1
Amengel'dy	76	M7
American Falls	126	D2
American Samoa	112	J7
Americus	130	E3
Amersfoort	54	H2
Amery	122	N5
Amery Ice Shelf	144	(2)M2
Ames	128	B2
Amfilochia	68	D6
Amfissa	68	E6
Amga	78	L5
Amga	78	N4
Amguid	102	F2
Amgun'	78	P6
Amherst	122	U7
Amiens	54	E5
Amirante Islands	108	(2)B2
Amistad Reservoir	132	F3
Amlekhganj	88	D3
Åmli	48	E7
'Amm Adam	100	G5
'Ammān	94	C5
Ammerland	54	K1
Ammersee	62	F2
Ammochostos	92	E6
Ammochostos Bay	94	A1
Amo	84	C2
Amol	90	F2
Amorgos	68	H8
Amos	128	E1
Amourj	102	D5
Ampana	87	B3
Ampanihy	108	G4
Amparai	88	D7

Name	Page	Ref
Ampezzo	62	H4
Amposta	60	L4
Amrān	90	D6
Amravati	88	C4
Amritsar	88	B2
Amroha	88	C3
Amrum	52	D2
Amsterdam, *Netherlands*	54	G2
Amsterdam, *US*	128	F2
Amstetten	62	K2
Am Timan	100	D5
Amudar'ya	76	L9
Amundsen Gulf	122	G2
Amundsen Sea	144	(2)GG3
Amungen	48	H6
Amuntai	86	F3
Amur	78	P6
Amursk	78	P6
Amvrakikos Kolpos	68	C6
Anabanua	87	B3
Anabar	78	J2
Anaconda	126	D1
Anacortes	126	B1
Anadarko	126	G3
Anadolu Dağlari	92	H3
Anadyr'	78	X4
Anadyrskaya Nizmennost'	78	X3
Anadyrskiy Zaliv	78	Y3
Anafi	68	H8
'Ānah	92	J6
Anaheim	132	C2
Anáhuac	132	F3
Analalava	108	H2
Anamur	92	E5
Anan	82	H7
Anantapur	88	C6
Anan'yiv	66	T2
Anapa	92	G1
Anápolis	140	H7
Anār	95	F1
Anārak	90	F3
Anardara	90	H3
Anatolia	68	M6
Añatuya	142	J4
Anchorage	132	(1)H3
Ancona	64	H5
Ancud	142	G7
Anda	80	H1
Andalgalá	142	H4
Åndalsnes	48	D5
Andalusia	130	D3
Andaman Islands	84	A4
Andaman Sea	84	A4
Andapa	108	H2
Andarāb	90	J2
Andenne	54	H4
Andéramboukane	104	E1
Andermatt	62	D4
Andernach	54	K4
Anderson	122	F3
Anderson	130	E3
Andes	138	D5
Andfjorden	48	J2
Andijan	76	N9
Andilamena	108	H3
Andipsara	68	H6
Andkhvoy	90	J2
Andoas	140	B4
Andong	82	E5
Andorra	60	L2
Andorra la Vella	60	M2
Andover	54	A3
Andøya	48	H2
Andradina	142	L3
Andrews	132	F2
Andria	64	L7
Andriamena	108	H3
Andros	68	G7
Andros, *Greece*	68	G7
Andros, *The Bahamas*	130	F5
Andros Town	130	F5
Andrott	88	B6
Andrychów	50	J8
Andújar	60	F7
Andulo	108	B2
Aneto	60	L2
Angara	78	G5
Angarsk	78	G6
Ånge	48	H5
Angel de la Guarda	132	D3
Ángeles	84	G3
Ängelholm	48	G8
Angeln	52	E2
Angermünde	52	K4
Angern	62	M2
Angers	58	E6
Anglesey	56	H8
Angmagssalik = Tasiilaq	122	Z3
Ango	106	D3
Angoche	108	F3
Angohrān	95	G3
Angol	142	G6
Angola	98	E7
Angola	128	D2
Angostura Reservoir	126	F2
Angoulême	58	F8
Angren	76	M9
Anguilla	134	M5
Aniak	132	(1)F3
Anina	66	J4
Anıyaman	92	H5
Ankang	80	D4
Ankara	92	E4
Ankazoabo	108	G4
Anklam	52	J3
Ankpa	104	F3
Ånn	48	G5
Anna	70	H4
Annaba	102	G1
Annaberg-Buchholz	52	H6
An Nabk, *Saudi Arabia*	94	E5
An Nabk, *Syria*	94	D2
An Nafud	100	G2
An Nāiriyah	90	E3
An Najaf	90	D3
Annapolis	128	E3
Annapurna	88	D3
Ann Arbor	128	D2
An Nāsiriyah	100	J1
Annecy	62	B5
Annemasse	62	B4
Anniston	130	D3
Annobón	104	F5
Annonay	58	K8
An Nukhayb	90	D3
Anqing	80	F4
Ansbach	52	F7
Anshan	82	B3
Anshun	80	D5
Ansley	126	G2
Anson	130	B3
Ansongo	102	F5
Antakya	92	G5
Antalaha	108	J2
Antalya	68	N8
Antalya Körfezi	68	N8
Antananarivo	108	H3
Antarctic Peninsula	144	(2)LL3
Antequera	60	F7
Anti-Atlas	102	D3
Antibes	62	C7
Antigo	128	C1
Antigua	134	M5
Antigua and Barbuda	134	M5
Antikythira	68	F9
Antiparos	68	G7
Antipaxoi	68	C5
Antipayuta	76	P4
Antipodes Islands	116	(3)A1
Antlers	130	B3
Antofagasta	142	G3
Antonito	126	E3
Antrim	56	F7
Antropovo	70	H3
Antsalova	108	G3
Antsirabe	108	H3
Antsirañana	108	H2
Antu	82	E2
Antwerp = Antwerpen	54	G3
Antwerpen	54	G3
Anuradhapura	88	D7
Anveh	95	F3
Anxi	80	B2
Anyang, *China*	80	E3
Anyang, *South Korea*	82	D5
Anyuysk	78	U3
Anzhero-Sudzhensk	76	R6
Anzi	106	C4
Anzio	64	G7
Aoga-shima	82	K7
Aomori	82	L3
Aoraki (Mount Cook)	116	C6
Aosta	62	C5
Aoukâr	102	C5
Aoukoukar	104	C1
Apalachee Bay	130	E4
Apalachicola	130	D4
Aparri	84	G3
Apatin	66	F4
Apatity	70	F1
Ape	48	P8
Apeldoorn	54	H2
Api	88	D2
Apia	112	J7
Apoera	140	F2
Apolda	52	G5
Apollo Bay	114	H7
Aporé	140	G5
Apostle Islands	128	B1
Apoteri	140	F3
Appalachian Mountains	130	E3
Appennino	64	G5
Appennino Abruzzese	64	H6
Appennino Calabro	64	K10
Appennino Lucano	64	K8
Appennino Tosco-Emiliano	62	E6
Appennino Umbro-Marchigiano	64	H6
Appleton	128	C2
Aprilia	64	G7
Apure	140	D2
Apurimac	140	C6
Āqā	90	H3
'Aqaba	94	C7
Aquidauana	140	F8
Ara	88	D3
Aracaju	140	K6
Aracati	140	K4
Araçatuba	140	G8
Aracuca	134	L7
Arad	66	J3
Arādah	90	F5
Arafura Sea	87	D5
Aragarças	140	G7
Araguaia	138	F4
Araguaína	140	H5
Araguari	140	H7
Araguatins	140	H5
Arāk	90	E3
Arak	102	F3
Aral Sea	76	K5
Aral'sk	70	M5
Aranda de Duero	60	G3
Arandjelovac	66	H5
Aran Island	56	D6
Aran Islands	56	B8
Aranjuez	60	G4
Aranos	108	B4
Aranyaprathet	84	C4
Araouane	102	E5
Arapahoe	126	G2
Arapiraca	140	K5
'Ar'ar	90	D3
Araras	140	G5
Ararat	92	L4
Arauca	140	D2
Araxá	140	H7
Araz	92	L4
Arbīl	92	K5
Arbon	62	E3
Arbre du Ténéré	102	G5
Arbroath	56	K5
Arcachon	58	D9
Arcadia	130	E4
Arcata	126	B2
Archidona	60	F7
Archipelago of the Recherche	114	D6
Archipel de la Société	112	L7
Archipel des Tuamotu	112	M7
Archipiélago de Camagüey	134	J4
Archipiélago de la Reina Adelaida	142	F9
Archipiélago de los Chonos	142	F7
Arco, *Italy*	62	F5
Arco, *US*	126	D2
Arcos de la Frontera	60	E8
Arctic Bay	122	P2
Arctic Ocean	144	(1)A1
Arctic Red River	122	E3
Arda	68	H3
Ardabīl	92	N4
Ardahan	92	K3
Årdalstangen	48	D6
Ardas	68	J3
Ardatov	70	J4
Ardennes	54	G4
Ardestān	90	F3
Ardila	60	C7
Ardmore	124	G5
Aredo	87	D3
Areia Branca	140	K5
Arendal	48	E7
Arenys de Mar	60	N3
Areopoli	68	E8
Arequipa	140	C7
Arere	140	G4
Arévalo	60	F3
Arezzo	64	F5
Argan	76	R9
Argenta	62	G6
Argentan	54	B6
Argentera	62	B6
Argentina	142	H6
Argenton-sur-Creuse	58	G7
Argeş	66	N5
Argolikos Kolpos	68	E7
Argos	68	E7
Argos Orestiko	68	D4
Argostoli	68	C6
Argun'	78	K6
Argungu	104	E2
Argunsk	78	L6
Argyll	56	G5
Ar Horqin Qi	80	G2
Ariano Irpino	64	K7
Ari Atoll	88	B8
Arica	140	C7
Ariège	58	G11
Arihge	60	M2
Arinos	140	F6
Aripuanã	140	E5
Aripuanã	140	E5
Ariquemes	140	E5
Arizona	132	D2
Arjäng	48	G7
Arjasa	86	F4
Arka	78	Q5
Arkadak	70	H4
Arkadelphia	130	C3
Arkalyk	76	M7
Arkansas	130	C3
Arkansas	130	C3
Arkansas City	130	B2
Arkhalts'ikhe	92	K3
Arkhangel'sk	70	H2
Arkhipelag Nordenshel'da	76	R2
Arklow	56	F9
Arkoudi	68	C6
Arles	58	K10
Arlington, *Oreg., US*	126	B1
Arlington, *Tex., US*	130	B3
Arlington, *Va., US*	128	E3
Arlit	102	G5
Arlon	54	H4
Armagh	56	F7
Armavir	92	J1
Armenia	92	K3
Armenia	140	B3
Armentières	54	E4
Armidale	114	K6
Armstrong	122	P6
Armyans'k	70	F5
Arnedo	60	H2
Arnett	130	B2
Arnhem	54	H3
Arnhem Land	114	F2
Arno	62	F7
Arnøy	48	G3
Arnprior	128	E1
Arnsberg	54	L3
Arnstadt	52	F6
Aroab	108	B5
Arolsen	52	L5
Aroma	100	G4
Arorae	112	H6
Arquipélago dos Bijagós	104	A2
Ar Ramādī	90	D3
Ar Ramlah	94	C7
Arran	56	G5
Ar Raqqah	92	H6
Arras	54	E4
Arrasate	60	H1
Ar Rastan	94	D2
Ar Rawdah	90	E7
Ar Rayn	95	A5
Arrecife	102	C3
Ar Riyāḍ	90	E5
Arrow Lake	126	C1
Arroyo Grande	132	B1
Ar Ruşāfah	92	H6
Ar Rustāq	90	G5
Ar Ruṭba	90	D3
Ar Ruways	90	F5
Årsandøy	48	G4
Arta, *Greece*	68	C5
Arta, *Mallorca*	60	P5
Artem	82	G2
Artemovsk	76	S7
Artemovskiy	78	K5
Artesia	132	F2
Arthur	126	F2
Arthur's Town	130	F5
Artigas	142	K5
Artillery Lake	122	J4
Artsyz	66	S4
Artux	76	P10
Artvin	92	J3
Artyk	78	Q4
Aru	112	D6
Arua	106	E3
Aruba	134	K6
Arumā	140	E4
Arusha	106	F4
Arvayheer	80	C1
Arviat	122	N4
Arvidsjaur	48	K4
Arvika	48	G7
Ary	76	Y3
Aryta	78	M4
Arzamas	70	H3
Arzew	60	K9
Arzignano	62	G5
Asahi-dake	82	M2
Asahikawa	82	M2
Āsalē	100	G5
Asansol	88	E4
Asarum	50	D1
Asbest	70	M3
Ascea	64	K8
Ascension	98	B6
Ascensión	140	E7
Aschaffenburg	52	E7
Aschersleben	52	G5
Ascoli Piceno	64	H6
Āsela	106	F2
Åsele	48	J4
Asenovgrad	68	G3
Asha	70	L3
Ashburton	116	C6
Ashdod	94	B5
Asherton	130	B4
Asheville	128	D3
Ashford	54	C3
Ash Fork	132	D1
Ashgabat	90	G2
Ashington	56	L6
Ashizuri-misaki	82	G7
Ashkhabad = Ashgabat	90	G2
Ashland, *Kans., US*	126	G3
Ashland, *Ky., US*	128	D3
Ashland, *Mont., US*	126	E1
Ashland, *Oreg., US*	126	B2
Ashland, *Wis., US*	128	B1
Ashoro	82	M2
Ashqelon	94	B5
Ash Shadādah	92	J5
Ash Shāriqah	95	F4
Ash Sharqāt	92	K6
Ash Shihr	90	E7
Ash Shu'bah	95	A2
Ash Shuqayq	100	H4
Ash Shurayf	100	G2
Ash Shuwayrif	102	H3
Ashtabula	128	D2
Ashuanipi	122	T6
Ashuanipi Lake	122	T6
Asia	112	B2
Āsika	88	D5
Asilah	102	D1
Asinara	64	C7
Asino	76	R6
Asīr	100	H3
Aşkale	92	J4
Askim	48	F7
Askot	88	D3
Asmara	100	G4
Åsnen	48	H8
Āsosa	106	E1
Aspang Markt	62	M3
Aspe	60	K6
Aspermont	132	F2
As Pontes de Garcia Rodriguez	60	C1
As Sa'an	94	E1
Assab	100	H5
Aş Şalīf	90	D6
As Salmān	90	E3
As Salwā	95	D4
Assamakka	102	G5
Aş Şanamayn	94	D3
As Sarīr	100	D2
Asse	54	G4
Assemini	64	C9
Assen	54	J2
Assens	52	E1
As Sīb	95	H5
As Sidrah	100	C1
Assiniboia	122	K7
Assiniboine	122	M7
Assis	142	L3
Assisi	64	G5
As Sukhnah	92	H6
As Sulaymānīyah	92	L6

152

Bosa 64 C8
Bosanska Dubica 66 D4
Bosanska Gradiška 66 E4
Bosanska Kostajnica 62 M5
Bosanska Krupa 66 D5
Bosanski Brod 66 F4
Bosanski Novi 66 D4
Bosanski Petrovac 66 D5
Bosansko Grahovo 62 M6
Boşca 66 J4
Bose 84 D2
Bosilegrad 66 K7
Boskovice 50 F8
Bosna 66 F5
Bosnia and Herzegovina 66 E5
Bosobolo 106 B3
Bosporus = İstanbul Boğazı 68 M3
Bosporus 90 A1
Bossambélé 106 B2
Bossangoa 106 B2
Bossier City 130 C3
Bosten Hu 76 R9
Boston, *UK* 56 M9
Boston, *US* 128 F2
Botevgrad 66 L7
Botlikh 90 E1
Botna 66 R3
Botoşani 66 P2
Botou 80 F3
Botrange 54 J4
Botswana 108 C4
Bottrop 54 J3
Bou Ahmed 60 F9
Bouaké 104 C3
Bouar 106 B2
Bouârfa 102 E2
Boufarik 60 N8
Bougainville Island 112 F6
Bougainville Reef 114 J3
Bougouni 104 C2
Bougzoul 60 N9
Bouira 102 F1
Bou Ismaïl 60 N8
Bou Izakarn 102 D3
Boujdour 102 C3
Bou Kadir 60 M8
Boukra 102 C3
Boulder 126 E2
Boulder City 132 D1
Boulia 114 G4
Boulogne-sur-Mer 54 D4
Bouna 104 D3
Boundiali 104 C3
Bounty Islands 112 H10
Bourem 102 E5
Bourg 58 E8
Bourg-de-Piage 58 L9
Bourg-en-Bresse 58 L7
Bourges 58 H6
Bourgoin-Jallieu 58 L8
Bourke 114 J6
Bournemouth 56 L11
Bou Saâda 102 F1
Bousso 100 C5
Boussu 54 F4
Boutilimit 102 C5
Bouzghaïa 60 M8
Bowbells 126 F1
Bowen 114 J4
Bowie, *Ariz., US* 132 E2
Bowie, *Tex., US* 132 G2
Bowkan 92 M5
Bowling Green, *Fla., US* 130 E4
Bowling Green, *Ky., US* 130 D2
Bowling Green, *Mo., US* 130 C2
Bowman 126 F1
Bowman Bay 122 R3
Bo Xian 80 F4
Boxwood Hill 114 C6
Boyabat 92 F3
Boyang 80 F5
Boyarka 78 F2
Boyle 56 D8
Boysen Reservoir 126 E2
Boyuibe 142 J3
Bozcaada 68 H5
Boz Dağ 68 M7
Bozeman 126 D1
Bozkır 68 Q7
Bozoum 106 B2
Bozova 92 H5
Bozüyük 68 N5
Bra 62 C6
Brač 66 D6
Bracciano 64 G6
Bräcke 48 H5
Bracknell 54 B3
Brad 66 K3
Bradano 64 L8
Bradford 56 L8
Brady 130 B3
Braga 60 B3
Bragança, *Brazil* 140 H4
Bragança, *Portugal* 60 D3
Brahmapur 88 D5
Brahmaputra 88 F3
Brăila 66 Q4
Brainerd 128 B1
Braintree 54 C3
Brake 52 D3
Bramming 52 D1
Brampton 128 E2
Bramsche 52 D4
Branco 140 E3
Brandberg 108 A4
Brandenburg 52 H4
Brandenton 130 E4
Brandon 122 M7
Brandvlei 108 C5
Brandýs 50 D7
Braniewo 50 J3
Brasileia 140 D6
Brasília 140 H7
Braslaw 48 P9
Braşov 66 N4
Bratislava 50 G9
Bratsk 78 G5
Bratskoye Vodokhranilishche 78 G5
Brattleboro 128 F2
Braţul 66 R4
Bratunac 66 G5
Braunau 62 J2
Braunschweig 52 F4
Brawley 132 C2
Bray 56 F8
Brazil 138 F4
Brazzaville 106 B4
Brčko 66 F5
Brda 50 G4
Bream Bay 116 E2
Breckenridge 132 G2
Břeclav 50 F9
Breda 54 G3
Bredasdorp 108 C6
Bredstedt 52 E2
Bredy 70 M4
Bree 54 H3
Bree 58 L2
Bregenz 62 E3
Breiðafjörður 48 (1)A2
Bremangerlandet 48 B6
Bremen, *Germany* 52 D3
Bremen, *US* 130 D3
Bremerhaven 52 D3
Bremerton 126 B1
Bremervörde 52 E3
Brenham 130 B3
Brennero 62 G4
Breno 62 F5
Brentwood 54 C3
Brescia 62 F5
Breslau = Wrocław 50 G6
Bressanone 62 G4
Bressay 56 M1
Bressuire 58 E7
Brest, *Belarus* 70 D4
Brest, *France* 58 A5
Breteuil 54 E5
Bretten 52 D7
Breves 140 G4
Brewarrina 114 J5
Brewton 130 D3
Brežice 66 C4
Brézina 102 F2
Brezno 50 J9
Bria 106 C2
Briançon 62 B6
Briceni 66 Q1
Bridgend 56 J10
Bridgeport, *Calif., US* 132 C1
Bridgeport, *Conn., US* 128 F2
Bridgeport, *Nebr., US* 126 F2
Bridgetown 140 F1
Bridgewater 122 U8
Bridgwater 56 J10
Bridlington 56 M7
Brienzer See 62 D4
Brig 62 C4
Brigham City 126 D2
Brighton, *UK* 54 B4
Brighton, *US* 126 F3
Brignoles 62 B7
Brikama 104 A2
Brilon 52 D5
Brindisi 64 M8
Brinkley 130 C3
Brisbane 114 K5
Bristol, *UK* 56 K10
Bristol, *US* 130 E2
Bristol Bay 132 (1)E4
Bristol Channel 56 H10
British Columbia 122 F5
Britstown 108 C6
Brive-la-Gaillarde 58 G8
Briviesca 60 G2
Brixham 56 J11
Brlik 76 N9
Brno 50 F8
Broad Sound 114 J4
Broadus 126 E1
Brockton 128 F2
Brockville 128 E2
Brod 66 J9
Brodeur Peninsula 122 P2
Brodick 56 G6
Brodnica 50 J4
Broken Arrow 134 E1
Broken Bow 130 C3
Broken Hill 114 H6
Brokopondo 140 F2
Bromölla 50 D1
Bromsgrove 56 K9
Brønderslev 48 E8
Broni 62 E5
Brooke's Point 84 F5
Brookhaven 124 H5
Brookhaven 130 C3
Brookhaven 134 F2
Brookings, *Oreg., US* 126 B2
Brookings, *S.D., US* 126 G2
Brooks 122 J6
Brooks Range 132 (1)F2
Brooksville 130 E4
Broome 114 D3
Brora 56 J3
Brösarp 48 H9
Broughton Island 122 U3
Brovary 70 F4
Brownfield 132 F2
Browning 126 D1
Brownsville, *Tenn., US* 130 D2
Brownsville, *Tex., US* 130 B4
Brownwood 130 B3
Bruchsal 52 D7
Bruck, *Austria* 62 L3
Bruck, *Austria* 62 M2
Bruck an der Mur 66 C2
Brugge 54 F3
Brühl 54 J4
Bruint 88 G3
Brumado 140 J6
Brumath 62 C2
Bruneau 126 C2
Brunei 86 E2
Brunflo 48 H5
Brunico 64 F2
Brunsbüttel 52 E3
Brunswick, *Ga., US* 130 E3
Brunswick, *Me., US* 128 G2
Bruntal 50 G8
Brush 126 F2
Brussels = Bruxelles 54 G4
Bruxelles 54 G4
Bryan 130 B3
Bryanka 76 S6
Bryansk 70 F4
Brzeg 50 G7
Brzeg Dolny 50 F6
Brzeziny 50 J6
B-Spandau 50 C5
Bubi 108 E4
Bucak 92 D5
Bucaramanga 140 C2
Buchanan 104 B3
Buchan Gulf 122 S2
Bucharest = Bucureşti 66 P5
Buchen 52 E7
Buchholz 52 E3
Buchy 58 M5
Bückeburg 52 E4
Bučovice 50 F8
Bucureşti 66 P5
Budapest 66 G2
Bude 56 H11
Budennovsk 92 L1
Büdingen 52 E6
Budoni 64 D8
Budrio 62 G6
Budva 66 F7
Buenaventura, *Colombia* 140 B3
Buenaventura, *Mexico* 132 E3
Buena Vista 126 E3
Buenos Aires 142 K5
Buffalo, *Okla., US* 130 B2
Buffalo, *N.Y., US* 128 E2
Buffalo, *S.D., US* 126 F1
Buffalo, *Tex., US* 130 B3
Buffalo, *Wyo., US* 126 E2
Buffalo Lake 122 J4
Buffalo Narrows 122 K5
Buftea 66 N5
Bug 50 L5
Bugojno 66 E5
Bugrino 76 H4
Bugsuk 84 F5
Bugul'ma 70 K4
Buguruslan 70 K4
Buhayrat al Asad 92 H5
Buhayrat ath Tharthār 92 K6
Buhuşi 66 P3
Builth Wells 56 J9
Buinsk 70 J3
Buir Nuur 80 F1
Bujanovac 66 J7
Buje 62 J5
Bujumbura 106 D4
Bukachacha 78 K6
Bukavu 106 D4
Bukhara 90 H2
Bukkittinggi 86 C3
Bukoba 106 E4
Bula, *Indonesia* 87 D3
Bula, *Papua New Guinea* 87 F4
Bülach 62 D3
Bulan 84 G4
Būlāq 100 F2
Bulawayo 108 D4
Buldir Island 78 X6
Bulgan 78 G7
Bulgaria 66 M7
Buli 87 C2
Bulle 62 C4
Bullhead City 132 D1
Bulls 116 E5
Bulukumba 87 B4
Bulun 78 M2
Bumba 106 C3
Bumbeşti Jiu 66 L4
Buna 106 F3
Bunbury 114 C6
Buncrana 56 E6
Bunda 106 E4
Bundaberg 114 K4
Bünde 52 D4
Bungunya 114 J5
Bunia 106 E3
Bunkie 130 C3
Bunnell 130 E4
Bünyan 92 F4
Bu ol Kheyr 95 D2
Buôn Mê Thuột 84 D4
Buotama 78 M4
Bura 106 F4
Buran 76 R8
Buranj 88 D2
Burao 106 H2
Burāq 94 D3
Buraydah 90 D4
Burco 100 J6
Burdur 92 D5
Burdur Gölü 68 N7
Burē 100 G5
Büren 54 L3
Burg 52 G4
Burgas 66 Q7
Burgaski Zaliv 66 Q7
Burgdorf 62 C3
Burghausen 62 H2
Burglengenfeld 52 H7
Burgos 60 G2
Burgsvik 48 K8
Burhaniye 68 K5
Burhanpur 88 C4
Burjassot 60 K5
Burj Şāfitā 94 D2
Burketown 114 G3
Burkeville 128 E3
Bur-Khaybyt 78 P3
Burkina 104 D2
Burlin 70 K4
Burlington, *Colo., US* 132 F1
Burlington, *Ia., US* 128 B2
Burlington, *Vt., US* 128 F2
Burma = Myanmar 84 B2
Burnet 130 B3
Burney 126 B2
Burnie 114 J8
Burns 126 C2
Burns Junction 126 C2
Burns Lake 122 F6
Burqin 76 R8
Burra 114 G6
Burrel 68 C3
Bursa 68 M4
Būr Safāga 100 F2
Būr Sa'īd 100 F1
Bur Sudan 100 G4
Burtnieks 48 N8
Burton-upon-Trent 56 L9
Buru 87 C3
Burundi 106 D4
Bururi 106 D4
Burwell 126 G2
Buryatiya 78 J6
Bury St. Edmunds 54 C2
Būshehr 95 D2
Bushire = Būshehr 95 D2
Businga 106 C3
Busira 106 C4
Buşrá ash Shām 94 D4
Bussum 54 H2
Busto Arsizio 62 D5
Buta 106 C3
Butare 106 D4
Butaritari 112 H5
Bute 56 G6
Butembo 106 D3
Búðardalur 48 (1)C2
Buton 87 B3
Butte, *Mont., US* 126 D1
Butte, *Nebr., US* 126 G2
Butuan 84 H5
Butwal 88 D3
Butzbach 52 D6
Bützow 52 G3
Buulobarde 106 H3
Buur Gaabo 106 G4
Buurhabaka 106 G3
Buxtehude 52 E3
Buxton 54 A1
Buy 70 H3
Buynaksk 92 M2
Büyükada 68 L4
Büyükçekmece 68 L4
Buzai Gumbad 90 K2
Buzançais 58 G7
Buzău 66 P4
Buzău 66 Q4
Buzuluk 70 K4
Byala, *Bulgaria* 66 N6
Byala, *Bulgaria* 66 Q7
Byala Slatina 66 L6
Byam Martin Island 122 L2
Byaroza 48 N10
Bydgoszcz 50 H4
Bygdin 48 D6
Bygland 48 D7
Bykovskiy 78 M2
Bylot Island 122 R2
Byskeälven 48 L4
Bystřice 50 G8
Bystrzyca Kłodzka 50 F7
Bytatay 78 N3
Bytča 50 H8
Bytom 50 H7
Bytów 50 G3
Bzura 50 J5

C

Caaguazú 142 K4
Caballococha 140 C5
Caballo Reservoir 132 E2
Cabañaquinta 60 E1
Cabanatuan 84 G3
Cabano 128 G1
Cabdul Qaadir 100 H5
Cabeza del Buey 60 E6
Cabezas 140 E7
Cabimas 140 C1
Cabinda 104 G6
Cabinda 104 G6
Cabo Bascuñán 142 G4
Cabo Beata 134 K5
Cabo Camarón 134 G5
Cabo Carvoeiro 60 A5
Cabo Catoche 134 G4
Cabo Corrientes, *Colombia* 140 B2
Cabo Corrientes, *Mexico* 134 C4
Cabo Corrubedo 60 A2
Cabo Cruz 134 J5
Cabo de Espichel 60 A6
Cabo de Gata 60 H8
Cabo de Hornos 142 H10
Cabo de la Nao 60 L6
Cabo Delgado 108 G2
Cabo de Palos 60 K7

Cabo de São Roque 140 K5
Cabo de Sao Tomé 142 N3
Cabo de São Vicente 60 A7
Cabo de Trafalgar 60 D8
Cabo dos Bahías 142 H8
Cabo Fisterra 60 A2
Cabo Frio 142 N3
Cabo Gracias á Dios 134 H6
Cabo Mondego 60 A4
Cabo Norte 140 H3
Cabo Orange 140 G3
Cabo Ortegal 60 B1
Cabo Peñas 60 E1
Caborca 132 D2
Cabo Rojo 134 E4
Cabo Roxo 104 A2
Cabo San Diego 142 H9
Cabo San Francisco de Paula 142 H8
Cabo San Juan 104 F4
Cabo San Lucas 124 D7
Cabo Santa Elena 134 J7
Cabo Tortosa 60 L4
Cabo Tres Puntas 142 H8
Cabot Strait 122 U7
Cabrera 60 N5
Čačak 66 H6
Cáceres, *Brazil* 140 F7
Cáceres, *Spain* 60 D5
Cacheu 104 A2
Cachimbo 140 G5
Cachoeira do Sul 142 L4
Cachoeiro de Itapemirim 140 J8
Cacola 108 B2
Caconda 108 B2
Čadca 50 H8
Cadillac, *Mich., US* 128 C2
Cadillac, *Mont., US* 124 E2
Cádiz 60 D8
Caen 54 B5
Caernarfon 56 H8
Cagayan de Oro 84 G5
Cagli 62 H7
Cagliari 64 D9
Cagnes-sur-Mer 62 C7
Caguas 134 L5
Cahama 108 A3
Cahersiveen 56 B10
Cahir 56 E9
Cahors 58 G9
Cahuapanas 140 B5
Cahul 66 R4
Caia 108 F3
Caianda 108 C2
Caicos Islands 134 K4
Cairns 114 J3
Cairo = El Qâhira, *Egypt* 100 F1
Cairo, *US* 130 D2
Cairo Montenotte 62 D6
Caiundo 108 B3
Cajamarca 140 B5
Čakovec 66 D3
Calabar 104 F3
Calabozo 140 D2
Calabro 64 L9
Calafat 66 K6
Calagua Islands 84 G4
Calahorra 60 J2
Calais 54 D4
Calama, *Brazil* 140 E5
Calama, *Peru* 142 H3
Calamar 140 C3
Calamian Group 84 F4
Calamocha 60 J4
Călan 66 L4
Calanscio Sand Sea 100 D2
Calapan 84 G4
Călăraşi, *Moldova* 66 R2
Călăraşi, *Romania* 66 Q5
Calatafim 64 G11
Calatayud 60 J3
Calauag 84 G4
Calbayog 84 G4
Calçoene 140 G3
Calcutta = Kolkata 88 E4
Caldas da Rainha 60 A5
Caldera 142 G4
Caldwell, *Id., US* 126 C2
Caldwell, *Kans., US* 130 B2
Calf of Man 56 H7
Calgary 122 J6
Calhoun 130 E3
Calhoun City 130 D3
Calhoun Falls 130 E3
Cali 140 B3
Calicut = Kozhikode 88 C6
Caliente 126 D3
California 124 B4
Calilabad 92 N4
Callao 140 B6
Caloundra 114 K5
Caltagirone 64 J11
Caltanissetta 64 J11
Caluquembe 108 A2
Caluula 106 J1
Calvi 64 C6
Calvin 130 B3
Calvinia 108 B6
Calw 62 D2
Camaçari 140 K6
Camacupa 108 B2
Camagüey 134 J4
Camaiore 62 F7
Camana 140 C7
Camargue 58 K10
Camariñas 60 A1
Camarones 142 H7
Ca Mau 84 D5
Camberley 56 M10
Cambodia 84 C4
Cambrai 54 F4
Cambre 60 B1
Cambria 126 B3
Cambrian Mountains 56 H10
Cambridge, *New Zealand* 116 E3
Cambridge, *UK* 56 N9
Cambridge, *Md., US* 128 E3
Cambridge, *Mass., US* 128 F2
Cambridge, *Oh., US* 128 D3
Cambridge Bay 122 K3
Cambrils 60 M3
Camden, *Ark., US* 130 C3
Camden, *S.C., US* 130 E3
Cameron, *La., US* 130 C4
Cameron, *Mo., US* 130 C2
Cameron, *Tex., US* 130 B3
Cameroon 104 G3
Cametá 140 H4
Çamiçigölü 68 K7
Caminha 60 B3
Camiranga 140 H4
Camocim 140 J4
Camooweal 114 G3
Camopi 140 G3
Campbell Island 116 (2)C2
Campbell River 122 F7
Campbellsville 128 C3
Campbellton 128 G1
Campbeltown 56 G6
Campeche 134 F5
Câmpeni 66 L3
Câmpia Turzii 66 L3
Câmpina 66 N4
Campina Grande 140 L5
Campinas 142 M3
Campobasso 64 J7
Campo de Criptana 60 G5
Campo de Diauarum 140 G6
Campo Gallo 142 J4
Campo Grande 142 L3
Campo Maior 140 J4
Campo Mourão 142 L3
Campos 142 N3
Câmpulung 66 N4
Câmpulung Moldovenesc 66 N2
Cam Ranh 84 D4
Çan 68 K4
Canada 120 M4
Canadian 132 F1
Canadian 132 F1
Çanakkale 68 J4
Çanakkale Boğazı 68 J4
Canal de Panamá 134 J7
Cananea 132 D2
Canary Islands = Islas Canarias 98 A3
Canary Islands = Islas Canarias 102 B3
Cañaveras 60 H4
Canberra 114 J7
Cancún 134 G4
Çandarli Körfezi 68 J6
Candelaro 66 C8
Candlemas Island 138 J9
Cangamba 108 B2
Cangas 60 B2
Cangas de Narcea 60 D1
Cangyuan 84 B2
Cangzhou 80 F3
Canicatti 64 H11
Canindé 140 K4
Çankiri 92 E3
Canna 56 F4
Cannanore 88 B6
Cannanore 88 C6
Cannes 62 C7
Cannock 54 A2
Canon City 132 E1
Cantanduanes 84 G4
Canterbury 54 D3
Canterbury Bight 116 C7
Canterbury Plains 116 C6
Cân Tho 84 D5
Canto do Buriti 140 J5
Canton, *Miss., US* 130 D3
Canton, *Oh., US* 130 E1
Canton, *S.D., US* 126 G2
Canumã 140 F4
Canumã 140 F5
Canutama 140 E5
Canyon 132 F1
Canyon Ferry Lake 126 D1
Cao Bǎng 84 D2
Caorle 62 H5
Cap Blanc 64 D11
Cap Bon 102 H1
Cap Corse 64 D5
Cap d'Agde 58 J10
Cap d'Antifer 54 C5
Cap de Fer 102 G1
Cap de Formentor 60 P5
Cap de la Hague 58 D4
Cap-de-la-Madeleine 128 F1
Cap de Nouvelle-France 122 S4
Cap de ses Salines 60 P5
Cap des Trois Fourches 60 H9
Cape Agulhas 108 C6
Cape Alexandra 142 P9
Cape Andreas 90 B2
Cape Apostolos Andreas 92 F6
Cape Arid 114 D6
Cape Arnaoutis 92 D6
Cape Arnhem 114 G2
Cape Barren Island 114 J8
Cape Bauld 122 V6
Cape Blanco 126 B2
Cape Borda 114 G7
Cape Breton Island 122 U7
Cape Brett 116 E2
Cape Byron 114 K5
Cape Campbell 116 E5
Cape Canaveral 130 E4
Cape Canaveral 130 E4
Cape Carnot 114 F6
Cape Charles 128 E3
Cape Chidley 122 U4
Cape Christian 122 T2
Cape Churchill 122 N5
Cape Clear 56 C10
Cape Cleare 132 (1)H4
Cape Coast 104 D3
Cape Cod 128 G2
Cape Columbine 108 B6
Cape Colville 116 E3
Cape Comorin 88 C7
Cape Constantine 132 (1)E4
Cape Coral 130 E4
Cape Crawford 114 G3
Cape Croker 114 F2
Cape Dalhousie 132 (1)L1
Cape Direction 114 H2
Cape Disappointment 142 P9
Cape Dominion 122 R3
Cape Dorchester 122 Q3
Cape Dorset 122 R4
Cape Dyer 122 U3
Cape Egmont 116 D4
Cape Eleaia 94 B1
Cape Farewell, *Greenland* 120 F4
Cape Farewell, *New Zealand* 116 D5
Cape Fear 130 F3
Cape Finisterre = Cabo Fisterra 60 A2
Cape Flattery, *Australia* 114 J2
Cape Flattery *United States* 126 A1
Cape Forestier 114 J8
Cape Foulwind 116 C5
Cape Fria 108 A3
Cape Girardeau 128 C3
Cape Greko 92 F6
Cape Grenville 114 H2
Cape Grim 114 H8
Cape Harrison 122 V6
Cape Hatteras 130 F2
Cape Henrietta Maria 122 Q5
Cape Horn = Cabo de Hornos 142 H10
Cape Howe 114 K7
Cape Inscription 114 B5
Cape Jaffa 114 G7
Cape Karikari 116 D2
Cape Kellett 122 F2
Cape Kidnappers 116 F4
Cape Leeuwin 114 B6
Cape Lévêque 114 D3
Cape Londonderry 114 E2
Cape Lookout 134 J2
Cape May 128 F3
Cape Melville 114 H2
Cape Mendenhall 132 (1)D4
Cape Mendocino 126 A2
Cape Mercy 122 U4
Cape Meredith 142 J9
Cape Naturaliste 114 B6
Capenda-Camulemba 108 B1
Cape Negrais 84 A3
Cape Nelson 114 H7
Cape Newenham 132 (1)E4
Cape of Good Hope 108 B6
Cape Palliser 116 E5
Cape Palmas 104 C4
Cape Parry 122 G2
Cape Providence 116 A8
Cape Race 120 G5
Cape Ray 122 V7
Cape Reinga 116 D2
Cape Romanzof 132 (1)D3
Cape Runaway 116 G3
Cape Sable 122 T8
Cape St. Elias 132 (1)J4
Cape St. Francis 108 C6
Cape San Agustin 84 H5
Cape San Blas 130 D4
Cape Saunders 116 C7
Cape Scott 114 E1
Cape Stephens 116 D5
Cape Terawhiti 116 E5
Cape Three Points 104 D4
Cape Town 108 B6
Cape Turnagain 116 F5
Cape Verde 104 (1)B2
Cape Wessel 114 G2
Cape Wrangell 78 W6
Cape Wrath 56 G3
Cape York 114 H2
Cape York Peninsula 114 H2
Cap Figalo 60 J9
Cap Fréhel 58 C5
Cap Gris-Nez 54 D4
Cap-Haïtien 134 K5
Cap Juby 102 C3
Čapljina 66 E6
Cap Lopez 104 F5
Cap Negro 60 E9
Capo Carbonara 64 D10
Capo Colonna 64 M9
Capo Gallo 64 H10
Capo Granitola 64 G11
Capo Murro di Porco 64 K11
Capo Palinuro 64 J8
Capo Passero 64 K12
Capo Santa Maria di Leuca 64 N9
Capo San Vito 64 G10
Capo Spartivento, *Italy* 64 C10
Capo Spartivento, *Italy* 64 L11
Capo Vaticano 64 K10
Capraia 64 D5
Cap Rhir 102 C2
Capri 64 J8
Capri 64 J8
Capricorn Group 114 K4
Cap Rosa 64 C11
Cap Serrat 64 D11
Cap Spartel 60 E9
Cap Timiris 102 B5
Capua 64 J7
Cap Verga 104 B2
Cap Vert 104 A2
Caquetá 140 C4
Caracal 66 M5
Caracarai 140 E3
Caracas 140 D1
Caransebeş 66 K4
Carauari 140 D4
Caravaca de la Cruz 60 J6
Caravelas 140 K7
Carazinho 142 L4
Carballiño 60 B2
Carballo 60 B1
Carbondale, *Ill., US* 130 D2
Carbondale, *Pa., US* 130 F1
Carboneras 60 J7
Carbonia 64 C9
Carcar 84 G4
Carcassonne 58 H10
Cardiff 56 J10
Cardigan 56 H9
Cardigan Bay 56 H9
Cardston 126 D1
Carei 66 K2
Carentan 58 D4
Cariacica 142 N3
Cariati 64 L9
Caribbean Sea 134 J6
Caripito 140 E1
Carlet 60 K5
Carleton Place 128 E1
Carlisle, *UK* 56 K7
Carlisle, *US* 128 E2
Carlow 56 F9
Carlsbad 132 F2
Carlyle 126 F1
Carmacks 122 D4
Carmagnola 62 C6
Carmarthen 56 H10
Carmarthen Bay 56 G10
Carmaux 58 H9
Carmen 134 B3
Carmona 60 E7
Carnarvon, *Australia* 114 B4
Carnarvon, *South Africa* 108 C6
Car Nicobar 88 F7
Carnot 106 B2
Carnsore Point 56 F9
Carolina 140 H5
Carolina Beach 130 F3
Caroline Island 112 L6
Caroline Islands 112 E5
Carpathian Mountains 50 J8
Carpații Meridionali 66 K4
Carpentras 58 L9
Carpi 62 F6
Carrabelle 130 E4
Carrara 62 F6
Carrickfergus 56 G7
Carrick-on-Suir 56 E9
Carrington 126 G1
Carrizozo 132 E2
Carroll 128 B2
Carrollton, *Ky., US* 128 D3
Carrollton, *Mo., US* 130 C1
Çarşamba 92 G3
Carson City 126 C3
Cartagena, *Colombia* 140 B1
Cartagena, *Spain* 60 K7
Carthage 130 C3
Cartwright 122 V6
Caruarú 140 K5
Carúpano 140 E1
Casablanca 102 D2
Casa Grande 132 D2
Casale Monferrato 62 D5
Casalmaggiore 62 F6
Casamozza 64 D6
Casarano 64 N9
Cascade, *Id., US* 126 C2
Cascade, *Mont., US* 126 C1
Cascade Range 126 B2
Cascade Reservoir 126 C2
Cascais 60 A6
Cascavel 142 L3
Caserta 64 J7
Cashel, *Ireland* 56 E9
Cashel, *Zimbabwe* 108 E3
Casiguran 84 G3
Casino 114 K5
Čašma 62 M5
Caspe 60 K3
Casper 126 E2
Caspian Sea 46 J3
Cassiar 122 F5
Cassino 64 H7
Castanhal 140 H4
Castelbuono 64 J11
Castèl di Sangro 64 J7
Castelfidardo 64 H5
Castellammare del Golfo 64 G10
Castellane 62 B7
Castellaneta 64 L8
Castelli 142 J4
Castelló de la Plana 60 K5
Castelnaudary 58 G10
Castelo Branco 60 C5
Castelsarrasin 58 G10
Castelvetrano 64 G11
Castets 58 D10
Castiglion Fiorentino 62 G7
Castlebar 56 C8
Castleford 56 L8
Castle Point 116 F5
Castres 58 H10
Castricum 54 G2
Castries 134 M6
Castro 142 M3
Castro Verde 60 B7
Castrovillari 64 L9
Castuera 60 E6
Çatak 92 K5
Catamarca 142 H4

Catandica 108 E3
Catania 64 K11
Catanzaro 64 L10
Catanzaro Marina 64 L10
Catarman 84 G4
Catbalogan 84 H4
Catió 104 A2
Cat Island 130 F5
Cat Lake 122 N6
Cato Island 114 L4
Catriló 142 J6
Catrimani 140 E3
Catskill Mountains 124 M3
Cattolica 62 H7
Cauayan 84 G5
Cauca 140 C2
Caucaia 140 K4
Caucasia 140 B2
Caucasus 92 K2
Caudry 54 F4
Cauquenes 142 G6
Caura 140 E2
Causapscal 128 G1
Căușeni 66 S3
Cavaillon 58 L10
Cavalese 62 G4
Cavan 56 E8
Cavarzere 62 H5
Cavinas 140 D6
Cavtat 66 F7
Caxias 140 J4
Caxias do Sul 142 L4
Caxito 104 G6
Çay 68 P6
Cayce 130 E3
Çaycuma 68 Q3
Cayenne 140 G3
Cayman Islands 134 H5
Caynabo 106 H2
Cayos Miskitos 134 H6
Cay Sal Bank 130 E5
Cazorla 60 H7
Ceanannus Mor 56 F8
Ceará 140 J4
Cebu 84 G4
Cebu 84 G4
Cecina 62 F7
Cedar City 126 D3
Cedar Falls 128 B2
Cedar Lake 122 L6
Cedar Rapids 128 B2
Cedros 124 C6
Ceduna 114 F6
Ceerigaabo 106 H1
Cefalù 64 J10
Cegléd 66 G2
Celaya 134 D4
Celebes = Sulawesi 87 A3
Celebes Sea 87 B2
Celje 66 C3
Celldömölk 66 E2
Celle 52 F4
Celtic Sea 56 E10
Centerville 128 B2
Cento 62 G6
Central African Republic 106 C2
Central City 126 G2
Centralia, *Ill., US* 128 C3
Centralia, *Wash., US* 126 B1
Central Range 87 F3
Central Siberian Plateau = Srednesibirskoye Ploskogor'ye 74 N2
Cenxi 84 E2
Cerea 62 G5
Ceres, *Argentina* 142 J4
Ceres, *Brazil* 140 H7
Cerezo de Abajo 60 G3
Cerignola 64 K7
Çerikli 92 E4
Çerkes 68 Q4
Çerkezköy 68 K3
Cerknica 62 K5
Cernavodă 66 R5
Cero Champaqui 142 J5
Cerralvo 124 E7
Cërrik 68 C3
Cerritos 132 F4
Cerro Aconcagua 142 G5
Cerro Bonete 142 H4
Cerro de la Encantada 124 C5
Cerro de Pasco 140 B6
Cerro Huehuento 134 C4
Cerro Las Tórtolas 142 H5
Cerro Marahuaca 140 D3
Cerro Mercedario 142 G5
Cerro Murallón 142 G8
Cerro Nevado 142 H6
Cerro Pena Nevade 134 D4
Cerro San Lorenzo 142 G8
Cerro San Valentín 142 G8
Cerros de Bala 140 D6
Cerro Tres Picos 142 J6
Cerro Tupungato 142 H5
Cerro Yaví 140 D2
Cerro Yogan 142 H9
Certaldo 62 G7
Cervaro 64 K7
Cervia 62 H6
Cervionne 64 D6
Cervo 60 C1
Cesano 62 J7
Cesena 62 H6
Cesenatico 62 H6
Cēsis 48 N8
Česka Lípa 52 K6
České Budějovice 62 K2
Český Krumlov 62 K2
Çeşme 68 J6
Česna 62 M5
Cessnock 114 K6
Cestas 58 E9
Cetate 66 L5
Cetinje 66 F7
Cetraro 64 K9
Ceuta 102 D1
Cevizli 68 P7
Chachapoyas 140 B5
Chaco Boreal 142 K3
Chad 100 C5
Chadan 76 S7
Chadron 126 F2
Chagai 90 H4
Chagda 78 N5
Chaghcharān 90 J3
Chagyl 90 G1
Chāh Bahār 90 H4
Chāībāsa 88 E4
Chainat 84 C3
Chaiyaphum 84 C3
Chalais 58 F8
Chalhuanca 140 C6
Chalinze 106 F5
Chalki 68 K8
Chalkida 68 F6
Chalkidiki 68 F4
Challans 58 D7
Challapata 140 D7
Challenger Deep 112 E4
Challis 126 D2
Châlons-sur-Marne 54 G6
Chalon-sur-Saône 58 K7
Cham 52 H7
Chama 108 E2
Chamba 88 C2
Chambal 88 C3
Chamberlain 126 G2
Chambersburg 128 E3
Chambéry 62 A5
Chambly 54 E5
Chamonix 62 B5
Champagnole 62 A4
Champaign 128 C2
Champaubert 54 F6
Champlitte 62 A3
Chañaral 142 G4
Chandalar 122 B3
Chandeleur Islands 134 G3
Chandigarh 88 C2
Chandler 132 D2
Chandrapur 88 C5
Changane 108 E4
Changara 108 E3
Changchun 82 C2
Changde 80 E5
Chang-hua 80 G6
Chang Jiang 80 D4
Changsha 80 E5
Changshou 80 D5
Changshu 80 G4
Changting 80 F5
Changzhi 80 E3
Changzhou 80 F4
Chania 68 G9
Channel Islands, *UK* 56 K12
Channel Islands, *US* 124 C5
Channel-Port aux Basques 122 V7
Chanthaburi 84 C4
Chantilly 54 E5
Chanute 130 B2
Chao Phraya 84 C4
Chaouèn 102 D1
Chao Xian 80 F4
Chaoyang 80 G2
Chaozhou 80 F6
Chapada Diamantina 140 J6
Chapais 128 F1
Chapayev 70 K4
Chapayevo 78 K4
Chapayevskoye 76 N7
Chapecó 142 L4
Chapleau 128 D1
Chapra 88 D3
Chara 78 K5
Charcas 132 F4
Chard 122 J5
Chardara 90 J1
Chardzhev 90 H2
Chari 100 C5
Chārīkār 90 J2
Charleroi 54 G4
Charlesbourg 128 F1
Charleston, *New Zealand* 116 C5
Charleston, *S.C., US* 130 F3
Charleston, *W. Va., US* 130 E2
Charlestown 130 D2
Charleville 114 J5
Charleville-Mézières 54 G5
Charlevoix 128 C1
Charlotte, *Mich., US* 128 D2
Charlotte, *N.C., US* 130 E2
Charlottesville 130 F2
Charlottetown 122 U7
Charlton Island 122 Q6
Charrat 62 C4
Charsk 76 Q8
Charters Towers 114 J4
Chartres 58 G5
Charymovo 70 Q3
Chasel'ka 78 C3
Chastyye 70 K3
Châteaguay 128 F1
Châteaubriant 58 D6
Châteaudun 58 G5
Châteaulin 58 A5
Châteauneuf-sur-Loire 58 H6
Châteauroux 58 G7
Château-Thierry 54 F5
Châtellerault 58 F7
Châtenois 62 A2
Chatham 128 D2
Chatham Island 116 (1)B1
Chatham Islands 116 (1)B1
Châtillon-sur Seine 58 K6
Chattanooga 124 J4
Chauffayer 62 B6
Chauk 88 F4
Chaumont 58 L5
Chaunskaya Guba 78 V3
Chauny 54 F5
Chaves, *Brazil* 140 G4
Chaves, *Portugal* 60 C3
Chavuma 108 C2
Cheb 52 H6
Cheboksary 70 J3
Chechnya 92 L2
Cheduba Island 88 F5
Cheektowaga 128 E2
Chegdomyn 78 N6
Chegga 102 D3
Chegutu 108 E3
Chehalis 126 B1
Cheju 82 D7
Cheju do 82 D7
Chekhov 78 Q7
Chelan 126 C1
Cheleken 90 F2
Chélif 60 L8
Chelkar 76 K8
Chełm 50 N6
Chełmno 50 H4
Chelmsford 54 C3
Chełmża 50 H4
Cheltenham 56 L10
Chelyabinsk 70 M3
Chelyuskin 76 U2
Chemnitz 52 H6
Chenab 88 B2
Chenachane 102 E3
Cheney Reservoir 130 B2
Chengde 80 F2
Chengdu 80 C4
Chengshan Jiao 82 B5
Chennai 88 D6
Chenzhou 80 E5
Chepes 142 H5
Cher 58 G6
Cheraw 130 F3
Cherbaniani Reef 88 B6
Cherbourg 58 D4
Cherchell 60 N8
Cherdyn 70 L2
Cheremkhovo 78 G6
Cherepovets 70 G3
Cherkasy 70 F5
Cherkessk 92 K1
Chermoz 70 L3
Chernihiv 70 F4
Chernivtsi 70 E5
Chernushka 70 L3
Chernyakhovsk 50 L3
Chernyayevo 78 M6
Chernyshevsk 78 K6
Chernyshevskiy 78 J4
Chernyye Zemli 70 J5
Cherokee 128 A2
Cherskiy 78 U3
Cherven Bryag 66 M6
Červonohrad 70 D4
Chesapeake 130 F2
Cheshskaya Guba 70 J1
Cheshunt 54 C3
Chester, *UK* 56 K8
Chester, *Calif., US* 126 B2
Chester, *Mont., US* 126 D1
Chesterfield 56 L8
Chesterfield Inlet 122 N4
Chetumal 134 G5
Chetwynd 122 G5
Cheviot 116 D6
Cheviot Hills 56 K6
Ch'ew Bahir 106 F3
Cheyenne 126 F2
Cheyenne 126 F2
Cheyenne Wells 132 F1
Cheyne Bay 114 C6
Chhatarpur 88 C4
Chhindwara 88 C4
Chhuka 88 E3
Chia-i 80 G6
Chiang Khan 84 C3
Chiang-Mai 84 B3
Chiang Rai 84 B3
Chiavari 62 E6
Chiavenno 62 E4
Chiba 82 L6
Chibougamau 122 S6
Chibuto 108 E4
Chicago 128 C2
Chicapa 106 C5
Chichagof Island 132 (1)K4
Chichaoua 102 D2
Chichester 54 B4
Chickasha 130 B3
Chiclana de la Frontera 60 D8
Chiclayo 140 B5
Chico 142 H8
Chicopee 128 F2
Chicoutimi 122 S7
Chicualacuala 108 E4
Chiemsee 62 H3
Chieri 62 C5
Chiese 62 F5
Chieti 64 J6
Chifeng 80 F2
Chiganak 76 N8
Chigubo 108 E4
Chihuahua 132 E3
Chiili 76 M9
Chikwa 108 E2
Chilas 88 B1
Childress 132 F2
Chile 138 D8
Chile Chico 142 G8
Chilik 76 P9
Chilika Lake 88 D4
Chillán 142 G6
Chillicothe, *Mo., US* 128 B3
Chillicothe, *Oh., US* 128 D3
Chilliwack 126 B1
Chiloquin 126 B2
Chilpancingo 134 E5
Chi-lung 80 G5
Chimbay 76 K9
Chimborazo 140 B4
Chimbote 140 B5
Chimchememel' 78 V3
Chimec 66 J1
Chimoio 108 E3
China 74 N6
Chincha Alta 140 B6
Chincilla de Monte-Aragón 60 J6
Chinde 108 F3
Chin do 82 C6
Chindwin 84 A2
Chingola 108 D2
Chinguetti 102 C4
Chinhoyi 108 E3
Chiniot 88 B2
Chinju 82 E6
Chinmen 84 F2
Chinnur 88 C5
Chino 82 K6
Chioggia 62 H5
Chios 68 H6
Chios 68 J6
Chipata 108 E2
Chippewa Falls 128 B2
Chipping Norton 54 A3
Chirala 88 D5
Chirchik 76 M9
Chirikof Island 132 (1)F5
Chiromo 108 F3
Chirpan 68 H2
Chirripo 134 H7
Chişinău 66 R2
Chişineu-Criş 66 J3
Chita 78 J6
Chitado 108 A3
Chitato 106 C5
Chitembo 108 B2
Chitipa 106 E5
Chitradurga 88 C6
Chitral 88 B1
Chitré 134 H7
Chittagong 88 F4
Chittaurgarh 88 B4
Chittoor 88 C6
Chitungwiza 108 E3
Chiume 108 C3
Chivasso 62 C5
Chizha 70 H1
Chodov 52 H6
Chodzież 50 F5
Choiseul 112 F6
Chojnice 50 G4
Chojnów 50 F6
Chokurdakh 78 R2
Chókwé 108 E4
Cholet 58 E6
Choma 108 D3
Chomutov 50 C7
Chona 78 H4
Chonan 82 D5
Chone 140 A4
Ch'ŏngjin 82 E3
Chŏngju 82 C4
Ch'ŏngju 82 D6
Chŏngp'yŏng 82 D4
Chongqing 74 P7
Chŏngŭp 82 D6
Ch'ŏnju 82 D5
Chonogol 80 F1
Chon Thanh 84 D4
Chop 50 M9
Chornobyl' 70 F4
Chornomors'ke 70 F5
Ch'osan 82 C3
Chōshi 82 L6
Choszczno 50 E4
Choteau 126 D1
Chott el Hodna 102 F1
Chott el Jerid 102 G2
Chott Melrhir 102 G2
Choûm 102 C4
Choybalsan 78 J7
Choyr 80 D1
Chre 58 H9
Christchurch 116 D6
Christiansburg 128 D3
Christiansø 50 E2
Christmas Island 86 D5
Chrudim 50 E8
Chrysi 68 H10
Chrysoupoli 66 M9
Chu 76 N9
Chubut 142 H7
Chugach Mountains 122 B4
Chūgoku-sanchi 80 J3
Chugwater 126 F2
Chukchi Sea 132 (1)C2
Chukotskiy Khrebet 78 W3
Chukotskiy Poluostrov 78 Z3
Chula Vista 132 C2
Chulucanas 140 A5
Chulym 76 R6
Chum 70 M1
Chumikan 78 P6
Chum Phae 84 C3
Chumphon 84 B4
Ch'unch'ŏn 82 D5
Chunchura 88 E4
Chundzha 76 P9
Ch'ungju 82 D5
Chuquicamata 142 H3
Chur 62 E4
Churapcha 78 N4
Churchill 122 N5

Churchill, *Man., Canada*	122	M5
Churchill, *Nfld., Canada*	122	U6
Churchill Falls	122	U6
Churchill Peak	122	F5
Churu	88	B3
Chuska Mountains	132	E1
Chusovoy	70	L3
Chute des Passes	122	S7
Chuuk	112	F5
Chuvashiya	70	J3
Chuxiong	84	C2
Chuya	78	J5
Ciadîr-Lunga	66	R3
Cide	92	E3
Ciechanów	50	K5
Ciechocinek	50	H5
Ciego de Avila	134	J4
Cienfuegos	134	H4
Cieza	60	J6
Cihanbeyli	92	E4
Cijulang	86	D4
Cilacap	86	D4
Cili	80	E5
Cimarron	130	B2
Cimișlia	66	R3
Cîmpeni	50	N11
Cinca	60	L3
Cincinnati	128	D3
Cine	68	L7
Ciney	54	H4
Cintalapa	134	F5
Circle, *Ak., US*	132	(1)J2
Circle, *Mont., US*	126	E1
Circleville	128	D3
Cirebon	86	D4
Cirò Marina	64	M9
Cisco	130	B3
Cistierna	60	E2
Čitluk	66	E6
Citronelle	130	D3
Cittadella	62	G5
Città di Castello	62	H7
Ciucea	66	K3
Ciudad Acuña	132	F3
Ciudad Bolívar	140	E2
Ciudad Camargo	132	E3
Ciudad del Carmen	134	F5
Ciudad del Este	142	L4
Ciudad Delicias	132	E3
Ciudad del Maíz	132	G4
Ciudad de Valles	134	E4
Ciudad Guayana	140	E2
Ciudad Juárez	132	E2
Ciudad Madero	132	G4
Ciudad Mante	134	E4
Ciudad Obregón	134	C3
Ciudad Real	60	G6
Ciudad-Rodrigo	60	D4
Ciudad Valles	132	G4
Ciudad Victoria	124	G7
Ciutadella	60	P4
Cividale del Friuli	62	J4
Civita Castellana	64	G6
Civitanova Marche	64	H5
Civitavecchia	64	F6
Cizre	92	K5
Clacton-on-Sea	54	D3
Clair Engle Lake	126	B2
Clairview	114	J4
Clamecy	58	J6
Clare Island	56	B8
Claremorris	56	D8
Clarence	116	D6
Clarence Strait	114	E2
Clarendon	132	F2
Clarkdale	132	D2
Clarksburg	130	E2
Clarksdale	130	C3
Clarks Junction	116	C7
Clarkston	126	C1
Clarksville, *Ark., US*	130	C2
Clarksville, *Tenn., US*	130	D2
Claro	140	G7
Clausthal-Zellerfeld	52	F5
Claveria	84	G3
Clayton	132	F1
Clear Island	56	C10
Clear Lake	128	B2
Clear Lake Reservoir	126	B2
Clearwater	126	C1
Clearwater	130	E4
Clearwater Mountains	126	C1
Cleburne	130	B3
Clermont, *Australia*	114	J4
Clermont, *France*	54	E5
Clermont-Ferrand	58	J8
Clervaux	54	J4
Cles	62	F4
Cleveland, *Oh., US*	128	D2
Cleveland, *Tenn., US*	130	E2
Cleveland, *Tex., US*	130	B3
Clifden	116	A7
Clifton	132	E2
Climax	126	E1
Clines Corners	132	E2
Clinton, *Canada*	122	G6
Clinton, *New Zealand*	116	B8
Clinton, *Ark., US*	128	B3
Clinton, *Ia., US*	124	H3
Clinton, *Miss., US*	130	C3
Clinton, *Mo., US*	128	B3
Clinton, *N.C., US*	130	F3
Clinton, *Okla., US*	130	B2
Clipperton Island	134	C6
Clonakilty	56	D10
Cloncurry	114	H4
Clonmel	56	E9
Cloppenburg	52	D4
Cloquet	128	B1
Cloud Peak	126	E2
Clovis, *Calif., US*	126	C3
Clovis, *N. Mex., US*	132	F2
Cluj-Napoca	66	L3
Cluny	58	K7
Cluses	62	B4
Clyde	56	H6
Clyde River	122	T2
Coaldale	126	C3
Coalville	126	C2
Coari	140	E4
Coast Mountains	122	E5
Coast Range	126	B3
Coatbridge	56	J6
Coats Island	122	Q4
Coatzacoalcos	134	F5
Cobalt	122	R7
Cobán	134	F5
Cobija	140	D6
Cobourg	124	L3
Cobourg Peninsula	114	F2
Cóbuè	108	E2
Coburg	52	F6
Cochabamba	140	D7
Cochin = Kochi	88	C7
Cochrane	128	D1
Cockburn Town	130	G5
Coco	134	H6
Cocoa	130	E4
Cocobeach	104	F4
Coco Channel	84	A4
Coco Island	84	A4
Codajás	140	E4
Codigoro	62	H6
Cod Island	122	U5
Codlea	66	N4
Codó	140	J4
Codogno	62	E5
Codroipo	62	J5
Cody	126	E2
Coen	114	H2
Coesfeld	52	C5
Coëtivy Island	98	J6
Coeur d'Alene	126	C1
Coeur d'Alene Lake	126	C1
Coevorden	54	J2
Coffs Harbour	114	K6
Cofrents	60	J5
Cognac	58	E8
Cogne	62	C5
Coiba	138	C3
Coihaique	142	G8
Coimbatore	88	C6
Coimbra	60	B4
Colchester	54	C3
Colebrook	128	F1
Coleman	130	B3
Coleraine	56	F6
Colesberg	108	D6
Colfax	126	C1
Colibași	66	M5
Colico	62	E4
Coll	56	F5
Collado-Villalba	60	F4
Collecchio	62	F6
College Station	130	B3
Collier Bay	114	D3
Collingwood	128	E2
Collins	130	D3
Collooney	56	D7
Colmar	62	C2
Colmenar Viejo	60	G4
Colombia	140	C3
Colombo	88	C7
Colomiers	58	G10
Colonia Las Heras	142	H8
Colonial Heights	128	E3
Colonsay	56	F5
Colorado	126	E3
Colorado, *Colo., US*	132	E1
Colorado, *Tex., US*	132	G2
Colorado Plateau	132	D1
Colorado Springs	126	F3
Columbia	126	C1
Columbia, *La., US*	130	C3
Columbia, *Md., US*	130	F2
Columbia, *Mo., US*	130	C2
Columbia, *S.C., US*	130	E3
Columbia, *Tenn., US*	130	D2
Columbia Mountains	122	G6
Columbus, *Ga., US*	130	E3
Columbus, *Ind., US*	130	D2
Columbus, *Miss., US*	130	D3
Columbus, *Mont., US*	126	E1
Columbus, *Nebr., US*	126	G2
Columbus, *N. Mex., US*	132	E2
Columbus, *Oh., US*	130	E1
Columbus, *Tex., US*	130	B4
Colville	116	E3
Colville	132	(1)G2
Colville Lake	132	(1)M2
Comacchio	62	H6
Comănești	66	P3
Comarnic	66	N4
Combarbalá	142	G5
Combeaufontaine	58	M6
Comilla	84	A2
Comino = Kemmuna	64	J12
Commentry	58	H7
Commercy	54	H6
Como	62	E5
Comoé	104	D3
Comondú	124	D6
Comoros	108	G2
Compiègne	54	E5
Comrat	66	R3
Comstock	132	F3
Conakry	104	B3
Concarneau	58	B6
Conceição do Araguaia	140	H5
Concepción, *Bolivia*	140	E7
Concepción, *Chile*	142	G6
Conches-en-Ouche	54	C6
Conchos	134	C3
Concord, *Calif., US*	132	B1
Concord, *N.H., US*	128	F2
Concord, *N.C., US*	130	E2
Concordia, *Argentina*	142	K5
Concordia, *US*	130	B2
Condé-sur-Noireau	54	B6
Condobolin	114	J6
Condom	58	F10
Conegliano	62	H5
Conggar	88	F3
Congo	98	E6
Congo	104	G5
Connecticut	128	F2
Connemara	56	C8
Conrad	126	D1
Côn Son	84	D5
Constanța	92	C1
Constantina	60	E7
Constantine	102	G1
Consul	126	E1
Contact	126	D2
Contamana	140	B5
Contwoyto Lake	122	J3
Convay	130	F3
Conway	130	C2
Conwy	56	J8
Conwy Bay	56	H8
Coober Pedy	114	F5
Cookeville	128	C3
Cook Inlet	132	(1)G4
Cook Islands	112	K7
Cook Strait	116	E5
Cooktown	114	J3
Coolabah	114	J6
Coolgardie	114	D6
Cooma	114	J7
Coonabarabran	114	J6
Coon Rapids	128	B1
Coopers Town	130	F4
Coorabie	114	F6
Coos Bay	126	B2
Cootamundra	114	J6
Copenhagen = København	48	G9
Copertino	64	N8
Copiapó	142	G4
Copper Harbor	128	C1
Cöqen	88	E2
Coquille	126	B2
Coquimbo	142	G4
Corabia	66	M6
Coral	124	K1
Coral Harbour	122	Q4
Coral Sea	114	K2
Coral Sea Islands Territory	112	F7
Coral Sea Islands Territory	114	J2
Coral Springs	130	E4
Corantijn	140	F3
Corbeil-Essonnes	58	H5
Corbigny	58	J6
Corbu	66	R5
Corby	54	B2
Cordele	130	E3
Cordillera Cantábrica	60	D2
Cordillera Central	138	E5
Cordillera del Condor	140	B5
Cordillera de Mérida	138	D3
Cordillera de Oliva	142	G4
Cordillera Isabella	134	G6
Cordillera Occidental	138	E5
Cordillera Oriental	138	D5
Cordillera Penibética	60	F8
Cordillera Vilcabamba	140	C6
Córdoba, *Argentina*	142	J5
Córdoba, *Spain*	60	F7
Corfu = Kerkyra	68	B5
Coria	60	D5
Corinth	130	D3
Corinto	140	H7
Cork	56	D10
Cork Harbour	56	D10
Corleone	64	H11
Çorlu	68	K3
Corn Islands	138	C2
Cornwall	124	M2
Cornwallis Island	122	M2
Coro	140	D1
Corocoro	140	D7
Coromandel	116	E3
Coromandel Coast	88	D6
Coromandel Peninsula	116	E3
Coron	84	G4
Coronation Gulf	122	J3
Coronel Oviedo	142	K4
Coronel Pringles	142	J6
Coronel Suárez	142	J6
Corpus Christi	130	B4
Corrientes	142	K4
Corrigan	130	C3
Corriverton	140	F2
Corse	64	D6
Corsica = Corse	64	D6
Corsicana	130	B3
Corte	64	D6
Cortegana	60	D7
Cortez	132	E1
Cortina d'Ampezzo	62	H4
Cortland	128	E2
Cortona	64	F5
Coruche	60	B6
Çorum	92	F3
Corumbá	140	F7
Corvallis	126	B2
Corvo	102	(1)A2
Cosenza	64	L9
Cosmoledo Group	108	(2)A2
Cosne-sur-Loire	58	H6
Cossato	62	D5
Costa Blanca	60	K7
Costa Brava	60	P3
Costa del Sol	60	F8
Costa de Mosquitos	134	H6
Costa Dorada	60	M4
Costa do Sol	60	A6
Costa Rica	134	G7
Costa Smeralda	64	D7
Costa Verde	60	D1
Costești	66	M5
Coswig	52	H5
Cotabato	84	G5
Côte d'Ivoire	104	C3
Cotonou	104	E3
Cottage Grove	126	B2
Cottbus	50	D6
Cotulla	130	B4
Couhe	58	F7
Coulommiers	54	F6
Council Bluffs	126	F2
Courland Lagoon	50	L2
Courtacon	54	F6
Courtenay	124	B2
Coushatta	130	C3
Coutances	58	D4
Couvin	54	G4
Covasna	66	P4
Coventry	56	L9
Covilhã	60	C4
Covington, *Ga., US*	130	E3
Covington, *Ky., US*	130	E2
Covington, *Va., US*	128	D3
Cowell	114	G6
Cowes	54	A4
Cowra	114	J6
Cox's Bazar	88	F4
Coy Aike	142	H9
Cradock	108	D6
Craig	126	E2
Crailsheim	52	F7
Craiova	66	L5
Cranbrook, *Australia*	114	C6
Cranbrook, *US*	124	C2
Crater Lake	126	B2
Crato	140	K5
Crawford	126	F2
Crawfordsville	128	C2
Crawley	54	B3
Cree Lake	122	K5
Creil	54	E5
Crema	62	E5
Cremona	62	F5
Crépy-en-Valois	54	E5
Cres	62	K6
Cres	62	K6
Crescent City	126	B2
Crest	58	L9
Creston	128	B2
Crestview	124	J5
Crestview	134	G2
Crete = Kriti	68	H10
Créteil	54	E6
Creuse	58	G7
Crevillent	60	K6
Crewe	56	K8
Crianlarich	56	H5
Criciúma	142	M4
Cristalina	140	H7
Cristóbal Colón	120	J8
Crna Gora	66	F7
Croatia	66	C4
Crockett	130	B3
Croker Island	114	F2
Cromer	56	P9
Cromwell	116	B7
Crooked Island	134	K4
Crookston	124	G2
Cross City	130	E3
Cross Lake	122	M6
Crossville	128	C3
Crotone	64	M9
Crowley	130	C3
Crownest Pass	124	D2
Crown Point	128	C2
Croydon	114	H3
Cruz Alta	142	L4
Cruz del Eje	142	J5
Cruzeiro do Sul	140	C5
Crvenka	66	G4
Crystal City	130	B4
Crystal Falls	128	C1
Crystal River	130	E4
Crystal Springs	130	C3
Csorna	66	E2
Csurgó	62	N4
Cuamba	108	F2
Cuando	108	C3
Cuangar	108	B3
Cuango	106	B5
Cuanza	106	B5
Cuatro Ciénegas	132	F3
Cuauhtémoc	132	E3
Cuba	126	E3
Cuba	134	H4
Cubal	106	A6
Cubali	108	A2
Cubango	108	B3
Çubuk	68	R4
Cucuí	140	D3
Cúcuta	140	C2
Cuddalore	88	C6
Cuddapah	88	C6
Cuemba	108	B2
Cuenca, *Ecuador*	140	B4
Cuenca, *Spain*	60	H4
Cuernavaca	134	E5
Cuero	130	B4
Cuiabá	140	F7
Cuilo	106	B5
Cuio	106	A6
Cuito	108	B3
Cuito Cuanavale	108	B3
Culbertson	126	E1
Culfa	92	L4
Culiacán	134	C4
Cullera	60	K5
Cullman	130	D3
Culpepper	140	(1)A1

Eleuthera	**124**	L6
El Fahs	**64**	D12
El Faiyûm	**100**	F2
El Fasher	**100**	E5
El Geneina	**100**	D5
Elgin, *UK*	**56**	J4
Elgin, *Ill., US*	**128**	C2
Elgin, *N.D., US*	**126**	F1
El'ginskiy	**78**	Q4
El Gîza	**100**	F1
El Goléa	**102**	F2
El Homr	**102**	F3
El Iskandarîya	**100**	E1
Elista	**70**	H5
Elizabeth	**128**	F2
Elizabeth City	**130**	F2
Elizabethton	**130**	E2
El Jadida	**102**	D2
El Jafr	**94**	D6
El Jafr	**94**	D6
Ełk	**50**	M4
Ełk	**50**	M4
El Kala	**64**	C12
Elk City	**132**	G1
El Kef	**64**	C12
El Kelaâ des Srarhna	**102**	D2
El Khandaq	**100**	F4
El Khârga	**100**	F2
Elkhart, *Ind., US*	**128**	C2
Elkhart, *Kans., US*	**130**	A2
El Khartum	**100**	F4
El Khartum Bahri	**100**	F4
Elkhorn	**126**	G2
Elkhorn	**128**	C2
Elkhovo	**68**	J2
Elkins	**128**	E3
Elko, *Canada*	**126**	C1
Elko, *US*	**126**	C2
Elk River	**128**	B1
El Kuntilla	**94**	B7
Ellendale	**124**	G2
Ellensburg	**126**	B1
Ellesmere Island	**120**	K1
Ellice Islands	**112**	H6
Elliot	**108**	D6
Ellis	**122**	J8
Ellisras	**108**	D4
Elliston	**114**	F6
Ellsworth	**128**	G2
Ellwangen	**62**	F2
Elmadağ	**68**	R5
Elmali	**68**	M8
El Mansûra	**100**	F1
El Mazâr	**94**	A5
El Minya	**100**	F2
Elmira	**128**	E2
Elmshorn	**52**	E3
El Muglad	**100**	E5
El Nido	**84**	F4
El Obeid	**100**	F5
El Odaiya	**100**	E5
El Oued	**102**	G2
El Paso	**132**	E2
El Portal	**132**	C1
El Potosi	**132**	F4
El Prat de Llobregat	**60**	N3
El Puerto de Santa María	**60**	D8
El Qâhira	**100**	F1
El Qasr	**100**	E2
El Quseima	**94**	B6
El Quweira	**94**	C7
El Reno	**130**	B2
El Sahuaro	**132**	D2
El Salvador	**134**	F6
Elster	**52**	H5
Elsterwerda	**52**	J5
El Sueco	**132**	E3
El Suweis	**100**	F2
Eltanin Bay	**144**	(2)JJ2
El Tarf	**64**	C12
El Thamad	**94**	B7
El Tigre	**140**	E2
El Turbio	**142**	G9
Eluru	**88**	D5
Elvas	**60**	C6
Elverum	**48**	F6
Elvira	**140**	C5
El Wak	**106**	G3
Ely, *UK*	**56**	N9
Ely, *US*	**126**	D3
Emajõgi	**48**	P7
Emāmrūd	**90**	F2
Emba	**70**	L5
Emba	**70**	L5
Embalse de Alarcon	**60**	H5
Embalse de Alcántara Uno	**60**	D5
Embalse de Almendra	**60**	D3
Embalse de Contreras	**60**	J5
Embalse de Gabriel y Galán	**60**	D4
Embalse de Garcia Sola	**60**	E5
Embalse de Guadalhorce	**60**	F8
Embalse de Guadalmena	**60**	G6
Embalse de Guri	**140**	E2
Embalse de la Serena	**60**	E6
Embalse de la Sotonera	**60**	K2
Embalse del Bembézar	**60**	E6
Embalse del Ebro	**60**	G1
Embalse del Río Negro	**138**	F7
Embalse de Negratín	**60**	G7
Embalse de Ricobayo	**60**	E3
Embalse de Santa Teresa	**60**	E4
Embalse de Yesa	**60**	J2
Embalse Toekomstig	**140**	F3
Embarcación	**142**	J3
Emden	**52**	C3
Emerald	**114**	J4
Emi Koussi	**100**	C4
Emin	**76**	Q8
Emirdağ	**68**	P5
Emmeloord	**54**	H2
Emmen	**54**	J2
Emmendingen	**62**	C2
Emmerich	**54**	J3
Emory Peak	**132**	F3
Empalme	**132**	D3
Empangeni	**108**	E5
Empoli	**62**	F7
Emporia	**130**	B2
Empty Quarter = Rub' al Khālī	**90**	E6
Ems	**54**	J1
Ems-Jade-Kanal	**52**	C3
Enafors	**70**	B2
Encarnación	**142**	K4
Encs	**66**	J1
Ende	**87**	B4
Enderby Island	**116**	(2)B1
Energetik	**70**	L4
Enewetak	**112**	F4
Enez	**68**	J4
Enfida	**64**	E12
Enfield	**54**	B3
Engel's	**70**	J4
Enggano	**86**	C4
Enghien	**54**	G4
England	**56**	L9
English Channel	**56**	J12
Engozero	**48**	S4
'En Hazeva	**94**	C6
Enid	**130**	B2
Enkhuizen	**54**	H2
Enköping	**48**	J7
Enna	**64**	J11
En Nahud	**100**	E5
Enngonia	**114**	J5
Ennis, *Ireland*	**56**	D9
Ennis, *US*	**126**	D1
Enniscorthy	**56**	F9
Enniskillen	**56**	E7
Enn Nâqoûra	**94**	C3
Enns	**62**	K2
Enns	**62**	K3
Enschede	**54**	J2
Ensenada	**132**	C2
Enshi	**80**	D4
Entebbe	**106**	E3
Enterprise	**126**	C1
Entrevaux	**62**	B7
Entroncamento	**60**	B5
Enugu	**104**	F3
Enurmino	**78**	Z3
Envira	**140**	C5
Enz	**62**	D2
Enza	**62**	F6
Epanomi	**68**	E4
Epéna	**106**	B3
Épernay	**58**	J4
Épinal	**62**	B2
Episkopi	**68**	Q10
Epsom	**54**	B3
Eqlīd	**95**	E1
Equatorial Guinea	**104**	F4
Erbach	**52**	D7
Erçek	**92**	K4
Erciş	**92**	K4
Ercolano	**64**	J8
Érd	**66**	F2
Erdek	**68**	K4
Erdemli	**68**	S8
Erdenet	**78**	G7
Erding	**62**	G2
Erechim	**142**	L4
Ereğli, *Turkey*	**92**	D3
Ereğli, *Turkey*	**92**	F5
Ereikoussa	**68**	B5
Erenhot	**80**	E2
Erfurt	**52**	G6
Ergani	**92**	H4
Erg Chech	**102**	D4
Erg du Ténéré	**102**	H5
Ergel	**80**	D2
Erg Iguidi	**102**	D3
Er Hai	**80**	C5
Erie	**128**	D2
Erimo	**82**	M2
Erimo-misaki	**82**	M3
Eriskay	**56**	E4
Eritrea	**100**	G4
Erlangen	**52**	G7
Ermenek	**92**	E5
Ermoupoli	**68**	G7
Erode	**88**	C6
Er Rachidia	**102**	E2
Er Rahad	**100**	F5
Er Renk	**106**	E1
Errol	**128**	F2
Er Ruseifa	**94**	D4
Ersekë	**68**	C4
Erskine	**128**	A1
Ertai	**76**	S8
Ertix	**76**	R8
Erzgebirge	**52**	H6
Erzin	**76**	S7
Erzincan	**92**	H4
Erzurum	**92**	J4
Esan-misaki	**82**	L3
Esashi, *Japan*	**82**	L3
Esashi, *Japan*	**82**	M1
Esbjerg	**48**	E9
Escanaba	**128**	C1
Escárcega	**134**	F5
Esch	**54**	J5
Eschwege	**52**	F5
Eschweiler	**54**	J4
Escondido	**132**	C2
Eséka	**104**	G4
Eşfahān	**90**	F3
Eskifjöður	**48**	(1)G2
Eskilstuna	**48**	J7
Eskimo Lakes	**132**	(1)L2
Eskişehir	**92**	D4
Esla	**60**	E3
Eslāmābād e Gharb	**92**	M6
Eslamshahr	**90**	F2
Esler Dağ	**68**	M7
Eslö	**50**	C2
Esmeraldas	**140**	B3
Esneux	**54**	H4
Espalion	**58**	H9
Espanola, *Canada*	**128**	D1
Espanola, *US*	**126**	E3
Espelkamp	**52**	D4
Esperance	**114**	D6
Esperance Bay	**114**	D6
Esperanza	**140**	C5
Espinho	**60**	B4
Espírito Santo	**140**	J7
Espíritu Santo	**112**	G7
Esplanada	**140**	K6
Espoo	**48**	N6
Espungebera	**108**	E4
Es Samrā	**94**	D4
Essaouira	**102**	D2
Es Semara	**102**	C3
Essen, *Belgium*	**54**	G3
Essen, *Germany*	**54**	K3
Essequibo	**140**	F2
Esslingen	**62**	E2
Eşţahbānāt	**95**	F2
Este	**62**	G5
Estella	**60**	H2
Estepona	**60**	E8
Esteros	**142**	J3
Estevan	**124**	F2
Estonia	**48**	M7
Estoril	**60**	A6
Estrecho de Le Maire	**142**	H10
Estrecho de Magallanes	**142**	G9
Estrela	**60**	C4
Estremoz	**60**	C6
Estuário do Rio Amazonaz	**140**	H3
Esztergom	**66**	F2
Étain	**54**	H5
Étampes	**58**	H5
Étang de Berre	**58**	L10
Étaples	**54**	D4
Etawah	**88**	C3
Ethiopia	**98**	G5
Etolin Strait	**132**	(1)D3
Etosha Pan	**108**	B3
Étretat	**54**	C5
Ettelbruck	**52**	B7
Ettlingen	**52**	D8
Eucla	**114**	E6
Euclid	**128**	D2
Eufala	**130**	D3
Eufaula Lake	**130**	B2
Eugene	**126**	B2
Eupen	**52**	B6
Euphrates = Firat	**92**	H4
Eure	**54**	D6
Eureka, *Calif., US*	**126**	B2
Eureka, *Mont., US*	**126**	C1
Eureka, *Nev., US*	**132**	C1
Eureka, *Ut., US*	**126**	D3
Europoort	**54**	F3
Euskirchen	**52**	B6
Eutin	**52**	F2
Eutsuk Lake	**122**	F6
Evans Strait	**122**	Q4
Evanston, *Ill., US*	**128**	C2
Evanston, *Wyo., US*	**126**	D2
Evansville	**130**	D2
Evaz	**95**	F3
Everett	**126**	B1
Everglades City	**130**	E4
Evergreen	**130**	D3
Evesham	**54**	A2
Évora	**60**	C6
Évreux	**54**	D5
Evron	**58**	E5
Evros	**68**	J3
Evvoia	**68**	F6
Ewo	**104**	G5
Exaltación	**140**	D6
Exe	**56**	J11
Exeter	**56**	J11
Exmouth, *Australia*	**114**	B4
Exmouth, *UK*	**56**	J11
Exuma Sound	**124**	L7
Eyl	**106**	H2
Eyre Peninsula	**114**	G2
Ezine	**68**	J5

F

Faadippolu Atoll	**88**	B8
Fåborg	**52**	F1
Fabriano	**62**	H7
Fachi	**102**	H5
Fada	**100**	D4
Fada Ngourma	**104**	E2
Faenza	**62**	G6
Færingehavn = Kangerluarsoruseq	**122**	W4
Faeroes	**46**	D1
Fafanlap	**87**	D3
Făgăraş	**66**	M4
Fagernes	**48**	E6
Fagersta	**48**	H6
Făget	**66**	K4
Fagurhólsmýri	**48**	(1)E3
Fahraj	**95**	H2
Faial	**102**	(1)B2
Fairbanks	**132**	(1)H3
Fair Isle	**56**	L2
Fairlie	**116**	C7
Fairmont	**128**	B2
Faisalabad	**88**	B2
Faith	**126**	F1
Faizabad	**88**	D3
Fakfak	**87**	D3
Fakse	**52**	H1
Fakse Bugt	**48**	G9
Faku	**80**	G2
Falaise	**54**	B6
Falaise de Tiguidit	**102**	G5
Falconara Marittima	**62**	J7
Falcon Lake	**130**	B4
Fălești	**66**	Q2
Falfurrias	**130**	B4
Falkenberg	**48**	G8
Falkensee	**52**	J4
Falkland Islands	**142**	K9
Falkland Sound	**142**	J9
Falköping	**48**	G7
Fallingbostel	**52**	E4
Fallon	**126**	C3
Fall River	**128**	F2
Falls City	**124**	G3
Falmouth, *UK*	**56**	G11
Falmouth, *US*	**128**	F2
Falster	**52**	H2
Fălticeni	**66**	P2
Falun	**48**	H6
Famagusta = Ammochostos	**94**	A1
Fanchang	**80**	F4
Fandriana	**108**	H4
Fangzheng	**80**	H1
Fannūj	**90**	G4
Fanø	**52**	D1
Fano	**62**	J7
Fanø Bugt	**52**	D1
Faradje	**106**	D3
Farafangana	**108**	H4
Farāh	**90**	H3
Farah Rud	**90**	H3
Faranah	**104**	B2
Fareham	**54**	A4
Farewell Spit	**116**	D5
Fargo	**124**	G2
Faribault	**128**	B2
Faridabad	**88**	C3
Farihy Alaotra	**108**	H3
Färjestaden	**50**	F1
Farmington, *Me., US*	**128**	F2
Farmington, *N. Mex., US*	**132**	E1
Farnborough	**54**	B3
Farne Islands	**56**	L6
Fårö	**48**	K8
Faro, *Brazil*	**140**	F4
Faro, *Portugal*	**60**	C7
Fårösund	**48**	K8
Farquhar Group	**108**	(2)B3
Farrāshband	**95**	E2
Farson	**126**	E2
Fasā	**95**	E2
Fasano	**64**	M8
Fategarh	**88**	C3
Fatehpur	**88**	D3
Făurei	**66**	Q4
Fauske	**48**	H3
Fauville-en-Caux	**54**	C5
Favara	**64**	H11
Faversham	**54**	C3
Favignana	**64**	G11
Faxaflói	**48**	(1)B2
Faya	**100**	C4
Fayette	**130**	D3
Fayetteville, *Ark., US*	**130**	C2
Fayetteville, *N.C., US*	**128**	E3
Fayetteville, *Tenn., US*	**130**	D2
Faylakah	**95**	C2
Fažana	**64**	H4
Fdérik	**102**	C4
Featherston	**116**	E5
Fécamp	**54**	C5
Federated States of Micronesia	**112**	E5
Fedorovka	**70**	M4
Fehmarn	**52**	G2
Feijó	**140**	C5
Feilding	**116**	E5
Feira de Santana	**140**	K6
Feistritz	**62**	L3
Fejø	**52**	G2
Feldbach	**62**	L4
Feldkirch	**62**	E3
Feldkirchen	**62**	K4
Felidu Atoll	**88**	B8
Felixstowe	**54**	D3
Feltre	**62**	G4
Femø	**52**	G2
Femund	**48**	F5
Fengcheng	**82**	C3
Fenghua	**80**	G5
Fengning	**80**	F2
Feng Xian	**80**	D4
Feni	**88**	F4
Fenyang	**80**	E3
Feodosiya	**92**	F1
Feres	**68**	J4
Fergana	**90**	K1
Fergus Falls	**124**	G2
Ferkessédougou	**104**	C3
Ferlach	**62**	K4
Fermo	**64**	H5
Fernandina Beach	**130**	E3
Fernandópolis	**142**	L3
Ferrara	**62**	G6
Ferreira do Alentejo	**60**	B7
Ferrol	**60**	B1
Ferry Lake	**130**	C2
Fès	**102**	E2
Festus	**128**	B3
Fetești	**66**	Q5
Fethiye	**68**	M8
Fetisovo	**90**	F1
Fetlar	**56**	M1
Feucht	**52**	G7
Feuchtwangen	**52**	F7
Feyzābād	**90**	K2
Fianarantsoa	**108**	H4
Fianga	**106**	B2
Fichē	**106**	F2
Fidenza	**62**	F6
Fieni	**66**	N4
Fier	**68**	B4

Name		Page	Grid
Figari	●	64	D7
Figeac	●	58	G9
Figline Valdarno	●	62	G7
Figueira da Foz	●	60	B4
Figueres	●	60	N2
Figuig	●	102	E2
Figuil	●	104	G3
Fiji	A	112	H8
Filadélfia	●	142	J3
Fiľakovo	●	50	J9
Filiași	●	66	L5
Filicudi	☒	64	J10
Fīltu	●	106	G2
Finale Ligure	●	62	D6
Findlay	●	128	D2
Fingoè	●	108	E3
Finike	●	68	N8
Finland	A	48	P3
Finlay	◿	122	F5
Finley	●	114	J7
Finnsnes	●	48	K2
Finsterwalde	●	52	J5
Fırat	◿	92	H4
Firenze	●	62	G7
Firminy	●	58	K8
Firozabad	●	88	C3
Firozpur	●	88	B2
Firth of Clyde	⬔	56	G6
Firth of Forth	⬔	56	K5
Firth of Lorn	⬔	56	G5
Firth of Thames	⬔	116	E3
Fish	◿	108	B5
Fisher Strait	●	122	Q4
Fishguard	●	56	H9
Fiskenæsset = Qeqertarsuatsiaat	●	122	W4
Fismes	●	54	F5
Fitzroy Crossing	●	114	E3
Fivizzano	●	62	F6
Fizi	●	106	D4
Flå	●	48	E6
Flaming Gorge Reservoir	◪	126	E2
Flamingo	●	130	E4
Flannan Islands	☒	56	E3
Flåsjön	◪	48	H4
Flateyri	●	48	(1)B1
Flathead Lake	◪	126	D1
Flat Point	▱	116	E5
Flekkefjord	●	48	D7
Flensburg	●	52	E2
Flensburg Fjorde	⬔	52	E2
Flers	●	54	B6
Flinders Island	☒	114	J7
Flinders Ranges	▲	114	G6
Flinders Reefs	●	114	J3
Flin Flon	●	122	L6
Flint	●	128	D2
Flint Island	☒	112	L7
Flirey	●	62	A2
Flöha	●	52	J6
Florac	●	58	J9
Florence = Firenze, Italy	●	62	G7
Florence, Al., US	●	130	D3
Florence, S.C., US	●	130	F3
Florencia	●	140	B3
Florennes	●	54	G4
Florenville	●	54	H5
Flores, Azores	☒	102	(1)A2
Flores, Indonesia	☒	87	B4
Florești	●	66	R2
Floriano	●	140	J5
Florianópolis	▣	142	M4
Florida	a	130	E4
Florida	●	142	K5
Florida Keys	☒	120	K7
Florina	●	68	D4
Florissant	●	128	B3
Florø	●	48	C6
Floydada	●	132	F2
Flumendosa	◿	64	D9
Fly	◿	87	F4
Foča	●	66	F6
Foça	●	68	J6
Focșani	●	66	Q4
Foggia	●	64	K7
Fogo	☒	104	(1)B1
Fogo Island	●	122	W7
Fohnsdorf	●	62	K3
Föhr	☒	52	D2
Foix	●	58	G11
Folegandros	☒	68	G8
Foleyet	●	128	D1
Foligno	●	64	G6
Folkestone	●	54	D3
Folkston	●	130	E3
Follonica	●	64	E6
Fomboni	●	108	G2
Fond du Lac	●	128	C2
Fondi	●	64	H7
Fongafale	■	112	H6
Fontainebleau	●	58	H5
Fontana	●	64	M8
Fonte Boa	●	140	D4
Fontenay-le-Comte	●	58	E7
Fontur	▱	48	(1)F1
Fonyód	●	64	M2
Forbach, France	●	54	J5
Forbach, Germany	●	54	L6
Forchheim	●	52	G7
Førde	●	48	C6
Fordyce	●	130	C3
Forest, Canada	●	128	D2
Forest, US	●	130	D3
Forestville	●	128	G1
Forfar	●	56	K5
Forges-les-Eaux	●	54	D5
Forks	●	126	B1
Forlì	●	62	H6
Formazza	●	62	H6
Formentera	☒	60	M6
Formia	●	64	H7
Formiga	●	142	M3
Formosa, Brazil	●	140	H7
Formosa, Paraguay	●	142	K4
Fornovo di Taro	●	62	F6
Forsayth	●	114	H3
Forssa	●	48	M6
Forst	●	52	K5
Forsyth	●	126	E1
Fort Abbas	●	88	B3
Fortaleza	▣	140	K4
Fort Augustus	●	56	H4
Fort Bayne	●	128	C4
Fort Beaufort	●	108	D6
Fort Benton	●	126	D1
Fort Bragg	●	132	B1
Fort Chipewyan	●	122	J5
Fort Cobb Reservoir	◪	130	B2
Fort Collins	●	126	E2
Fort-de-France	●	134	M6
Fort Dodge	●	128	B2
Forte dei Marmi	●	62	F7
Fortezza	●	62	G4
Fort Frances	●	128	B1
Fort George	●	122	R6
Fort Gibson Lake	◪	130	B2
Fort Good Hope	●	122	F3
Forth	◿	56	H5
Fort Hope	●	122	P6
Fortín Coronel Eugenio Garay	●	142	J3
Fort Kent	●	128	G1
Fort Lauderdale	●	130	E4
Fort Liard	●	122	G4
Fort Mackay	●	122	J5
Fort Macleod	●	126	D1
Fort McMurray	●	122	J5
Fort McPherson	●	132	(1)L2
Fort Munro	●	90	J4
Fort Myers	●	130	E4
Fort Nelson	●	122	G5
Fort Norman	●	132	(1)M3
Fort Payne	●	130	D3
Fort Peck Reservoir	◪	126	E1
Fort Pierce	●	130	E4
Fort Pierre	●	126	F2
Fort Portal	●	106	E3
Fort Providence	●	122	H4
Fortrose	●	116	B8
Fort Rupert	●	122	R6
Fort St. John	●	122	G5
Fort Saint Lucie	●	130	E4
Fort Scott	●	130	C2
Fort Severn	●	122	P5
Fort Shevchenko	●	76	J9
Fort Simpson	●	122	G4
Fort Smith, Canada	●	122	J4
Fort Smith, US	●	130	C2
Fort Stockton	●	132	F2
Fort Summer	●	132	F2
Fortuna	●	126	F1
Fortune Bay	⬔	122	V7
Fort Vermilion	●	122	H5
Fort Wayne	●	130	D1
Fort William	●	56	G5
Fort Worth	●	130	B3
Fort Yates	●	126	F1
Foshan	●	84	E2
Fosna	◿	48	F5
Fossano	●	62	C6
Fossombrone	●	62	H7
Fougamou	●	104	G5
Fougères	●	58	D5
Foula	☒	56	K1
Foulness	●	54	C3
Foumban	●	104	G3
Fourmies	●	54	G4
Fournoi	☒	68	J7
Fouta Djallon	◉	104	B2
Foveaux Strait	◿	116	A8
Foxe Basin	⬔	122	R3
Foxe Channel	⬔	122	R4
Foxe Peninsula	◉	122	R4
Fox Glacier	●	116	B6
Fox Islands	☒	132	(1)D5
Foz	●	60	C1
Foz do Cunene	●	108	A3
Foz do Iguaçu	●	142	L4
Fraga	●	60	L3
Franca	●	142	M3
Francavilla al Mare	●	64	J6
France	A	58	G7
Franceville	●	104	G5
Francisco I. Madero	●	132	F4
Francistown	●	108	D4
Francs Peak	▲	126	E2
Franeker	●	54	H1
Frankenberg	●	52	D5
Frankenthal	●	52	D7
Frankfort, Ind., US	●	130	D1
Frankfort, Ky., US	▣	130	E2
Frankfurt, Germany	●	52	K4
Frankfurt, Germany	●	52	D6
Franklin, N.C., US	●	128	D3
Franklin, Tenn., US	●	128	C3
Franklin Bay	⬔	122	F2
Franklin D. Roosevelt Lake	◪	126	C1
Franklin Mountains	◉	122	F3
Franklin Strait	⬔	122	M2
Franz Josef Glacier	●	116	C6
Franz Josef Land = Zemlya Frantsa-Iosifa	☒	76	J2
Fraser	◿	122	G6
Fraserburg	●	108	C6
Fraserburgh	●	56	L4
Fraser Island	●	114	K5
Frasertown	●	116	F4
Frater	●	128	D1
Frauenfeld	●	62	D3
Fredensborg	●	50	B2
Frederick, Md., US	●	128	E3
Frederick, Okla., US	●	130	B3
Fredericksburg, Tex., US	●	130	B3
Fredericksburg, Va., US	●	128	E3
Fredericktown	●	128	B3
Fredericton	▣	122	T7
Frederikshåb = Paamiut	●	122	X4
Frederikshavn	●	48	F8
Frederikssund	●	50	B2
Frederiksværk	●	48	G9
Fredrikstad	●	48	F7
Freeport, Ill., US	●	128	C2
Freeport, Tex., US	●	130	B4
Freeport City	●	130	F4
Freer	●	130	B4
Free State	a	108	D5
Freetown	■	104	B3
Fregenal de la Sierre	●	60	D6
Freiberg	●	52	J6
Freiburg	●	62	C3
Freilassing	●	62	H3
Freising	●	62	G2
Freistadt	●	62	K2
Fréjus	●	58	M10
Fremantle	●	114	C6
Fremont, Calif., US	●	132	B1
Fremont, Nebr., US	●	124	G3
Frenchglen	●	126	C2
French Guiana	a	140	G3
French Pass	●	116	D5
French Polynesia	●	112	L7
Frenda	●	102	F1
Fresnes-sur-Apances	●	62	A3
Fresnillo	●	134	D4
Fresno	●	132	C1
Fresno Reservoir	◪	126	E1
Freudenstadt	●	62	D2
Freyung	●	52	J8
Frias	●	142	H4
Fribourg	●	62	C4
Friedburg	●	62	G2
Friedrichshafen	●	62	E3
Friesach	●	62	K4
Friesoythe	●	52	C3
Frisian Islands	☒	54	H1
Fritzlar	●	52	E5
Frobisher Bay	⬔	122	T4
Frolovo	●	70	H5
Frome	●	56	K10
Frontera	●	134	F5
Frontignan	●	58	J10
Frosinone	●	64	H7
Frøya	●	48	D5
Fruges	●	54	E4
Frýdek Místek	●	50	H8
Fudai	●	82	L4
Fuding	●	80	G5
Fuengirola	●	60	F8
Fuentesauco	●	60	E3
Fuerte Olimpo	●	142	K3
Fuerteventura	☒	102	C3
Fugu	●	80	E3
Fuhai	●	76	R8
Fujieda	●	82	K6
Fujin	●	78	N7
Fuji-san	▲	82	K6
Fukuchiyama	●	82	H6
Fukue	●	82	E7
Fukue-jima	☒	82	E7
Fukui	●	82	J5
Fukuoka	●	82	F7
Fukushima	●	82	L5
Fukuyama	●	82	G6
Fulda	●	52	E6
Fulda	◿	52	E6
Fuling	●	80	D5
Fulton	●	130	D2
Funabashi	●	82	L6
Funafuti	☒	112	H6
Funchal	●	102	B2
Fundão	●	60	C4
Funing	●	84	D2
Funtua	●	104	F2
Furano	●	82	M2
Fürg	●	95	F2
Furmanovka	●	76	N9
Furmanovo	●	70	J5
Furneaux Group	☒	114	J8
Furqlus	●	94	E2
Fürstenberg	●	52	J3
Fürstenfeldbruck	●	62	G2
Fürstenwalde	●	52	K4
Fürth	●	52	F7
Furukawa	●	82	L4
Fushun	●	82	B3
Fusong	●	82	D2
Füssen	●	62	F3
Futog	●	66	G4
Fuxhou	●	80	F5
Fu Xian	●	80	D3
Fuxin	●	80	G2
Fuyang	●	80	F4
Fuyu	●	80	G1
Fuyun	●	76	R8
Fuzhou	●	84	F1
Fyn	☒	52	F1
Fynshav	●	52	F2

G

Name		Page	Grid
Gaalkacyo	●	106	H2
Gabès	●	102	H2
Gabon	A	104	G5
Gaborone	■	108	D4
Gäbrik	●	95	H4
Gabrovo	●	66	N7
Gacé	●	54	C6
Gacko	●	66	F6
Gäddede	●	48	H4
Gadsden	●	130	D3
Găești	●	66	N5
Gaeta	●	64	H7
Gafsa	●	102	G2
Gaggenau	●	62	D2
Gagnoa	●	104	C3
Gagra	●	92	J2
Gaildorf	●	62	E2
Gaillac	●	58	G10
Gainesville, Fla., US	●	130	E4
Gainesville, Ga., US	●	130	E3
Gainesville, Mo., US	●	130	C2
Gainesville, Tex., US	●	130	B3
Gai Xian	●	82	B3
Gala	●	48	E3
Galana	◿	106	F4
Galanta	●	62	N2
Galapagos Islands = Islas Galápagos	☒	140	(1)B1
Galashiels	●	56	K6
Galatas	●	68	F7
Galați	●	66	R4
Galdhøpiggen	▲	48	D6
Galena	●	132	(1)F3
Galesburg	●	128	B2
Galich	●	70	H3
Gallabat	●	100	G5
Galle	●	88	D7
Gallipoli	●	64	N8
Gallipolis	●	130	E2
Gällivare	●	48	L3
Gallup	●	132	E1
Galtat Zemmour	●	102	C3
Galveston Bay	⬔	124	G6
Galway	●	56	C8
Galway Bay	⬔	56	C8
Gamalakhe	●	108	E6
Gambēla	●	106	E2
Gambell	●	78	Z4
Gambier Islands	☒	112	N8
Gamboma	●	106	B4
Gamboula	●	106	B3
Gan	◿	78	L7
Ganado	●	132	E1
Gäncä	●	92	M3
Gandajika	●	106	C5
Gander	●	122	W7
Ganderkesee	●	52	D3
Gandesa	●	60	L3
Gāndhīdhām	●	88	B4
Gandhinagar	●	88	B4
Gandia	●	60	K6
Gandu	●	140	K6
Ganganagar	●	88	B3
Gangara	●	104	F2
Gangdise Shan	●	88	D2
Ganges	●	58	J10
Ganges	◿	88	E3
Gangi	●	64	J11
Gangtok	●	88	E3
Gannett Peak	▲	126	E2
Ganta	●	104	C3
Ganye	●	104	G3
Ganzhou	●	80	E5
Gao	●	102	E5
Gaoual	●	102	C6
Gap	●	62	B6
Gapan	●	84	G3
Garanhuns	●	140	K5
Garba	●	104	J3
Garbsen	●	52	E4
Gardelegen	●	52	G4
Garden City	●	126	F3
Gardēz	●	90	J3
Gardone Val Trompia	●	62	F5
Gargždai	●	50	L2
Gariau	●	87	D3
Garies	●	108	B6
Garissa	●	106	F4
Garland	●	130	B3
Garlasco	●	62	D5
Garliava	●	50	N3
Garmisch-Partenkirchen	●	62	G3
Garnett	●	130	B2
Garonne	◿	58	E9
Garoowe	●	106	H2
Garoua	●	104	G3
Garoua Boulaï	●	104	G3
Garry Lake	◪	122	L3
Garsen	●	106	G4
Garut	●	86	D4
Garwa	●	88	D4
Garwolin	●	50	L6
Gary	●	124	J3
Garyarsa	●	88	D2
Garzē	●	80	B4
Gasan Kuli	●	90	F2
Gasht	●	90	H4
Gashua	●	104	G2
Gastonia	●	130	E2
Gastre	●	142	H7
Gatchina	●	70	F3
Gateshead	●	56	L7
Gatesville	●	130	B3
Gatineau	●	128	E1
Gatrūyeh	●	95	F2
Gauja	◿	48	N8
Gaula	◿	48	F5
Gaurella	●	88	D4
Gauteng	a	108	D5
Gava	●	60	N3
Gävbandī	●	95	E3
Gavdos	☒	68	G10
Gävle	●	48	J6
Gawler	●	114	G6
Gawler Ranges	▲	114	G6
Gaxun Nur	●	80	C2
Gaya, India	●	88	E4
Gaya, Niger	●	104	E2
Gaylord	●	128	D1
Gayndah	●	114	K5
Gayny	●	70	K2
Gaza	●	94	B5
Gaz-Achak	●	76	L9
Gazandzhyk	●	76	K10
Gaza Strip	a	94	B5
Gaziantep	●	92	G5
Gazipaşa	●	68	Q8
Gazli	●	76	L9
Gaz Şāleh	●	95	G2

Gbaaka	**104**	C3
Gbarnga	**104**	C3
Gdańsk	**50**	H3
Gdov	**48**	P7
Gdyel	**60**	K9
Gdynia	**50**	H3
Gebel el Tîh	**94**	A7
Gebel Halâl	**94**	A6
Gebel Katherina	**100**	F2
Gebel Yi'allaq	**94**	A6
Gebze	**68**	M4
Gedaref	**100**	G5
Gediz	**68**	K6
Gediz	**68**	M6
Gedser	**52**	G2
Geel	**54**	H3
Geelong	**114**	H7
Geesthacht	**52**	F3
Gê'gyai	**88**	D2
Geidam	**104**	G2
Geilenkirchen	**54**	J4
Geilo	**48**	E6
Geinhausen	**52**	E6
Geislingen	**62**	E2
Geita	**106**	E4
Gejiu	**84**	C2
Gela	**64**	J11
Geladī	**106**	H2
Geldern	**54**	J3
Geleen	**54**	H4
Gelendzhik	**92**	H1
Gelibolu	**68**	J4
Gelibolu Yarimadasi	**68**	J4
Gelsenkirchen	**54**	K3
Gembloux	**54**	G4
Gembu	**104**	G3
Gemena	**106**	B3
Gemlik	**68**	M4
Gemlik Körfezi	**68**	L4
Gemona del Friuli	**62**	J4
Genalē Wenz	**106**	G2
General Acha	**142**	J6
General Alvear	**142**	H6
General Pico	**142**	J6
General Pinedo	**142**	J4
General Roca	**142**	H6
General Santos	**84**	H5
Geneva	**128**	E2
Genève	**62**	B4
Gengma	**84**	B2
Genil	**60**	F7
Genk	**54**	H4
Genoa = Genova	**62**	D6
Genova	**62**	D6
Gent	**54**	F3
Genteng	**86**	D4
Genthin	**52**	H4
Geographe Bay	**114**	B6
George	**108**	C6
George	**122**	T5
George Town, *Australia*	**114**	J8
George Town, *Malaysia*	**86**	C1
George Town, *US*	**130**	F5
Georgetown, *Australia*	**114**	H3
Georgetown, *Gambia*	**104**	B2
Georgetown, *Guyana*	**140**	F2
Georgetown, *Ky., US*	**130**	E2
Georgetown, *S.C., US*	**130**	F3
Georgetown, *Tex., US*	**130**	B3
George West	**130**	B4
Georgia	**92**	K2
Georgia	**130**	E3
Georgian Bay	**128**	D1
Gera	**52**	H6
Geraldine	**116**	C7
Geraldton, *Australia*	**114**	B5
Geraldton, *Canada*	**124**	J2
Gérardmer	**62**	B2
Gerāsh	**95**	F3
Gerede	**92**	E3
Gerefsried	**62**	G3
Gereshk	**90**	H3
Gérgal	**60**	H7
Gerik	**84**	C5
Gerlach	**126**	C2
Germantown	**128**	C3
Germany	**52**	E6
Germencik	**68**	K7
Germering	**62**	G2
Germersheim	**54**	L5
Gernika	**60**	H1
Gerolzhofen	**52**	F7
Gêrzê	**88**	D2
Geser	**87**	D3
Getafe	**60**	G4
Gettysburg	**126**	F2
Getxo	**60**	H1
Geugnon	**58**	K7
Gevaş	**92**	K4
Gevgelija	**68**	E3
Gewanē	**100**	H5
Geyik Dağ	**68**	Q8
Geyser	**126**	D1
Geyve	**68**	N4
Ghabāghib	**94**	D3
Ghadāmis	**102**	G2
Ghadīr Minqār	**94**	E3
Ghana	**104**	D3
Ghanzi	**108**	C4
Gharandal	**94**	C6
Ghardaïa	**102**	F2
Gharo	**90**	J5
Gharyān	**102**	H2
Ghāt	**100**	B2
Ghazaouet	**102**	E1
Ghaziabad	**88**	C3
Ghazipur	**88**	D3
Ghazn	**90**	J3
Gheorgheni	**66**	N3
Gherla	**66**	L2
Ghizar	**88**	B1
Ghotāru	**88**	B3
Ghōwrī	**95**	F2
Ghunthur	**94**	E2
Giannitsa	**68**	E4
Giannutri	**64**	F6
Giarre	**64**	K11
Gibraleón	**60**	D7
Gibraltar	**60**	E8
Gibson Desert	**114**	D4
Gideån	**48**	K5
Gien	**58**	H6
Gießen	**52**	D6
Gifhorn	**52**	F4
Gifu	**82**	J6
Gigha	**56**	G6
Giglio	**64**	E6
Giglio Castello	**64**	E6
Gijón	**60**	E1
Gila	**132**	E2
Gila Bend	**132**	D2
Gilan Garb	**92**	L6
Gilău	**66**	L3
Gilazi	**92**	N3
Gilbert Islands	**112**	H5
Gilbués	**140**	H5
Gilching	**62**	G2
Gilf Kebir Plateau	**100**	E3
Gilgandra	**114**	J6
Gilgit	**88**	B1
Gilgit	**90**	K2
Gilimanuk	**86**	E4
Gillam	**122**	N5
Gillette	**126**	E2
Gillingham	**54**	C3
Gills Rock	**128**	C1
Gilroy	**126**	B3
Gīmbī	**106**	F2
Gimli	**122**	M6
Gimol'skoe Ozero	**48**	R5
Gīnīr	**106**	G2
Gioia del Colle	**64**	L8
Gioia Tauro	**64**	K10
Gioura	**68**	F5
Giresun	**92**	H3
Girga	**100**	F2
Girona	**60**	N3
Gironde	**58**	E8
Girvan	**56**	H6
Gisborne	**116**	G4
Gisenyi	**106**	D4
Gitega	**106**	D4
Giurgiu	**66**	N6
Givet	**54**	G4
Givors	**58**	K8
Giyon	**106**	F2
Gizhiga	**78**	U4
Gizhiginskaya Guba	**78**	T4
Giżycko	**50**	L3
Gjiri i Vlorës	**68**	B4
Gjirokaster	**68**	C4
Gjoa Haven	**122**	M3
Gjøvik	**48**	F6
Glacier Peak	**126**	B1
Gladstone	**114**	K4
Glamoč	**66**	D5
Glan	**52**	C7
Glan	**87**	C1
Glarner Alpen	**62**	D4
Glasgow, *UK*	**56**	H6
Glasgow, *Ky., US*	**128**	C3
Glasgow, *Mont., US*	**126**	E1
Glauchau	**52**	H6
Glazov	**76**	J6
Gleisdorf	**62**	L3
Glendale, *Ariz., US*	**132**	D2
Glendale, *Calif., US*	**132**	C2
Glendambo	**114**	G6
Glendive	**126**	F1
Glenmorgan	**114**	J5
Glennallen	**132**	(1)H3
Glenn Innes	**114**	K5
Glenrothes	**56**	J5
Glens Falls	**128**	F2
Glenwood, *Ark., US*	**128**	B4
Glenwood, *Minn., US*	**128**	A1
Glenwood, *N. Mex., US*	**132**	E2
Glenwood Springs	**126**	E3
Glidden	**128**	B1
Glina	**62**	M5
Gliwice	**50**	H7
Glodeni	**66**	Q2
Głogów	**50**	F6
Glomfjord	**48**	H3
Glomma	**48**	F5
Glorieuses	**98**	H7
Gloucester, *UK*	**56**	K10
Gloucester, *US*	**128**	F2
Głowno	**50**	J6
Głuchołazy	**50**	G7
Glückstadt	**52**	E3
Gmünd, *Austria*	**62**	J4
Gmünd, *Austria*	**62**	L2
Gmunden	**62**	J3
Gniezno	**50**	G5
Gnjilane	**68**	D2
Gnoien	**52**	H3
Goalpara	**88**	F3
Goba	**106**	F2
Gobabis	**108**	B4
Gobernador Gregores	**142**	G8
Gobi Desert	**80**	C2
Gobo	**82**	H7
Gobustan	**90**	E1
Goch	**54**	J3
Gochas	**108**	B4
Godbout	**128**	G1
Godé	**106**	G2
Goderich	**128**	D2
Godhra	**88**	B4
Gödöllő	**66**	G2
Gods Lake	**122**	N6
Godthåb = Nuuk	**122**	W4
Goeree	**54**	F3
Goes	**54**	F3
Gogama	**128**	D1
Goiânia	**140**	H7
Goiás	**140**	G6
Goiás	**140**	G7
Gökçeada	**68**	H4
Gökova Körfezi	**68**	K8
Göksun	**92**	G5
Golaghat	**88**	F3
Golan Heights	**94**	C3
Golbāf	**95**	G2
Gölbasi	**92**	G5
Gol'chikha	**76**	Q3
Gölcük	**68**	K5
Gołdap	**50**	M3
Gold Coast	**114**	K5
Golden Bay	**116**	D5
Goldendale	**126**	B1
Golden Gate	**132**	B1
Goldfield	**126**	C3
Goldsboro	**128**	E3
Göle	**92**	K3
Goleniów	**50**	D4
Golestānak	**95**	F1
Golfe d'Ajaccio	**64**	C7
Golfe de Gabès	**102**	H2
Golfe de Hammamet	**102**	H1
Golfe de Porto	**64**	C6
Golfe de Sagone	**64**	C6
Golfe de Saint-Malo	**58**	C5
Golfe de Tunis	**64**	E11
Golfe de Valinco	**64**	C7
Golfe du Lion	**58**	J10
Golfo de Almería	**60**	H8
Golfo de Batabanó	**134**	H4
Golfo de Cádiz	**60**	C7
Golfo de California	**134**	B3
Golfo de Chiriquí	**134**	H7
Golfo de Corcovado	**142**	F7
Golfo de Cupica	**140**	B2
Golfo de Fonseca	**134**	G6
Golfo de Guayaquil	**140**	A4
Golfo de Honduras	**134**	G5
Golfo del Darién	**140**	B2
Golfo dell' Asinara	**64**	C7
Golfo de los Mosquitos	**140**	A2
Golfo de Mazarrón	**60**	J7
Golfo de Morrosquillo	**140**	B1
Golfo de Panamá	**134**	J7
Golfo de Penas	**142**	F8
Golfo de San Jorge	**142**	H8
Golfo de Santa Clara	**132**	D2
Golfo de Tehuantepec	**134**	E5
Golfo de València	**60**	L5
Golfo de Venezuela	**140**	C1
Golfo di Augusta	**64**	K11
Golfo di Catania	**64**	K11
Golfo di Gaeta	**64**	H7
Golfo di Gela	**64**	J11
Golfo di Genova	**64**	C4
Golfo di Manfredonia	**64**	L7
Golfo di Olbia	**64**	D8
Golfo di Oristano	**64**	C9
Golfo di Orosei	**64**	D8
Golfo di Palmas	**64**	C10
Golfo di Policastro	**64**	K9
Golfo di Salerno	**64**	J8
Golfo di Santa Eufemia	**64**	K10
Golfo di Squillace	**64**	L10
Golfo di Taranto	**64**	L8
Golfo di Trieste	**62**	J5
Golfo di Venezia	**62**	H5
Golfo San Matías	**142**	J6
Gölhisar	**68**	M8
Golin Baixing	**82**	A1
Gölköy	**92**	G3
Gölmarmara	**68**	K6
Golyshmanovo	**76**	M6
Goma	**106**	D4
Gombe	**104**	G2
Gombi	**104**	G2
Gomera	**102**	B3
Gómez Palacio	**132**	F3
Gonam	**78**	M5
Gonbad-e Kavus	**90**	G2
Gonda	**88**	D3
Gonder	**100**	G5
Gondia	**88**	D4
Gondomar	**60**	B3
Gönen	**68**	K4
Gonfreville-Orcher	**54**	C5
Gongga Shan	**80**	C5
Gonghe	**80**	C3
Gongliu	**76**	Q9
Gongpoquan	**80**	B2
Gongshan	**84**	B1
Gonzáles	**124**	G7
Gonzales	**130**	B4
González	**132**	G4
Goodland	**126**	F3
Goolgowi	**114**	J6
Goomalling	**114**	C6
Goondiwindi	**114**	K5
Goose Lake	**126**	B2
Göppingen	**62**	E2
Góra	**50**	F6
Gora Bazardyuzi	**92**	M3
Gora Kamen	**76**	S4
Gorakhpur	**88**	D3
Gora Ledyanaya	**78**	W4
Gora Pobeda	**78**	R4
Gora Yenashimskiy Polkan	**76**	S6
Goražde	**66**	F6
Gorbitsa	**78**	K6
Goré	**104**	H3
Gorē	**106**	F2
Gore	**116**	B8
Gorgān	**90**	F2
Gorgona	**62**	E7
Gori	**92**	L2
Gorinchem	**54**	H3
Goris	**92**	M4
Gorizia	**62**	J5
Gorki	**70**	N1
Gorlice	**50**	L8
Görlitz	**50**	D6
Gorna Oryakhovitsa	**66**	N6
Gornji Milanovac	**66**	H5
Gorno-Altaysk	**76**	R7
Gorno Oryakhovitsa	**68**	H1
Gorodets	**70**	H3
Gorontalo	**87**	B2
Goryachiy Klyuch	**92**	H1
Gory Belukha	**76**	R8
Gory Ulutau	**70**	N5
Gorzów Wielkopolski	**50**	E5
Goslar	**52**	F5
Gospić	**64**	K4
Gosport	**58**	D3
Gossau	**62**	E3
Gossi	**104**	D1
Gostivar	**68**	C3
Gostyń	**50**	G6
Gostynin	**50**	J5
Göteborg	**48**	F8
Gotha	**52**	F6
Gothèye	**104**	E2
Gotland	**48**	K8
Gotō-rettō	**82**	E7
Gotse Delchev	**68**	F3
Gotska Sandön	**48**	K7
Göttingen	**52**	E5
Gouda	**54**	G2
Gough Island	**98**	B10
Goundam	**102**	E5
Gouraya	**60**	M8
Gourcy	**104**	D2
Gourdon	**58**	G9
Gournay-en-Bray	**54**	D5
Governador Valadares	**140**	J7
Governor's Harbour	**130**	F4
Govorovo	**78**	M3
Gowārān	**90**	J4
Goya	**142**	K4
Gozha Co	**88**	D1
Gozo = Gwardex	**64**	J12
Graaff-Reinet	**108**	C6
Grabovica	**66**	K5
Gračac	**62**	L6
Gračanica	**66**	F5
Gradačac	**66**	F5
Gräfenhainichen	**52**	H5
Grafton, *Australia*	**114**	K5
Grafton, *US*	**126**	G1
Graham Island	**132**	(1)L5
Grajaú	**140**	H5
Grajewo	**50**	M4
Gram	**52**	E1
Gramat	**58**	G9
Grampian Mountains	**56**	H5
Granada, *Nicaragua*	**134**	G6
Granada, *Spain*	**60**	G7
Granby	**128**	F1
Gran Canaria	**102**	B3
Grand Bahama	**130**	F4
Grand Ballon	**58**	N6
Grand Bank	**122**	V7
Grand Canyon	**126**	D3
Grande, *Bolivia*	**140**	E7
Grande, *Brazil*	**140**	J6
Grande Cache	**122**	H6
Grande Prairie	**122**	H5
Grand Erg de Bilma	**102**	H5
Grand Erg Occidental	**102**	E3
Grand Erg Oriental	**102**	F3
Grand Falls, *N.B., Canada*	**128**	G1
Grand Falls, *Nfld., Canada*	**122**	V7
Grand Forks, *Canada*	**124**	C2
Grand Forks, *US*	**126**	G1
Grand Haven	**128**	C2
Grand Island	**126**	G2
Grand Junction	**126**	E3
Grand Marais, *Mich., US*	**128**	C1
Grand Marais, *Minn., US*	**128**	B1
Grand-Mère	**128**	F1
Grândola	**60**	B6
Grand Portage	**128**	C1
Grand Rapids, *Canada*	**122**	M6
Grand Rapids, *Mich., US*	**128**	C2
Grand Rapids, *Minn., US*	**128**	B1
Grand Teton	**126**	D2
Grangeville	**126**	C1
Granite Falls	**128**	A2
Granollers	**60**	N3
Gran Paradiso	**62**	C5
Grantham	**56**	M9
Grants	**132**	E1
Grants Pass	**126**	B2
Granville	**58**	D5
Granville Lake	**122**	M5
Gräsö	**48**	K6
Grasse	**62**	B7
Grassrange	**126**	E1
Grass Valley	**126**	B3
Graulhet	**58**	G10
Graus	**60**	L2
Gravelines	**54**	E3
Gravenhurst	**128**	E2
Gravesend	**54**	C3
Gravina in Puglia	**64**	L8
Gray	**58**	L6
Grayling	**128**	D2
Grays	**54**	C3
Grays Lake	**126**	D2
Grayville	**128**	C3
Graz	**62**	L3
Great Abaco	**130**	F4
Great Artesian Basin	**114**	H4
Great Australian Bight	**114**	E6
Great Bahama Bank	**134**	J4
Great Barrier Island	**116**	E3
Great Barrier Reef	**114**	J2
Great Basin	**126**	C3
Great Bear Lake	**132**	(1)M2

165

Name	Page	Grid
Kettle Falls	124	C2
Kewanee	128	C2
Keweenaw Peninsula	128	C1
Key Largo	130	E4
Keystone Lake	130	B2
Key West	130	E5
Kezhma	78	G5
Kežmarok	50	K8
Khabarovsk	78	P7
Khadyzhensk	92	H1
Khakasiya	76	R7
Khairwāra	88	B4
Khalafābād	95	C1
Khalīg el Suweis	100	F2
Khalīj Surt	100	C1
Khalūf	90	G5
Khambhat	88	B4
Khamis Mushay	90	D6
Khamis Mushayt	100	H4
Khamkkeut	84	C3
Khampa	78	L4
Khamrà	78	J4
Khān al Baghdād	92	K7
Khān az Zabīb	94	D5
Khandagayty	76	S7
Khandwa	88	C4
Khanewal	88	B2
Khannya	76	X4
Khanpur	88	B3
Khān Shaykhūn	94	D1
Khantau	76	N9
Khantayka	78	D3
Khanty-Mansiysk	70	N2
Khān Yūnis	94	B5
Khapalu	88	C1
Kharabali	70	J5
Kharagpur	88	E4
Kharampur	78	B4
Kharan	90	J4
Khargon	88	C4
Kharkiv	70	G5
Kharlu	48	R6
Kharmanli	68	H3
Kharnmam	88	D5
Kharovsk	70	H3
Khartoum = El Khartum	100	F4
Khasavyurt	92	M2
Khāsh	90	H4
Khashgort	70	N1
Khashm el Girba	100	G4
Khashuri	92	K3
Khaskovo	68	H3
Khatanga	78	G2
Khātūnābād	95	F1
Khatyrka	78	X4
Khavda	90	J5
Khawr Fakkān	95	G4
Khaydarken	90	K2
Khayelitsha	108	B6
Khemis Miliana	102	F1
Khemisset	102	D2
Khenchela	102	G1
Kherāmeh	95	E2
Kherson	70	F5
Kheta	76	T3
Kheta	76	T3
Kheygiyakha	70	P2
Khilok	78	J6
Khirbat Isrīyah	94	E1
Khīyāv	92	M4
Khmel'nyts'kyy	70	E5
Khodā Afarīn	92	M4
Kholmsk	78	Q7
Khonj	95	E3
Khon Kaen	84	C3
Khonuu	78	Q3
Khoper	70	H4
Khor	78	P7
Khor	78	P7
Khoreyver	70	L1
Khorinsk	78	H6
Khorramābād	90	E3
Khorramshahr	95	C1
Khorugh	90	K2
Khoseda Khard	70	L1
Khouribga	102	D2
Khrebet Cherskogo	78	P3
Khrebet Dzhagdy	78	N6
Khrebet Dzhugdzhur	78	N5
Khrebet Khamar Daban	78	G6
Khrebet Kolymskiy	74	U3
Khrebet Kopet Dag	90	G2
Khrebet Suntar Khayata	78	P4
Khrebet Tarbagatay	76	Q8
Khroma	78	Q2
Khudoseya	78	C3
Khudzhakh	78	R4
Khujand	90	J1
Khulna	88	E4
Khurays	95	B4
Khushab	88	B2
Khust	66	L1
Khuwei	100	E5
Khuzdar	90	J4
Khvormūj	95	D2
Khvoy	92	L4
Khyber Pass	90	K3
Kibaya	106	F4
Kibombo	106	D4
Kibondo	106	E4
Kibre Mengist	106	F2
Kičevo	68	C3
Kichmengskiy Gorodok	70	J3
Kicking Horse Pass	122	H6
Kidal	102	F5
Kidderminster	56	K9
Kidira	104	B2
Kiel	52	F2
Kielce	50	K7
Kieler Bucht	52	F2
Kiev = Kyyiv	70	F4
Kiffa	102	C5
Kigali	106	E4
Kigoma	106	D4
Kihnu	48	M7
Kıkıköy	68	L3
Kikinda	66	H4
Kikonai	82	L3
Kikori	87	F4
Kikwit	106	B5
Kilchu	82	E3
Kilifi	106	F4
Kilindoni	106	F5
Kilingi-Nõmme	48	N7
Kilis	92	G5
Kiliya	66	S4
Kilkenny	56	E9
Kilkis	68	E4
Killarney, Canada	128	D1
Killarney, Ireland	56	C9
Kilmarnock	56	H6
Kil'mez	70	K3
Kilosa	106	F5
Kilrush	56	C9
Kilttan	88	B6
Kilwa	106	D5
Kilwa Masoko	106	F5
Kimberley	108	C5
Kimberley Plateau	114	E3
Kimch'aek	82	E3
Kimolos	68	G8
Kimongo	104	G5
Kimry	70	G3
Kinango	106	F4
Kincardine	128	D2
Kinda	106	C5
Kinder	130	C3
Kindia	104	B2
Kindu	106	D4
Kineshma	70	H3
Kingaroy	114	K5
King City	126	B3
King George Islands	122	R5
Kingisepp	48	Q7
King Island, Australia	114	H7
King Island, Canada	78	AA3
Kingman	132	D1
Kingri	90	J3
Kingscote	114	G7
Kingsland	130	E3
King's Lynn	56	N9
King Sound	114	D3
Kings Peak	126	D2
Kingsport	130	E2
Kingston, Canada	128	E2
Kingston, Jamaica	134	J5
Kingston, US	128	F2
Kingston-upon-Hull	56	M8
Kingston upon Thames	54	B3
Kingstown	140	E1
Kingsville	130	B4
Kingville	134	E3
King William Island	122	M3
King William's Town	108	D6
Kinik	68	K5
Kinka-san	82	L4
Kinna	48	G8
Kinsale	56	D10
Kinshasa	106	B4
Kinsley	130	B2
Kinston	128	E3
Kintampo	104	D3
Kintyre	56	G6
Kinyeti	106	E3
Kinzig	52	E6
Kipini	106	G4
Kipnuk	132	(1)E3
Kirchheim	62	E2
Kirchheimbolanden	54	L5
Kirenga	78	H5
Kirensk	78	H5
Kiribati	112	J6
Kırıkhan	92	G5
Kırıkkale	92	E4
Kirillov	70	G3
Kirinyaga	106	F4
Kirishi	70	F3
Kiritimati	112	L5
Kırkağaç	68	K5
Kirk Bulāg Dāgh	90	E2
Kirkcaldy	56	J5
Kirkcudbright	56	H7
Kirkjubæjarklaustur	48	(1)E3
Kirkland Lake	128	D1
Kırklareli	68	K3
Kirkūk	92	L6
Kirkwall	56	K3
Kirov, Kyrgyzstan	76	N9
Kirov, Russia	70	F4
Kirov, Russia	70	J3
Kirovohrad	70	F5
Kiroyo-Chepetsk	70	K3
Kirriemuir	56	K5
Kirs	70	K3
Kirsanov	70	H4
Kırşehir	92	F4
Kiruna	48	L3
Kiryū	82	K5
Kisangani	106	D3
Kisbér	66	F2
Kiselevsk	76	R7
Kishanganj	88	E3
Kishangarh, India	88	B3
Kishangarh, India	88	B3
Kishi	104	E3
Kishiwada	82	H6
Kishtwar	88	C2
Kisii	106	E4
Kiska Island	132	(3)B1
Kiskőrös	66	G3
Kiskunfélegyháza	66	G3
Kiskunhalas	66	G3
Kiskunmajsa	66	G3
Kislovodsk	92	K2
Kismaayo	106	G4
Kissidougou	104	B3
Kisumu	106	E4
Kisvárda	66	K1
Kita	104	C2
Kitakami	82	L4
Kita-Kyūshū	80	H4
Kita-Kyūshū	82	F7
Kitami	82	M2
Kitchener	128	D2
Kitgum	106	E3
Kitimat	122	F6
Kittilä	48	N3
Kitunda	106	E5
Kitwe	108	D2
Kitzingen	52	F7
Kiuruvesi	48	N5
Kivijärvi	48	N5
Kivik	50	D2
Kiya	78	D5
Kiyiköy	92	C3
Kizel	70	L3
Kizilalan	68	R8
Kızılcahamam	92	E3
Kızılırmak	92	F3
Kızılkaya	68	N7
Kizil'skoye	70	L4
Kızıltepe	92	J5
Kizlyar	92	M2
Kizlyarskiy Zaliv	92	M1
Kizyl-Atrek	76	J10
Kladanj	66	F5
Kladno	50	D7
Klagenfurt	62	K4
Klaipėda	48	L9
Klamath	126	B2
Klamath	126	B2
Klamath Falls	126	B2
Klarälven	48	G6
Klatovy	52	J7
Klaus	62	K3
Klerksdorp	108	D5
Kleve	52	B5
Klin	70	G3
Klingenthal	52	H6
Klínovec	52	H6
Klintsy	70	F4
Ključ	62	M6
Kłobuck	50	H7
Kłodzko	50	F7
Kløfta	48	F6
Klosterneuburg	62	M2
Klosters	62	E4
Kluane	122	D4
Kluane Lake	132	(1)J3
Kluczbork	50	H7
Klyuchevskaya Sopka	78	U5
Klyuchi	78	U5
Knezha	66	M6
Knin	66	D5
Knittelfeld	66	B2
Knjaževac	66	K6
Knokke-Heist	54	F3
Knoxville	128	D3
Knysna	108	C6
Koba	86	D3
Kōbe	82	H6
Kobe	87	C2
København	48	G9
Kobenni	102	D5
Koblenz	52	C6
Kobo	88	G3
Kobroör	87	E4
Kobryn	70	P5
Kobuk	132	(1)F2
Kobuk	132	(1)F2
Kočani	68	E3
Koçarli	68	K7
Kočevje	66	B4
Kōch'ang	82	E6
Ko Chang	84	C4
Kochechum	78	F3
Kōchi	82	G7
Kochi	88	C7
Kochkor	76	P9
Kochki	76	Q7
Kochubey	92	M1
Kodiak	132	(1)G4
Kodiak Island	132	(1)G4
Kodino	70	G2
Kodinsk	78	F5
Kodomari-misaki	82	L3
Kodyma	66	S1
Köflach	66	C2
Kōfu	82	K6
Køge	50	B2
Køge Bugt	50	B2
Kohat	88	B2
Kohima	88	F3
Koh-i-Qaisir	90	H3
Koh-i-Sangan	90	J3
Kohtla-Järve	48	P7
Koidu	104	B3
Koi Sanjaq	92	L6
Koitere	48	R5
Kokenau	87	E3
Kokkola	48	M5
Kokomo	130	C2
Kokpekty	76	Q8
Kokshetau	70	N4
Kokstad	108	D6
Kolaka	87	B3
Kolar	88	C6
Kolari	48	M3
Kolašin	66	G7
Kolda	104	B2
Kolding	48	E9
Kole	106	D4
Kolhapur	88	B5
Kolín	50	E7
Kolkata	88	E4
Kollam	88	C7
Köln	52	B6
Kolno	50	L4
Koło	50	H5
Kołobrzeg	50	E3
Kologriv	70	H3
Kolomna	70	G3
Kolomyya	66	N1
Kolonedale	87	B3
Kolosovka	70	P3
Kolpashevo	76	Q6
Kolpos Agiou Orous	68	F4
Kolpos Kassandras	68	F4
Kolpos Murampelou	68	H9
Kolskijzaliv	48	S2
Kolskiy Poluostrov	70	G1
Kolumadulu Atoll	88	B8
Koluton	70	N4
Kolva	70	L2
Kolwezi	108	D2
Kolyma	78	R4
Kolymskaya Nizmennost'	78	S3
Kolymskaye	78	T3
Komandorskiye Ostrova	78	V5
Komárno	66	F2
Komárom	66	F2
Komatsu	82	J5
Kombe	106	D4
Komi	70	K2
Komló	66	F3
Kom Ombo	100	F3
Komotini	68	H3
Komsa	76	R5
Komsomol'skiy	70	J5
Komsomol'sk-na-Amure	78	P6
Konārka	88	E5
Konda	78	N3
Kondagaon	88	D5
Kondinskoye	70	N3
Kondoa	106	F4
Kondopoga	70	F2
Kondrat'yeva	76	V5
Konduz	90	J2
Kong Frederik VI Kyst	122	Y4
Kongi	76	R9
Kongola	108	C3
Kongolo	106	D5
Kongsberg	48	E7
Kongur Shan	76	N10
Königsberg = Kaliningrad	50	K3
Königswinter	52	C6
Königs-Wusterhausen	52	J4
Konin	50	H5
Konispol	68	C5
Konitsa	68	C4
Köniz	62	C4
Konjic	66	E6
Konosha	70	H2
Konotop	70	F4
Konstanz	62	E3
Konstinbrod	66	L7
Kontagora	104	F2
Kon Tum	84	D4
Konya	92	E5
Konz	52	B7
Kookynie	114	D5
Kootenai	126	C1
Kootenay Lake	124	C2
Kópasker	48	(1)E1
Kópavogur	48	(1)C2
Koper	62	J5
Kopeysk	70	M3
Köping	48	J7
Koplik	66	G7
Koprivnica	66	D3
Korba, India	88	D4
Korba, Tunisia	64	E12
Korbach	52	D5
Korçë	68	C4
Korčula	66	D7
Kord Sheykh	95	E2
Korea Bay	82	B4
Korea Strait	82	E6
Korf	78	V4
Korhogo	104	C3
Korinthiakos Kolpos	68	E6
Korinthos	68	E7
Kōriyama	82	L5
Korkino	70	M4
Korkuteli	92	D5
Korla	76	R9
Korliki	78	C4
Körmend	66	D2
Kornat	66	C6
Koroba	87	F4
Koroğlu Dağları	68	Q4
Koroğlu Tepesi	68	P4
Korogwe	106	F5
Koronowo	50	G4
Koror	112	D5
Korosten'	70	E4
Koro Toro	100	C4
Korsakov	78	Q7
Korsør	52	G1
Korti	100	F4
Kortrijk	54	F4
Korumburra	114	J7
Koryakskiy Khrebet	78	V4
Koryazhma	70	H5
Kos	68	K8
Kosa	70	L3
Ko Samui	84	C5
Kościan	50	F5
Kościerzyna	50	H3
Kosciusko	130	D3
Kosh Agach	76	R8
Koshoba	90	F1
Košice	66	L9
Koslan	70	J2
Kosŏng	82	E4
Kosovo	68	C2
Kosovska Mitrovica	68	C2

167

L

La Habana	**134**	H4
Lahad Datu	**84**	F5
Lahat	**86**	C3
La Haye-du-Puits	**54**	A5
Lāhījān	**90**	F2
Lahn	**54**	L4
Lahnstein	**54**	K4
Laholmsbukten	**50**	B1
Lahore	**88**	B2
Lahr	**62**	C2
Lahti	**48**	N6
Laï	**106**	B2
Laiagam	**87**	F4
Lai Chau	**84**	C2
L'Aigle	**54**	C6
Laihia	**48**	M5
Laingsburg	**108**	C6
Laiwu	**80**	F3
Laiyuan	**80**	E3
Lajanurpekhi	**92**	K2
Lajes	**142**	L4
Lajosmizse	**50**	J10
La Junta	**126**	F3
Lake Abbe	**106**	G1
Lake Abitibi	**128**	E1
Lake Albert, *Dem. Rep. of the Congo/Uganda*	**106**	D3
Lake Albert, *US*	**126**	B2
Lake Almanor	**126**	B2
Lake Amadeus	**114**	F4
Lake Andes	**126**	G2
Lake Argyle	**114**	E3
Lake Athabasca	**122**	K5
Lake Austin	**114**	C5
Lake Balkhash = Ozero Balkhash	**74**	L5
Lake Bangweulu	**108**	E2
Lake Barlee	**114**	C5
Lake Benmore	**116**	C7
Lake Blanche	**114**	H5
Lake Buchanan	**132**	G2
Lake Callabonna	**114**	H5
Lake Carey	**114**	D5
Lake Carnegie	**114**	D5
Lake Chad	**100**	B5
Lake Charles	**130**	C3
Lake Chelan	**126**	B1
Lake Chilwa	**108**	F3
Lake City	**130**	E3
Lake Claire	**122**	J5
Lake Coleridge	**116**	C6
Lake Constance	**62**	E3
Lake Crowley	**126**	C3
Lake C. W. McConaughy	**126**	F2
Lake Diefenbaker	**122**	K6
Lake Disappointment	**114**	D4
Lake District	**56**	J7
Lake Dojran	**68**	E3
Lake Dora	**114**	D4
Lake Dundas	**114**	B6
Lake Edward	**106**	D4
Lake Elwall	**126**	D1
Lake Erie	**128**	D2
Lake Eyasi	**106**	E4
Lake Eyre	**112**	D8
Lake Eyre Basin	**114**	G5
Lake Eyre North	**114**	G5
Lake Eyre South	**114**	G5
Lake Francis Case	**126**	G2
Lake Frome	**114**	H6
Lake Gairdner	**114**	G6
Lake Geneva	**62**	B4
Lake Gordon	**114**	H8
Lake Grace	**114**	C6
Lake Harbour	**122**	T4
Lake Hauroko	**116**	A7
Lake Havasu	**132**	C2
Lake Havasu City	**132**	D2
Lake Hopkins	**114**	E4
Lake Hudson	**130**	B2
Lake Huron	**128**	D1
Lake Jackson	**130**	B4
Lake Kariba	**108**	D3
Lake Kemp	**130**	B2
Lake Kerkinitis	**66**	L8
Lake Kivu	**106**	D4
Lake Kyoga	**106**	E3
Lake Ladoga = Ladozhskoye Ozero	**70**	F2
Lakeland	**130**	E4
Lake Lefroy	**114**	D6
Lake Louis	**122**	H6
Lake Macdonald	**114**	E4
Lake Mackay	**114**	E4
Lake Macleod	**114**	B4
Lake Manapouri	**116**	A7
Lake Manitoba	**122**	M6
Lake Manyara	**106**	F4
Lake Maurice	**114**	F5
Lake McDonald	**126**	D1
Lake McMillan	**132**	F2
Lake Mead	**126**	D3
Lake Melville	**122**	U6
Lake Michigan	**128**	C2
Lake Moore	**114**	C5
Lake Murray	**87**	F4
Lake Mweru	**106**	D5
Lake Mweru Wantipa	**106**	E5
Lake Nasser	**100**	F3
Lake Natron	**106**	F4
Lake Neale	**114**	E4
Lake Nipigon	**122**	P6/7
Lake Nipissing	**128**	E1
Lake Nyasa	**108**	E2
Lake Oahe	**126**	F2
Lake of the Woods	**128**	B1
Lake Ohau	**116**	B7
Lake Ohrid	**68**	C4
Lake Okeechobee	**130**	E4
Lake Onega = Onezhskoye Ozero	**46**	H1
Lake Ontario	**128**	E2
Lake O' The Cherokees	**128**	B3
Lake O' The Pines	**130**	C3
Lake Paringa	**116**	B6
Lake Peipus	**48**	P7
Lake Placid	**130**	E4
Lakeport	**126**	B3
Lake Poteriteri	**116**	A8
Lake Powell	**126**	D3
Lake Prespa	**68**	D4
Lake Providence	**130**	C3
Lake Pskov	**48**	P7
Lake Pukaki	**116**	C7
Lake Rotorua	**116**	F4
Lake Rukwa	**106**	E5
Lake St. Lucia	**108**	E5
Lake Sakakawea	**126**	F1
Lake Scutari	**66**	G7
Lake Simcoe	**128**	E2
Lake Superior	**128**	C1
Lake Tahoe	**126**	B3
Lake Tanganyika	**106**	D5
Lake Taupo	**116**	E4
Lake Te Anau	**116**	A7
Lake Tekapo	**116**	C6
Lake Tekapo	**116**	C6
Lake Texoma	**130**	B3
Lake Torrens	**114**	G6
Lake Travis	**132**	G2
Lake Tschida	**126**	F1
Lake Turkana	**106**	F3
Lake Victoria	**106**	E4
Lakeview	**126**	B2
Lake Volta	**104**	D3
Lake Waikare	**116**	E3
Lake Waikaremoana	**116**	F4
Lake Wakatipu	**116**	B7
Lake Wanaka	**116**	B7
Lake White	**114**	E4
Lake Wills	**114**	E4
Lake Winnipeg	**122**	M6
Lake Winnipegosis	**122**	L6
Lakewood	**126**	E3
Lake Woods	**114**	F3
Lake Xau	**108**	C4
Lake Yamma Yamma	**114**	H5
Lakhdaria	**60**	P8
Lakhimpur	**88**	D3
Lakhnadon	**88**	C4
Lakhpat	**88**	A4
Lakin	**130**	A2
Lakki	**88**	B2
Lakonikos Kolpos	**68**	E8
Lakota	**126**	G1
Lakselv	**48**	N1
Lalín	**60**	B2
La Línea	**60**	E8
Lalitpur	**88**	C4
Lal-Lo	**84**	G3
La Loche	**122**	K5
La Louvière	**54**	G4
La Maddalena	**64**	D7
Lamar, *Colo., US*	**132**	F1
Lamar, *Mo., US*	**130**	C2
Lamard	**95**	E3
La Marsa	**64**	E12
Lamballe	**58**	C5
Lambaréné	**104**	G5
Lambay Island	**56**	G8
Lambert's Bay	**108**	B6
Lam Chi	**84**	C3
Lamesa	**132**	F2
Lamia	**68**	E6
Lamone	**62**	G6
Lampang	**84**	B3
Lampasas	**132**	G2
Lampedusa	**102**	H1
Lamu	**106**	G4
Lanai	**132**	(2)D3
Lanai City	**132**	(2)E3
Lancang	**84**	B2
Lancaster, *UK*	**56**	K7
Lancaster, *Mo., US*	**128**	B2
Lancaster, *N.H., US*	**128**	F2
Lancaster, *Oh., US*	**128**	D3
Lancaster, *Pa., US*	**128**	E2
Lancaster, *S.C., US*	**130**	E3
Lancaster Sound	**122**	Q2
Lanciano	**64**	J6
Landau, *Germany*	**54**	L5
Landau, *Germany*	**62**	H2
Landeck	**62**	F3
Lander	**126**	E2
Landerneau	**58**	A5
Landsberg	**62**	F2
Land's End	**56**	F11
Landshut	**62**	H2
Landskrona	**50**	B2
Landstuhl	**54**	K5
Land Wursten	**52**	D3
La'nga Co	**88**	D2
Langarūd	**92**	N5
Langdon	**126**	G1
Langebæk	**52**	H1
Langeland	**52**	F2
Langen, *Germany*	**52**	D3
Langen, *Germany*	**54**	L5
Langenau	**62**	F2
Langenhagen	**52**	E4
Langeoog	**52**	C3
Langeoog	**52**	C3
Langfang	**80**	F3
Langjökull	**48**	(1)C2
Langkawi	**84**	B5
Langkon	**84**	F5
Langogne	**58**	J9
Langon	**58**	E9
Langøya	**48**	H2
Langreo	**60**	E1
Langres	**62**	A3
Langsa	**84**	B6
Langtry	**132**	F3
Langvatnet	**48**	G3
Länkäran	**92**	N4
Lannion	**58**	B5
L'Anse	**128**	C1
Lansing	**128**	D2
Lanxi	**80**	H1
Lanya	**106**	E2
Lanzarote	**102**	C3
Lanzhou	**80**	C3
Laoag	**84**	G3
Lao Cai	**84**	C2
Laohekou	**80**	E4
Laon	**54**	F5
La Oroya	**140**	B6
Laos	**84**	C3
Laotougou	**82**	E2
Lapa	**142**	M4
La Palma	**102**	B3
La Palma	**134**	J7
La Paragua	**140**	E2
La Paz, *Argentina*	**142**	K5
La Paz, *Bolivia*	**140**	D7
La Paz, *Mexico*	**134**	B4
La Pedrera	**140**	D4
La Perla	**132**	F3
La Pérouse Strait	**80**	L1
La Pesca	**130**	B5
La Pine	**126**	B2
Lapithos	**94**	A1
La Plant	**126**	F1
La Plata	**142**	K5
Lappajärvi	**48**	M5
Lappeenranta	**48**	Q6
Lappland	**48**	M2
Laptev Sea = More Laptevykh	**78**	L1
Lapua	**48**	M5
Łapy	**50**	M5
La Quiaca	**142**	H3
L'Aquila	**64**	H6
Lār	**95**	F3
Larache	**102**	D1
Laramie	**126**	E2
Laramie Range	**126**	E2
Larantuka	**87**	B4
Larat	**87**	D4
Larba	**60**	P8
Laredo, *Spain*	**60**	G1
Laredo, *US*	**132**	G3
Largo	**130**	E4
L'Ariana	**64**	E12
Lariang	**87**	A3
La Rioja	**142**	H4
Larisa	**68**	E5
Larkana	**90**	J4
Larnaka	**94**	A2
Larne	**56**	G7
La Rochelle	**58**	D7
La Roche-sur-Yon	**58**	D7
La Roda	**60**	H5
La Romana	**134**	L5
La Ronge	**122**	K5
Larrimah	**114**	F3
Lar'yak	**76**	Q5
La Sarre	**128**	E1
Las Cabezas de San Juan	**60**	E7
Las Cruces	**132**	E2
La Serena	**142**	G4
La Seu d'Urgell	**60**	M2
La Seyne-sur-Mer	**58**	L10
Lashio	**84**	B2
Lashkar Gāh	**90**	H3
Las Horquetas	**142**	G8
Łask	**50**	J6
Las Lomitas	**142**	J3
La Solana	**60**	G6
Las Palmas	**102**	B3
Las Petas	**140**	F7
La Spezia	**62**	E6
Las Plumas	**142**	H7
Las Taques	**140**	C1
Last Chance	**126**	F3
Lastoursville	**104**	G5
Lastovo	**66**	D7
Las Varas	**124**	E7
Las Varillas	**142**	J5
Las Vegas, *Nev., US*	**126**	C3
Las Vegas, *N. Mex., US*	**132**	E1
La Teste	**58**	D9
Latina	**64**	G7
Latisana	**62**	J5
La Toma	**142**	H5
La Tuque	**128**	F1
Latur	**88**	C5
Latvia	**48**	M8
Lauchhammer	**52**	J5
Lauenburg	**52**	F3
Lauf	**52**	G7
Lau Group	**112**	J7
Launceston, *Australia*	**114**	J8
Launceston, *UK*	**56**	H11
La Union	**60**	K7
Laupheim	**62**	E2
Laura	**114**	H3
Laurel	**130**	D3
Lauria	**64**	K8
Laurinburg	**130**	F3
Lausanne	**62**	B4
Laut Banda	**87**	C3
Laut, *Indonesia*	**86**	F3
Laut, *Malaysia*	**86**	D2
Lauter	**54**	K5
Lauterbach	**52**	E6
Laut Flores	**87**	A4
Laut Java	**86**	E4
Laut Molucca	**87**	C2
Laut Sawu	**87**	B4
Laut Seram	**87**	C3
Lava	**50**	L3
Laval, *Canada*	**128**	F1
Laval, *France*	**58**	E5
La Vall d'Uixo	**60**	K5
Lavant	**62**	K4
Lāvar Kabkān	**95**	D2
La Vega	**134**	K5
Laviana	**60**	E1
La Vila Joiosa	**60**	K6
Lavras	**142**	N3
Lavrentiya	**78**	Z3
Lavrio	**68**	G7
Lawdar	**100**	J5
Lawra	**104**	D2
Lawrence, *New Zealand*	**116**	B7
Lawrence, *Kans., US*	**128**	A3
Lawrence, *Mass., US*	**128**	F2
Lawrenceville	**130**	D2
Lawton	**130**	B3
Laya	**70**	L1
Laylā	**100**	J3
Laysan Island	**112**	J3
Layton	**126**	D2
Lazarev	**78**	Q6
Lázaro Cárdenas	**134**	D5
Lazdijai	**50**	N3
Lāzeh	**95**	E3
Lazo	**78**	P3
Leadville	**126**	E3
Leamington	**128**	D2
Leavenworth, *Kans., US*	**128**	A3
Leavenworth, *Wash., US*	**126**	B1
Lebach	**54**	J5
Lebanon	**94**	C3
Lebanon, *Mo., US*	**128**	B3
Lebanon, *N.H., US*	**128**	F2
Lebanon, *Pa., US*	**128**	E2
Lebanon, *Tenn., US*	**128**	C3
Lebel-sur-Quévillon	**128**	E1
Lębork	**50**	G3
Lebrija	**60**	D8
Lebu	**142**	G6
Lecce	**64**	N8
Lecco	**62**	E5
Lech	**62**	F3
Leck	**52**	D2
Le Creusot	**58**	K7
Le Crotoy	**54**	D4
Łeczna	**50**	M6
Łęczyca	**50**	J5
Ledmozero	**48**	R4
Lee	**56**	D10
Leech Lake	**128**	B1
Leeds	**56**	L8
Leek, *Netherlands*	**54**	J1
Leek, *UK*	**54**	A1
Leer	**54**	K1
Leesburg	**130**	E4
Leeston	**116**	D6
Leesville	**130**	C3
Leeuwarden	**54**	H1
Leeward Islands	**134**	M5
Lefkada	**68**	C6
Lefkada	**68**	C6
Lefkimmi	**68**	C5
Lefkonikon	**94**	A1
Lefkosia	**68**	R9
Legaspi	**84**	G4
Legionowo	**50**	K5
Legnago	**62**	G5
Legnica	**50**	F6
Leh	**88**	C2
Le Havre	**54**	C5
Lehre	**52**	F4
Lehrte	**52**	F4
Leiah	**88**	B2
Leibnitz	**62**	L4
Leicester	**54**	A2
Leiden	**54**	G2
Leie	**54**	F4
Leigh Creek	**114**	G6
Leighton Buzzard	**54**	B3
Leine	**52**	E4
Leinster	**114**	D5
Leipzig	**52**	H5
Leiria	**60**	B5
Leiyang	**80**	E5
Lek	**54**	G3
Lelystad	**54**	H2
Le Mans	**58**	F6
Le Mars	**128**	A2
Lemberg	**52**	D8
Lemesos	**68**	Q10
Lemgo	**54**	L2
Lemieux Islands	**122**	U4
Lemmer	**54**	H2
Lemmon	**126**	F1
Le Muret	**58**	E9
Lena	**60**	E1
Lena	**78**	L4
Lendava	**62**	M4
Lendinare	**62**	G5
Lengerich	**54**	K2
Lengshuijiang	**80**	E5
Lengshuitan	**80**	E5
Leninisk-Kuznetskiy	**76**	R7
Leninskoye	**70**	J3
Lenmalu	**87**	D3
Lenne	**54**	K3
Lennestadt	**54**	L3
Lens	**54**	E4
Lensk	**78**	K4
Lenti	**62**	M4
Lentini	**64**	J11
Léo	**104**	D2
Leoben	**62**	L3
León, *Mexico*	**134**	D4
León, *Nicaragua*	**134**	G6
León, *Spain*	**60**	E2
Leonardville	**108**	B4
Leonberg	**62**	E2
Leonforte	**64**	J11
Leonidi	**68**	E7
Leonora	**114**	D5
Leova	**66**	R3
Le Palais	**58**	B6
Lepe	**60**	C7

Mano River	104	B3
Manosque	58	L10
Manouane	128	F1
Manouane Lake	122	S6
Manp'o	82	D3
Manra	112	J6
Manresa	60	M3
Mansa	108	D2
Mansel Island	122	Q4
Mansfield, *UK*	54	A1
Mansfield, *La., US*	130	C3
Mansfield, *Oh., US*	128	D2
Manta	140	A4
Manteo	130	F2
Mantes-la-Jolie	54	D5
Mantova	62	F5
Manturovo	70	H3
Manú	140	C6
Manuelzinho	140	G5
Manūjān	95	G3
Manukan	84	G5
Manukau	116	E3
Manukau Harbour	116	E3
Manyberries	126	D1
Manyinga	108	C2
Manyoni	106	E5
Manzanares	60	G5
Manzanillo	134	J4
Manzhouli	78	K7
Manzil	94	D5
Manzini	108	E5
Mao	100	C5
Maoming	84	E2
Mapam Yumco	88	D2
Mapi	87	E4
Mapinhane	108	F4
Maple Creek	124	E2
Mapuera	140	E4
Maputo	108	E5
Maqueda	60	F4
Maquela do Zombo	106	B5
Maquinchao	142	H7
Maquoketa	128	B2
Māra	88	D4
Maraã	140	D4
Maraba	140	H5
Maracaibo	140	C1
Maracay	140	D1
Marādah	100	C2
Maradi	104	F2
Marāgheh	92	M5
Maralal	106	F3
Marand	92	L4
Maranhão	140	H5
Marañón	140	B4
Marans	58	E7
Marari	140	D5
Mărășești	66	Q4
Marathon, *Canada*	128	C1
Marathon, *US*	132	F2
Marbella	60	F8
Marble Bar	114	C4
Marburg	54	L4
Marcal	62	N3
Marcali	62	N4
March	54	C2
Marche	54	H4
Marchena	60	E7
Mardan	88	B2
Mar del Plata	142	K6
Mardin	92	J5
Maré	112	G8
Mareeba	114	J3
Marettimo	64	F11
Marfa	132	F2
Margate	54	D3
Margherita di Savoia	64	L7
Marghita	66	K2
Margilan	90	K1
Marguerite Bay	144	(2)KK3
María Elena	142	H3
Marianas Trench	112	E4
Marianna	130	D3
Mariánská Lázně	52	H7
Mariazell	62	L3
Mar'ib	100	J4
Maribo	52	G2
Maribor	62	L4
Maridi	106	D2
Marie Byrd Land	144	(2)FF2
Marie Galante	134	M5
Mariehamn	48	K6
Marienberg	52	J6
Mariental	108	B4
Mariestad	48	G7
Marietta	130	E2
Marietta, *Oh., US*	128	D3
Marietta, *Okla., US*	130	B3
Mariinsk	76	R6
Marijampolė	50	N3
Marília	142	M3
Marin	60	B2
Marinette	128	C1
Maringá	142	L3
Marino	64	G7
Marion, *Ill., US*	128	C3
Marion, *Ind., US*	128	C2
Marion, *Oh., US*	128	D2
Maripa	140	D2
Mariscal Estigarribia	142	J3
Maritime Alps	62	C6
Mariupol'	70	G5
Marīvān	92	M6
Mariy El	70	J3
Marjayoûn	94	C3
Marka	106	G3
Markam	80	B5
Markaryd	50	C1
Marked Tree	130	C2
Marken	54	H2
Markermeer	54	H2
Market Harborough	54	B2
Markham	128	E2
Marki	50	L5
Markit	76	P10
Markkleeberg	52	H5
Markovo	78	W4
Marktoberdorf	62	F3
Marktredwitz	52	H7
Marla	114	F5
Marle	54	F5
Marmande	58	F9
Marmara Adası	68	K4
Marmara Denizi	68	L4
Marmaris	68	L8
Marmolada	62	G4
Marne	54	F5
Marne-la-Vallée	54	E6
Maro	104	H3
Maroansetra	108	H3
Marolambo	108	H4
Maroni	140	G3
Maros	87	A3
Marotiri	112	M8
Maroua	104	G2
Marquesas Islands	112	M6
Marquette	128	C1
Marradi	62	G6
Marrakech	102	D2
Marra Plateau	100	D5
Marree	114	G5
Marrupa	108	F2
Marsa Alam	100	F2
Marsabit	106	F3
Marsala	64	G11
Marsberg	54	L3
Marsden	114	J6
Marseille	58	L10
Marseille-en-Beauvaisis	54	D5
Marshall, *Ill., US*	130	D2
Marshall, *Tex., US*	130	C3
Marshall Islands	112	G4
Marshalltown	128	B2
Marsh Harbour	130	F4
Marsh Island	130	C4
Martapura, *Indonesia*	86	C3
Martapura, *Indonesia*	86	E3
Martigny	62	C4
Martigues	58	L10
Martin, *Slovakia*	50	H8
Martin, *US*	126	F2
Martina Franca	64	M8
Martinborough	116	E5
Martinique	134	M6
Martinsburg	128	E3
Martinsville, *Ind., US*	128	C3
Martinsville, *Va., US*	128	E3
Marton	116	E5
Martos	60	G7
Maruchak	90	H2
Mårvatn	48	E6
Mary	90	H2
Maryborough	114	K5
Maryland	128	E3
Marysville, *Canada*	128	G1
Marysville, *Calif., US*	132	B1
Marysville, *Kans., US*	130	B2
Maryville	128	B2
Masai Steppe	106	F4
Masaka	106	E4
Masalembu Besar	86	E4
Masallı	92	N4
Masamba	87	B3
Masan	82	E6
Masasi	106	F6
Masbate	84	G4
Masbate	84	G4
Mascara	102	F1
Maseru	108	D5
Mashhad	90	G2
Masi-Manimba	106	B4
Masindi	106	E3
Maṣīrah	90	G5
Masjed Soleymān	90	E3
Maskanah	92	H5
Mason	130	B3
Mason Bay	116	A8
Mason City	128	B2
Masqaṭ	95	H5
Massa	62	F6
Massachusetts	128	F2
Massachusetts Bay	128	G2
Massafra	64	M8
Massa Marittimo	64	E5
Massawa	100	G4
Massena	128	F2
Masset	122	E6
Massif Central	58	H8
Massif de Guéra	100	C5
Massif de l'Aïr	102	G5
Massif des Écrins	62	B5
Massif du Chaillu	104	G5
Massif du Tsaratanana	108	H2
Massif Ennedi	100	D4
Massillon	128	D2
Massinga	108	F4
Masteksay	70	K5
Masterton	116	E5
Mastung	90	J4
Masty	48	N10
Masuda	82	F6
Masuguru	108	F2
Masvingo	108	E4
Maşyāf	94	D1
Matadi	106	A5
Matagami	128	E1
Matagorda Island	130	B4
Matakana Island	116	F3
Matakawau	116	E3
Matale	88	D7
Matam	104	B1
Matamoros, *Mexico*	132	F3
Matamoros, *Mexico*	132	G3
Matane	128	G1
Matanzas	124	K7
Matara	88	D7
Mataram	86	F4
Mataranka	114	F3
Mataró	60	N3
Mataura	116	B8
Matawai	116	F4
Matehuala	132	F4
Matera	64	L8
Mátészalka	66	K2
Mateur	64	D11
Matheson	128	D1
Mathraki	68	B5
Mathura	88	C3
Mati	84	H5
Matlock	54	A1
Matmata	102	G2
Mato Grosso	140	F6
Mato Grosso	140	F6
Mato Grosso do Sul	140	F7
Matosinhos	60	B3
Maṭraḥ	95	H5
Matrei	62	H4
Matrûh	100	E1
Matsiatra	108	H4
Matsu	80	G5
Matsue	82	G6
Matsumae	82	L3
Matsumoto	82	J5
Matsusaka	82	J6
Matsuyama	82	G7
Mattawa	128	E1
Matterhorn	62	C5
Matthews Ridge	140	E2
Mattighofen	52	J8
Mattoon	128	C3
Maturín	140	E2
Maubeuge	54	F4
Mauganj	88	D4
Maui	132	(2)F3
Maullín	142	G7
Maun	62	K6
Maun	108	C3
Mauna Kea	132	(2)F4
Mauna Loa	132	(2)F4
Mauritania	102	C5
Mauritius	108	(1)B2
Mauron	58	C5
Mauthen	62	H4
Mavinga	108	C3
Mawlaik	84	A2
Max	126	F1
Maya	78	P5
Maya	86	D3
Mayādīn	92	J6
Mayaguana	134	K4
Mayagüez	134	L5
Mayamba	106	B4
Maych'ew	100	G5
Maydh	106	H1
Mayenne	58	E5
Mayenne	58	E5
Mayer	132	D2
Maykamys	76	P8
Maykop	92	J1
Mayly-Say	90	K1
Maymecha	78	G3
Mayn	78	W4
Mayo	122	D4
Mayor Island	116	F3
Mayotte	108	H2
Mayrhofen	62	G3
Mayskiy	78	M6
Mayumba	104	G5
Mayya	78	N4
Mazagão	140	G4
Mazagran	58	K4
Mazama	126	B1
Mazamet	58	H10
Mazar	76	P10
Mazār	94	C5
Mazara del Vallo	64	G11
Mazār-e Sharīf	90	J2
Mazatlán	134	C4
Mažeikiai	50	M1
Mazocahui	132	D3
Mazomora	106	F5
Mazra	94	C5
Mazyr	70	E4
Mazzarino	64	J11
Mbabane	108	E5
Mbaïki	104	H4
Mbala	106	E5
Mbale	106	E3
Mbalmayo	104	G4
Mbamba Bay	108	E2
Mbandaka	106	B3
Mbanga	104	F4
M'banza Congo	106	A5
Mbarara	106	E4
Mbeya	106	E5
Mbomou	106	C3
Mbour	104	A2
Mbout	102	C5
Mbuji-Mayi	106	C5
Mbuyuni	106	F5
McAlester	130	B3
McBride	122	G6
McCamey	132	F2
McCammon	126	D2
McClintock	122	N5
McClintock Channel	122	L2
McComb	130	C3
McCook	126	F2
McDermitt	126	C2
McGehee	130	C3
McGrath	132	(1)F3
Mchinga	106	F5
McKinlay	114	H4
McKinney	130	B3
McLaughlin	126	F1
McLennan	122	H5
McMinnville	128	C3
McPherson	130	B2
McRae	130	E3
Meadow Lake	122	K6
Meadville	128	D2
Meander River	122	H5
Meaux	54	E6
Mecca = Makkah	100	G3
Mechelen	54	G3
Mechernich	54	J4
Mecidiye	68	J4
Mecklenburger Bucht	52	G2
Mecula	108	F2
Meda	60	C4
Medak	88	C5
Medan	86	B2
Médéa	60	N8
Medellín	140	B2
Medenine	102	H2
Mederdra	102	B5
Medford	126	B2
Medgidia	66	R5
Mediaş	66	M3
Medicine Bow	126	E2
Medicine Hat	122	J7
Medicine Lodge	130	B2
Medina = Al Madīnah	100	G3
Medinaceli	60	H3
Medina de Campo	60	F3
Medina Sidonia	60	E8
Mediterranean Sea	46	E4
Mednogorsk	70	L4
Medveditsa	70	H4
Medvezh'yegorsk	70	F2
Meekatharra	114	C5
Meeker	126	E2
Meerane	52	H6
Meerut	88	C3
Mega	87	D3
Mēga	106	F3
Megalopoli	68	E7
Meganisi	68	C6
Megara	68	F6
Megisti	68	M8
Mehrān	92	M7
Mehriz	90	F3
Meiktila	84	B2
Meiningen	52	F6
Meiringen	62	D4
Meißen	52	J5
Meizhou	84	F2
Mejez El Bab	64	D12
Mékambo	104	G4
Mek'elē	100	G5
Meknès	102	D2
Mekong	84	D4
Melaka	86	C2
Melanesia	112	F5
Melbourne, *Australia*	114	H7
Melbourne, *US*	130	E4
Melchor de Mencos	134	G5
Meldorf	52	D2
Meldrum Bay	128	D1
Meleuz	70	L4
Mélfi	100	C5
Melfi	64	K8
Melfort	122	L6
Melide	60	B2
Melilla	60	H9
Melita	126	F1
Melitopol'	70	G5
Melk	62	L2
Melkosopochnik	76	N8
Mělník	52	K6
Melo	142	L5
Melton Mowbray	54	B2
Melun	58	H5
Melut	100	F5
Melvern Lake	130	B2
Melville	122	L6
Melville Island, *Australia*	114	F2
Melville Island, *Canada*	120	N2
Melville Peninsula	122	P3
Memba	108	G2
Memberamo	87	E3
Memboro	87	A4
Memmert	54	J1
Memmingen	62	F3
Mempawah	86	D2
Memphis, *Mo., US*	128	B2
Memphis, *Tenn., US*	128	C3
Mena	130	C3
Menai Strait	56	H8
Ménaka	102	F5
Mendawai	86	E3
Mende	58	J9
Menden	54	K3
Mendī	106	F2
Mendoza	142	H5
Menemen	68	K6
Menen	54	F4
Menfi	64	G11
Menggala	86	D3
Meniet	102	F4
Menindee	114	H6
Menkere	78	L3
Menominee	128	C1
Menomonee Falls	128	C2
Menongue	108	B2
Menorca	60	Q4
Mentok	86	D3
Menunu	87	B2
Menyuan	80	C3
Menzel Bourguiba	64	D11
Menzel Bouzelfa	64	E12
Menzel Temime	64	E12
Menzies	114	D5
Meppel	54	J2
Meppen	54	K2
Merano	62	G4
Merauke	87	F4
Mercato Saraceno	62	H7

Merced 126 B3
Mercedes, *Argentina* 142 H5
Mercedes, *Argentina* 142 K4
Mercedes, *US* 130 B4
Mercedes, *Uruguay* 142 K5
Mercury Islands 116 E3
Mere 54 F4
Mergenevo 70 K5
Mergui 84 B4
Mergui Archipelago 84 B4
Merichas 68 G7
Mérida, *Mexico* 134 G4
Mérida, *Spain* 60 D6
Mérida, *Venezuela* 134 K7
Meridian 130 D3
Mérignac 58 E9
Merinha Grande 60 B5
Meriruma 140 G3
Merke 76 N9
Merkys 48 N9
Merowe 100 F4
Merredin 114 C6
Merrill 128 C1
Merriman 126 F2
Merritt 122 G6
Mersch 54 J5
Merseburg 52 H5
Mers el Kébir 60 K9
Mersey 56 J8
Mersin = İçel 68 S8
Mersing 86 C2
Mērsrags 48 M8
Merthyr Tydfil 56 J10
Méru 54 E5
Meru 106 F3
Merzifon 92 F3
Merzig 54 J5
Mesa 132 D2
Mesa de Yambi 140 C3
Mesagne 64 M8
Meschede 54 L3
Mesöaria Plain 94 A1
Mesolongi 68 D6
Mesopotamia 92 K6
Messaad 102 F2
Messina, *Italy* 64 K10
Messina, *South Africa* 108 D4
Messini 68 E7
Messiniakos Kolpos 68 D8
Mestre 62 H5
Meta 140 C2
Metairie 130 C4
Metaline Falls 126 C1
Metán 142 J4
Metangula 108 E2
Metema 100 G5
Meteor Depth 138 J9
Metković 66 E6
Metlika 62 L5
Metro 86 D4
Metsovo 68 D5
Mettet 54 G4
Mettlach 54 J5
Metz 54 J5
Metzingen 62 E2
Meulaboh 84 B6
Meuse 54 G4
Mexia 130 B3
Mexicali 132 C2
Mexican Hat 132 E1
Mexico 128 B3
Mexico 134 D4
México 134 E5
Meymaneh 90 H2
Meynypil'gyno 78 X4
Mezdra 66 L6
Mezen' 70 H1
Mezenskaya Guba 70 H1
Mezhdurechensk 76 R7
Mezőberény 66 J3
Mezőkövesd 66 H2
Mezőtúr 66 H2
Mfuwe 108 E2
Miajadas 60 E5
Miami, *Fla., US* 130 E4
Miami, *Okla., US* 130 C2
Miandowāb 92 M5
Miandrivazo 108 H3
Mīāneh 92 M5
Miangyang 80 E4
Mianning 80 C5
Mianwali 88 B2
Mianyang 80 C4
Miaodao Qundao 80 G3
Miao'ergou 76 Q8
Miass 70 M4
Miastko 50 G4
Michalovce 50 L9
Michigan 128 C1
Michipicoten Island 128 C1
Michurin 66 Q7
Michurinsk 70 H4
Micronesia 112 F4
Mid-Atlantic Ridge 138 G1
Middelburg, *Netherlands* 54 F3
Middelburg, *South Africa* 108 D6
Middelfart 52 E1
Middelkerke 54 E3
Middle America Trench 120 L8
Middle Andaman 84 A4
Middlebury 128 F2
Middle Lake 126 C2
Middlesboro 128 D3
Middlesbrough 56 L7
Middletown, *N.Y., US* 128 F2
Middletown, *Oh., US* 128 D3
Mīdī 100 H4
Midland, *Canada* 128 E2
Midland, *Mich., US* 128 D2
Midland, *Tex., US* 132 F2
Midway Islands 112 J3
Midwest City 130 B2
Midzor 66 K6
Miechów 50 K7
Międzyrzec Podlaski 50 M5
Miedzyrzecz 50 E5
Mielan 58 F10
Mielec 50 L7
Miembwe 106 F5
Mien 50 D1
Miercurea-Ciuc 66 N3
Mieres 60 E1
Miesbach 62 G3
Mī'ēso 106 G2
Miging 88 F3
Miguel Auza 132 F4
Mikhaylovka 70 H4
Mikhaylovskiy 76 P7
Mikino 78 U4
Mikkeli 48 P6
Mikulov 62 M2
Mikun' 70 K2
Mikuni-sammyaku 82 K5
Mikura-jima 82 K7
Mila 102 G1
Milaca 128 B1
Miladhunmadulu Atoll 88 B7
Milan = Milano, *Italy* 62 E5
Milan, *US* 130 D2
Milano 62 E5
Milas 68 K7
Milazzo 64 K10
Mildura 114 H6
Miles 114 K5
Miles City 126 E1
Milford, *Del., US* 128 E3
Milford, *Ut., US* 126 D3
Milford Haven 56 G10
Milford Sound 116 A7
Milford Sound 116 A7
Miliana 60 N8
Milicz 50 G6
Milk 122 J7
Mil'kovo 78 T6
Millau 58 J9
Millbank 126 G1
Milledgeville 130 E3
Miller 126 G2
Millerovo 70 H5
Millington 128 C3
Millinocket 128 G1
Miloro 106 E5
Milos 68 G8
Milton, *New Zealand* 116 B8
Milton, *US* 130 D3
Milton Keynes 54 B2
Miluo 80 E5
Milwaukee 128 C2
Mily 76 L8
Mimizan-Plage 58 D9
Mīnāb 95 G3
Mina Jebel Ali 95 F4
Minas, *Indonesia* 86 C3
Minas, *Uruguay* 142 K5
Mīnā' Sa'ūd 95 C2
Minas Gerais 140 H7
Minas Novas 140 J7
Minatitlán 134 F5
Minbu 84 A2
Minchinmávida 142 G7
Mincivan 92 M4
Mindanao 84 G5
Mindelheim 62 F2
Mindelo 104 (1)B1
Minden 54 L2
Mindoro 84 G4
Mindoro Strait 84 G4
Minehead 56 J10
Mineola 130 B3
Mineral'nyye Vody 92 K1
Minerva Reefs 112 J8
Minfeng 76 Q10
Minga 106 D6
Mingäçevir 92 M3
Mingäçevir Su Anbarı 92 M3
Mingulay 56 D5
Minhe 80 C3
Minicoy 88 B7
Minilya Roadhouse 114 B4
Minna 104 F3
Minneapolis 128 B2
Minnesota 128 A1
Minnesota 128 A2
Miño 60 C2
Minot 126 F1
Minsk 70 E4
Minturn 126 E3
Minusinsk 76 S7
Min Xian 80 C4
Min'yar 70 L3
Miquelon 128 E1
Miraflores 140 C3
Miramas 58 K10
Mirambeau 58 E8
Miranda 140 F8
Miranda de Ebro 60 H2
Miranda do Douro 60 D3
Mirandela 60 C3
Mirbāt 90 F6
Mīrjāveh 90 H4
Mirnyy 78 J4
Mirow 52 H3
Mirpur Khas 88 A3
Mirtoö Pelagos 68 F7
Mirzapur 88 D3
Miskolc 66 H1
Misoöl 87 D3
Miṣrātah 100 C1
Missinaibi 122 Q6
Missinipe 122 L5
Mission 126 F2
Mississippi 130 C3
Mississippi 130 D2
Mississippi River Delta 130 D4
Missoula 126 D1
Missouri 126 F1
Missouri 128 B3
Missouri City 130 B4
Mistassibi 122 S7
Mistelbach 62 M2
Mitchell 126 G2
Mithankot 90 K4
Mithaylov 70 G4
Mithymna 68 J5
Mito 82 L5
Mitsamiouli 108 G2
Mitsinjo 108 H3
Mits'iwa 90 C6
Mittellandkanal 54 K2
Mittersill 62 H3
Mittweida 52 H6
Mitú 140 C3
Mitzic 104 G4
Miyake-jima 82 K6
Miyako 82 L4
Miyakonojō 82 F8
Miyazaki 82 F8
Miyoshi 82 G6
Mīzan Teferī 106 F2
Mizdah 102 H2
Mizen Head 56 B10
Mizhhir"ya 66 L1
Mizil 66 P4
Mizpe Ramon 94 B6
Mjölby 48 H7
Mjøsa 48 F6
Mkuze 108 E5
Mladá Boleslav 50 D7
Mladenovac 66 H5
Mława 50 K4
Mljet 66 E7
Mmabatho 108 D5
Moa 114 H2
Moanda 104 G5
Moapa 126 D3
Moba 106 D5
Mobaye 106 C3
Mobayi-Mbongo 106 C3
Moberly 128 B3
Mobile 130 D3
Moçambique 108 G3
Môc Châu 84 C2
Mochudi 108 D4
Mocimboa da Praia 108 G2
Mocuba 108 F3
Modane 62 B5
Modena 62 F6
Modesto 126 B3
Modica 64 J12
Mödling 62 M2
Modowi 87 D3
Modriča 66 F5
Moenkopi 132 D1
Moers 54 J3
Moffat 56 J6
Moffat Peak 116 B7
Mogadishu = Muqdisho 106 H3
Mogaung 84 B1
Mogilno 50 G5
Mogocha 78 K6
Mogochin 76 Q6
Mogok 84 B2
Mohács 66 F4
Mohammadia 60 L9
Mohe 78 L6
Mohembo 108 C3
Mohoro 106 F5
Mohyliv-Podil's'kyy 66 Q1
Moi 48 D7
Moincêr 88 D2
Moinești 66 P3
Mo i Rana 48 H3
Moissac 58 G9
Mojave 132 C1
Mojave Desert 132 C2
Mokau 116 E4
Mokohinau Island 116 E2
Mokolo 104 G2
Mokoreta 116 B8
Mokp'o 82 D6
Mol 54 H3
Mola di Bari 64 M7
Molat 62 K6
Molde 48 D5
Moldova 66 P2
Moldova 66 R2
Moldova Nouă 66 J5
Molepolole 108 C4
Molfetta 64 L7
Molina de Aragón 60 J4
Molina de Segura 60 J6
Moline 128 B2
Möll 62 J4
Mollendo 140 C7
Molokai 132 (2)D2
Molopo 108 C5
Molsheim 62 C2
Moma 108 F3
Mombasa 106 G4
Momchilgrad 66 N8
Møn 52 H2
Monach Islands 56 E4
Monaco 62 C7
Monaco 62 C7
Monahans 132 F2
Mona Passage 134 L5
Monbetsu, *Japan* 82 M1
Monbetsu, *Japan* 82 M2
Moncalieri 62 C5
Monchegorsk 48 S3
Mönchengladbach 54 J3
Monchique 60 B7
Monclova 132 F3
Moncton 122 U7
Mondovi 62 C6
Mondragone 64 H7
Mondy 78 G6
Monemvasia 68 F8
Monfalcone 62 J5
Monforte 60 C5
Monforte de Lemos 60 C2
Monfredónia 64 K7
Monga 106 C3
Mongkung 84 B2
Mongo 100 C5
Mongolia 80 B2
Mongonu 104 G2
Mongora 88 B2
Mongu 108 C3
Mong Yai 84 B2
Mong Yu 84 B2
Monkoto 106 C4
Monmouth 128 B2
Mono 104 E3
Mono Lake 126 C3
Monopoli 64 M8
Monor 50 J10
Monowai 116 A7
Monreal del Campo 60 J4
Monreale 64 H10
Monroe, *La., US* 130 C3
Monroe, *Mich., US* 128 D2
Monroe, *N.C., US* 130 E3
Monroe, *Wash., US* 126 B1
Monroe City 130 C2
Monrovia 104 B3
Mons 54 F4
Monschau 54 J4
Monselice 62 G5
Montabaur 54 K4
Montague Island 138 J9
Montalbán 60 K4
Montalto Uffugo 64 L9
Montana 66 L6
Montana 126 E1
Montargis 58 H6
Montauban 58 G10
Montauk 128 F2
Mont aux Sources 108 D5
Montbard 58 K6
Montbéliard 62 B3
Montblanc 60 M3
Mont Blanc 62 B5
Montbrison 58 K8
Mont Cameroun 104 F4
Montceau-les-Mines 58 K7
Mont-de-Marsan 58 E10
Montdidier 54 E5
Monte Alegre 140 G4
Monte Azul 140 J7
Montebello 128 F1
Montebello Islands 114 B4
Montebelluna 62 H5
Monte Calvo 64 K7
Monte Cinto 64 C6
Montecristo 64 E6
Monte Etna 64 J11
Montefiascone 64 G6
Montego Bay 134 J5
Montélimar 58 K9
Monte Limbara 64 D8
Monte Lindo 142 K4
Montemorelos 130 B4
Monte Namuli 108 F3
Monte Perdino 60 L2
Monte Pollino 64 L9
Montepuez 108 F2
Montepulciano 64 F5
Monte Quemado 142 J4
Montereau-faut-Yonne 58 H5
Monterey 128 E3
Monterey Bay 126 B3
Montería 140 B2
Montero 140 E7
Monte Rosa 62 C5
Monterotondo 64 G6
Monterrey 132 F3
Monte Sant'Angelo 64 K7
Montes Claros 140 J7
Montesilvano 64 J6
Montevarchi 62 G7
Montevideo, *US* 128 A1
Montevideo, *Uruguay* 142 K5
Monte Viso 62 C6
Monte Vista 132 E1
Montgomery 130 D3
Monthey 62 B4
Monticello 126 E3
Montijo 60 D6
Montilla 60 F7
Mont Joli 128 G1
Mont-Laurier 128 E1
Montluçon 58 H7
Montmagny 128 F1
Montmedy 54 H5
Mont Mézenc 58 K9
Montone 62 G6
Montoro 60 F6
Mont Pelat 58 M9
Montpelier, *Id., US* 126 D2
Montpelier, *Vt., US* 128 F2
Montpellier 58 J10
Montréal 128 F1
Montreul 54 D4
Montreux 62 B4
Montrose, *UK* 56 K5
Montrose, *US* 126 E3
Monts Bagzane 102 G5
Mont Serkout 102 G4
Montserrat 134 M5
Monts Nimba 104 C3
Monts Otish 122 S6
Mont Tahat 102 G4
Monywa 84 A2
Monza 62 E5
Monzón 60 L3
Moonie 114 K5
Moorcroft 126 F2

Moorhead 128 A1
Moosburg 62 G1
Moose Jaw 122 K6
Moose Lake 122 M6
Moosomin 122 L6
Moosonee 122 Q6
Mopeia 108 F3
Mopti 102 E6
Moqor 90 J3
Mór 66 F2
Mora 48 H6
Móra 60 B6
Moradabad 88 C3
Morafenobe 108 G3
Morag 50 J4
Moramanga 108 H3
Moran 126 D2
Morane 112 N8
Moratuwa 88 D7
Morava 50 G8
Moravské Budějovice 62 L1
Morawhanna 140 F2
Moray Firth 56 J4
Morbach 54 K5
Morbegno 62 E4
Morbi 88 B4
Morcenx 58 E9
Mordaga 78 L6
Mordoviya 70 H4
Moreau 126 F1
Morecambe 56 K7
Moree 114 J5
Morehead, *Papua New Guinea* 87 F4
Morehead, *US* 128 D3
More Laptevykh 78 L1
Morelia 134 D5
Morella 60 K4
Moresby Island 132 (1)L5
Moreton Island 114 K5
Morez 58 M7
Morfou 68 Q9
Morgan 114 G6
Morgan City 130 C4
Morgantown 128 D3
Morges 62 B4
Mori 82 L2
Morioka 82 L4
Morkoka 78 J4
Morlaix 58 B5
Mornington Island 114 G3
Morocco 98 C2
Morogoro 106 F5
Moro Gulf 84 G5
Morombe 108 G4
Mörön 78 G7
Morondava 108 G4
Morón de la Frontera 60 E7
Moroni 108 G2
Moron Us He 88 F2
Morotai 87 C2
Moroto 106 E3
Morpeth 56 L6
Morris 126 G1
Morristown 130 E2
Mors 48 E8
Morshansk 70 H4
Mortain 54 B6
Morteros 142 J5
Morvern 56 G5
Morwell 114 J7
Mosbach 52 E7
Mosby 126 D1
Moscow = Moskva 70 G3
Mosel 54 K4
Moselle 54 G6
Moses Lake 126 C1
Mosgiel 116 C7
Moshi 106 F4
Mosjøen 48 G4
Moskenesøy 48 F3
Moskva 70 G3
Mosonmagyaróvár 62 N3
Mosquero 132 F1
Moss 48 F7
Mossburn 116 B7
Mosselbaai 108 C6
Mossoró 140 K5
Most 52 J6
Mostaganem 60 L9
Mostar 66 E6
Mostoles 60 G4
Møsvatn 48 E7
Mot'a 100 G5
Motala 48 H7
Motherwell 56 J6
Motihari 88 D3
Motilla del Palancar 60 J5
Motiti Island 116 F3
Motril 60 G8
Motru 66 K5
Motu One 112 L7
Motygino 76 S6
Mouchard 62 A4
Moudjéria 102 C5
Moudros 68 H5
Mouila 104 G5
Moulins 58 J7
Moulmein 84 B3
Moultrie 130 E3
Moundou 100 C6
Mount Adam 142 J9
Mount Adams 126 B1
Mountain Grove 128 B3
Mountain Home 128 B3
Mountain Nile = Bahr el Jebel 106 E2
Mount Alba 116 B7
Mount Aloysius 114 E5
Mount Anglem 116 A8
Mount Apo 84 H5
Mount Ararat 92 L4
Mount Arrowsmith 116 C6
Mount Aspiring 116 B7
Mount Assiniboine 122 H6
Mount Augustus 114 C4
Mount Baco 84 G3
Mount Baker 126 B1
Mount Bartle Frere 114 J3
Mount Bogong 114 J7
Mount Brewster 116 B7
Mount Bruce 114 C4
Mount Cameroun 98 D5
Mount Carmel 126 D3
Mount Columbia 122 H6
Mount Cook = Aoraki 116 C6
Mount Cook 116 C6
Mount Donald 116 A7
Mount Douglas 114 J4
Mount Egmont 116 E4
Mount Elbert 126 E3
Mount Elgon 106 E3
Mount Essendon 114 D4
Mount Evelyn 114 F2
Mount Everest 88 E3
Mount Fairweather 122 D5
Mount Gambier 114 H7
Mount Garnet 114 J3
Mount Hermōn 94 C3
Mount Hood 126 B1
Mount Hutt 116 C6
Mount Huxley 116 B7
Mount Isa 114 G4
Mount Jackson 144 (2)MM2
Mount Karisimbi 106 D4
Mount Kendall 116 D5
Mount Kenya = Kirinyaga 106 F4
Mount Kilimanjaro 106 F4
Mount Kirkpatrick 144 (2)AA1
Mount Kosciuszko 114 J7
Mount Liebig 114 F4
Mount Lloyd George 122 G5
Mount Logan 122 C4
Mount Magnet 114 C5
Mount Maunganui 116 F3
Mount McKinley 132 (1)G3
Mount Meharry 114 C4
Mount Menzies 144 (2)L2
Mount Minto 144 (2)Y2
Mount Mulanje 108 F3
Mount Murchison 116 C6
Mount Nyiru 106 F3
Mount Olympus 126 B1
Mount Ord 114 E3
Mount Ossa 114 J8
Mount Owen 116 D5
Mount Paget 142 P9
Mount Pleasant, *Ia., US* 128 B2
Mount Pleasant, *Mich., US* 128 D2
Mount Pleasant, *S.C., US* 130 F3
Mount Pleasant, *Tex., US* 130 B3
Mount Pleasant, *Ut., US* 126 D3
Mount Pulog 84 G3
Mount Rainier 126 B1
Mount Ratz 122 E5
Mount Richmond 116 D5
Mount Roberts 114 K5
Mount Robson 122 H6
Mount Roosevelt 122 F5
Mount Roraima 140 E2
Mount Ross 116 E5
Mount Shasta 126 B2
Mount Somers 116 C6
Mount Stanley 106 D3
Mount Tahat 98 D3
Mount Travers 116 D6
Mount Tuun 82 D3
Mount Usborne 142 K9
Mount Vernon, *Al., US* 130 D3
Mount Vernon, *Ill., US* 128 C3
Mount Vernon, *Oh., US* 128 D2
Mount Vernon, *Wash., US* 126 B1
Mount Victoria, *Myanmar* 84 A2
Mount Victoria, *Papua New Guinea* 112 E6
Mount Waddington 122 F6
Mount Washington 122 S8
Mount Whitney 126 C3
Mount Wilson 126 E3
Mount Woodroffe 114 F5
Mount Ziel 114 F4
Moura 60 C6
Mousa 56 L2
Moussoro 100 C5
Moutamba 104 G5
Mouth of the Shannon 56 B9
Mouths of the Amazon 138 G3
Mouths of the Danube 66 S4
Mouths of the Ganges 88 E4
Mouths of the Indus 90 J5
Mouths of the Irrawaddy 84 A3
Mouths of the Krishna 88 D5
Mouths of the Mekong 84 D5
Mouths of the Niger 104 F4
Moûtiers 62 B5
Moutong 87 B2
Mouzarak 104 H2
Moyale 106 F3
Moyen Atlas 102 D2
Moyenvic 54 J6
Moyeroo 76 U4
Moyynty 76 N8
Mozambique 108 E3
Mozambique Channel 108 F4
Mozdok 92 L2
Mozhga 70 K3
Mozirje 62 K4
Mpanda 106 E5
Mpika 108 E2
Mporokoso 106 E5
Mpumalanga 108 D5
Mrągowo 50 L4
Mrkonjić-Grad 62 N6
M'Sila 102 F1
Mtsensk 70 G4
Mtwara 106 G6
Muang Khammouan 84 C3
Muang Không 84 D4
Muang Khôngxédôn 84 D3
Muang Khoua 84 C2
Muang Pakxan 84 C3
Muang Phin 84 D3
Muang Sing 84 C2
Muang Xai 84 C2
Muar 86 C2
Muarabungo 86 C3
Muaradua 86 C3
Muarasiberut 86 B3
Muaratewen 86 E3
Muarawahau 86 F2
Mubarek 76 M10
Mubende 106 E3
Mubrani 87 D3
Muck 56 F5
Muckadilla 114 J5
Muconda 106 C6
Mucur 68 S5
Mudanjiang 82 E1
Mudanya 68 L4
Muddy Gap 126 E2
Mudurnu 68 P4
Mufulira 108 D2
Mughshin 90 F6
Muğla 68 L7
Mugodzhary 70 L5
Muhammad Qol 100 G3
Mühldorf 62 H2
Mühlhausen 52 F5
Muhos 48 N4
Muhu 48 M7
Muhulu 106 D4
Mukacheve 50 M9
Mukdahan 84 C3
Mukomuko 86 C3
Mukry 90 J2
Mukuku 108 D2
Mulaku Atoll 88 B8
Mulde 52 H5
Muleshoe 132 F2
Mulgrave Island 114 H2
Mulhacén 60 G7
Mülheim 54 J3
Mulhouse 62 C3
Muling 82 G1
Mull 56 G5
Mullaittivu 88 D7
Mullewa 114 C5
Müllheim 62 C3
Mullingar 56 E8
Mulobezi 108 D3
Multan 90 K3
Mumbai 88 B5
Mumbwa 108 D2
Muna 87 B4
Münchberg 52 G6
München 62 G2
Münden 52 E5
Mundo Novo 140 J6
Mundrabilla 114 E6
Muneðarnes 48 (1)C1
Munera 60 H5
Mungbere 106 D3
Munger 88 E3
Munich = München 62 G2
Munster, *France* 62 C2
Munster, *Germany* 52 F4
Münster, *Germany* 54 K3
Munte 87 A2
Muojärvi 48 Q4
Muonio 48 M3
Muqdisho 106 H3
Mur 62 L4
Muradiye 92 K4
Murang'a 106 F4
Murashi 70 J3
Murat 92 K4
Muratlı 68 K3
Murchison 116 D5
Murcia 60 J7
Murdo 126 F2
Mureș 66 J3
Muret 58 G10
Murfreesboro, *N.C., US* 130 F2
Murfreesboro, *Tenn., US* 130 D2
Murghob 90 K2
Muriaé 140 J8
Müritz 52 H3
Muriwai 116 F4
Murmansk 48 S2
Murnau 62 G3
Murom 70 H3
Muroran 82 L2
Muros 60 A2
Muroto 82 H7
Murphy 130 E2
Murray 114 H6
Murray 128 C3
Murray Bridge 114 G7
Murray River Basin 114 H6
Murska Sobota 62 M4
Murter 62 L7
Murtosa 60 B4
Murud 88 B5
Murupara 116 F4
Mururoa 112 M8
Murwara 88 D4
Murzūq 102 H3
Mürzzuschlag 62 L3
Muş 92 J4
Mūša 50 N1
Musala 68 F2
Musandam Peninsula 95 G3
Musay'īd 95 D4
Muscat = Masqaț 95 H5
Musgrave Ranges 114 E5
Mushin 104 E3
Muskegon 128 C2
Muskogee 130 B2
Musmar 100 G4
Musoma 106 E4
Mussende 106 B6
Mustafakemalpaşa 68 L4
Mut, *Egypt* 100 E2
Mut, *Turkey* 68 R8
Mutare 108 E3
Mutarnee 114 J3
Mutnyy Materik 70 L1
Mutoray 76 U5
Mutsamudu 108 G2
Mutsu 82 L3
Mutsu-wan 82 L3
Muttaburra 114 H4
Mutur 88 D7
Muyezerskiy 48 R5
Muyinga 106 E4
Muynak 76 K9
Muzaffarnagar 88 C3
Muzaffarpur 88 E3
Muzillac 58 C6
Múzquiz 132 F3
Muztagata 76 N10
Mwali 108 G2
Mwanza 106 E4
Mweka 106 C4
Mwenda 106 D6
Mwene-Ditu 106 C5
Mwenezi 108 E4
Mwenezi 108 E4
Mwinilunga 108 C2
Myanmar 84 B2
Myaungmya 84 A3
Myingyan 84 B2
Myitkyina 84 B1
Myjava 62 N2
Myjava 62 N2
Mykolayiv 50 N8
Mykonos 68 H7
Mymensingh 88 F4
Mynbulak 76 L9
Myndagayy 78 N4
Myōjin 80 K4
Myonggan 82 E3
Myrdalsjökull 48 (1)D3
Myrina 68 H5
Myrtle Beach 130 F3
Mys Alevina 78 S5
Mys Aniva 80 L1
Mys Buorkhaya 78 N2
Mys Dezhneva 78 Z3
Mys Elizavety 78 Q6
Mys Enkan 78 P5
Mys Govena 78 V5
Mys Kanin Nos 70 H1
Mys Kekurskij 48 S2
Mys Kril'on 80 L1
Myślenice 50 J8
Myślibórz 50 D5
Mys Lopatka, *Russia* 78 T6
Mys Lopatka, *Russia* 78 S2
Mys Navarin 78 X4
Mys Olyutorskiy 78 W5
Mysore 88 C6
Mys Peschanyy 76 J9
Mys Povorotnyy 82 G2
Mys Prubiynyy 70 F5
Mys Shelagskiy 78 V2
Mys Sivuchiy 78 U5
Mys Terpeniya 78 Q7
Mys Tolstoy 78 T5
Mys Yuzhnyy 78 T5
Mys Zhelaniya 76 M2
Myszków 50 J7
My Tho 84 D4
Mytilini 68 J5
Mývatn 48 (1)E2
Mže 52 H7
Mzimba 108 E2
Mzuzu 108 E2

N

Naalehu 132 (2)F4
Naas 56 F8
Nabas 84 G4
Naberezhnyye Chelny 70 K3
Nabeul 64 E12
Nabīd 95 G2
Nabire 87 E3
Nablus 94 C4
Nacala 108 G2
Nacaroa 108 F2
Náchod 50 F7
Nacogdoches 130 C3
Nadiad 88 B4
Nador 102 E2
Nadvirna 66 M1
Nadym 70 P1
Nadym 70 P2
Næstved 52 G1
Nafpaktos 68 D6
Nafplio 68 E7
Naga 84 G4
Nagano 82 K5
Nagaoka 82 K5
Nagaon 88 F3
Nagarzê 88 F3
Nagasaki 82 E7
Nagaur 88 B3
Nagercoil 88 C7
Nago 80 H5
Nagold 52 D8
Nagorsk 70 K3
Nagoya 82 J6
Nagpur 88 C4
Nagqu 88 F2
Nagyatád 62 N4
Nagykálló 66 J2
Nagykanizsa 62 N4
Nagykáta 50 J10
Nagykőrös 66 G2

175

Place	Page	Grid
Pakistan	90	J4
Pakokku	84	A2
Pakotai	116	D2
Pakrac	62	N5
Paks	66	F3
Pakxé	84	D3
Pala	100	B6
Palafrugell	60	P3
Palagonia	64	J11
Palagruža	64	L6
Palaiochora	68	F9
Palamós	60	P3
Palana	78	U5
Palanan	84	G3
Palanga	50	L2
Palangkaraya	86	E3
Palanpur	88	B4
Palantak	90	H4
Palapye	108	D4
Palatka, Russia	78	S4
Palatka, US	130	E4
Palau	64	D7
Palau	112	D5
Palau	112	D5
Palaw	84	B4
Palawan	84	F5
Palazzolo Arceide	64	J11
Palembang	86	C3
Palencia	60	F2
Paleokastritsa	68	B5
Palermo	64	H10
Palestine	130	B3
Palestrina	64	G7
Paletwa	84	A2
Palghat	88	C6
Pali	88	B3
Palikir	112	F5
Palimbang	84	G5
Pälkohda	88	D5
Palk Strait	88	C7
Palma	60	N5
Palma del Rio	60	E7
Palma di Montechiaro	64	H11
Palmanova	62	J5
Palmares	140	K5
Palmarola	64	G8
Palmas	140	H6
Palmas	142	L4
Palm Bay	130	E4
Palmdale	132	C2
Palmerston	116	C7
Palmerston Island	112	K7
Palmerston North	116	E5
Palm Harbor	130	E4
Palmi	64	K10
Palmira	140	B3
Palmyra Island	112	K5
Palojärvi	48	M2
Palopo	87	B3
Palu, Indonesia	87	A3
Palu, Turkey	92	J4
Palyavaam	78	W3
Pama	104	E2
Pamekasan	86	E4
Pamhagen	62	M3
Pamiers	58	G10
Pamlico Sound	130	F2
Pampa	132	F1
Pampas	142	J6
Pamplona, Colombia	134	K7
Pamplona, Spain	60	J2
Pana	128	C3
Panagyurishte	66	M7
Panaji	88	B5
Panama	134	H7
Panamá	140	B2
Panama Canal = Canal de Panamá	134	J7
Panama City	130	D3
Panarea	64	K10
Panarik	86	D2
Panaro	62	G6
Panay	84	G4
Pančevo	66	H5
Panciu	66	Q4
Pandan	84	G4
Pandharpur	88	C5
Panevėžys	50	P2
Pangani	106	F5
Pangin	88	F3
Pangkajene	87	A3
Pangkalanbuun	86	E3
Pangkalpinang	86	D3
Pangnirtung	122	T3
Panguitch	126	D3
Pangutaran Group	84	G5
Panhandle	132	F1
Panipat	88	C3
Panjāb	90	J3
Panjgur	90	H4
Pankshin	104	F3
Pantanal	140	F7
Pantar	87	B4
Pantelleria	102	H1
Pantemakassar	87	B4
Paola	64	L9
Paoua	106	B2
Pápa	66	E2
Papa	132	(2)F4
Papakura	116	E3
Papantla	134	E4
Paparoa	116	E3
Papa Stour	56	L1
Papatowi	116	B8
Papa Westray	56	K2
Papenburg	52	C3
Papey	48	(1)F2
papua	87	E3
Papua New Guinea	112	E6
Papun	84	B3
Pará	140	G5
Para	140	H4
Parabel'	76	Q6
Paracatu	140	H7
Paracel Islands	84	E3
Paraćin	66	J6
Pará de Minas	140	J7
Paragould	130	C2
Paragua, Bolivia	140	E6
Paragua, Venezuela	140	E2
Paraguay	138	F6
Paraguay	142	J3
Paraíba	140	K5
Parakou	104	E3
Paralia	68	E8
Paralimni	94	A1
Paramaribo	140	F2
Paraná	140	H6
Paraná	140	H6
Paraná	142	J5
Paraná	142	L3
Paraná	142	L3
Paranaguá	142	M4
Paranaíba	140	G7
Paranaíba	140	G7
Paranavaí	142	L3
Paranestio	68	G3
Paraparaumu	116	E5
Paray-le Monial	58	K7
Parbhani	88	C5
Parchim	52	G3
Pardo	140	J7
Pardubice	50	E7
Pareh	92	L4
Parepare	87	A3
Parga	68	C5
Parigi	87	B3
Parika	140	F2
Parintins	140	F4
Paris, France	58	H5
Paris, Tenn., US	130	D2
Paris, Tex., US	130	B3
Parkersburg	128	D3
Park Rapids	128	A1
Parla	60	G4
Parma	62	F6
Parma, Italy	62	F6
Parma, US	128	D2
Parnaíba	140	J4
Parnassus	116	D6
Pärnu	48	N7
Pärnu	48	N7
Paros	68	H7
Paros	68	H7
Parry Bay	122	Q3
Parry Islands	122	L1
Parry Sound	128	D2
Parsons	130	B2
Parthenay	58	E7
Partinico	64	H10
Partizansk	82	G2
Paru	140	G4
Parvatipuram	88	D5
Paryang	88	D2
Pasadena, Calif., US	132	C2
Pasadena, Tex., US	130	B4
Paşalimani Adası	68	K4
Pasawng	84	B3
Paşcani	66	P2
Pasco	126	C1
Pascual	84	G4
Pasewalk	52	K3
Pasig	84	G4
Pasinler	92	J3
Pasłęk	50	J3
Pasłęk	50	J3
Pasleka	48	L9
Pašman	62	L7
Pasni	90	H4
Paso de Hachado	142	G6
Paso de Indios	142	H7
Paso de la Cumbre	142	H5
Paso de San Francisco	142	H4
Paso Río Mayo	142	G8
Paso Robles	132	B1
Passau	52	J8
Passo Fundo	142	L4
Passos	140	H8
Pastavy	48	P9
Pasto	140	B3
Pastos Bons	140	J5
Pasvalys	50	P1
Pásztó	66	G2
Patagonia	142	G8
Patan, India	88	B4
Patan, Nepal	88	E3
Patea	116	E4
Pate Island	106	G4
Paterna	60	K5
Paternò	64	J11
Paterson	128	F2
Pathankot	88	C2
Pathein	84	A3
Pathfinder Reservoir	126	E2
Patia	140	B3
Patiala	88	C2
Patmos	68	J7
Patna	88	E3
Patnos	92	K4
Patos de Minas	140	H7
Patra	68	D6
Patraikis Kolpos	68	D6
Patreksfjörður	48	(1)B2
Pattani	84	C5
Pattaya	84	C4
Patti	64	J10
Paturau River	116	D5
Pau	60	K1
Pauini	140	D5
Pauini	140	D5
Paulatuk	132	(1)N2
Paulo Afonso	140	K5
Paul's Valley	130	B3
Pāveh	92	M6
Pavia	62	E5
Pãvilosta	48	L8
Pavlikeni	66	N6
Pavlodar	76	P7
Pavlohrad	70	G5
Pavlovsk	70	H4
Pavlovskaya	70	G5
Pavullo nel Frignano	62	F6
Paxoi	68	C5
Paxson	132	(1)H3
Payerne	62	B4
Payette	126	C2
Paynes Find	114	C5
Paysandu	142	K5
Payson	132	D2
Payturma	76	S3
Pazar	92	J3
Pazardzhik	66	M7
Pazin	62	J5
Peace	122	H5
Peace River	122	H5
Peach Springs	132	D1
Pearsall	130	B4
Pebane	108	F3
Pebas	140	C5
Peć	66	H7
Pecan Island	130	C4
Pechora	70	K1
Pechora	70	L1
Pechorskoye More	76	J4
Pechory	48	P8
Pecos	132	F2
Pecos	132	F2
Pécs	66	F3
Pedja	48	P7
Pedra Azul	140	J7
Pedra Lume	104	(1)B1
Pedreiras	140	J4
Pedro Afonso	140	H5
Pedro Juan Caballero	142	K3
Pedro Luro	142	J6
Peel Sound	122	M2
Peene	52	J3
Peenemünde	52	J2
Pegasus Bay	116	D6
Pegnitz	52	G7
Pegu	84	B3
Pegunungan Barisan	86	B2
Pegunungan Iban	86	F2
Pegunungan Maoke	87	E3
Pegunungan Meratus	86	F3
Pegunungan Schwaner	86	E3
Pegunungan Van Rees	87	E3
Pehuajó	142	J6
Peine	52	F4
Peißenberg	62	G3
Peixe	140	H6
Pekalongan	86	D4
Pekanbaru	86	C2
Peking = Beijing	80	F3
Pelaihari	86	E3
Peleduy	78	J5
Peleng	87	B3
Pelhřimov	50	E8
Pelješac	64	M6
Pello	48	N3
Pellworm	52	D2
Pelly Bay	122	P3
Peloponnisos	68	D7
Pelotas	142	L5
Pelym	70	M2
Pemangkat	86	D2
Pematangsiantar	86	B2
Pemba	108	G2
Pemba Island	106	F5
Pembina	126	G1
Pembine	128	C1
Pembroke, Canada	128	E1
Pembroke, UK	56	H10
Pembroke, US	130	E3
Peñafiel	60	F3
Peñaranda de Bracamonte	60	E4
Peñarroya-Pueblonuevo	60	E6
Pendik	68	M4
Pendleton	126	C1
Pendolo	86	G3
Pend Oreille Lake	126	C1
Pen Hills	128	E2
Peniche	60	A5
Península de Azuero	134	H7
Península de Guajira	134	K6
Península Valdés	142	J7
Péninsule de Gaspé	122	T7
Péninsule d'Ungava	122	R4
Penmarch	58	A6
Penne	64	H6
Pennines	56	K7
Pennsylvania	128	E2
Penrith	56	K7
Pensacola	134	G2
Penticton	126	C1
Penza	70	J4
Penzance	56	G11
Penzhina	78	V4
Penzhinskaya Guba	78	U4
Penzhinskiy Khrebet	78	V4
Peoria, Ariz., US	132	D2
Peoria, Ill., US	128	C2
Percival Lakes	114	D4
Peregrebnoye	70	N2
Pereira	140	B3
Pergamino	142	J5
Périers	58	D4
Périgueux	58	F8
Peristera	68	G5
Perito Moreno	142	G8
Perleberg	52	G3
Perm'	70	L3
Përmet	68	C4
Pernambuco	140	K5
Pernik	66	L7
Péronne	54	E5
Perpignan	58	H11
Perrine	130	E4
Perry, Fla., US	130	E3
Perry, Ga., US	130	E3
Persepolis	95	C2
Persian Gulf	95	C2
Perth, Australia	114	C6
Perth, UK	56	J5
Pertuis Breton	58	D7
Peru	128	C2
Peru	140	C6
Peru-Chile Trench	138	D5
Perugia	64	G5
Pervomays'k	70	F5
Pervoural'sk	70	L3
Pesaro	62	H7
Pescara	64	J6
Pescia	62	F7
Peshawar	88	B2
Peshkopi	68	C3
Peshtera	68	L8
Peski Karakumy	90	G2
Peski Kzyylkum	76	L9
Peski Priaral'skiye Karakumy	76	L8
Pesnica	62	L4
Pessac	58	E9
Petah Tiqwa	94	B4
Petalioi	68	G7
Petaluma	126	B3
Pétange	54	H5
Petare	134	L6
Petauke	108	E2
Peterborough, Canada	128	E2
Peterborough, UK	56	M9
Peterhead	56	L4
Peter I Øy	144	(2)JJ3
Petersburg	128	E3
Petersfield	54	B3
Petershagen	52	D4
Petit Mécatina	122	U6
Peto	134	G4
Petre Bay	116	(1)B1
Petrich	68	F3
Petrila	66	L4
Petrinja	62	M5
Petrolina	140	J5
Petropavlovka	78	H6
Petropavlovsk	70	N4
Petropavlovsk-Kamchatskiy	78	T6
Petrópolis	142	N3
Petroşani	66	L4
Petrovac	66	J5
Petrovsk-Zabaykal'skiy	78	H6
Petrozavodsk	70	F2
Petukhovo	70	N3
Petrun	70	M1
Pevek	78	W3
Pezinok	50	G9
Pfaffenhofen	52	G8
Pfarrkirchen	52	H8
Pflach	62	F3
Pforzheim	52	D8
Pfunds	62	F4
Pfungstadt	52	D7
Phalaborwa	108	E4
Phalodi	88	B3
Phan Rang	84	D4
Phan Thiêt	84	D4
Phatthalung	84	C5
Phet Buri	84	B4
Phichit	84	C3
Philadelphia, Miss., US	130	D3
Philadelphia, Pa., US	128	F2
Philippeville	54	G4
Philippines	84	G4
Philippine Trench	74	R8
Philips	122	K7
Phillipsburg	126	G3
Phitsanulok	84	C3
Phnum Penh	84	C4
Phoenix	108	(1)B2
Phoenix	132	D2
Phoenix Islands	112	K6
Phôngsali	84	C2
Phuket	84	B5
Phumĩ Sâmrâong	84	C4
Piacenza	62	E5
Piadena	62	F5
Pianoro	62	G6
Pianosa	64	P3
Piatra-Neamţ	66	P3
Piauí	140	J5
Piazza Armerina	64	J11
Pibor Post	106	E2
Picacho del Centinela	132	F3
Picayune	130	D4
Pichilemu	142	G5
Pico	102	(1)B2
Pico Almanzor	60	E4
Pico Cristóbal Colón	134	K6
Pico da Bandeira	142	N3
Pico da Neblina	140	D3
Pico de Itambé	142	N2
Pico de Teide	102	B3
Pico Duarte	134	K5
Picos	140	J5
Picton, New Zealand	116	D5
Picton, US	128	E2
Pic Tousside	100	C3
Piedras Negras	132	F3
Pieksämäki	48	P5
Pielinen	48	Q5
Pierre	126	F2
Pierrelatte	58	K9
Piers do Rio	140	H7
Piešťany	50	G9
Pietermaritzburg	108	E5
Pietersburg	108	D4
Pietrasanta	62	F6
Piet Retief	108	E5
Pieve di Cadore	62	H4
Pihlájavesi	48	P6

Prince Edward Island 122 U7
Prince George 122 G6
Prince of Wales Island, *Australia* 114 H2
Prince of Wales Island, *Canada* 122 L2
Prince of Wales Island, *US* 122 E5
Prince of Wales Strait 122 H2
Prince Patrick Island 120 Q2
Prince Regent Inlet 122 N2
Prince Rupert 122 E6
Princess Charlotte Bay 114 H2
Princeton, *Canada* 126 B1
Princeton, *Ill., US* 128 C2
Princeton, *Ky., US* 128 C3
Princeton, *Mo., US* 128 B2
Prince William Sound 122 B4
Príncipe 104 F4
Prineville 126 B2
Priozersk 48 R6
Priština 66 J7
Pritzwalk 52 H3
Privas 58 K9
Privolzhskaya Vozvyshennost 70 H4
Prizren 66 H7
Probolinggo 86 E4
Proddatur 88 C6
Progreso 134 G4
Prokhladnyy 92 L2
Prokop'yevsk 76 R7
Prokuplje 66 J6
Proletarsk 70 H5
Proliv Longa 78 X2
Proliv Matochkin Shar 76 K3
Proliv Vil'kitskogo 76 U2
Prophet 122 G5
Propriano 64 C7
Prorer Wiek 52 J2
Proserpine 114 J4
Prosna 50 G6
Prosperidad 84 H5
Prostojov 50 G8
Proti 68 D7
Provadiya 66 Q6
Prøven = Kangersuatsiaq 122 W2
Providence 128 F2
Providence Island 108 (2)B2
Provideniya 78 Z4
Provincetown 128 F2
Provins 58 J5
Provo 126 D2
Provost 122 J6
Prudhoe Bay 132 (1)H1
Prudnik 50 G7
Prüm 54 J4
Pruszków 50 K5
Prut 66 R4
Pružany 50 P5
Prvić 62 K6
Pryluky 70 F4
Prypyats' 46 G2
Przasnysz 50 K4
Przemyśl 50 M8
Przeworsk 50 M7
Psara 68 H6
Psebay 92 J1
Pskov 70 E3
Ptolemaïda 68 D4
Ptuj 62 L4
Pucallpa 140 C5
Pucheng 80 F5
Puch'ŏn 82 D5
Púchov 50 H8
Pucioasa 66 N4
Puck 50 H3
Pudasjärvi 48 P4
Pudozh 70 G2
Puebla 134 E5
Puebla de Don Rodrigo 60 F5
Pueblo 126 F3
Puelches 142 H6
Puelén 142 H6
Puente-Genil 60 F7
Puerto Acosta 140 D7
Puerto Aisén 142 G8
Puerto Alegre 140 E6
Puerto Angel 134 E5
Puerto Ayacucho 134 L7
Puerto Barrios 134 G5
Puerto Berrío 140 C2
Puerto Cabezas 134 H6
Puerto Carreño 134 L7
Puerto del Rosario 102 C3
Puerto de Navacerrada 60 G4
Puerto Guarini 140 F8
Puerto Heath 140 D6
Puerto Inírida 140 D3
Puerto Leguizamo 140 C4
Puerto Libertad 132 D3
Puerto Limón 140 B3
Puertollano 60 F6
Puerto Madryn 142 J7
Puerto Maldonado 140 D6
Puerto Montt 142 G7
Puerto Natáles 142 G9
Puerto Nuevo 134 K7
Puerto Páez 140 D2
Puerto Peñasco 132 D2
Puerto Princesa 84 F5
Puerto Real 60 D8
Puerto Rico 134 L5
Puerto Rico 140 D6
Puerto Rico Trench 138 E1
Puerto Santa Cruz 142 H9
Puerto Suárez 140 F7
Pukapuka 112 N7
Pukatawagen 122 L5
Pukch'ŏng 82 E3
Pukë 66 G7
Pukeuri Junction 116 C7
Pula 62 J6
Pulaski 128 E2
Puławy 50 M6
Pullman 126 C1
Pułtusk 48 L10
Pultusk 50 L5
Pulu 76 Q10
Pülümür 92 H4
Puncak Jaya 87 E3
Puncak Mandala 87 F3
Pune 88 B5
P'ungsan 82 E3
Punia 106 D4
Puno 140 C7
Punta Albina 108 A3
Punta Alice 64 M9
Punta Angamos 142 G3
Punta Arena 126 B3
Punta Arenas 142 G9
Punta Ballena 142 G4
Punta da Estaca de Bares 60 C1
Punta Dungeness 142 H9
Punta Eugenia 134 A3
Punta Galera 142 G6
Punta Gallinas 134 K6
Punta Gorda 130 E4
Punta La Marmora 64 D8
Punta Lavapié 142 G6
Punta Lengua de Vaca 142 G5
Punta Mala 140 B2
Punta Mariato 134 H7
Punta Medanosa 142 H8
Punta Negra 140 A5
Punta Norte, *Argentina* 142 J7
Punta Norte, *Argentina* 142 K6
Punta Pariñas 140 A5
Punta Rasa 142 J7
Puntarenas 134 H6
Punta San Gabriel 132 D3
Punta San Telmo 134 D5
Punta Sarga 102 B4
Puponga 116 D5
Puqi 80 E5
Pur 76 P4
Puri 88 E5
Purmerend 54 G2
Purpe 78 B4
Purukcahu 86 E3
Purus 140 E5
Puruvesi 48 Q6
Pusan 82 E6
Pushkin 70 F3
Püspökladany 50 L10
Putao 84 B1
Putaruru 116 E3
Putian 80 F5
Putna 66 P4
Putrajaya 86 C2
Puttalami 88 C7
Putten 54 G3
Puttgarden 52 G2
Putumayo 140 C4
Putusibau 86 E2
Puuwai 132 (2)A2
Puvurnituq 122 R5
Puy de Dôme 58 H8
Puy de Sancy 58 H8
Puysegur Point 116 A8
Pweto 106 D5
Pwllheli 56 H9
Pyal'ma 70 G2
Pyasina 76 R3
Pyatigorsk 92 K1
Pyè 84 B3
Pyhäjärvi 48 M6
Pylos 68 D8
Pyŏktong 82 C3
P'yŏnggang 82 D4
P'yŏngyang 82 C4
Pyramid Island 116 (1)B2
Pyramid Lake 126 C2/3
Pyrenees 58 E11
Pyrgos 68 D7
Pyrzyce 50 D4
Pyshchug 70 J3
Pytalovo 48 P8

Q

Qā 'Aẓamān 94 E5
Qadīmah 90 C5
Qādub 90 F7
Qagan Nur 80 F2
Qal'aikhum 90 K2
Qalamat Nadqān 95 D5
Qalāt 90 J3
Qal'at Bīshah 90 D5
Qal'eh-ye Now 90 H3
Qamdo 80 B4
Qamīnīs 100 C1
Qandala 106 H1
Qaraaoun 92 F7
Qardho 106 H2
Qartaba 94 C2
Qasr el Azraq 94 D5
Qasr el Kharana 94 D5
Qasr Farafra 100 E2
Qaṭanā 94 D3
Qatar 95 D4
Qatrāna 94 D5
Qattâra Depression 100 E2
Qax 92 M3
Qāyen 90 G3
Qazangöldag 92 M4
Qazax 92 L3
Qazımämmäd 92 N3
Qazvīn 90 E2
Qena 100 F2
Qeqertarsuatsiaat 122 W4
Qeqertarsuatsiaq 122 V2
Qeqertarsuup Tunua 122 V3
Qeshm 95 F3
Qeshm 95 G3
Qeys 95 E3
Qezel Owzan 92 N5
Qezi'ot 94 B6
Qianshanlaoba 76 Q8
Qiaowan 80 B2
Qidukou 88 G2
Qiemo 76 R10
Qijiang 80 D5
Qijiaojing 76 S9
Qila Saifullah 90 J3
Qilian 80 C3
Qilian Shan 80 B3
Qingdao 80 G3
Qinghai Hu 80 B3
Qinghai Nanshan 80 B3
Qingjiang 80 F4
Qingshuihe 80 E3
Qingyang 80 D3
Qingyuan, *China* 80 E6
Qingyuan, *China* 80 G2
Qinhuangdao 80 F3
Qinzhou 84 D2
Qionghai 84 E3
Qiqian 78 L6
Qiqihar 78 L7
Qīr 95 E2
Qira 76 Q10
Qiryat Ata 94 C4
Qiryat Motzkin 94 C4
Qiryat Shemona 94 C3
Qishn 90 F6
Qolleh-ye Damāvand 90 F2
Qom 90 F3
Qornet es Saouda 94 D2
Qorveh 92 M6
Qoṭbābād 95 G3
Qotūr 92 L4
Quang Ngai' 84 D3
Quangolodougou 104 C3
Quang Tri 84 D3
Quanzhou 84 F2
Quaqtaq 122 T4
Quarto Sant'Elena 64 D9
Quba 92 N3
Quchan 90 G2
Québec 128 F1
Quedlinburg 52 G5
Queen Charlotte 122 E6
Queen Charlotte Islands 122 E6
Queen Charlotte Sound 122 E6
Queen Charlotte Strait 122 F6
Queen Elizabeth Islands 120 M2
Queen Maud Gulf 122 L3
Queensland 114 G4
Queenstown, *Australia* 114 J8
Queenstown, *New Zealand* 116 B7
Queenstown, *South Africa* 108 D6
Queets 126 B1
Quelimane 108 F3
Quemado 132 E2
Querétaro 134 D4
Quesnel 122 G6
Quetta 90 J3
Quezaltenango 134 F6
Quezon 84 F5
Quezon City 84 G4
Qufu 80 F3
Quibala 108 A2
Quibdó 134 J7
Quiberon 58 B6
Quijotoa 132 D2
Quillagua 142 H3
Quilmes 142 K5
Quilpie 114 H5
Quimbele 106 B5
Quimilí 142 J4
Quimper 58 A5
Quimperlé 58 B6
Quincy 128 B3
Qui Nhon 84 D4
Quionga 106 G6
Quirindi 114 K6
Quito 140 B4
Qujing 84 C1
Qumar He 88 F1
Qumaryan 88 F1
Qurayyāt 90 G5
Qurghonteppa 90 J2
Qurlurtuuq 122 H3
Qus 100 F2
Qusar 92 N3
Quseir 100 F2
Quzhou 80 F5

R

Raab 62 L3
Raahe 48 N4
Raalte 54 J2
Raasay 56 G4
Raas Caseyr 90 F7
Rab 62 K6
Rab 62 K6
Rába 66 E2
Raba 87 A4
Răbăgani 66 K3
Rabak 100 F5
Rabat, *Malta* 64 J13
Rabat, *Morocco* 102 D2
Rabca 62 N3
Rābigh 90 C5
Rabka 50 K8
Rach Gia 84 D5
Racine 128 C2
Ráckeve 66 F2
Rădăuţi 66 N2
Radbuza 52 H7
Radeberg 52 J5
Radebeul 52 J5
Radhanpur 88 B4
Radnevo 66 N7
Radom 50 L6
Radomir 66 K7
Radomsko 50 J6
Radoviš 68 E3
Radstadt 50 C10
Raduznny 76 P5
Radviliškis 50 N2
Radzyń Podlaski 50 M6
Rae-Edzo 122 H4
Raevavae 112 M8
Rafaela 142 J4
Rafah 94 B5
Rafaï 106 C3
Rafḥā 90 D4
Rafsanjān 95 G1
Raglan 116 E3
Ragusa 64 J12
Raha 87 B3
Rahad el Berdi 100 D5
Rahimyar Khan 90 K4
Raichur 88 C5
Raiganj 88 E3
Raigarh 88 D4
Rainach 62 L4
Rainbow Lake 122 H5
Rainier 126 B1
Rainy Lake 128 B1
Rainy River 128 B1
Raipur 88 D4
Rai Valley 116 D5
Rajahmundry 88 D5
Raja-Jooseppi 48 Q2
Rajapalaiyam 88 C7
Rajgarh 88 C3
Rajkot 90 K5
Rajnandgaon 88 D4
Rajsamand 88 B3
Rajshahi 88 E4
Rakhiv 66 M1
Rakovica 62 L6
Rakovník 50 C7
Rakovski 66 M7
Rakvere 48 P7
Raleigh 130 F2
Ralik Chain 112 G5
Ram 94 C7
Rama 134 H6
Ramallah 94 C5
Rambouillet 58 G5
Rameswaram 88 C7
Rāmhormoz 95 C1
Ramla 94 B5
Ramlat Rabyānah 100 C3
Râmnicu Sărat 66 Q4
Râmnicu Vâlcea 66 M4
Ramonville-St-Agne 58 G10
Rampur, *India* 88 C2
Rampur, *India* 88 C3
Ramree Island 84 A3
Ramsgate 56 P10
Ramtha 94 D4
Ranau 86 F1
Rancagua 142 G5
Ranchi 88 E4
Randazzo 64 J11
Randers 48 F8
Randijaure 48 K3
Randolph 126 G2
Rånes 54 B6
Rangamati 88 F4
Rangiora 116 D6
Rangoon = Yangon 84 B3
Rankin 132 F2
Rankin Inlet 122 N4
Ranong 84 B5
Ransiki 87 D3
Rānya 92 L5
Rapa 112 M8
Rapalla 64 D4
Rapallo 62 E6
Rapar 90 K5
Raperswil 62 D3
Rapid City 126 F2
Rapid River 128 C1
Rapla 48 N7
Rapur 90 J5
Raroia 112 N7
Rarotonga 112 K8
Râs Abu Shagara 100 G3
Ra's al Hadd 90 G5
Ra's al Ḥazrah 95 D4
Ra's al Hilāl 100 D1
Ra's al Khajī 95 C2
Ra's al Khaymah 95 F4
Ra's al Kūh 95 G4
Ra's al Muraysah 100 E1
Ra's al 'Udayd 95 D4
Ra's az Zawr 95 C3
Râs Banâs 100 G3
Ras Beddouza 102 C1
Ras Bir 100 H5
Ras Dashen Terara 100 G5
Ra's-e Barkan 95 C2
Raseiniai 48 M9
Râs el Nafas 94 B7
Ra's Fartak 90 F6
Râs Ghârib 100 F2
Rasht 92 N5
Rāsk 90 H4
Raška 66 H6
Ras Kasar 100 G4
Ra's Madrakah 90 G6
Râs Nouâdhibou 102 B4
Rason Lake 114 D5
Rass Ajdir 102 H2
Rass Jebel 64 E11
Rass Mostefa 64 F12
Rassokha 78 H2
Rast 66 L6
Ras Tannūrah 95 D3
Rastatt 54 L6
Rastede 52 D3
Ratak Chain 112 H4
Ratangarh 90 K4

Name	Page	Grid
Rat Buri	84	B4
Rath	88	C3
Rathenow	52	H4
Rathlin Island	56	F6
Rathluirc	56	D9
Ratlam	88	C4
Ratnagiri	90	K6
Raton	126	F3
Ratta	78	C4
Ratten	62	D4
Ratzeburg	52	F3
Rauđamýri	48	(1)B2
Raudhatain	95	B1
Raukumara Range	116	F4
Rauma	48	L6
Raurimu	116	E4
Rausu	82	N1
Răut	66	R2
Ravalli	126	D1
Ravānsar	92	M6
Rāvar	95	G1
Ravenna	62	H6
Ravensburg	62	E3
Ravensthorpe	114	D6
Ravnina	90	H2
Rāwah	92	J6
Rawaki	112	J6
Rawalpindi	90	K3
Rawa Mazowiecka	50	K6
Rawāndiz	92	L5
Rawicz	50	F6
Rawlinna	114	E6
Rawlins	126	E2
Rawson	142	J7
Rawu	88	G3
Raychikhinsk	78	M7
Raymond	126	B1
Raymondville	132	G3
Rayong	84	C4
Razdol'noye	82	F2
Razgrad	66	P6
Razlog	66	L8
Reading, *UK*	56	M10
Reading, *US*	128	E2
Realicó	142	J6
Rebaa	102	G2
Rebbenesøya	48	J1
Rebun-tō	80	L1
Rechytsa	70	F4
Recife	140	L5
Recklinghausen	54	K3
Recknitz	52	H3
Reconquista	142	K4
Recreo	142	H4
Red, *Canada/US*	126	G1
Red, *US*	130	B3
Reda	50	H3
Red Bluff	132	B1
Red Cloud	130	B1
Red Deer	122	J6
Redding	126	B2
Redditch	54	A2
Redfield	126	G2
Red Lake	122	N6
Red Lakes	124	H2
Red Lodge	126	E1
Red Oak	128	A2
Redon	58	C6
Redondela	60	B2
Red River = Song Hông	84	C2
Red Sea	100	G3
Redwater	122	J6
Red Wing	128	B2
Redwood City	126	B3
Redwood Falls	128	A2
Reed City	128	C2
Reedsport	126	B2
Reefton	116	C6
Rega	50	E4
Regen	52	H7
Regen	52	J8
Regensburg	52	H7
Regenstauf	52	H7
Reggane	102	F3
Reggio di Calabria	64	K10
Reggio nell'Emilia	62	F6
Reghin	66	M3
Regina, *Brazil*	140	G3
Regina, *Canada*	124	F1
Rehau	52	H6
Rehoboth	108	B4
Rehovot	94	B5
Reichenbach	52	H6
Reigate	56	M10
Reims	54	G5
Reinach Bad	62	C3
Reindeer Lake	122	L5
Reinosa	60	F1
Reisi	64	J11
Reliance	122	K4
Relizane	102	F1
Remada	102	H2
Remagen	54	K4
Rembang	86	E4
Remeshk	95	H3
Remiremont	58	M6
Remscheid	54	K3
Rena	48	F6
Rendina	68	F4
Rendsburg	52	E2
Rengat	86	C3
Reni	66	R4
Renmark	114	H6
Rennes	58	D5
Reno	62	G6
Reno	126	C3
Renteria	60	J1
Renton	126	B1
Renukut	88	D4
Reo	87	B4
Replot	48	L5
Reprêsa de Balbina	140	F4
Represa de Samuel	140	E5
Represa de Sao Simao	140	G7
Represa Ilha Solteira	140	G7
Represa Tucuruí	140	H4
Republic	126	C1
Repulse Bay	114	J4
Repulse Bay	122	P3
Requena, *Peru*	140	C5
Requena, *Spain*	60	J5
Reşadiye	92	G3
Resen	66	J8
Réservoir Cabonga	128	E1
Réservoir Caniapiscau	122	T6
Réservoir de La Grande 2	122	R6
Réservoir de La Grande 3	122	R6
Réservoir de La Grande 4	122	S6
Réservoir Gouin	128	F1
Réservoir Manicouagan	122	T6
Réservoir Opinaca	122	R6
Réservoir Pipmuacan	128	G1
Reshteh-ye Kūhhā-ye Alborz	90	F2
Resistencia	142	K4
Reşiţa	66	J4
Resolute	122	N2
Resolution Island, *Canada*	122	U4
Resolution Island, *New Zealand*	116	A7
Resovo	68	K3
Rethel	54	G5
Rethymno	68	G9
Réunion	108	(1)B2
Reus	60	M3
Reutlingen	52	E8
Revda	70	L3
Revillagigedo Island	132	(1)L4
Revin	54	G5
Revivim	94	B5
Revúca	50	K9
Rewa	88	D4
Rexburg	126	D2
Reykjanes	48	(1)B3
Reykjavík	48	(1)C2
Reynosa	130	B4
Rezat	52	F7
Rezé	58	D6
Rēzekne	48	P8
Rezina	66	R2
Rezovo	66	R8
Rezzato	62	F5
Rheda-Wiedenbrück	52	D5
Rhein = Rhine	62	C2
Rheinbach	54	K4
Rheine	54	K2
Rheinfelden	62	C3
Rhin = Rhine	62	C2
Rhine	62	C2
Rhinelander	128	C1
Rho	62	E5
Rhode Island	128	F2
Rhodes = Rodos	68	L8
Rhondda	56	J10
Rhône	58	K9
Rhyl	56	J8
Ribadeo	60	C1
Ribas do Rio Pardo	142	L3
Ribe	48	E9
Ribeauvillé	58	N5
Ribeirão Prêto	142	M3
Ribeiria = Santa Eugenia	60	A2
Ribera	64	H11
Riberalta	140	D6
Ribnica	64	J3
Rîbniţa	66	S2
Ribnitz-Damgarten	52	H2
Ričany	52	K6
Riccione	62	H7
Richardson Mountains	132	(1)K2
Richfield	126	D3
Richland	126	C1
Richlands	128	D3
Richmond, *Australia*	114	H4
Richmond, *New Zealand*	116	D5
Richmond, *Ky., US*	128	D3
Richmond, *Va., US*	128	E3
Ridgecrest	132	C1
Ridgway	128	E2
Ried	62	J2
Riesa	52	J5
Rieti	64	G6
Rifle	126	E3
Rīga	48	N8
Rīgān	95	H2
Riggins	126	C1
Rigolet	122	V6
Rijeka	62	K5
Riley	126	C2
Rimava	50	J9
Rimavská Sobota	50	K9
Rimini	62	H6
Rimouski	128	G1
Rineia	68	H7
Ringe	52	F1
Ringkøbing	48	E8
Ringkøbing Fjord	48	D9
Ringsted	52	G1
Ringvassøya	48	J1
Rinteln	52	E4
Rio Branco	140	D5
Río Colorado	142	J6
Río Cuarto	142	J5
Rio de Janeiro	142	N3
Rio de Janeiro	142	N3
Río de la Plata	142	K6
Río Gallegos	142	H9
Rio Grande	132	E2
Río Grande, *Argentina*	142	H9
Río Grande, *Mexico*	132	F4
Rio Grande	142	L5
Rio Grande City	130	B4
Rio Grande do Norte	140	K5
Rio Grande do Sul	142	L4
Ríohacha	134	K6
Río Largartos	134	G4
Riom	58	J8
Río Mulatos	140	D7
Rionero in Vulture	64	K8
Río Tigre	140	B4
Rio Verde, *Brazil*	140	G7
Río Verde, *Chile*	142	G9
Rio Verde de Mato Grosso	140	G7
Ripley, *Oh., US*	128	D3
Ripley, *Tenn., US*	128	C3
Ripley, *W.Va., US*	128	D3
Ripoll	60	N2
Ripon	56	L7
Rishiri-tō	78	Q7
Rishon le Ẕiyyon	94	B5
Risør	48	E7
Ritchie's Archipelago	84	A4
Ritzville	126	C1
Rivadavia	142	G4
Riva del Garda	62	F5
Rivarolo Canavese	62	C5
Rivas	134	G6
Rivera, *Argentina*	142	J6
Rivera, *Uruguay*	142	K5
River Cess	104	C3
Riversdale	108	C6
Riversdale Beach	116	E5
Riverton, *Canada*	122	M6
Riverton, *New Zealand*	116	A8
Rivesaltes	58	H11
Rivière-du-Loup	128	G1
Rivne	70	E4
Rivoli	62	C5
Riwoqê	88	G2
Riyadh = Ar Riyāḍ	95	B4
Rize	92	J3
Rizhao	80	F3
Roanne	58	K7
Roanoke	128	D3
Roanoke Rapids	130	F2
Robāţ	95	G1
Robe	114	G7
Robertsfors	48	L4
Robertval	128	F1
Roboré	140	F7
Robstown	130	B4
Roccastrada	64	F6
Rochefort, *Belgium*	54	H4
Rochefort, *France*	58	E8
Rochelle	128	C2
Rocher River	122	J4
Rochester, *UK*	54	C3
Rochester, *Minn., US*	128	B2
Rochester, *N.H., US*	128	F2
Rochester, *N.Y., US*	128	E2
Rockall	46	C2
Rockefeller Plateau	144	(2)EE2
Rockford	128	C2
Rockhampton	114	K4
Rock Hill	128	D4
Rock Island	128	B2
Rocklake	126	G1
Rockport	126	B1
Rock Rapids	128	A2
Rock Springs	126	E2
Rocksprings	132	F3
Rocky Mount	128	E3
Rocky Mountains	122	F5
Rødby Havn	52	G2
Roddickton	122	V6
Roden	54	J1
Rodez	58	H9
Rodi Garganico	64	K7
Roding	52	H7
Rodney	128	D2
Rodopi Planina	66	M7
Rodos	68	L8
Rodos	68	L8
Roebourne	114	C4
Roermond	54	J3
Roeselare	54	F4
Roes Welcome Sound	122	P4
Rogers City	128	D1
Rogerson	126	D2
Rogliano	64	D6
Rogozno	50	G5
Rogue	126	B2
Rohrbach	62	K2
Rohtak	88	C3
Roi Et	84	C3
Roja	48	M8
Rokiškis	48	N9
Rokycany	50	C8
Rolla	128	B3
Rolleston	116	D6
Rolvsøya	48	M1
Roma	87	C4
Roma, *Australia*	114	J5
Roma, *Italy*	64	G7
Roman	66	P3
Romania	66	L4
Romans-sur-Isère	58	L8
Rombas	54	J5
Rome = Roma	64	G7
Rome, *Ga., US*	130	D3
Rome, *N.Y., US*	128	E2
Romney	128	E3
Romny	70	F4
Rømø	52	D1
Romorantin-Lanthenay	58	G6
Romsey	54	A3
Rona	56	G2
Ronan	124	D2
Roncesvalles	60	J2
Ronda	60	E8
Rondônia	140	E6
Rondônia	140	E6
Rondonópolis	140	G7
Rondu	90	L2
Rongcheng	80	G3
Rønne	50	D2
Ronneby	48	H8
Ronne Entrance	144	(2)JJ3
Ronne Ice Shelf	144	(2)MM2
Ronse	54	F4
Roosendaal	54	G3
Roper Bar	114	F2
Roquetas de Mar	60	H8
Roraima	140	E3
Røros	48	F5
Rosário	140	J4
Rosario, *Argentina*	142	J5
Rosario, *Mexico*	124	D6
Rosario, *Mexico*	124	E7
Rosario, *Paraguay*	142	K3
Rosário Oeste	140	F6
Rosarito	124	C6
Rosarno	64	K10
Roscommon	56	D8
Roscrea	56	E9
Roseau	134	M5
Roseburg	126	B2
Roseires Reservoir	100	F5
Rose Island	112	K7
Rosenburg	132	G3
Rosenheim	62	H3
Roses	60	P2
Rosetown	122	K6
Rosica	66	N6
Rosignano Marittimo	62	F7
Roşiori de Vede	66	N5
Rosita	66	Q6
Roskilde	48	G9
Roslavl'	70	F4
Rossano	64	L9
Ross Ice Shelf	144	(2)Z1
Ross Lake	126	B1
Rosslare	56	F9
Roßlau	52	H5
Rosso	102	B5
Rossosh'	70	G4
Ross River	122	E4
Ross Sea	144	(2)AA2
Røssvatnet	48	G4
Røst	48	G3
Rostāq	95	E3
Rosthern	122	K6
Rostock	52	H2
Rostov	70	G3
Rostov-na-Donu	70	G5
Rostrenen	58	B5
Roswell	132	F2
Rota	112	E4
Rote	87	B5
Rotenburg, *Germany*	52	E3
Rotenburg, *Germany*	52	E5
Roth	52	G7
Rothenburg	52	F7
Roto	114	J6
Rotorua	116	F4
Rott	62	H2
Rottenmann	62	K3
Rotterdam	58	K2
Rottnen	50	E1
Rottumeroog	54	J1
Rottumerplaat	54	J1
Rottweil	62	D2
Rotuma	112	H7
Roubaix	54	F4
Rouen	54	D5
Rouiba	60	P8
Round Mountain	114	K6
Round Rock	130	B3
Roundup	126	E1
Rousay	56	J2
Rouyn	128	E1
Rovaniemi	48	N3
Rovato	62	E5
Rovereto	62	G5
Rovigo	62	G5
Rovinari	66	L5
Rovinj	62	J5
Rovuma	106	F6
Rowley Island	122	R3
Rowley Shoals	114	C3
Roxas	84	G4
Roxburgh	116	B7
Royal Leamington Spa	54	A2
Royal Tunbridge Wells	54	C3
Royan	58	D8
Roye	54	E5
Royston	54	C2
Rozdil'na	66	T3
Rožňava	50	K9
Rozzano	62	E5
Rrëshen	68	B3
Rtishchevo	70	H4
Ruacana	108	A3
Ruahine Range	116	E5
Ruapehu	116	E4
Ruapuke Island	116	B8
Ruarkela	88	D4
Ruatahuna	116	F4
Ruatoria	116	G3
Ruawai	116	D3
Rub' al Khālī	90	E6
Rubeshibe	82	M2
Rubi	106	C3
Rubtsovsk	76	Q7
Ruby	132	(1)F3
Rudan	95	G3
Ruda Śląska	50	H7
Rudbar	90	H3
Rüdersdorf	52	J4
Rudkøbing	52	F2
Rudnaya Pristan'	82	H2
Rudnyy	70	M4
Rudolstadt	52	G6
Rue	54	D4
Ruffec	58	F7
Rufiji	106	F5
Rugby, *UK*	54	A2
Rugby, *US*	124	G2
Rügen	50	C3
Ruhnu	48	M8

Sanghar 90 J4
San Gimignano 62 G7
San Giovanni in Fiore 64 L9
San Giovanni Valdarno 62 G7
Sangir 87 C2
Sangkhla Buri 84 B3
Sangkulirang 86 F2
Sangli 88 B5
Sangmélima 104 G4
Sangre de Cristo Range 132 E1
Sangsang 88 E3
Sangue 140 F6
Sangüesa 60 J2
Sanjō 82 K5
San Joaquin Valley 126 B3
San Jose 126 B3
San José 134 H7
San Jose de Buenavista 84 G4
San José de Chiquitos 140 E7
San Jose de Jáchal 142 H5
San José del Cabo 134 C4
San José de Ocuné 140 C3
San Juan 134 H4
San Juan, *Argentina* 142 H5
San Juan, *Costa Rica* 134 H6
San Juan, *Puerto Rico* 134 L5
San Juan, *US* 132 E1
San Juan, *Venezuela* 140 D2
San Juan Bautista, *Paraguay* 142 K4
San Juan Bautista, *Spain* 60 M5
San Juan de los Cayos 140 D1
San Juan de los Morros 140 D2
San Juan Mountains 126 E3
San Julián 142 H8
Sankt-Peterburg 70 F3
Sankuru 106 C4
Sanlıurfa 92 H5
San Lorenzo 132 D3
Sanlúcar de Barrameda 60 D8
San Lucas 134 C4
San Luis 142 H5
San Luis Obispo 132 B1
San Luis Potosí 134 D4
San Luis Rio Colorado 132 D2
San Marcos 130 B4
San Marino 62 H7
San Marino 62 H7
San Martín 140 E6
Sanmenxia 80 E4
San Miguel 134 G6
San Miguel 140 E7
San Miguel de Tucumán 142 H4
San Miguel Island 132 B2
San Miniato 62 F7
San Nicolas de los Arroyos 142 J5
San Nicolás de los Garzas 130 A4
San Nicolas Island 132 C2
Sânnicolau Mare 66 H3
Sanok 50 M8
San Pablo 84 G4
San-Pédro 104 C4
San Pedro, *Argentina* 142 J3
San Pedro, *Bolivia* 140 E7
San Pedro, *Paraguay* 142 K3
San Pedro, *Philippines* 84 G4
San Pedro de las Colonias 132 F3
San Pedro Sula 134 G5
San Pellegrino Terme 62 E5
San Pietro 64 C9
Sanqaçal 92 N3
San Rafael 142 H5
San Remo 62 C7
San Roque 60 E8
Sansalé 104 B2
San Salvador 130 G5
San Salvador 134 G6
San Salvador de Jujuy 142 H3
Sansar 88 C4
San Sebastián = Donostia 60 J1
San Sebastian de los Reyes 60 G4
Sansepolcro 62 H7
San Severo 64 K7
Sanski Most 62 M6
Santa Ana, *Bolivia* 140 D7
Santa Ana, *El Salvador* 134 G6
Santa Ana, *Mexico* 132 D2
Santa Ana, *US* 132 C2
Santa Bárbara 124 E6
Santa Barbara 132 C2
Santa Barbara Island 132 C2
Santa Catalina 142 H4
Santa Catalina Island 132 C2
Santa Catarina 142 L4
Santa Clara, *Columbia* 140 D4
Santa Clara, *Cuba* 124 K7
Santa Clarita 132 C2
Santa Comba Dão 60 B4
Santa Cruz 142 G9
Santa Cruz, *Bolivia* 140 E7
Santa Cruz, *Philippines* 84 G3
Santa Cruz, *US* 132 B1
Santa Cruz de Tenerife 102 B3
Santa Cruz Island 132 B2
Santa Cruz Islands 112 G7
Santa Elena 140 E3
Santa Eugenia 60 A2
Santa Fe 126 E3
Santa Fé 142 J5
Sant'Agata di Militello 64 J10
Santa Isabel 112 F6
Santa Isabel 142 H6
Santa la Grande 124 K7
Santa Margarita 124 D7
Santa Margherita Ligure 62 E6
Santa Maria 102 (1)B2
Santa Maria, *Brazil* 142 L4
Santa Maria, *US* 132 B2
Santa Maria das Barreiras 140 H5
Santa Marinella 64 F6
Santa Marta, *Colombia* 134 K6
Santa Marta, *Spain* 60 D6
Santana do Livramento 142 K5
Santander 60 G1
Sant'Antioco 64 C9
Sant'Antioco 64 C9
Santanyí 60 P5
Santa Pola 60 K6
Santarém, *Brazil* 140 G4
Santarém, *Spain* 60 B5
Santa Rosa, *Argentina* 142 J6
Santa Rosa, *R.G.S., Brazil* 142 L4
Santa Rosa, *Acre, Brazil* 140 C5
Santa Rosa, *Calif., US* 126 B3
Santa Rosa, *N. Mex., US* 132 F2
Santa Rosa Island 132 B2
Santa Vitória do Palmar 142 L5
Sant Boi 60 N3
Sant Carlos de la Ràpita 60 L4
Sant Celoni 60 N3
Sant Feliu de Guixols 60 P3
Santiago 142 G5
Santiago, *Brazil* 142 L4
Santiago, *Dominican Republic* 134 K5
Santiago, *Philippines* 84 G3
Santiago, *Spain* 60 B2
Santiago de Cuba 134 J5
Santiago del Estero 142 J4
Santo André 142 M3
Santo Antão 104 (1)A1
Santo Antônio de Jesus 140 K6
Santo Antônio do Içá 140 D4
Santo Domingo 134 L5
Santo Domingo de los Colorados 140 B4
Santoña 60 G1
Santos 142 M3
San Vicente 84 G3
San Vincenzo 64 E5
Sanya 84 D3
Sao Bernardo do Campo 140 E4
São Borja 142 K4
São Carlos 142 M3
São Félix, *M.G., Brazil* 140 G6
São Félix, *Pará, Brazil* 140 G5
São Filipe 104 (1)B2
São Francisco 140 J6
São João de Madeira 60 B4
São Jorge 102 (1)B2
São José do Rio Prêto 142 L3
São Luís 140 J4
São Miguel 102 (1)B2
Saône 58 K7
São Nicolau 104 (1)B1
São Paulo 142 L3
São Paulo 142 M3
São Paulo de Olivença 140 D4
São Raimundo Nonato 140 J5
São Tiago 104 (1)B1
São Tomé 104 F4
São Tomé 104 F4
São Tomé and Príncipe 104 F4
São Vicente 104 (1)A1
São Vicente 142 M3
Sapanca 68 M4
Saparua 87 C3
Sapele 104 F3
Sapes 68 H4
Sapientza 68 D8
Sa Pobla 60 P5
Sapporo 82 L2
Sapri 64 K8
Sapudi 86 E4
Sapulpa 130 B2
Saqqez 92 M5
Sarāb 92 M5
Sara Buri 84 C4
Sarajevo 66 F6
Sarakhs 90 H2
Saraktash 70 L4
Saramati 88 G3
Saran 76 N8
Saranac Lake 128 F2
Sarandë 68 C5
Sarangani Islands 87 C1
Saranpul 70 M2
Saransk 70 J4
Sarapul 70 K3
Sarapul'skoye 78 P7
Sarasota 130 E4
Sarata 66 S3
Saratoga 126 E2
Saratoga Springs 128 F2
Saratov 70 J4
Saravan 90 H4
Sarawak 86 E2
Saray 68 K3
Sarayköy 68 L7
Sarayönü 68 Q6
Sarbāz 90 H4
Sarbīsheh 90 G3
Sárbogárd 66 F3
Sar Dasht 92 L5
Sardegna 64 E8
Sardinia = Sardegna 64 E8
Sardis Lake 130 B3
Sar-e Pol 90 J2
Sargodha 90 K3
Sarh 104 H3
Sārī 90 F2
Saria 68 K9
Sarıkamış 92 K3
Sarıkaya 92 F4
Sarikei 86 E2
Sarina 114 J4
Sariñena 60 K3
Sarīr Tibesti 100 C3
Sariwŏn 82 C4
Sar'yer 68 M3
Sark 58 C4
Sarkad 66 J3
Sarkand 76 P8
Şarkikaraağaç 68 P6
Şarkişla 92 G4
Şarköy 68 K4
Sarmi 87 E3
Särna 48 G6
Sarnia 128 D2
Sarny 70 E4
Sarolangun 86 C3
Saronno 62 E5
Saros Körfezi 68 J4
Sárospatak 50 L9
Sarre 58 M5
Sarrebourg 58 N5
Sarreguemines 58 N4
Sarria 60 C2
Sartène 64 C7
Sartyn'ya 70 M2
Saruhanli 68 K6
Sarur 92 L4
Sárvár 62 M3
Sarvestān 95 E2
Sarviz 66 F2
Sarykamyshkoye Ozero 76 K9
Saryozek 76 P9
Saryshagan 76 N8
Sarysu 76 M8
Sary-Tash 90 K2
Sarzana 62 E6
Sasaram 88 D4
Sasebo 82 E7
Saskatchewan 122 K6
Saskatchewan 122 L6
Saskatoon 122 K6
Saskylakh 76 W3
Sassandra 104 C4
Sassari 64 C8
Sassnitz 52 J2
Sasso Marconi 62 G6
Sassuolo 62 F6
Satadougou 104 B2
Satara 88 B5
Satna 88 D4
Sátoraljaújhely 50 L9
Satti 88 C2
Sättna 48 J5
Satu Mare 66 K2
Satun 86 B1
Sauce 142 K5
Saudi Arabia 90 D4
Sauk Center 128 B1
Saulgau 62 E2
Saulieu 58 K6
Sault Ste. Marie, *Canada* 128 D1
Sault Ste. Marie, *US* 128 D1
Saumlakki 87 D4
Saumur 58 E6
Saunders Island 138 J9
Saura 76 J9
Saurimo 106 C5
Sauðarkrókur 48 (1)D2
Sava 62 L5
Savaii 112 J7
Savalou 104 E3
Savannah 120 K6
Savannah, *Ga., US* 130 E3
Savannah, *Tenn., US* 130 D2
Savannakhet 84 C3
Savaştepe 68 K5
Savè 104 E3
Save 108 E4
Sāveh 90 F2
Saverne 52 C8
Savigliano 62 C6
Savona 62 D6
Savonlinna 48 Q6
Savu 87 B5
Sawahlunto 86 C3
Sawai Madhopur 88 C3
Sawqirah 90 G6
Sayanogorsk 76 S7
Sayansk 78 G6
Sayhūt 90 F6
Sāylac 100 H5
Saynshand 80 E2
Sayram Hu 76 Q9
Say'ūn 90 E6
Say-Utes 76 J9
Sazan 68 B4
Sazin 90 K2
Sbaa 102 E3
Scafell Pike 56 J7
Scalea 64 K9
Scarborough 56 M7
Scargill 116 D6
Scarp 56 E3
Schaalsee 52 F3
Schaffhausen 62 D3
Schagen 54 G2
Scharbeutz 52 F2
Schärding 62 J2
Scharhörn 52 D3
Scheeßel 52 E3
Schefferville 122 T6
Scheibbs 62 L3
Schelde 54 F3
Schenectady 128 F2
Scheveningen 54 G2
Schiedam 54 G3
Schiermonnikoog 54 H1
Schiermonnikoog 54 J1
Schio 62 G5
Schiza 68 D8
Schkeuditz 52 H5
Schlei 52 E2
Schleiden 54 J4
Schleswig 52 E2
Schlieben 52 J5
Schlüchtern 52 E6
Schneeberg 52 G6
Schneeberg 52 H6
Schönebeck 52 G4
Schongau 62 F3
Schöningen 52 F4
Schouwen 54 F3
Schramberg 62 D2
Schreiber 128 C1
Schrems 62 L2
Schull 56 C10
Schwabach 52 G7
Schwäbische Alb 62 E2
Schwäbisch-Gmünd 62 E2
Schwäbisch-Hall 52 E7
Schwalmstadt 52 E6
Schwandorf 52 H7
Schwarzenbek 52 F3
Schwarzenberg 52 H6
Schwarzwald 62 D3
Schwaz 62 G3
Schwechat 50 F9
Schwedt 50 D4
Schweich 54 J5
Schweinfurt 52 F6
Schwenningen 62 D2
Schwerin 52 G3
Schweriner See 52 G3
Schwetzingen 52 D7
Schwyz 62 D3
Sciacca 64 H11
Scicli 64 J12
Scobey 126 E1
Scotia Ridge 142 K9
Scotia Sea 144 (2)A4
Scotland 56 H5
Scott City 126 F3
Scott Inlet 122 T2
Scott Island 144 (2)Z3
Scott Reef 114 D2
Scottsbluff 126 F2
Scottsboro 128 C4
Scotty's Junction 132 C1
Scranton 128 E2
Scunthorpe 56 M8
Seal 122 M5
Sea of Azov 70 G5
Sea of Galilee 94 C4
Sea of Japan 82 G3
Sea of Marmara = Marmara Denizi 68 L4
Sea of Okhotsk 78 Q5
Sea of the Hebrides 56 E4
Searchlight 132 D1
Searcy 128 B3
Seaside 126 B1
Seattle 126 B1
Sebeş 66 L4
Sebkha Azzel Matti 102 F3
Sebkha de Timimoun 102 E3
Sebkha de Tindouf 102 D3
Sebkha Mekerrhane 102 F3
Sebkha Oum el Drouss Telli 102 C4
Sebkhet de Chemchâm 102 C4
Sebnitz 52 K6
Sebring 130 E4
Secchia 62 F6
Sechura 140 A5
Secretary Island 116 A7
Secunderabad 88 C5
Sécure 140 D7
Sedalia 128 B3
Sedan 54 G5
Sedano 60 G2
Seddon 116 D5
Sede Boqer 94 B6
Sedeh 90 G3
Sederot 94 B5
Sedico 62 H4
Sedom 94 C5
Seeheim 108 B5
Seelow 52 K4
Sées 58 F5
Seesen 52 F5
Seevetal 52 E3
Séez 62 B5
Seferihisar 68 J6
Segamat 86 C2
Segezha 70 F2
Seghnān 90 K2
Ségou 104 C2
Segovia 60 F4
Segré 58 E6
Séguédine 102 H4
Seguin 130 B4
Segura 60 H6
Sehithwa 108 C4
Sehnde 52 E4
Seiland 48 M1
Seiling 130 B2
Seinäjoki 48 M5
Seine 58 F4
Sekayu 86 C3
Sekondi 104 D3
Selassi 87 D3
Selat Bangka 86 D3
Selat Berhala 86 C3
Selat Dampir 87 D3
Selat Karimata 86 D3
Selat Makassar 86 F3
Selat Mentawai 86 B3
Selat Sunda 86 D4
Selawik 132 (1)F2
Selb 52 H6
Selby 126 G1
Selçuk 68 K7
Selebi-Phikwe 108 D4
Sélestat 62 C2
Selfoss 48 (1)C3
Sélibabi 102 C5
Seligman 132 D1
Seljord 48 E7
Selkirk 124 G1
Selkirk Mountains 124 C1
Sells 132 D2
Selm 54 K3
Selmer 128 C3
Selpele 87 D3
Selvas 140 C5
Selwyn Lake 122 L5

Name	Page	Grid
Tanahjampea	87	A4
Tanahmerah	87	F4
Tanami Mine	114	E4
Tanami Desert	114	E4
Tanaro	62	C6
Tanch'ŏn	82	E3
Tanda	104	D3
Tandag	84	H5
Tăndărei	66	Q5
Tandil	142	K6
Tanega-shima	82	F8
Tanew	50	M7
Tanezrouft	102	E4
Tanga, Russia	78	J6
Tanga, Tanzania	106	F5
Tanger	102	D1
Tangermünde	52	G4
Tanggu	80	F3
Tangmai	88	G2
Tangra Yumco	88	E2
Tangshan	80	F3
Tanimbar	112	D6
Tanjona Ankaboa	108	G4
Tanjona Bobaomby	108	H2
Tanjona Masoala	108	J3
Tanjona Vilanandro	108	G3
Tanjona Vohimena	108	H5
Tanjung	86	F3
Tanjungbalai	86	B2
Tanjung Cangkuang	86	C4
Tanjung Datu	86	D2
Tanjung d'Urville	87	E3
Tanjung Libobo	87	C3
Tanjung Lumut	86	D3
Tanjung Mengkalihat	86	F2
Tanjungpandan	86	D3
Tanjung Puting	86	E3
Tanjungredeb	86	F2
Tanjung Selatan	86	E3
Tanjungselor	86	F2
Tanjung Vals	87	E4
Tankovo	76	R5
Tankse	88	C2
Tanlovo	70	P1
Tanney	54	G5
Tanout	104	F2
Tanta	100	F1
Tan-Tan	102	C3
Tanzania	106	E5
Tao'an	80	G1
Taomasina	108	H3
Taongi	112	J4
Taormina	64	K11
Taos	132	E1
Taoudenni	102	E5
Taourirt	102	E2
T'ao-yuan	84	G2
Tapa	48	N7
Tapachula	134	F6
Tapajós	140	F4
Tapauá	140	E5
Tapolca	66	E3
Tappahannock	130	F2
Tapsuy	70	M2
Tapuaenuku	116	D6
Taquarí	140	F7
Tara	70	Q3
Tara	76	N6
Tarābulus	102	H2
Taraclia	66	R4
Taracua	140	D3
Tarāghin	102	H3
Tarakan	84	F6
Taran	76	N3
Taranaki = Mount Egmont	116	E4
Tarancón	60	H5
Taranto	64	M8
Tarapoto	140	B5
Tarare	58	K8
Tarascon	58	K10
Tarauacá	140	C5
Tarauacá	140	C5
Tarawa	112	H5
Tarawera Lake	116	F4
Tarazona	60	J3
Tarbert, UK	56	G6
Tarbes	58	F10
Tarbet, UK	56	F4
Tarcoola	114	F6
Taree	114	K6
Tareya	76	S3
Tarfaya	102	C3
Târgovişte	66	N5
Târgu Frumos	66	Q2
Târgu Jiu	66	L4
Târgu Lăpuş	66	L2
Târgu Mureş	66	M3
Târgu-Neamţ	66	P2
Târgu Ocna	66	P3
Târgu Secuiesc	66	P3
Tarhunah	102	H2
Tarif	95	E4
Tarifa	60	E8
Tarija	142	J3
Tarim	76	Q9
Tarīm	90	E6
Tarim Pendi	76	Q10
Tarīn Kowt	90	J3
Tariskay Shan	76	Q9
Taritatu	87	E3
Tarkio	130	B1
Tarko Sale	76	P5
Tarlac	84	G3
Tarn	58	H10
Tarna	50	K10
Tärnaby	48	H4
Tărnăveni	66	M3
Tarnogskiy Gorodok	70	H2
Tărnovo	68	K2
Tarnów	50	K7
Tarnowskie Góry	50	H7
Taro	62	E6
Tārom	95	F2
Taroom	114	J5
Taroudannt	102	D2
Tarquinia	64	F6
Tarragona	60	M3
Tarras	116	B7
Tàrrega	60	M3
Tarso Emissi	100	C3
Tarsus	92	F5
Tartagal	142	J3
Tartu	48	P7
Tarţūs	94	C2
Tarutyne	66	S3
Tarvisio	62	J4
Tasbuget	76	M9
Tashigang	88	F3
Tashir	92	L3
Tashkent = Toshkent	76	M9
Tash-Körmür	76	N9
Tashtagol	76	R7
Tasiilaq	122	Z3
Tasikmalaya	86	D4
Taskesken	76	Q8
Taşköprü	92	F3
Tasman Bay	116	D5
Tasmania	112	E10
Tasmania	114	H8
Tasman Mountains	116	D5
Tasman Sea	116	B3
Tăşnad	66	K2
Taşova	92	G3
Tassili du Hoggar	102	F4
Tassili-n'-Ajjer	102	G3
Tasty	76	M9
Tasūj	92	L4
Tata, Hungary	66	F2
Tata, Morocco	102	D3
Tataba	87	B3
Tatabánya	66	F2
Tataouine	102	H2
Tatarbunary	66	S4
Tatariya	70	J3
Tatarsk	76	P6
Tatarskiy Proliv	78	P7
Tateyama	82	K6
Tathlina Lake	122	H4
Tatta	90	J5
Tatvan	92	K4
Tauá	140	J5
Tauberbischofsheim	52	E7
Tauern	62	J4
Taumarunui	116	E4
Taungdwingyi	84	B2
Taung-gyi	88	G4
Taungup	88	F5
Taunsa	88	B2
Taunton, UK	56	J10
Taunton, US	128	F2
Taunus	54	L4
Taunusstein	54	L4
Taupo	116	F4
Tauragė	50	M2
Tauranga	116	F3
Tauroa Point	116	D2
Tavda	70	N3
Tavda	70	N3
Tavira	60	C7
Tavoy	84	B4
Tavşanli	92	C4
Taw	56	J11
Tawas City	128	D2
Tawau	86	F2
Tawitawi	86	F1
Taxkorgan	76	P10
Tay	56	J5
Tayga	76	R6
Taylorville	130	D2
Taym	90	C4
Taymā'	100	G2
Taymura	78	F4
Taymylyr	78	L2
Tay Ninh	84	D4
Tayshet	78	F5
Tayuan	78	L6
Tayyebād	90	H3
Taza	102	E2
Tazeh Kand	92	M4
Tazenakht	102	D2
Tăzirbū	100	D2
Tazovskaya Guba	76	N4
Tazovskiy	76	P4
Tazovskiy Poluostrov	76	N4
Tazungdam	84	B1
T'bilisi	92	L3
Tchamba	104	G3
Tchibanga	104	G5
Tchin Tabaradene	102	G5
Tczew	50	H3
Te Anau	116	A7
Te Araroa	116	G3
Te Aroha	116	E3
Te Awamutu	116	E4
Teberda	92	J2
Tébessa	102	G1
Tebingtinggi	86	B2
Téboursouk	64	D12
Techa	70	M3
Techiman	104	D3
Tecuala	132	D4
Tecuci	66	Q4
Tedzhen	90	H2
Tees	56	L7
Tegal	86	D4
Tegernsee	62	G3
Tegina	104	F2
Teglio	62	F4
Tegucigalpa	134	G6
Tegul'det	76	R6
Te Hapua	116	D2
Te Haroto	116	F4
Tehek Lake	122	M3
Teheran = Tehrān	90	F2
Tehrān	90	F2
Teignmouth	56	J11
Tejo = Tagus	60	B5
Te Kaha	116	F3
Te Kao	116	D2
Tekirdağ	68	K4
Tekirdağ	92	B3
Teknaf	88	F4
Teku	87	B3
Te Kuiti	116	E4
T'elavi	92	L3
Tel Aviv-Yafo	94	B4
Telegraph Creek	132	(1)L4
Telén	142	H6
Teles Pires	140	F5
Telford	56	K9
Telfs	62	G3
Teller	132	(1)D2
Telsen	142	H7
Telšiai	50	M2
Teltow	52	J4
Teluk Berau	87	D3
Teluk Bone	87	B3
Teluk Cenderawasih	87	E3
Telukdalem	86	B2
Teluk Kumai	86	E3
Telukpakedai	86	D3
Teluk Sampit	86	E3
Teluk Sukadana	86	D3
Teluk Tomini	87	B2
Tema	104	D3
Tembenchi	76	T4
Temerin	66	G4
Temerloh	84	C6
Teminabuan	87	D3
Temochic	132	E3
Tempe	132	D2
Tempio Pausaria	64	D8
Temple	132	G2
Temryuk	92	G1
Temuco	142	G6
Tenali	88	D5
Tendaho	100	H5
Ten Degree Channel	88	F7
Tendo	82	L4
Tendrara	102	E2
Ténéré	102	G5
Ténéré du Tafassasset	102	G4
Tenerife	102	B3
Ténès	102	F1
Tenggarong	86	F3
Tenke	108	D2
Tenkodogo	104	D2
Tennant Creek	114	F3
Tennessee	120	K6
Tennessee	124	J4
Tenojoki	48	P2
Tenteno	87	B3
Tenterfield	114	K5
Teo	60	B2
Teófilo Otoni	140	J7
Tepa	87	C4
Tepehuanes	124	E6
Tepic	124	F7
Teplice	50	C7
Ter	60	N2
Terceira	102	(1)B2
Terek	92	L2
Teresina	140	J5
Tergnier	54	F5
Terme	92	G3
Termez	90	J2
Termini Imerese	64	H11
Termirtau	76	N7
Termoli	66	C8
Ternate	87	C2
Terneuzen	54	F3
Terni	64	G6
Ternitz	62	M3
Ternopil'	70	E5
Ternuka	116	C7
Terracina	64	H7
Terrassa	60	N3
Terre Haute	130	D2
Terry	126	E1
Tersa	70	H4
Terschelling	54	H1
Teruel	60	J4
Tervel	92	B2
Tervola	48	N3
Teseney	100	G4
Teshekpuk Lake	132	(1)F1
Teshikaga	82	N2
Teshio	82	L1
Teslin	132	(1)L3
Teslin	132	(1)L3
Tessalit	102	F4
Têt	58	H11
Tete	108	E3
Teterow	52	H3
Teteven	68	G2
Tétouan	102	D1
Tetovo	68	H8
Teuco	142	J3
Teulada	64	C10
Tevere	64	G6
Teverya	94	C4
Tevriz	70	P3
Te Waewae Bay	116	A8
Texarkana	130	C3
Texas	124	F5
Texel	54	G1
Teya	76	S5
Teykovo	70	H3
Tfarity	102	C3
Thaba Putsoa	108	D5
Thabazimbi	108	D4
Thailand	84	C4
Thai Nguyên	84	D2
Thal	88	B2
Thale Luang	84	C5
Thamarīt	90	F6
Thames	56	L10
Thamūd	90	E6
Thane	88	B5
Thanh Hoa	84	D3
Thanjavur	88	C6
Thann	62	C3
Tharad	88	B4
Thar Desert	88	B3
Thargomindah	114	H5
Tharwäniyyah	95	E5
Thasos	68	G4
Thasos	68	G4
Thaton	84	B3
Thaya	50	E9
The Bahamas	130	F4
The Bluff	130	F4
The Dalles	126	B1
Thedford	126	F2
The Fens	54	B2
The Gambia	104	A2
The Granites	114	E4
The Hague = 's-Gravenhage	54	G2
Thelon	122	L4
The Minch	56	F3
The Naze	54	D3
Thenia	60	P8
Theniet el Had	60	N9
Theodore Roosevelt	140	E5
Theodore Roosevelt Lake	132	D2
The Pas	122	L6
Thermaikos Kolpos	68	E4
Thermopolis	126	E2
The Sisters	116	(1)B1
The Solent	54	A4
Thessalon	128	D1
Thessaloniki	68	E4
Thetford	56	N9
Thetford Mines	128	F1
The Twins	116	D5
The Wash	56	N9
The Weald	54	B3
The Whitsundays	114	J4
Thief River Falls	128	A1
Thiers	58	J8
Thiès	104	A2
Thika	106	F4
Thimphu	88	E3
Þingvallavatn	48	(1)C2
Thionville	54	J5
Thira	68	H8
Thira	68	H8
Thirasia	68	H8
Thirsk	56	L7
Thiruvananthapuram	88	C7
Thisted	48	E8
Þistilfjöður	48	(1)F1
Thiva	68	F6
Thiviers	58	F8
Þjórsá	48	(1)D2
Tholen	54	G3
Thomasville	130	E3
Thompson	122	H6
Thompson	122	M5
Thompson Falls	126	C1
Thomson	130	E3
Thonon-les-Bains	62	B4
Þórisvatn	48	(1)D2
Þorlákshöfn	48	(1)C3
Þorshöfn	48	(1)F1
Thouars	58	E7
Thrakiko Pelagos	68	H4
Three Forks	126	D1
Three Kings Island	116	C2
Three Rivers	128	C2
Throckmorton	130	B3
Thuin	54	G4
Thun	62	C4
Thunder Bay	128	C1
Thuner See	62	C4
Thung Song	84	B5
Thüringer Wald	52	F6
Thurso	56	J3
Thusis	62	E4
Tiäb	95	G3
Tianjin	80	F3
Tianmen	80	F4
Tianqiaoling	82	E2
Tianshifu	82	C3
Tianshui	80	D4
Tianshuihai	90	L2
Tianyang	80	D6
Tiaret	102	F1
Tibati	104	G3
Tibesti	100	C3
Tibet = Xizang	88	G2
Tibooburra	114	H5
Tiburón	134	B3
Tîchît	102	D5
Tichla	102	C4
Ticino	62	D4
Ticul	134	G4
Tidjikdja	102	C5
Tieling	82	B2
Tielongtan	88	C1
Tielt	54	F4
Tienen	54	G4
Tien Shan	76	Q9
Tien Yen	84	D2
Tierra Amarilla	126	E3
Tiétar	60	E4
Tiflis = T'bilisi	98	H1
Tifton	130	E3
Tifu	87	C3
Tighina	66	S3
Tignère	104	G3
Tigre	140	E4
Tigris	92	K6
Tijuana	124	C5
Tikanlik	76	R9
Tikhoretsk	70	H5
Tikhvin	70	F3
Tikrīt	92	K6

Name	Page	Grid
Turpan Pendi	76	S9
Turquino	138	D2
Turtas	70	N3
Turtkul'	90	H1
Turtle Island	114	K3
Turu	76	U5
Turugart Pass	76	P9
Turukhan	78	C3
Turukhansk	76	R4
Turukta	78	K4
Tuscaloosa	130	D3
Tuscola	130	D2
Tuticorin	88	C7
Tutonchany	78	E4
Tutrakan	66	P5
Tuttle Creek Reservoir	130	B2
Tuttlingen	62	D3
Tutuila	112	K7
Tuvalu	112	H6
Tuxpan, Mexico	124	E7
Tuxpan, Mexico	124	G7
Tuxtla Gutiérrez	134	F5
Tuyên Quang	84	D2
Tuy Hoa	84	D4
Tuymazy	70	K4
Tuz Gölü	92	E4
Tuz Khurmātū	92	L6
Tuzla	66	F5
Tver'	70	G3
Tweed	56	K6
Twentynine Palms	132	C2
Twilight Cove	114	E6
Twin Buttes Reservoir	132	F2
Twin Falls	126	D2
Twizel	116	C7
Two Harbors	128	B1
Tyachiv	66	L1
Tygda	78	M6
Tyler	124	G5
Tylkhoy	78	U4
Tym	76	Q6
Tynda	78	L5
Tyne	56	K6
Tynemouth	56	L6
Tynset	48	F5
Tyra	76	S7
Tyrifjorden	48	F6
Tyrnavos	68	E5
Tyrrhenian Sea	64	F8
Tyry	78	P4
Tysa	50	N9
Tyukyan	78	K4
Tyumen'	76	M6
Tyung	78	K3
Tyva	78	F6

U

Name	Page	Grid
Uarini	140	D4
Uaupés	140	D3
Ubá	140	J8
Ubaitaba	140	K6
Ubangi	106	B3
Ube	82	F7
Úbeda	60	G6
Uberaba	140	H7
Uberlândia	140	H7
Überlingen	62	E3
Ubon Ratchathani	84	C3
Ubrique	60	E8
Ucayali	140	B5
Uchami	76	T5
Ucharal	76	Q8
Uchiura-wan	82	L2
Uchkuduk	76	L9
Uckermark	52	J3
Ucluelet	126	A1
Uda, Russia	78	F5
Uda, Russia	78	N6
Udachnyy	78	J3
Udagamandalam	88	C6
Udaipur	88	B4
Uddevalla	48	F7
Uddjaure	70	C1
Uddjaure Storavan	48	K4
Udine	62	J4
Udmurtiya	70	K3
Udon Thani	84	C3
Udupi	88	B6
Uecker	52	J3
Ueckermünde	52	J3
Ueda	82	K5
Uele	106	C3
Uelen	78	AA3
Uel'kal	78	Y3
Uelzen	52	F4
Ufa	70	L3
Ufa	70	L4
Uganda	106	E3
Ugep	104	F3
Ugine	62	B5
Uglegorsk	78	Q7
Uglich	70	G3
Ugljan	62	L6
Ugol'naya Zyryanka	78	R3
Ugol'nyye Kopi	78	X4
Ugulan	78	S4
Uh	66	K1
Uherské Hradiště	50	G8
Uherský Brod	50	G8
Uiju	82	C3
Uil	70	K5
Uil	70	K5
Uinta Mountains	126	D2
Uitenhage	108	D6
Újfehértó	66	J2
Ujiji	106	D4
Ujjain	88	C4
Ukerewe Island	106	E4
Ukhta	76	J5

Name	Page	Grid
Ukiah	126	B3
Ukkusissat	122	W2
Ukmerge	50	P2
Ukraine	46	G3
Ulaanbaatar	78	H7
Ulaangom	76	S8
Ulan	80	B3
Ulan Bator = Ulaanbaatar	80	D1
Ulan-Ude	78	H6
Ulaş	92	G4
Ulchin	82	E5
Ulcinj	66	G8
Uldz	78	J7
Ulety	78	J6
Ulhasnagar	88	B5
Uliastay	76	T8
Ulindi	106	D4
Ullapool	56	G4
Ullŭng do	82	F5
Ulm	62	F2
Ulog	66	F6
Ulongue	108	E2
Ulsan	82	E6
Ulu	78	M4
Ulubat Gölü	68	L4
Ulugqat	90	K2
Ulukışla	92	F5
Ulungur Hu	76	R8
Ulunkhan	78	J5
Uluru	114	F5
Ulu-Yul	78	D5
Ulva	56	F5
Ulverston	56	J7
Ulya	78	Q5
Ul'yanovsk	70	J4
Ulytau	76	M8
Umag	64	H3
Uman'	70	F5
Umarkot	90	J4
Umba	70	F1
Umeå	48	L5
Umeälven	48	J4
Umfolozi	108	E5
Ummal Arānib	102	H3
Umm al Jamājim	95	A3
Umm Durman	100	F4
Umm Keddada	100	E5
Umm Lajj	100	G3
Umm Qaşr	95	B1
Umm Ruwaba	100	F5
Umnak Island	132	(1)E5
Umtata	108	D6
Umuarama	142	L3
Unalakleet	132	(1)E5
Unalaska Island	132	(1)E5
'Unayzah	94	C6
Underberg	108	D5
Ungava Bay	122	T5
Ungheni	66	Q2
Ungwana Bay	106	G4
União da Vitória	142	L4
Unije	62	K6
Unimak Island	132	(1)D5
Unim Bāb	95	D4
Unini	140	E4
Union	128	B3
Union City	134	G1
Union Springs	130	D3
United Arab Emirates	90	F5
United Kingdom	56	G6
United States	120	M5
Unna	54	K3
Unraven	132	E1
Unst	56	M1
Unstrut	52	G5
Unzha	70	H3
Upernavik	122	W2
Upernavik Kujalleq	122	V2
Upington	108	C5
Upolu	112	J7
Upper Hutt	116	E5
Upper Klamath Lake	126	B2
Upper Lake	126	C2
Upper Lough Erne	56	E7
Upper Sandusky	128	D2
Uppsala	48	J7
Upsala	128	B1
'Uqlat al 'Udhaybah	95	B2
Urad Houqi	80	D2
Urakawa	82	M2
Ural	70	K5
Ural Mountains = Ural'skiy Khrebet	46	L1
Ural'sk	70	K4
Ural'skiy Khrebet	46	L1
Urambo	106	E5
Uranium City	122	K5
Uraricoera	140	E3
Uraricoera	140	E3
Uray	70	M2
Urbana, Ill., US	128	C2
Urbana, Oh., US	128	D2
Urbania	62	H7
Urbino	62	H7
Urdzhar	76	Q8
Uren'	70	J3
Urengoy	76	P4
Urgench	90	H1
Urho	76	R8
Uritskiy	70	N4
Urla	68	J6
Urlaţi	66	P5
Uroševac	66	J7
Uro-teppa	90	J2
Urt	80	C2
Uruaçu	140	H6
Uruapan	134	D5
Urucurituba	140	F4
Uruguai	142	K4
Uruguay	142	K5
Uruguay	142	K5
Ürümqi	76	R9

Name	Page	Grid
Urus Martan	92	L2
Uruti	116	E4
Uryupino	78	L6
Uryupinsk	70	H4
Urzhum	70	K3
Urziceni	66	P5
Usa	76	L4
Usa	82	F7
Uşak	92	C4
Usedom	52	J3
Useless Loop	114	B5
Usfān	90	C5
Ushtobe	76	P8
Usingen	52	D6
Usk	56	J10
Usman'	70	G4
Usol'ye Sibirskoye	78	G6
Ussel	58	H8
Ussuri	82	G1
Ussuriysk	80	J2
Usta	70	J3
Ust'-Alekseyevo	70	J2
Ust'-Barguzin	78	H6
Ust' Chaun	78	W3
Ústí	50	F8
Ustica	64	H10
Ust'-Ilimsk	78	G5
Ústí nad Labem	50	D7
Ust'-Ishim	76	N6
Ustka	50	F3
Ust'-Kamchatsk	78	U5
Ust'-Kamenogorsk	76	Q8
Ust'-Kamo	78	T5
Ust'-Karenga	78	K6
Ust'-Khayryuzovo	78	T5
Ust'-Kulom	70	K2
Ust'-Kut	78	G5
Ust'-Kuyga	78	P3
Ust'-Labinsk	92	H1
Ust'-Maya	78	N4
Ust'-Mukduyka	76	R4
Ust'-Muya	78	K5
Ust' Nem	70	K2
Ust'-Nera	78	Q4
Ust'-Nyukzha	78	L5
Ust'-Olenek	78	K2
Ust'-Omchug	78	R4
Ust' Ozernoye	78	D5
Ust' Penzhino	78	V4
Ust'-Pit	78	E5
Ustrem	70	N2
Ust'-Sopochnoye	78	T5
Ust' Tapsuy	70	M2
Ust'-Tarka	76	P6
Ust'-Tatta	78	N4
Ust'-Tsil'ma	76	J4
Ust' Un'ya	70	L2
Ust'-Urkima	78	L5
Ust' Usa	70	L1
Ust'-Uyskoye	76	L7
Usu	76	Q9
Usuki	82	F7
Utah	124	D4
Utah Lake	126	D2
Utata	78	G6
Utena	48	N9
Uthal	90	J4
Utica	128	E2
Utiel	60	J5
Utrecht	54	H2
Utrera	60	E7
Utsjoki	48	P2
Utsunomiya	82	K5
Uttaradit	84	C3
Utva	70	K4
Uummannaq Fjord	122	V2
Uummannarsuaq	122	Y5
Uusikaupunki	48	L6
Uvalde	134	E3
Uvarin	78	X3
Uvat	70	N3
Uvinza	106	E5
Uvira	106	D4
Uvs Nuur	76	S7
Uwajima	82	G7
Uy	70	M4
Uyar	76	S6
Uyuk	76	N9
Uyuni	142	H3
Uzbekistan	76	L9
Uzhhorod	66	K1
Užice	66	G6
Uzunköprü	66	P8

V

Name	Page	Grid
Vaal	108	D5
Vaasa	48	L5
Vác	66	G2
Vacaria	142	M4
Vachi	90	E1
Vadodara	88	B4
Vado Ligure	62	D6
Vadsø	48	Q1
Vaduz	62	J4
Værøy	48	G3
Vaganski Vhr	64	L6
Vagay	70	N3
Váh	50	H8
Vakh	70	Q2
Valbonnais	62	A6
Valcheta	142	H7
Valdagno	62	G5
Valday	70	F3
Val-de-Meuse	62	A2
Valdemoro	60	G4
Valdepeñas	60	G6
Valdez	122	B4
Valdivia	142	G6
Val-d'Or	128	E1
Valdosta	124	K5

Name	Page	Grid
Valdres	48	E6
Valea lui Mihai	66	K2
Valence	58	K9
Valencia, Spain	60	K5
Valencia, Venezuela	140	D1
Valencia de Alcántara	60	C5
Valenciennes	54	F4
Vălenii de Munte	66	P4
Valentia Island	56	B10
Valentine	126	F2
Valenza	62	D5
Valera	140	C2
Valga	70	E3
Val Horn	124	F5
Valjevo	66	G5
Valka	48	N8
Val'karay	78	X3
Valkeakoski	48	N6
Valkenswaard	54	H3
Valladolid, Mexico	134	G4
Valladolid, Spain	60	F3
Valle	48	D7
Valledupar	140	C1
Vallée de Azaouagh	102	F5
Vallée du Tilemsi	102	F5
Vallée-Jonction	128	F1
Vallejo	126	B3
Vallentuna	48	K7
Valletta	64	J13
Valley City	126	G1
Valley Falls	126	B2
Valley of the Kings	100	F2
Valli di Comacchio	62	H6
Vallorbe	62	B4
Valls	60	M3
Valmiera	48	N8
Valognes	54	A5
Val-Paradis	128	E1
Valparai	88	C6
Valparaíso, Chile	142	G5
Valparaíso, Mexico	132	F4
Valsad	88	B4
Val'tevo	70	H2
Valuyki	70	G4
Valverde del Camino	60	D7
Vammala	48	M6
Van	92	K4
Vanadzor	92	L3
Vanavara	78	G4
Van Buren	128	G1
Vancouver, Canada	126	B1
Vancouver, US	126	B1
Vancouver Island	122	F7
Vandalia	130	D2
Vanderbijlpark	108	D5
Vanderhoof	122	G6
Van Diemen Gulf	114	F2
Vänern	48	G7
Vangaindrano	108	H4
Van Gölü	92	K4
Van Horn	132	F2
Vanimo	87	F3
Vanino	78	Q7
Vankarem	78	Y3
Vanna	48	K1
Vännäs	48	K5
Vannes	58	C6
Vanrhynsdorp	108	B6
Vantaa	48	N6
Vanua Levu	112	H7
Vanuatu	112	G7
Van Wert	128	D2
Vanzevat	70	N2
Vanzhil'kynak	78	C4
Varāmīn	90	F2
Varanasi	88	D3
Varangerfjorden	48	R2
Varaždin	66	D3
Varazze	62	D6
Varberg	48	G8
Varda	68	D6
Vardar	68	E3
Varde	48	E9
Vardenis	92	L3
Vardø	48	R1
Varel	52	D3
Varena	50	P3
Varese	62	D5
Vârful Moldoveanu	66	M4
Vârfurile	66	K3
Varginha	142	M3
Varkaus	48	P5
Varna	92	B2
Värnamo	48	H8
Varnsdorf	52	K6
Várpalota	66	F2
Varto	92	J4
Varzi	62	E6
Varzy	58	J6
Vásárosnamény	66	K1
Vasilikos	94	A2
Vaslui	66	Q3
Västerås	48	J7
Västervik	48	J8
Vasto	64	J6
Vasvár	62	M3
Vatan	58	G6
Vathia	68	E8
Vatican City	64	F7
Vatnajökull	48	(1)E2
Vatomandry	108	H3
Vatra Dornei	66	N2
Vättern	48	H7
Vaughn	132	E2
Vawkavysk	50	P4
Växjö	48	H8
Vayuniya	88	D7
Vazhgort	70	J2
Vecht	54	J2
Vechta	54	L2
Vecsés	66	G2
Vedaranniyam	88	C6

W